To Mark,
Best of l
Hopefully som
Coaches of the gam Walter, Fuzzy Naom-
Cothell, + bring your inspiration!

California

Baseball

From the Pioneers
To The Glory Years

Chris Goode

California Baseball: From the Pioneers to the Glory Years

Copyright 2009

ISBN 978-0-557-08760-0

Contact information: goode4@earthlink.net

(Eighth Version: July 24, 2009)

Table of Contents

Introduction

When America's founding fathers penned the Declaration of Independence, they patched together Democratic philosophies and ideals proffered from European pioneers including Hobbes, Locke, Diderot, Voltaire, and Rousseau. When Einstein founded modern physics, he built upon the works of Farraday, Lavosier, and du Châtelet. When Jackie Robinson broke the color barrier in major league baseball, he advanced the struggles of Cool Papa Bell, John Henry "Pop" Lloyd, and Rube Foster. And long before Curt Flood fought for free agency, Nap Lajoie and Hal Chase challenged baseball's restrictive reserve clause in court. Great institutions grow and evolve from the seeds of pioneers and their quest to improve the conditions of their respective eras. Baseball, in part, owes its richness as an American institution to the efforts of its pioneers – coaches who threw batting practice for decades, managers and moguls who risked their personal fortunes to entertain the fan, or the star player who served as an inspirational beacon for future generations. This book is about the California pioneers who helped shape baseball in the Golden State.

California baseball has enthused lives for generations. It derives its appeal from the familiar ritual, a desire for community, and the attraction of bonding with others against a common adversary. The significance of rituals manifests over decades; they are experienced and shared with generations, often growing in importance, as they evolve into traditions. Dating back to the Civil War, baseball has been laden with commonly understood rituals that distinguish it from other American sports.

Recall the day a relative or friend announced that they had tickets to opening day. "You can play hooky," they'd offer temptingly. "Bring your glove." Racing from the parking lot to witness the ceremonial first pitch, you heard the national anthem, the organist, and the umpire yelling, "Play ball." Purchasing peanuts thrown to your seat by the vendor, you smelled the beer that another salesman let flow over the edge of a souvenir cup and onto the hot cement. Wearing the ball cap of the home team, you bought a scorecard and pencil and kept score for at least two innings. The smell of freshly cut grass evoked memories of past springtimes and the anticipation of a pennant, the young prospect, and the possible comeback of an aging hero. You listened to the game on the radio so you could hear your favorite announcer do play-by-play even though you were closer to the field than he was. When the team fell behind, you made a "rally cap," and you watched the mascot for cues to cheer the home team to victory. When the umpire made a bad call, you muttered invectives under your breath, and then watched the manager take up your case, running out on the field and kicking dirt onto the umpire's sock.

The imagery may be cliché, but baseball fans likely feel a visceral tug when recounting an opening day ballgame. The rituals passed down through the generations sustain with an enduring allure.

The game's founding fathers began with a simple concept - to gather as a community to pass time in a friendly contest on the only day of rest. The game grew in popularity during the nineteenth century, fueled by newspaper accounts, sports gambling, and the romantic appeal of community.

In the earliest years, townspeople gathered for ballgames on a Sunday. Over time, towns assembled teams that challenged neighboring towns. For decades, hundreds and sometimes thousands of townspeople congregated at a field to watch their home team contest the adversary that hailed from a few stops away along the local railroad line. Before automobiles, the visiting crowd often paraded by foot, on horseback, and in buggies to the opponent's ballpark.

The games have always been played in a "park." Unlike the terms "stadium" or "coliseum" that conjure up images of battlegrounds for gladiators, baseball's quaint moniker portrays a natural and public gathering place. The ballpark took on greater significance as professional baseball developed; their control by owners represented an integral component in the establishment of professional monopolies. Most towns and cities had access to a single ballpark. As professional baseball grew in popularity, the owners who secured the single ballpark also secured the local franchise and the patrons that came with them. For many years, owners not only controlled usage of ballparks, but also constructed for the fans the requisite railroad transportation, sometimes adjoined by elaborate amusement parks that attracted the public on weekends. As people flocked to the parks to enjoy the game of baseball, the sport slowly assumed a distinction as America's pastime.

The term "pastime" did not have a place in the lexicon of the United States during the country's formative years. The original settlers, often first generation immigrants, worked sunrise to sunset seven days per week building the nation's foundation. They didn't know the luxury of "pastime," a term that evokes images of relaxation, entertainment, and a disregard for ambition. However, the second-generation immigrants, the native sons of the fledgling nation, did find time for recreation, even if only on Sundays. Sunday baseball broke the monotony of weekly toil.

The community embraced its team during this era, largely due to a sense of ownership and pride, as well as from the appeal of gambling. Sport owes much of its widespread appeal to gambling, a preoccupation that has survived to modern times. In town ball, locals frequently contributed to a pool that that was wagered against the opposing town before the weekly contest. The interest of fans on both sides piqued because of the wager. A low price of admission, reasonable for more than a century, reinforced the game's appeal, making baseball the sport of the people.

Ever since Civil War soldiers played baseball during idle periods between battles, the common man embraced the game. Upon the soldiers' return home, they transported a passion throughout the country. Its appeal grew as Americans identified with the contest that mirrored the unique character of the new nation. The fleeting nature of the game's successes and failures echoed the relationship that the common man had with struggle and survival. The appeal of gambling mimicked the nation's penchant for risk-taking. The game's scrappiness and brashness resonated with the country's confident individualists. And the affinity for creating rules while accommodating transgressions emulated the imperfections of capitalism, the justice system, and national politics in the 19th and 20th centuries.

The institution of baseball continues its battle with imperfection while striving for the ideal. It fails unrepentant. Its history is cloaked in tradition woven together through time, a closet filled with skeletons as well as a chest brimming with hope. Eventually, errors of the past are tested and corrected, the game evolving as well as embodying its richness and ritual.

Like America, baseball has developed an endearing split personality. On the one hand, fans are infatuated with the virtuous game, the game won by the best man in an honest contest among hard working and enterprising ballplayers. Conversely, the fans have been intrigued with the winner-at-any-cost. The American League, at its outset symbolized by manager Connie Mack and created by American League President Ban Johnson, represented clean baseball. The National League, whose dirty baseball principles were embodied by manager John McGraw, was the antithesis. Fans loved both – they loved baseball in spite of, and often because of, its many blemishes and warts.

Like baseball, America, endearing with all of its foibles, has been duplicitous, staging battles throughout its history between justice and injustice, idealism and pragmatism, struggle and success, welfare and self-reliance, labor and management. The social, political, and economic sentiment coursing from pool hall to church hall, barbershop to union shop, homemaker to book maker has swirled and churned in our major cities. The major metropolises, Chicago and New York, became the confluences of discord and progress on a national stage as well as in baseball. Carl Sandburg, in a poem entitled "Chicago," described the dichotomy that symbolized the city - the struggles within and the love affair that existed amidst the scars and disfigurement.

Hog Butcher for the World,
Tool Maker, Stacker of Wheat,
Player with Railroads and the Nation's Freight Handler;
Stormy, husky, brawling,
City of the Big Shoulders:
They tell me you are wicked and I believe them, for I have seen your
painted women under the gas lamps luring the farm boys.
And they tell me you are crooked and I answer: Yes, it is true I have seen

the gunman kill and go free to kill again.
And they tell me you are brutal and my reply is: On the faces of women
and children I have seen the marks of wanton hunger.
And having answered so I turn once more to those who sneer at this my
city, and I give them back the sneer and say to them:
Come and show me another city with lifted head singing so proud to be
alive and coarse and strong and cunning.
Flinging magnetic curses amid the toil of piling job on job, here is a tall
bold slugger set vivid against the little soft cities;

Carl Sandburg

During baseball's formative years, California ballplayers proliferated within teams in Chicago, New York, and the other major metropolises of the East. Starting in the 1880's, their stardom contributed to baseball's growing iconic status. But just as the players helped shape the cities, the cities also shaped the players. The corruption ever present in cities polluted the innocence of the youthful athletes. In time, the sport and its players mirrored society at large. Organized Baseball became a metaphor for what America has been, is, and would like to be.

Historian Jacques Barzun, who recently turned 100, has indulged himself with a lifetime love affair with erudition and scholarly rigor. Out of all of his writing, which spans diverse subjects and languages, his most frequently quoted sentence is inscribed on a plaque at the Baseball Hall of Fame.

Whoever wants to know the heart and mind of America had better learn baseball.

The history of baseball reveals the history of America. But for most fans, the most important history that baseball reveals is not of past eras, but about ourselves – our memories of the game and how those memories link us with past generations, our youth, and hopes for future generations. Just as we have memories of 4th of July ceremonies, Christmas days, or Passover feasts, we have recollections, as strong as any in our lives, of seasons past – of teams we rooted for, players we watched, players we played with and against, and of sitting around the dinner table with parents, aunts, and uncles talking about the day's game – the great catch, the long home run, or the bunt that scored the winning run. Around that dinner table, in addition to the outcomes of any one game, beliefs passed down from one generation to the next – not only of faith, morals, and social justice, but whether to take the extra base with one out, or throw a curve ball when behind in the count. In the history of baseball live memories of our past.

The regularity of play, unsurpassed by any other sport, engrained the game in our daily lives. During the long baseball season, fans have risen each morning to the habits of brushing their teeth, washing their faces, and reading the box scores. In its regularity, the sport has been accessible to the common man.

Even if a ticket was unaffordable, or a fan lived distant to a ballpark, for a few cents it could follow its team in the newspaper. Similarly, during the 1930's, the advent of the radio brought the game into the home. The voice of the local announcer became a sound as familiar and soothing as the wind blowing through the trees and the hum of cars rumbling down the street. The daily dose of baseball, relatively inexpensive, helped create a sense of ownership for the fan that appealed to the many immigrants and their children throughout the late 19th and early 20th centuries. The connection with their home team galvanized the hopes and dreams that many had to assimilate into America.

The relentless regularity of the game, symbolized by icons Lou Gehrig and Cal Ripken, became a hallmark. In the early years of the game, players sought a paycheck nearly every day of the year. In some minor leagues, teams played more than two hundred games per season. In 1904, George Van Haltren batted 941 times for Seattle of the Pacific Coast League. After the turn of the century, many major leaguers played a full season in the East, then traveled west to play a winter schedule. Other major leaguers toured in the off-season. A good player who could draw a crowd found employment throughout the year.

Professional baseball began in the East. But in spite of the separation from the East by thousands of miles, baseball firmly took root in California where the game could be played year round. Its popularity grew in the form of town ball, particularly from 1875 to 1890, as native sons, the children of the pioneer families who had settled the West, propagated the region, especially around San Francisco.

The first star ballplayers in California, many who played and starred in the major leagues in the 1880s, returned home from the East prior to the turn of the century and planted the seeds in the fertile California environs and cultivated the greatest hotbed of baseball talent in the United States. Over two thousand major leaguers have hailed from California, including more-than-thirty current and future major league Hall of Famers.

All Time California All Star Team

	1st Team	2nd Team	3rd Team	4th Team
Starting Pitchers	**Walter Johnson** Randy Johnson **Tom Seaver** **Don Drysdale**	Randy Jones Orval Overall Bret Saberhagen **Lefty Gomez**	Dave Stewart Jack McDowell Andy Messersmith Mike Mussina	Scott McGregor Dan Haren Tom Candiotti Dave Stieb
Relief Pitchers	**Dennis Eckersley** Trevor Hoffman	Robb Nen John Wetteland	Rod Beck Dan Quisenberry	Eddie Guardado Dave Righetti
First Base	**Eddie Murray**	**Willlie Stargell**	Mark McGwire	Hal Chase
Second Base	**Jackie Robinson**	**Joe Morgan**	Chase Utley	Jeff Kent
Shortstop	**Ozzie Smith**	Alan Trammell	**Joe Cronin**	Nomar Garciaparra
Third Base	Stan Hack	Gil McDougald	Matt Williams	Buck Weaver Ken Caminiti
Catcher	**Gary Carter**	**Ernie Lombardi**	Chief Meyers	Bob Boone
Outfield	**Joe DiMaggio** **Ted Williams** Barry Bonds	**Frank Robinson** Lefty O'Doul **Duke Snider**	**Tony Gwynn** **Harry Heilmann** **Paul Waner**	**Chick Hafey** **Lloyd Waner** George Van Haltren
Manager	**Casey Stengel**	Billy Martin	Bob Lemon	George Stallings

Honorable Mention: **Tony Lazzeri, Earl Averill,** Kevin Appier, C.C. Sabathia, Mark Prior, Willie McGee, Ryan Braun, Darryl Strawberry, George Hendrick, **Harry Hooper**, Mike Donlin, Dom DiMaggio, Fred Lynn, Jim Fogarty, Dusty Baker, Gavvy Cravath, Duffy Lewis, Dwight Evans, Willie Crawford, Garret Anderson, Darrell Evans, Bobby Bonds, Dave Kingman, Doug DeCinces, Bobby Doerr, Steve Sax, Keith Hernandez, **Frank Chance, George Kelly**, Bill Buckner, Tug McGraw, Bill Rigney.

Bold = Baseball Hall of Fame Member

Californians have played baseball as long as California has been a state - well before the formation of the professional major leagues in 1869. Immediately following the population explosions that followed the California gold rush of 1849, teams from San Francisco, Oakland, Sacramento, Sierra foothills, Santa Clara Valley, and San Joaquin Valley formed. In 1860, the San Francisco Board of Supervisors passed the Consolidation Act that created a park near Grove and Larkin Streets. The triangular piece of land, with a hill of sand at its peak, had been used as a cemetery. When the park was created, the dead were relocated and the sandy hill was leveled. Ballplayers soon frequented the park for games, and the local media referred to the players as "sand lotters." Over a period of decades, the term commonly known today as "sand lot " took on the meaning of any baseball field used by amateur or semi-pro baseball players.

Baseball emerged prominently from the State's population centers. In 1860, San Francisco contained over 56,000 citizens. By 1870, that figure nearly tripled. Sacramento maintained populations of nearly 14,000 and 16,000 during those periods. By 1870, Alameda County, across the Bay from San Francisco, crested the 10,000 figure and grew as the hub supporting goods flowing to and from the City. Stockton and Santa Clara Counties also approached 10,000 by 1870. While baseball was played throughout the State, most other cities and counties had comparatively small populations of a few thousand or less. Even Los Angeles did not achieve a population of 12,000 until 1880. The towns that initially fostered the tradition of elite baseball play in California were San Francisco, Sacramento, Oakland, Stockton, San Jose, and Fresno. The second tier teams included Santa Cruz, Sonoma, and Marysville. These cities remained the most prominent baseball towns for the next two decades.

Between 1880 and 1890, Los Angeles grew because of the railroad. The Southern Pacific completed its Los Angeles route in 1880, followed by the Santa Fe six years later. With a large investment in the transcontinental railroad, and with significant land holdings, the railroads set forth a long-term plan for growth. Citrus farming became the highest and best use of land. By 1890, San Francisco was still three times the size of Los Angeles. But in the 1890s, the Los Angeles population exploded, and its baseball team began to defeat its northern competitors with regularity. As the third largest county behind San Francisco and Alameda, Los Angeles attracted talent from throughout the state and delivered a superior product to what was becoming one of the largest fan bases in the West.

The three dominant cities in terms of population in 1900, San Francisco, Los Angeles, and Oakland produced eighteen Hall of Famers over the next three decades. After the turn of the century, the proportion of urban-born American players in the East declined proportionally as the importance of weather and open space in the West contributed to player development.

As players in the West from the 19th century returned home after playing in the major leagues, they coached the next generation of ballplayers who contributed heavily to the major leagues. The impact was undeniable. From 1920 to 1939, when compared to cities throughout the country, Oakland produced 6.2 times more players than its share of the population, followed by San Francisco (4.5 times), and Los Angeles (3.9 times). The three cities far exceeded the productivity of any other locale in the country.[1]

California Hall of Famers

SAN FRANCISCO	OAKLAND	LOS ANGELES
Harry Heilmann	Joe DiMaggio	Walter Johnson
George Kelly	Chick Hafey	Frank Chance
Tony Lazzeri	Harry Hooper	Bobby Doerr
Joe Cronin	Ernie Lombardi	Duke Snider
Lloyd Waner	Lefty Gomez	
Paul Waner		
Earl Averill		

* One of the greatest from San Franicsco, Lefty O'Doul, is not yet in the HOF.

Some academic institutions, both public and private, date back to the formative years in the State, particularly in the population centers. California is the only state that claims four different schools that have each produced two Hall of Fame baseball players. Frank Chance and Tom Seaver went to Fresno High School. Walter Johnson and Arky Vaughan attended Fullerton Union High. Harry Heilmann and Joe Cronin each attended Sacred Heart High School in San Francisco. And in more recent years, Ozzie Smith and Eddie Murray attended Los Angeles' Locke High School - at the same time. In addition to the academic institutions noted above, others dating back to the middle of the 19th century contributed significantly to the development of baseball in California, including Bellarmine High School, St. Ignatius High School, St. Mary's College, Santa Clara College, UC Berkeley, Whittier College, and St. Vincent's College (now Loyola High School and Loyola Marymount University).

The population growth in Southern California trailed that of Northern California in the 19th century. Although petroleum was discovered in Southern California in 1850 in Pico Canyon near the town now known as Santa Clarita, the oil boom in Los Angeles didn't begin until Edward Doheny discovered oil at 2nd Street and Glendale Boulevard in downtown Los Angeles in the 1890s. In the early 20th century, Los Angeles became a center for oil production. Agriculture also continued as an important component of the southland economy. Los Angeles annexed the San Fernando Valley, and between 1899 and 1903, the Los Angeles Times founder Harrison Gray Otis and son-in-law Harry Chandler purchased much of the cheap land on the northern outskirts of Los Angeles. By the end of 1913, they had secured a fortune by coordinating with William Mulholland to build an aqueduct, for which voters agreed to pay, which brought water from the Owens River to the San Fernando Valley.

The combination of the oil boom and the creation of the aqueduct fueled growth throughout Southern California. The population of Los Angeles, after quintupling between 1880 and 1890, doubled again by 1900. The city tripled between 1900 and 1910. Then by 1920, it nearly doubled once again, at which time it surpassed San Francisco in size. The population doubled again by 1930, exceeding the population of San Francisco by a two to one margin.

No major league baseball team would reside in California until 1958 when the Giants and Dodgers lugged their rivalry west from New York. But the Northern California versus Southern California antagonism dated back to the 1890s.

The book begins during this era and examines the personalities, schools, teams, managers, and owners that helped shape baseball in California. The book provides an insightful history of major league baseball from the perspective of the California minor leagues, particularly the California League and Pacific Coast League. While focusing on the lives of a select group of individuals integral to the development of baseball in California, it does not attempt to provide a complete history. Over decades, thousands of players stepped between the lines, some for a few years, and others for a few games. The intent is to truthfully reveal a representative and interesting sample of the achievements, events, and contributions.

One source for the book was <u>A History of Baseball in California and Pacific Coast Leagues 1847 – 1938, Memories and Musings of and Old Time Baseball Player</u>, written with love by Fred W. Lange, a former major leaguer in the 1880's and a founder of organized professional baseball in California in 1897. In his book, Mr. Lange wrote,

> *This has been my first venture into writing a book and I hope some young man may appreciate what I have written and that it will be a help for him later in life.*

His writing has been a help to this book, which is written with the heart of a young man and with eighty additional years of perspective since Lange last put pen to paper. And the book also corrects some of Lange's inaccuracies.

The additional historical distance allows for objectivity and sympathy as the actors are considered in relation to the conditions of their eras – conditions wherein primary sources of the day were party to the promotional objectives of the game. Over time, historians would reinforce the day's inaccuracies by referencing often-biased sources, many of which were, like the media that covers national politics today, part of the promotional machine.

The necessity for promotion created camps of players. There were those who became icons because they embodied commonly held American ideals – Cal Ripken for his durability, Lou Gehrig for his humility, and Jackie Robinson for his courage. Those with images, whether a product of perception or reality, that did not align with commonly held American ideals were soon forgotten as the years ushered in hundreds of new actors eager for the national stage. Memories of superstars such as Pete Rose, Mark McGwire, Barry Bonds and Shoeless Joe Jackson will take longer to fade. But the likes of Jose Canseco, Sammy Sosa, Rafael Palmeiro, Hal Chase, Buck Weaver, and Curt Flood may not resonate as decades pass. Baseball can be staunchly unforgiving, a tradition fostered from its inception by those, like Fred Lange, who loved the purity of the game. Lange wrote,

Baseball has always been conceded to be the cleanest and most healthful of sports, a great helper for the mind, for baseball is played as much by the head as by the body. Any player doing wrong in the game has never been taken back again.[A]

Unlike Lange's account, this book only dabbles in descriptions of balls, strikes, hits, and errors - just enough to give the rabid fan the requisite visceral fix. It doesn't chronicle various on-field events, but rather presents proceedings that reveal conditions in baseball in California, in baseball on a national level, and in society at large. It can't mention each player and all of the many personalities and events. The social and economic background is presented, and efforts have been made to prevent the chief personalities from being lost in a maze of tendencies and developments. At the same time, the book strives to be true to history.

With the characters in the book, one thing is certain. Many spent many hours of most days on the ball field for nearly fifty years, a period that created countless plays, players, and box scores. And while many baseball books successfully re-tell the "play of all plays," or draw comparisons between the greatest natural and supernatural on-field heroics in human history, the reality is more mundane. This book has as much to do with the off-season and player choices vis-à-vis Organized Baseball and the National Commission as it does the regular season. And in those off-seasons, life happened. This book is about lives – about people. It is about the people of California who influenced, and were influenced by, the growth of urban sports in America.

This book is also about Hal Chase. Nearly ninety years have passed since his major league career ended, and it is time for a fresh appraisal of his contribution. A great deal of new material has become available in the intervening decades, lending additional insight into the conditions and background of his life. After so many years, one might think that everything that was ever to be known about his life had already been disclosed, every speculation laid to rest, every clue pursued to its inevitable end. While much has been analyzed and written, none has accurately revealed Chase in a broader historical context.

Over a century after deadball era star Hal Chase played his first major league game, history has portrayed him as a villain. Many have called him baseball's "biggest crook." Once labeled as such by writers such as Eliot Asinof in his 1963 book "Eight Men Out" that documented the 1919 Chicago Black Sox scandal, future historians have relied on his and other secondary sources to form their view of Chase. And as they do their research and form their opinions, they often reach conclusions based on a pre-existing bias of "villain and crook" rather

---

[A] Not to imply that Curt Flood did wrong to the game, but he is included to highlight that at the time that he contested the reserve clause, he was perceived by many as a troublesome militant.

than by understanding motivations and the prevailing conditions and culture in baseball.

Chase may not be easily presented as victim, but equally he may not be accurately portrayed as villain. Perhaps with the passage of time, considering the various eras, including those of the deadball and steroids, the man and his role in the history of baseball will be better understood.

Parallels between players banished after the dead ball era and the issues of the steroid era are apparent. The steroid era transformed modern baseball. Prior to the 1980's, the ballplayer could be any size. Through the years, players like Johnny Evers, the Waner brothers, Pee Wee Reese, and even Pete Rose demonstrated that size didn't matter if you possessed the will to excel in the national game. Accessible to all young boys, the game presented no major physical barriers that couldn't be overcome by hard work and some basic athletic ability. In the 1980s, all of that changed. Baseball players began resembling football players. By the late 1980's, the "Bash Brothers"[A] of the Oakland A's symbolized what had transpired in the game. If the playing field was level, then it was made level by the widespread use of steroids. Good players faced the choice of using steroids or ending their baseball careers. Considering the escalating salaries during that era, many (the actual percentage we will never know) chose to become steroid users.

A visual comparison of games from the late 1970s with those from the late 1980s clearly reveals the increase in the girth of players. Steroid use resulted in the increase in home runs. Prior to the 1980s, only eleven players had hit over 50 home runs in a season. Yet, in the ensuing years, players who would weigh "a buck seventy-five soaking wet" without steroids were suddenly breaking the once elusive barrier. Soon, there would be ten players in a single season breaking the fifty-home run mark.

The playing field remained askew for many years without much scrutiny. Not until Jose Canseco spoke out about steroid use was there a challenge to the lack of oversight in major league baseball. And when Canseco spoke out, he was vilified. Few exhibit sympathy for a cheater. But over the next few years, proof of steroid use became more prevalent. Many stars have been implicated, including McGwire, Sosa, Tejada, Bonds, Clemens, Rodriguez. Only after a quarter of a century of steroid use has the issue finally been addressed. Why has it taken so long?

[A] Bash Brothers Jose Canseco and Mark McGwire, who allegedly used performance-enhancing drugs, were giants compared to players from the 1970s. Other large players on the team included Carney Lansford, Dave Henderson, and 2009 Hall of Fame inducteed Rickey Henderson.

The truth can take a long time to come to light. And when the truth is sought a quarter of a century later, the primary sources are hard to vet. And writers possess little incentive to find the truth about the alleged "cheaters." Readers tend to prefer the stories of heroes, particularly in sports, featuring the superlative, the superhero, the champion, the crusader, or the protector.

Writers tend to use a broad brush when telling tales of days past, simplistically categorizing "good versus evil" in what has become a tried and true theme. On the one hand we recount the winners of elections, the victors in wars, the All Stars and Hall of Famers. On the other hand, we distinguish the criminals, the villains, and the encroachers of men. But the truth can be more complex. That broad brush keeps us from understanding the context in which events occur.

Fixation on simplistic themes prevents us from understanding history; the loser is not always the villain, yet not always a victim either. Such is the case in today's game, with players such as Bonds, Clemens, Rodriquez, and McGwire, who in the context of history may not be considered as rogues, but part of a larger problem. Yet, as perpetrators of indiscretion, they also contributed to their own blemished reputations.

Just as Bonds, Clemens, Rodriguez, and McGwire were baseball's greatest players in the steroid era, Hal Chase was one of baseball's greatest players in the deadball era, an era in which gambling was pervasive, and when labor and management battled over the reserve clause and the treatment of the players. Chase took on a unique role by continually challenging the reserve clause. Even as baseball grew in popularity, Chase enigmatically demonstrated little allegiance with Organized Baseball. In a sense, he was a "baseball anarchist" at a time in American history when anarchists were considered criminals. Although not justified for his involvement with gambling, Chase was no more undeserving of recognition than the likes of many others including Comiskey, McGraw, Cobb, Speaker, and Ban Johnson who either directly gambled on the game, were complicit with gambling, or swept incidences of gambling under the rug for years.

In his actions as gambler, Chase was no different from Bonds, Clemens, Rodriguez, and McGwire who were party to a condition that was more widespread than is admitted or revealed. Chase was one of many who had involvement in baseball gambling during the deadball era. However, only when the sport's gambling problem became so great that action was required on the part of Organized Baseball, did the industry react. And similar to the current day's steroid issue, the reaction was often not even-handed or fair. A few of the accused were cast into the pot of "unfortunates." Those included Chase, Jimmy O'Connell, and the "eight men out" in Chicago, including Shoeless Joe Jackson and Buck Weaver. Yet many players from the era who were also involved with gambling ultimately received recognition in Cooperstown. Today's former players face a similar fate. Some may never achieve status in the Hall of Fame because of accusations, while others will continue to enter each year even though they used performance-enhancing drugs.

As historians build their cases regarding the legacies of players, much that is considered should be irrelevant. Questions about whether players were popular, good husbands, good fathers, alcoholics, good citizens, icons to the game, tax evaders, grouches, friends to the press, or dopes is of little significance. The list of ballplayers with little virtue is too long to enumerate. In that regard, baseball mirrors society. Thus, when considering the life of a player in the game, the noise that exists from the extraneous activities should be discounted. Analysis of Grover Cleveland Alexander as a drunk or Ty Cobb as an ass can be colorful, but it doesn't speak to their respective contributions as ballplayers. Rather than placing labels on the actors, such as hero or villain, this book uses the lives and events of the actors to reveal conditions and their reactions to those conditions.

The following book provides an historical backdrop to the career of Hal Chase, which in turn provides an historical backdrop for Baseball in America. It is not a biography. Even the most ardent baseball fan, who as some have noted are more willing than other sports fans to submit themselves to boredom, will be spared the granular details of "he said, she saids", at bats, and plays in the field over a long career. This book, with a western, minor league orientation, tells a broader story - of baseball from the perspective of California. The lives of Hal Chase and his associates during the deadball era reveal the prevailing conditions.

To this day, when springtime warms the ground, anxious and hopeful teeballers flock to the ballfield, struggling to shoulder a bat or find the batted ball with their diminutive gloves. In the stands, the proud grandparents watch, and in reverie, welcome the memory of days past - simpler times when their main concern was finding a field and deciding whose shirt would be used as a base. For that "baseball" - not "Organized Baseball" - but the universal game played in schoolyards throughout the world by children and the young at heart, Hal Chase was perhaps one of the greatest heroes.

Ok. Ok. Not a hero.

But at the very least, Hal Chase was not a baseball villain.

We begin in San Francisco in 1897 at the genesis of professional baseball in California – at the San Francisco Examiner Baseball Tournament.

---

[1] City Games, The Evolution of American Urban Society and the Rise of Sports, Steven A. Reiss

Chapter 1

The Birth of California Baseball

The summer of 1897 gave birth to California baseball. Surely talented players had graced ballfields in the Golden State for years. But that summer, California began to ascend into prominence on the national stage because of its impressive wealth of talent.

A San Francisco newspaper, the Examiner, sponsored an open baseball tournament that attracted much of that talent from throughout the State. Although organized baseball had been played in the state since 1859, the events of the Examiner Tournament of 1897 triggered the formation of what eventually became the Pacific Coast League. The tournament also marked the first widespread merger of the old and the new, the talent-laden teenagers competing against the iconic old-timers who would become the managers, owners, umpires, and scouts that would mentor the youth into major league all-stars and Hall of Famers.

The competition between the youth and the veterans was hardly collegial. The veterans didn't coach, coddle, or cradle the youngsters. Rather, they knocked them on their asses and challenged them to compete. Many a pitcher disregarded the target glove, and instead threw for the wetness behind the newcomers' ears. Frank Chance was known for getting hit so many times in the ear by a pitch that he lost the hearing in his left ear, the ear that faced the pitcher. Future Pacific Coast League manager Hap Hogan, known as Wallace Bray until he assumed the name Hogan, described the competitive atmosphere prior to 1900.

> Rickety stands, skinned diamonds with no dirt, low pay for the best players ... Now vets work with youngsters ... back then they threw obstacles in the way that required the youths to be thick-skinned.

California Baseball Prior to 1897

Even before the transcontinental railroad was completed in 1869 linking San Francisco to the East, immigrants migrated on foot, horseback, ship, and wagon train to realize the opportunity afforded by the great state of California. In 1849, the allure had been gold. By the 1860's, gold prospects diminished. The new immigrants moved west to reap the prosperity that trickled down from the burgeoning economy surrounding San Francisco.

Teams in the 1897 San Francisco Examiner Baseball Tournament		
Top Teams:	Other Teams:	Sacramento Corkers
Alameda Alerts (Bushnells)	S.F. Columbias	Lodi
SF California Markets	S.N. Wood and Co.	Petaluma Maroons
Sacramento Gilt Edge	Oakland Monarchs	Santa Rosa
Santa Cruz	SF Daily Reports	C.P. Nathans (Sacramento)
Sodality A.C. of Santa Clara	San Francisco Calls	Manhattans
Fresno Republicans	SF Monitors	Hollister
SF Will & Fincks	Vallejo Wizards	Grass Valley Monarchs
Los Angeles	Charles Bloomers	Hesseman's (Oakland)
Bakersfield	Redondos	Reliance Athletic Club
San Diego	LA Seventh Regiments	Judy Brothers (Winters)
Keegan Brothers (Santa Rosa)	Solicitors	Benicia
	San Francisco Monarchs	SF Examiners
S.F. Union Iron Works	Jacobs & Co. (Oakland)	Humboldt Steamship Pomonas
S.F. Violets	Fruitvale Steens (SF)	
S.F. Athletic Club	Westovers (Oakland)	San Carlos
United States Army Regulars	Davy Crocketts	Centerville
Riversides	Conway & Baumels Nationals	Irvington
	A.B. Smiths	Martinez
		Napa
	Monterey	Merced
		SF Acmes

Nearly sixty teams competed in the tournament that began on June 5, 1897. After a month of play, the top sixteen teams advanced to the semi-finals.

William and James Shepard were two pioneers who crossed the Overland Trail from St. Joseph, Missouri to San Francisco between May and September of 1861. Not alone, they traveled with caravans that literally cut grooves through the Plains that remained for more than a century. The Shepard brothers had played for the Knickerbockers of New York, the first team organized in the East. Upon their arrival in San Francisco, they joined the team credited as the first organized team in the City, the Eagles, which had formed in 1859.[1]

NOTABLE PARTIPANTS IN THE 1897 SAN FRANCISCO EXAMINER BASEBALL TOURNAMENT

Old Timers

Name	Significance
Geo. Van Haltren	Former Major League All Star. (SF Monarchs)
Bill Lange	Former Major League All Star and future scout who allegedly discovered future Hall of Famer Frank Chance at the Examiner Tourney
Fred W. Lange	Former battery mate to Van Haltren in majors and future co-founder of the Pacific Coast League. (Oakland Reliance)
Spike Hennessey	Current star and future scout who discovered multiple Hall of Famers, including, according to Hennessey, Joe Dimaggio. (Sacto Gilt Edge)
Pete Lohman	Former star and manager and future manager of Oakland Oaks. (Team Sponsor)
Phil Knell	Future manager of the SF Seals in early years. (Bakersfield)
Cal Ewing	Father of the Pacific Coast Leage (sponsor of Oakland Reliance)
Jerry Denny	Former major league star from 1881 – 1884
Jack Bodie	Part of Bodie family. Relative Ping would emerge as PCL star, major leaguer, and roommate of Babe Ruth. (California Markets)
Abe Arellanes	Star second baseman. Brother Frank would be local star pitcher and major leaguer. (Santa Cruz)
Charlie Geggus	Former St. Mary's player and major leaguer. Umpired tournament.
Fred Carroll	Former St. Mary's star and major leaguer. (SF Monarchs)
Tip O'Neill	Umpired in tournament. Star player since '80s. Became close friend of Comiskey and Chisox Secretary.

Newcomers

Name	Significance
Frank Chance	Future Hall of Famer (Fresno Republicans)
Charlie Graham	Current Santa Clara College player. Future major leaguer and owner of S.F. Seals (Sodality A.C. of Santa Clara)
Mike Donlin	Future perennial All Star for NY Giants (SF Calls)
George Hildebrand	Future long-time major league umpire. Co-inventor of spitball.
Henry Berry	Future Klondike gold rush king and owner of the Los Angeles Angels and SF Seals
Spider Baum	Pitching star and coach in PCL for five decades
Ham Iburg	Future major league pitcher. Taught Lefty O'Doul to pitch. (California Markets)
Ben Henderson	Dominant Newcomer
Jim Nealon	Dominant Newcomer
Doc Moskiman	Dominant Newcomer
Jimmy Whalen	Dominant Newcomer
Truck Eagan	Dominant Newcomer
Tommy Sheehan	Dominant Newcomer
Jay Hughes	Dominant Newcomer
Bill "Brick" Devereaux	Dominant Newcomer

A year later, the Shepards left the Eagles and formed a team called the Pacifics. By November of 1868, the team played its games in the first enclosed ball field on the Coast at 25th and Folsom against local teams called the Atlantics, the Brodericks, Phoenix, and the Oakland Wide Awakes.[2]

In 1869, professional leagues were founded in the East. The Cincinnati Red Stockings became the first openly professional baseball team in America. At the conclusion of its initial season, the Red Stockings traveled to San Francisco to play the Shepards and their team, the Pacifics. The locals were trounced 66-4 and 35-4 in two games.[3] But the game represented California's first brush with the elite Eastern teams.

At the time, equipment was scarce. Not even the catcher wore a glove. Even crude facemasks were not used for many more years. Into the 1880s, the only equipment a catcher wore was a rubber mouthpiece to prevent his teeth from getting knocked out. In 1875, Ed "Live" Taylor, became the first player from the Coast to wear a glove.[4]

In 1879, Cal McVey, a former Red Stockings star moved to Oakland.[A] With the repeal of blue laws that barred baseball on Sundays, McVey immediately formed the Bay City team in the Pacific Base Ball League. That same winter, McVey and his new squad challenged the National League Champion Chicago White Stockings. The San Francisco squad defeated the Eastern professionals in four out of six contests. For the first time, West Coast baseball made the Easterners take notice.

In the 1880s, St. Mary's College, which at that time operated in the city of Alameda near Oakland, turned out seven major leaguers who had played together at the school from 1881-1884. Whether they attended school is another matter. For another thirty years, the local schools recruited athletes who didn't always attend classes. In fact, rival colleges Santa Clara and St. Mary's entered into an agreement as late as 1909 that limited players to six years of eligibility and required them to attend class. Until that time, players competed for multiple colleges over a period of years.

With seven major leaguers from the same college team, the San Francisco Bay Area was making its mark on the national game. Jerry +Denny was one of the best fielders on the Coast throughout the 19th century, and amassed an impressive 1,286 hits professionally. Jim Fogarty was an all-star, known for his base stealing. His 102 stolen bases in 1887 and 99 steals in 1889 rank eighteenth and twenty-first respectively in major league history. Ed "Cannonball" Morris was one of the most dominating pitchers during his brief career. Hank O'Day became an esteemed umpire and assumed legendary status for his ruling on

---

[A] He played from 1871 to 1879 and posted a career batting average of .346.

the famous "Merkle Boner" that helped the Cubs win the 1908 pennant from the Giants.

Professional Players From St. Mary's College: 1880s -1890s

Name	Pos	Yrs	Teams	Yrs St. Mary's	Born	Key Stats
Jerry Denny	Third	13	Seven Teams	1881-1884	1859	1286 hits, 667 RBI, 130 SB, 112 RBI and 18 HR in 1889 in Indianapolis
Charlie Geggus	Pitch OF	1	Washington	1881-1884	1862	10-9 with 2.54 ERA in one season
Jim McElroy	Pitch OF	1	Philadelphia	1881-1884	1862	Won 1 and lost 13 in only season. ERA of 5.12
Ed Morris	Pitch	7	Pittsburgh	1881-1883	1862	Won 34, 39, 41, 14, and 29 games from 1884-1888. One of most dominant pitchers. 302, 298, and 326 K's in 1884, 1885, and 1886.
Hank O'Day	Pitch	7	Pittsburgh Washington	1881-1883	1862	Won 16 games in 1888. 73 and 110 lifetime – 3.74 ERA. Legendary Umpire
Fred Carroll	Catch OF	8	Pittsburgh	1883	1864	366 RBI and .284 BA. Stole 137 bases
Jim Fogarty	OF	7	Philadelphia	1883	1864	325 SBs, 709 hits, 102 SBs in 1887, 99 in 1889.
Joe Corbett	Pitch	4	Washington Baltimore St. Louis	1890-1893	1875	Coached Santa Clara, won 24 games for Baltimore in 1897
Bill Hanlon	1B	1	Chicago NL	1895-1902	1876	Went to Santa Clara as well

During the 1880's, Denny played at the same athletic field in Oakland, at 13th and Center streets, as Fred W. Lange and George Van Haltren. Van Haltren was the gifted athlete who could pitch, hit, and run better than anyone around. Lange was just sixteen when he first played with Van Haltren. One day in 1885, Van Haltren had been playing catcher in a game. Not using a glove, his hands tired, so Lange took over. Lange took to catching and Van Haltren became a dominant pitcher. Not long thereafter, the two became battery mates on the Chicago White Stockings.

Before playing in the major leagues, Van Haltren and Lange played for the Greenhood & Morans (G&Ms), which was the best team in the region in 1886. At the time, there were two dominant leagues, the California and the California State League. The California League had the Stars, Haverlys, and Pioneers of San Francisco, and the Atlas of Sacramento. The Haverlys dominated the California League behind star pitcher Billy Incell by winning the championships in 1883, 1884, 1885, and 1886. The Calfornia State League had the SF Californias, the SF Damians, G&M's of Oakland, and the Knickerbockers of SF.

Lange played under the name Dolan because his father didn't approve of his playing. One day, at a game in Alameda, umpired by the bare-knuckled heavyweight world-boxing champion, John L. Sullivan, Lange's father clandestinely spied on his son through a knothole in the fence. The crowd was standing room only that day. As more fans arrived, spectators were allowed to stand behind the outfielders on the field. Players received a cut of the gate, typically 35%. At the age of seventeen, Lange received $108 for the game. When he got home, his father didn't scold him for playing. Rather, he asked him for a $100 loan. Lange averaged $40 per Sunday game at a young age.[5]

Most players worked during the week and played on Sundays. There weren't many good ballplayers to choose from back then. And no coaches were paid to develop youngsters. Players didn't play for the money, according to Lange. They played for the love of the game.

In the 1880s, the rules were considerably different than they are today. There were nine balls and six strikes allowed. A foul ball didn't count as a strike. Players learned to foul the ball off to tire out the pitcher. The pitcher also took no warm-up tosses. In spite of the rules, the games were typically completed in ninety minutes.

"Inside baseball" was the standard. Hit and runs, steals, and bunts were the most common ways to reach base and advance runners. California products became known "back East" for their speed and defense, including Denny, Fogarty, and Van Haltren in the early years, and Hal Chase, Harry Hooper, and Frank Chance in subsequent years.

No regular schedules were created. Teams found opponents when and where they could, and then arranged games.

In 1888, George Van Haltren and Fred Lange traveled together via railroad to Chicago to play for the Nationals. Lange recounted their trip together.

Before we left Oakland, we fitted ourselves out with gray suits and overcoats. Both of our folks made up baskets of food for us to eat on the train. There were not accommodations in traveling then as at present, and at eating stops we were allowed but 20 minutes. Having our own food, we usually bought only a cup of coffee. Our car was not upholstered as they are now, and soon we were like one big family, playing cards and games. When we arrived in Chicago, George went to a boarding house that he had been to the year before. When located, we walked down to Spalding's Store on Madison Street, near the old McVickers Theater. In walking down, we had to go under the Chicago River, and icicles were hanging from the ceiling. People would turn and look at us as if we were a couple of Hoosiers just come to town, as we had on light gray suits and overcoats, and they were wearing fur coats. The snow was piled all around.[6]

Van Haltren and Lange in Chicago in 1888 and together at Seals Stadium at Old Timers Game fifty years later in 1937 as the oldest living battery in America.

Lange quit professional baseball in 1888 to work with his brother in his father's business, the American Biscuit Company, which became Nabisco when it merged with the New York Biscuit Company in 1898.

Van Haltren became the first great baseball star to come out of the Bay Area. He debuted in 1887 at the age of twenty-one with the Chicago White Stockings, the predecessor to the Chicago Cubs, under manager and future Hall of Famer Cap Anson. He was a fair pitcher, but a better hitter and fast on the base paths. Before his major league career ended in 1903 because of a broken ankle, the strong-armed outfielder played seventeen seasons and amassed a .316 lifetime batting average, 2,532 hits, and 582 stolen bases. He is the highest ranked player statistically in the history of the game who is not in the Hall of Fame.

In 1894, he joined the New York Giants and was voted by fans as the most popular player in New York, a distinction that earned him a silver bat. He batted a career high .351 in 1896. He later became roommates with the young Christy Mathewson.

In the off-season, Van Haltren returned to the West and played through the winter, as would be the custom and point of contention with major league owners for the next fifty years.[A] Following the 1888 season, superstar Van

---

[A] Even Babe Ruth would later be suspended from baseball for playing in barnstorming games in the off-season, sometimes in California.

Haltren pitched in front of his home crowd for a major league all-star exhibition team assembled to tour the world. Albert Spalding organized the 1888 World Tour in which members of the Chicago Nationals and other stars barnstormed the country playing exhibition games, then took their show abroad to Hawaii, Australia, New Zealand, Samoa, Ceylon, Egypt, Italy, France, England, Scotland, and Ireland before returning to New York and barnstorming back to Chicago. Jim Fogarty played for the All-Stars, as did St. Mary's teammate Fred Carroll, future Pennsylvania Governor John Tener, and future hall of famers Cap Anson, Ned Hanlon, John Montgomery Ward, and George Wright.[A]

Initially, the All-Stars played Stockton to a 2-2 tie behind a two-hitter thrown by Tener. They then defeated Stockton 16-1 and Haverly 6-1.

The tour played in Los Angeles, then returned to San Francisco on November 16. On November 17, the professionals held a big dinner at the Baldwin Hotel and invited seventy-five guests. The next day they boarded their shop at Folsom Street Wharf. In front of 2,000 fans that saw him and his team off, Spalding gave three cheers for California and California baseball.

In June of that same year, a humor columnist for the San Francisco Examiner named Ernest Lawrence Thayer penned a poem entitled "Casey." It would not become popular as "Casey at the Bat" for another two decades when it would appeal to baseball fans at vaudeville shows. The identity of the Mighty Casey is not known, but his team, the Mudville Nine, was likely the Stockton Millers. The Millers played their games a brief train ride east of San Francisco at Banner Island Park in an area along the delta known as Mudville.

In 1888, the formidable Stockton team was led by George Stallings, who would play briefly in the major leagues, then manage from 1897 to 1920 and become known for accomplishing a miraculous Worlds Series victory in 1914 for the Boston Braves.

By the 1890's, games were played on Saturdays as well as Sundays. San Jose fielded a team in 1891 after recruiting manager Mike Finn[B] from San Francisco. With Cal McVey and George Stallings, they edged out San Francisco, Oakland, and Sacramento for the championship. In 1892, Joe Corbett, brother of boxer Jim Corbett, led his St. Mary's squad to the Pacific Amateur Baseball title. The same year, Los Angeles began playing baseball professionally and immediately asserted itself on a level with its Northern California counterparts. Los Angeles won the state championship in 1892 by defeating rivals Oakland, San Francisco, and Sacramento. The Sacramento team featured ex-major leaguer and

---

[A] Van Haltren toured only for the U.S. leg; he didn't travel abroad.

[B] In 1901, Mike Finn moved to the Southern Association where he managed future Hall of Famer Tris Speaker with the Little Rock Travelers (1901-1909). Speaker would join former St. Mary's College players Duffy Lewis and Harry Hooper in the outfield of the Boston Red Sox and win four worlds series titles.

the future renowned Christian evangelist Billy Sunday, who by 1920 had preached Jesus Christ to more people than anyone in history. Ironically, throughout America, evangelicals fought successfully in many cities to ban baseball on Sundays. In 1896, the entire Chicago ball club had been arrested for playing on Sunday. The case of Walter Wilmot vs. City of Chicago Sunday Baseball, however was decided in favor of baseball and assured Sunday baseball in Chicago for the near future. Courts contested similar cases throughout the United States.

In 1893, the country fell into a great depression. The financial crisis was the worst to face the nation in its history. Three major railroads failed and hundreds of banks failed. The unemployment rate approached twenty percent. The California League blew up at the end of the season. No organized professional baseball would be played for the next three years. Only teams making their own arrangements played games.[A]

During this era of economic uncertainty, the San Francisco newspapers discovered the critical role that sports had in selling papers. During the depression, subscriptions dropped. Papers such as the San Francisco Call, San Francisco Monitor, San Francisco Daily, the San Francisco Bulletin, and the San Francisco Examiner sponsored baseball teams to create interest in their sports coverage. The San Francisco Bulletin touted the youthful star pitcher Charles "Spider" Baum, whose popularity rose each time he took the mound. The Examiner did one better than the other papers by sponsoring a tournament, beginning in 1894, featuring the West's best baseball players eighteen years of age and under. The tournament was the precursor to current day American Legion baseball. Stars of the tournaments included Ben Henderson, George Croll, Charlie Graham, and the handsome Doc Moskiman.

Teams from Oregon, Washington, and Nevada, San Diego, Sierra Nevada, Bay Area, Los Angeles, and Central Valley competed in the 1896 tournament. The finals between the Virginia City Stars from Nevada and the Tuft Lyons team from Los Angeles drew over 10,000 fans. The Tuft Lyons team won the championship.

The success of the tournament in the midst of the depression buoyed the local economies, spirits, and tax coffers. City officials in Oakland and San Francisco, including San Francisco's Mayor James Phelan, took an active administrative role planning for a grand tournament in 1897. President of the Oakland City Council had reason to be interested; William Pringle was a member of the Oakland Reliance Club that was the tournament favorite. George Newhall,

---

[A] Heinie Reitz was fortunate enough to dodge the financial crisis facing California baseball. A San Francisco club sold him to Baltimore in 1893 for $300. In Baltimore, the second baseman would play with future Hall of Famers John McGraw, Hugh Jennings, Willie Keeler, and Joe Kelley. He'd also play alongside local Joe Corbett, who posted 24 wins for the squad in 1897.

president of the prestigious Olympic Club of San Francisco, which entered a team, and businessman Henry J. Crocker, nephew of railroad magnate Charles Crocker, also helped plan the event. The enterprising officials and the Examiner decided to open up the Examiner Baseball Tournament to all ages, not just those eighteen or under. The tournament would be the first comprehensive statewide competition to decide a champion. Its success would indeed sell papers. For the entire summer of 1897, the Examiner sports page featured either results for the past week or promotion for the next week's contests.

The competing San Francisco Chronicle understandably never mentioned the Examiner Tournament in its newspaper. Even though the tournament was the most popular prolonged baseball event the state had ever known, the only mention of baseball in the Chronicle emanated from Cal Berkeley or down on "the farm" at Stanford.

Instead of putting all of its summer sports coverage on baseball, the Chronicle covered other popular sports of the day, including chess and checkers, bicycle racing, horse racing, cricket, diving, trap shooting, sailing and yachting, billiards, basketball, track and field, tennis, lawn tennis, football, volleyball, dog racing, hunting, fly fishing, swimming, and rowing. It covered the first event to be recorded on feature film, the "Fight of the Century" in Carson City, Nevada where Bob Fitzsimmons, with Bat Masterson and Wyatt Earp in the audience, knocked out champion Gentleman Jim Corbett.[A] The Chronicle also covered the fight between rising heavyweight contender Jim Jeffries versus Gus Ruhlin, and the arrival in town of one of the greatest "pound for pound" fighters, welterweight Joe Walcott.

Even though the Chronicle didn't cover the popular Examiner baseball tournament, it had little trouble selling newspapers during the summer of 1897. Another event captivated California, and the Chronicle brought it vividly to its readership.

1897 in San Francisco

Baseball and boxing weren't the only news items on the public's mind in San Francisco in the summer of 1897. The Chronicle featured regular coverage of international affairs such as the Greco Turkish war over Crete, political matters including President William McKinley taking office and William Jennings Bryan's summer visit to the City, the annexation of Hawaii on June 17, an exposé by journalist Annie Laurie on the conditions in sweatshops, and the formation of the new Social Democratic Party by Eugene Debs in Chicago.

But the biggest news was GOLD.

[A] Following the match, Fitzsimmons coined the phrase, "the bigger they are, the harder they fall." He was not so much referring to the much slighter and craftier Corbett, but to his stature and celebrity.

The California gold rush was long past. But the Klondike gold rush in Canada and Alaska had just begun. On August 16, 1896, John Carmack and Native American Skookum Jim discovered a large strike on Rabbit Creek near the town of Forty Mile in Canada. Clarence "C.J." Berry, former baseball player and farmer from Selma, California (near Fresno) had been in the northern region since 1893 after the California economy soured. Penniless after fruitless prospecting, C.J. took a job out of necessity in Bill McPhee's bar at Forty Mile. It was at McPhee's bar that Berry witnessed Carmack's arrival and announcement of his find. Berry immediately poled forty miles in a skiff, a raft no more than eight feet in length, in a six-mile-an-hour current, painstakingly criss-crossing the Yukon River. He then walked fifteen miles to stake claim number 40 above Rabbit Creek, which was soon renamed as Bonanza Creek. His wife Ethel and brother Clarence arrived soon thereafter on a riverboat to assist him. The claim turned out to be one of the richest strikes in the world.[7]

C.J. Berry's good fortune did not end with the strike at Bonanza. Clarence sold a portion of his claim on Bonanza Creek and purchased stakes in other claims. Two weeks after gold was found at Bonanza, it was also found at a tributary of Bonanza called Eldorado Creek, on which Berry purchased a share of a claim. While the strike at Bonanza became the most famous, Eldorado Creek turned out to be most prolific, producing the largest amount of gold during the Yukon gold rush.[A]

News of the gold in the Yukon slowly leaked out to the economically beleaguered citizens of the United States. The population of the town of Forty Mile, still limited to a small group of hopeful miners, exploded during 1897 after explorers, led by the Berry family, returned to the cities of the West Coast carrying large quantities of gold. In February of 1897, Henry Berry received a message from his brother C.J. It read:

> *"Quit your job. Come here. We have a very rich ground. We even have a 14 ounce nugget. Bring 100 lb each of dried raisins, peaches, and apricots. Dried fruit is worth 40-50 cents a pound and then it is no good . . . a wife is a very good thing in this country."[8]*

On July 14, 1897 the steamship Excelsior landed in San Francisco with passengers carrying $500,000 worth of gold from the Klondike. Clarence and Ethel Berry, and Clarence's brother Fred, brought back the largest bounty. While they were the most successful of the "Sourdoughs" thus far, they were far from done removing gold from the Yukon. In town, Clarence and Ethel Berry met with the press, friends, and interested parties while staying at the Grand Hotel in San Francisco.

[A] In today's dollars, the Eldorado Creek, although only five miles in length, yielded the approximate equivalent of $5 billion in gold.

The San Francisco Chronicle reported:

> *"Two million dollars taken from the Klondyke region in less than five months, and a hundred times that amount awaiting those who can handle a pick and shovel tells the story of the most marvelous placer digging the world has ever seen." This was the remark made yesterday by Clarence Berry of Fresno, who, with his wife, has just returned from the great frozen North, where gold is found in such quantities as to dazzle the imagination and startle the skeptical. At the Grand Hotel yesterday Mr. Berry was the recipient of many congratulations. Old miners called to see him and also to examine specimens of the wonderful region that yields nuggets as big as hens' eggs. . . Berry is regarded by miners as one of the luckiest men on earth. He went to the Klondyke as a tenderfoot, but came out a wealthy man and with prospects that may make him many times a millionaire. He bears the burden of his good fortune with easy grace, and is willing to tell what he knows of the Yukon country.*
>
> *I was rather lucky," said Berry yesterday. "In my trip to the Klondyke region. The first season's work has netted me something like $130,000, and I have nine-tenths of my claim yet to explore. In addition to this, I am interested in other locations which have been prospected and proved to be equally as rich as my own." [9]*

Throughout the summer of 1897, the craze of the Yukon gold rush pulsated through the Bay Area. Not a day went by when the newspapers didn't publish maps to the region, lists of recommended provisions, interviews with C.J. Berry or his wife Ethel, or additional accounts regarding the prospects and conditions. Each town assembled groups of young men to rush to the region, some raising funds by hosting baseball games and public dances.

Grand Ball in 1897 sponsored by the newly named Klondike Nugget Baseball Club in San Mateo, south of San Francisco, raised money for players heading to the Klondike.

Some of the local, young baseball prospects, with the ambition and vigor to embrace the challenge, chose adventure in the Yukon over a baseball career. One of those ballplayers was C.J.'s brother Henry.

The Berry brothers were handy with their fists, but baseball was their love. They all played ball in Selma at early ages.[10] When C.J. set sail for San Francisco from the Klondike in June of 1897, his brother Hen, future owner of the Los Angeles Angels and San Francisco Seals, was playing in the Examiner baseball tournament.

Examiner Baseball Tournament of 1897

The Examiner baseball tournament of 1897 began on June 5. It welcomed players from throughout the state. The only requirements were that participants wear the uniforms of their team and that the rosters be submitted prior to the tournament. The day before the tournament, the San Francisco Mayor worked out final details, such as the flexibility in the rosters. His participation in the decision to freeze rosters throughout the tournament and not allow for the recruitment of ringers attested to the level of interest the tournament engendered. The Examiner newspaper used the tournament, which ran from June to September, as a centerpiece in its sports page the entire summer.

The crowds, which ranged from a few hundred to over 10,000, created revenues for the city, particularly because the players were assured only a 10% cut of the gate as opposed to the 35% that was customary during that era. The grand prize was $1,000 in gold coin, a pennant, and a trophy created by Shreve and Company at an expense of $625. Considered a masterful creation, the trophy was put on display in the window of the company near Union Square where hundreds of thousands of people ogled it during a four-month period.

Nearly sixty teams from throughout California entered the double elimination tournament. Games were scheduled at parks throughout the State, including San Francisco's Central Park, Presidio, Sixteenth and Folsom Street grounds, Athletic Park in Fresno, Cycling Park in Santa Rosa, Vallejo, Bakersfield, Los Angeles, San Bernardino, Santa Cruz, Grass Valley, Alameda, Suisun, and Benicia.

Two thousand attended the opening game at 3:00 in Central Park between the San Francisco Columbias and the Alameda Bushnell Alerts. A procession preceded the game.

> *There will be a grand parade of players in uniform before the opening of the tournament... they will be met by Casassa's band, which will give a concert in the park. After the musical programs have been completed, a procession will be formed, headed by the band, and will proceed down Post Street to Kearny, thence to California, to Montgomery, to Market, to Eighth, to Mission, where the players will align and, headed by the music, march into Central Park, each balltosser carrying over his shoulder a small American flag. A drum major, the splendor of whose furnishings would turn a peacock green with envy, will lead the procession. Following him will march two ballplayers in uniform, one each from the Columbias and the Alerts, carrying a large bear flag and a big American flag. Then will come Casassa's musicians marching five abreast. Two open wagonettes, in each of which will be seated one of the ball teams in uniform, will bring up the rear.... The fences and stands will be tastefully decorated with bunting and American flags.*[11]

One of the strongest teams in the tournament was the Fresno Republicans, led by a powerful John McCarthy and fleet-footed young catcher named Frank Chance. Born on September 9, 1877, Chance had played in the tournament the previous year as an eighteen year old. During the tournament, All-Star outfielder Bill Lange of the Chicago Orphans (later Chicago Cubs) notified his team about Chance. The next season, Chance began his illustrious career with the Chicago franchise.[A]

Bill Lange, not to be confused with Fred W. Lange (no relation), hailed from San Francisco. He played for Chicago from 1893 to 1899 and put up a lifetime batting average of .330. And like the other stars from the West who turned professional in the East, Lange stole bases. He stole 399 bases in seven seasons. He averaged 72 stolen bases over four seasons. At 6'1" and 190 pounds, large for his era, he also hit for power. He averaged over ninety RBI per season his first five seasons as well as 98 runs his entire career. He batted .389 in 1895, still the individual single season record in Chicago Cub franchise history. In 1899, Lange retired from baseball in his prime at the age of twenty-eight to marry a woman whose father forbade her to marry a baseball player. When he later divorced, he refused offers to return to the East that would have made him the highest paid player of the day.[B]

Playing alongside Lange and Chance on the Cubs in 1898 were Bay Area native Sam Mertes, future Yankee and Pacific Coast League manager Harry Wolverton, Chicago baseball fixture Nixey Callahan, and future Hall of Famer Clark Griffith.

Another powerhouse team in the tournament hailed from Santa Cruz. It defeated Chance and his Fresno squad in consecutive games in late July. Led by power players Brick Devereaux, Julie Strieb, Abe Arellanes, and the Daubenbiss brothers, Santa Cruz won nearly all of its contests despite not signing the best player from the area, future New York Giant superstar Mike Donlin, who regrettably played for the weaker SF Calls that was eliminated before July.

Chance and his squad fared better than it had against Santa Cruz when it met the Sodality Athletic Club of Santa Clara in a hotly contested game at the end of June in Fresno. Charlie Graham, future owner of the San Francisco Seals, the slick-fielding Alfred Davis, and the rest of the Santa Clara squad jumped out to a

---

[A] Chance became the first major league player from California to play in the major leagues who reached the Hall of Fame. The first Californian to reach the Hall of Fame was Walter Johnson, who entered in the inaugural year. Chance remained with the Cubs until 1911. The Cubs won the pennant in 1906, 1907, 1908, and 1910 and won the World Series in 1907 and 1908. In 1913, he managed the New York Yankees. In 1916 he was with the Chisox and the Los Angeles Angels.

[B] His nephews were Hall of Famer George "High-Pockets" Kelly and his brother, Ren, who also played in the major leagues.

five-run lead in the second inning. But the Fresno Republicans shut out Santa Clara the remainder of the game and stormed back for an 8-5 win in Fresno in front of 1,000 fans. During the game, third baseman Davis ran for a foul fly, and after catching it, fell down an embankment at Athletic Park. Although injured badly, he played the game out. A few days later, he complained of pain. Steadily his condition worsened. On Monday, Alfred Davis tragically died from his injury. The team published a memorial in the Examiner dedicated to their fallen teammate and vowed to do their best through the remainder of the tournament under the circumstances.

Most of the Santa Clara team had been recycled from the San Jose team from the prior season. Charlie Graham was a star catcher for Santa Clara College who had just completed his junior season.[A] Graham was raised at the corner of Main and Reeves streets in Santa Clara. A native, and a devoted Catholic, he received his first communion at the Santa Clara Mission on May 19, 1881. He graduated from Bellarmine High School, and would graduate from Santa Clara College the following June.

Fortunately for Santa Clara Sodality, which was still shaken from the loss of their teammate when they faced rival Hollister, the tournament organizers decided to alter the tournament rules to require three losses for elimination. With the lesser teams eliminated in June, the Examiner sought to extend the competition among the stronger teams through July, August, and even September. In fact, they considered altering the format as the summer progressed to match the best and most popular teams.

The other strong teams in the tournament included the Oakland Reliance Athletic Club with stars Jim Nealon and Fred Lange, Sacramento Gilt Edge with first baseman Spike Hennessey and the unbeatable hurler Jay Hughes, SF Athletic Club and star Tommy Sheehan, Union Iron Works with Jimmy Whalen, California Markets with Ham Iburg and Jack Bodie, Bakersfield with Phil Knell and Bill Hanlon, SF Violets and stars Truck Eagan and

Five top West Coast ballplayers posing together in a light-hearted photo while in San Diego together in 1900. Top row: Truck Eagan, Abe Arellanes, Brick Devereaux. Bottom: Turkey Mike Donlin. Courtesy Fred Lange.

[A] His coach for the 1898 season would be major league pitcher Joe Corbett, who won 24 games for Baltimore the prior year.

Doc Moskiman,
circa 1900.
Courtesy Fred
Lange

Harry O'Day, Will and Fincks with George Hildebrand, the Bushnell Alerts with Doc Moskiman, and the Los Angeles squad.

On some teams, the best hitters were the best pitchers, as was the case with Moskiman. Over the next two decades, the major leagues would feature many players who could hit and pitch; many came from the West, including Walter Johnson, Hal Chase, Harry Wolter, Pop Dillon, Mike Donlin, Harry Wolverton, and George Van Haltren. Moskiman would remain atop the California and Pacific Coast leagues in hitting and pitching categories for most of the next decade. He became the anchor of the perennial powerhouse Stockton teams of the early 1900s. His cronies joked that his only weakness was that he didn't like to slide and dirty his uniform. Born in Oakland, he joined Van Haltren on the Monarchs as a fifteen year-old, excused by his father. In 1897, he joined the Bushnell Alerts, and then hitched up with Fred Lange's Oakland Reliance. He lived in Oakland with Fred Lange prior to the turn of the century at the corner of 12th and Chester Streets with players Lou Hardie, Claude Schmeer, Russ Steadman, and others. Doc was Lange's best man when Fred married Mary Nunan in 1900.[12]

Jay Hughes of the Gilt Edge, named for Sacramento's locally brewed Ruhstaller's Gilt Edge Lager, was virtually unbeatable on the mound; he averaged over ten strikeouts per game for the tournament. The Baltimore Orioles took notice, perhaps informed by team members and locals Joe Corbett and Heinie Reitz. Hughes immediately signed for the 1898 season and posted records of 23-12 and 28-6 in the next two seasons.[A]

The top teams competed furiously through July and August, giving the fans and promoters all they expected. Then on September 12, the tournament blew up amidst controversy.

When the tournament began, the rules posted in the papers allowed for teams to play exhibition games outside of the tournament. During the summer, some teams did play games for local fans. Yet, when the Reliance Athletic Club agreed to travel to Sacramento to play the Gilt Edge team in an exhibition, the Examiner Tournament organizers forbade the game. Fred Lange, who had organized the match, found himself in an uncomfortable predicament.

Much had been written about player and management controversies in past years that caused leagues to terminate and teams to realign. Undeniably, some animosity existed because the tournament paid players less than their normal percentage of the gate. But Fred Lange stated that the players played primarily for

---

[A] Jay Hughes would later coach at Santa Clara before his early death in 1924.

the love of the game. They required fairness, however, and they felt that the Examiner organizers had exploited them. The Tournament's ruling on the Reliance versus Gilt Edge exhibition game touched a nerve.

Lange recalled treating ballplayers with fairness. He wrote,

Sixteen or 17 of my players and friends used to have dinner together after the Saturday game and then all of us would go to the theater together at night. I used to give the theatrical people passes to ball games and they would give me passes to their show ... that is the reason I always had all the ball players I needed, as I gave them a square deal. I was making plenty of money in my business and played the game in those days for the sport I got out of it. I always have loved the game.[13]

The ban on exhibition games was an additional irritant to players already disgruntled over compensation. Even though the tournament organizers warned that if the two teams played the game they would be dismissed from the tournament, Fred Lange decided to play the game as he had agreed. The two top teams in the tournament, the Reliance and the Gilt Edge, had played their last game in the Examiner tournament.

Teams that remained in the tournament demanded 20% of gate receipts. At one game, six hundred fans showed up to watch Santa Cruz, but the team refused to play unless they received the 20%. The game was cancelled.

The strongest teams in the tournament snubbed the Examiner and secured new grounds at Eighth and Harrison known as Recreation Park. The park would become the center of baseball in San Francisco. By October, the teams formed the California League, the precursor to the Pacific Coast League, and played before 5,000 fans on opening day October 3, 1897. The new California League was comprised of four clubs – Lange's Oakland Reliance, the Sacramento Gilt Edges, Stockton, and the Olympic Club of San Francisco. The teams negotiated terms at Recreation Park that created a fair situation for fans and players. Admission was a reasonable 10 cents for general admission and 25 cents for reserved seating. The Examiner Tournament folded as the fans chose to attend the superior California League games.

Lange recounted that by expelling the two top teams in the tournament, the Examiner created the catalyst for what would eventually become the greatest baseball league in the West, the Pacific Coast League.

Pre 1920 California All Star Team

FIRST TEAM	SECOND TEAM	THIRD TEAM
Orval Overall	Harry Wolter	Frank Arellanes
Chief Meyers	Doc Moskiman	Fred Carroll
Gavvy Cravath	Rube Ellis	Tommy Sheehan
Bill Lange	Tillie Shafer	Jim Nealon
Duffy Lewis	Jim Fogarty	Truck Eagan
Ping Bodie	Phil Knell	George Hildebrand
Charlie Graham	Joe Corbett	Ham Iburg
Hal Chase	Sam Mertes	Ed "Live" Taylor
Frank Chance	Ossie Vitt	Mike Finn
Harry Hooper	Hank O'Day	Pete Lohman
George Van Haltren	Dutch Leonard	Hap Hogan
Jerry Denny	Rube Vickers	Spider Baum
Ed Morris	Fred Snodgrass	Ben Henderson
Mike Donlin	Kid Mohler	Brick Devereaux
Walter Johnson	Pop Dillon	Julie Strieb
Buck Weaver	George Stallings	Abe Arellanes
Harry Wolverton	Cal McVey	Fred W. Lange

Bold = Hall of Fame (Heilmann placed in post-1920)

Casey at the Bat

It looked extremely rocky for the Mudville nine that day;

The score stood two to four, with but an inning left to play.

So, when Cooney died at second, and Burrows did the same,

A pallor wreathed the features of the patrons of the game.

A straggling few got up to go, leaving there the rest,

With that hope which springs eternal within the human breast.

For if only Casey could get a whack at that,"

they'd put even money now, with Casey at the bat.

But Flynn preceded Casey, and likewise so did Blake,

And the former was a pudd'n and the latter was a fake.

So on that stricken multitude a deathlike silence sat;

For there seemed but little chance of Casey's getting to bat.

But Flynn let drive a "single," to the wonderment of all.

And the much-despised Blakey tore the cover off the ball.

And when the dust had lifted, and they saw what had occurred,

There was Blakey safe at second, and Flynn a-huggin' third.

Then from the gladdened multitude went up a joyous yell.

It rumbled in the mountaintops, it rattled in the dell;

It struck upon the hillside and rebounded on the flat;

For Casey, mighty Casey was advancing to the bat.

There was ease in Casey's manner as he stepped into his place,

There was pride in Casey's bearing and a smile on Casey's face;

And when responding to the cheers he lightly doffed his hat.

No stranger in the crowd could doubt 'twas Casey at the bat."

Ten thousand eyes were on him as he rubbed his hands with dirt,

Five thousand tongues applauded when he wiped them on his shirt;

Then when the writhing pitcher ground the ball into his hip,

Defiance glanced in Casey's eye, a sneer curled Casey's lip.

And now the leather-covered sphere came hurtling through the air,

And Casey stood a watching it in haughty grandeur there.

Close by the sturdy batsman the ball unheeded sped;

"That ain't my style," said Casey. "Strike one," the umpire said.

From the benches, black with people, there went up a muffled roar,

Like the beating of the storm waves on the stern and distant shore.

"Kill him! kill the umpire!" shouted someone in the stands;

And it's likely they'd have killed him had not Casey raised his hand.

With a smile of Christian charity great Casey's visage shone;

He stilled the rising tumault; he made the game go on;

He signaled to the pitcher, and once more the spheroid flew;

But Casey still ignored it, and the umpire said, "Strike Two."

"Fraud!" cried the maddened thousands, and the echo answered "Fraud!"

But one scornful look from Casey and the audience was awed;

They saw his face grow stern and cold, they saw his muscles strain,

And they knew that Casey wouldn't let that ball go by again.

The sneer is gone from Casey's lips, his teeth are clenched in hate,

He pounds with cruel violence his bat upon the plate;

And now the pitcher holds the ball, and now he lets it go,

And now the air is shattered by the force of Casey's blow.

Oh, somewhere in this favored land the sun is shining bright,

The band is playing somewhere, and somewhere hearts are light.

And somewhere men are laughing, and somewhere children shout,

But there is no joy in Mudville:

Mighty Casey has struck out.

1 History of Baseball in California and Pacific Coast Leagues 1847 - 1938. Memories and Musings of an Old Time Baseball Player. Fred W. Lange. Oakland, CA. 1938

2 A History of Baseball in the San Francisco Bay Area. San Francisco Giants Official 1985 Yearbook. Woodford Associates. 1985

3 History of Baseball in California and Pacific Coast Leagues 1847 - 1938. Memories and Musings of an Old Time Baseball Player. Fred W. Lange. Oakland, CA. 1938

4 History of Baseball in California and Pacific Coast Leagues 1847 - 1938. Memories and Musings of an Old Time Baseball Player. Fred W. Lange. Oakland, CA. 1938

5 History of Baseball in California and Pacific Coast Leagues 1847 - 1938. Memories and Musings of an Old Time Baseball Player. Fred W. Lange. Oakland, CA. 1938

6 History of Baseball in California and Pacific Coast Leagues 1847 - 1938. Memories and Musings of an Old Time Baseball Player. Fred W. Lange. Oakland, CA. 1938

7 Correspondence to author from Fred Berry's grandson William Berry.

8 "Pioneers of Alaska", Palma Berger, Klondike Sun, October 16, 1998 (oral history given by William Berry, grandson of Fred Berry).

9 "Mr. Berry of Fresno", Los Angeles Times, July 25, 1897

10 Correspondence to author from Fred Berry's grandson William Berry.

11 The Examiner, San Francisco, Saturday Morning, June 5, 1897

12 History of Baseball in California and Pacific Coast Leagues 1847 - 1938. Memories and Musings of an Old Time Baseball Player. Fred W. Lange. Oakland, CA. 1938

13 History of Baseball in California and Pacific Coast Leagues 1847 - 1938. Memories and Musings of an Old Time Baseball Player. Fred W. Lange. Oakland, CA. 1938

Chapter 2

The Boys of Santa Clara and Santa Cruz

Prior to the turn of the century, the baseball teams of the Santa Clara Valley and the Santa Cruz Mountains began assembling a nucleus of ballplayers that became the envy of Northern California. Some played for local college teams in the spring and local professional teams afterward. Others, like Mike Donlin, jumped straight into the California State League and then to the majors.

Donlin began as a pitcher for Watsonville in 1897 and 1898. He joined the Santa Cruz Beachcombers as an outfielder and pitcher in 1899. Santa Cruz, a beachfront town twenty miles over the Santa Cruz Mountains from the Santa Clara Valley and seventy-five miles down the coast from San Francisco, had a baseball team owned by Fred Stanton, who planned an oceanfront beach resort featuring entertainment and an amusement park. His team played their games at Dolphin Park across from where the Santa Cruz Beach Boardwalk now resides.

The idea of creating an entertainment center, particularly on the ocean, figured a popular enterprise over the ensuing years on both coasts. And often an integral component included baseball games, and sometimes boxing matches, to attract the population to the center. Frequently the planners were owners of local transportation systems, the two ventures enriching each other. For example, on the other side of the mountain, the owner of the San Jose and Santa Clara Railway purchased the San Jose ball club and built a park along the tracks at the major thoroughfares of Race Street and The Alameda.

Donlin featured a red neck, and people thought he walked with a strut. Thus, he earned the nickname "Turkey" Mike. Born in the Peoria, Illinois, Mike was orphaned at eight when his parents died tragically in a bridge collapse.1 And although he lived a rough life, he developed a sense of style; he was an

impeccable dresser off the field. On the diamond, however, his cheek was always filled with a plug of tobacco. He began as a pitcher, but then converted to the outfield when his natural ability to hit became apparent before he turned twenty. In 1899, his hitting attracted the attention of scouts.

Turkey Mike Donlin

Handsome, outgoing, and a natural athlete Donlin could also find trouble on occasion, particularly when he drank and partied. He had a scar on his face from one of those scrapes. When St. Louis sent notification in 1899 that they were interested in signing him, he received the news while in jail for public drunkenness.[A] They offered him the price of a train ticket and an opportunity to prove himself. He took it. He would return to California in the off-season, as was the custom among major leaguers, to play in the fall and winter. In March of 1901, for example, just prior to beginning his first season with Baltimore after two good seasons in St. Louis where he split duty in the outfield, he played for the All Californians. In a game against the Easterners, a team of major leaguers that included Frank Chance, Jake Beckley, and Van Haltren, who were staging exhibition games in the West, Donlin hit a home run to defeat the Easterners 7-6.

Other ballplayers in the San Jose and surrounding areas played for Santa Clara College, the oldest institution of higher learning in California, founded in 1851. The school fielded a baseball team as early as the 1860s when the college stood alone beside the Santa Clara Mission along the major thoroughfare known as "The Alameda" fifty miles south of San Francisco.

By the 1890s, the Santa Clara Valley expanded to support the growth of San Francisco, which had been connected with San Jose by a Southern Pacific Railroad line since 1864. Agriculture and lumber from the nearby mountains surrounding Los Gatos supported industry. And with San Francisco separated from the rest of the country by the San Francisco Bay, San Jose served as a connection for railroad traffic into the City.

Towards the turn of the century, plumbing and electricity were new, roads were unpaved, and horses outnumbered trolley cars as the western towns embraced modernity while still resembling the backward pioneer villages of the Wild West. In 1898, Charlie Graham, standout catcher for Santa Clara College graduated from the school and became the baseball coach and Professor of Mathematics.

Between 1896 and 1906, Santa Clara assembled many good players. A handful played in the majors briefly or filled in on teams in the West while holding down other full time jobs. Charles H. Graham, Elmer Stricklett, Charles Strub, Hal Chase, Hap Hogan, Frank Arellanes, Tillie Shafer, and Harry Wolter became colorful and influential figures in West Coast Baseball for much of their lives.

[A] Bill Lange was likely the scout that recommended Donlin to St. Louis. Lange recommended others to St. Louis during this period. Lange and Donlin would ironically have very similar statistics in the majors – Hall of Fame numbers, but in abbreviated careers.

Santa Clara College notables Charlie Graham, Elmer Stricklett, Charles "Doc" Strub, Walter Bray (Hap Hogan), Frank Arellanes, and Harry Wolter. Graham, Strub, Hogan, and Wolter photos courtesy of Santa Clara University Archives.

The young men were not an assemblage of rowdy country bumpkins, although all were from rural towns. With oversight from priests, who taught the classes and often assisted in coaching athletics at the private school, the boys were taught ethical behavior, social responsibility, and respectable conduct, as evidenced in the formal attire in the photographs. When they embarked on their respective careers, they assumed leading roles in ushering the golden age of sports on the West Coast. Through lives filled with uncertainty, instability, external challenges, internal battles, and political pitfalls, these individuals charted divergent paths in attempts to become pillars of baseball and sports in the West. Strub the owner, Graham the general manager, Hogan the manager, Chase the nationally acclaimed All Star, Wolter the batting champion and collegiate coach, Shafer the international baseball

Left: Hal Chase as player for Santa Clara College. Notation at the bottom reads "Prince Hal" Chase. Circa 1900. Right: Harry Wolter standing above Art "Tillie" Shafer circa 1906. Courtesy Santa Clara University Archives.

ambassador, and Stricklett and Arellanes the regional All Stars, made their mark on California baseball after 1900.[A]

Charlie Graham

After starring in the Examiner Baseball Tournament in 1897 with the Sodality Athletic Club of Santa Clara, Graham joined the best team in Northern

---

[A] It is not known who attended class. Graham and Wolter graduated. Strub graduated from UC Berkeley where he transferred in 1904.

California, the Sacramento Gilt Edge, where he played from 1897-1899. In Sacramento, he would eventually rise to prominence as a baseball manager, owner, and scout.

Charlie Graham coached at Santa Clara from 1898 to 1903 while in his early twenties. Young players who had recently graduated or retired from the game frequently coached the local college ball clubs. As a manager, Graham was pensive. Rarely animated, Graham bottled his emotions. He managed the way he saved his money; one run at a time, always conservative, never squandering opportunities to put one more tally in the bank, and worrying that whatever had been saved wasn't enough.

Unlike many young men of the era, he was not much of a gambler. A coach recalled how he never had much in his pocket as a youngster. When they traveled for road games, he would sometimes join the others in a poker game. Conservatively, he'd get the most distance from his paltry starter fund. And according to his coach, by the time the team returned home, invariably everyone owed Charlie.

He mastered "inside baseball," a style of play popular during the era. Today the style would be called "small ball," characterized by good pitching, good fielding, and runs manufactured by bunts, hit and runs, and steals. The number of hits and runs produced in games during the era was low. Not much offense was needed to win games. All most teams required to be competitive were two good pitchers, sound fielding, speed, two strong hitters, and a solid catcher.

Graham required that his players view baseball like any other trade. If a player didn't reach base, he would tell them that they didn't do their job. He was analytical. He could separate himself from the emotional aspects of player development. While known for his patience and unequaled ability to develop young talent, he was also able to make decisions with the calculating coolness of an accountant. He wasted little time dismissing anyone guilty of impropriety.

On the bench, Graham's face was often tortured, no matter the circumstances. If his team were up by ten, he'd grimace that the lead was insufficient. He would sit nervously on the edge of the bench grinding his molars and gripping a bat, ball, or glove convulsively in his hands. With the bases loaded and his best hitter up to the plate, Graham would bow his head as if saying his last prayer before facing a firing squad. If a player popped out, he would wince as if smacked in the head with a sledgehammer. When his player hit a double, he obsessed about whether he would be stranded. And even when he went to bat and successfully circled the bases for a score, he would inevitably stalk back to the bench seemingly without any joy in his soul.

Graham's legacy as a player and manager was his handling of pitchers, his brains, and his development of young talent. He learned that his temperament wasn't ideally suited for a bench coach; he'd eventually migrate to team ownership and general management instead. He replaced himself as manager three times in his career. He understood his weaknesses and complemented himself with those around him, such as Hap Hogan. And his abilities as a field general in the early years didn't go unnoticed. Early Los Angeles Angels owner Jim Morley reflected back on Graham as a player and manager during the first decade of the twentieth century.

> *We had to keep from being outguessed, and when Charley was behind the bat our fellows got mighty few balls to hit… He had them (his team) beating men of established class, and they were right off the lots, too, with no previous experience… I consider Graham and Frank Dillon two of the best managers who ever handled ball clubs on this Coast, and Graham had it all over Dillon in his judgment of young players. I consider Graham the best judge of a young ballplayer in the West. That is going pretty strong, but I mean it. I was given credit for digging up some pretty classy youngsters myself, for I came up here and snared such good ones as Hal Chase, Spider Baum, and Warren Hall right from under the noses of the San Francisco and Oakland magnates, but to my mind Charley Graham is the best judge of a young ballplayer I know, and what is more, he knows how to develop them.[2]*

One journalist pointed out that Graham was a man of considerable property. In essence, he was blessed with the ability and means to pursue any field. Not out of necessity, he chose baseball. Graham was a baseball man through and through. Over the next fifty years, he would exhibit his commitment to the game, meted out steadily, repetitively, and slowly, one pitch at a time, like the slow drip from a leaking faucet. Asked why he chose such a career, without hesitation Graham offered his customary, well-thought, succinct, and refreshingly simple response.

> **A man must live with a sigh of resignation, and it might as well be baseball as any other form of woe.**

Hap Hogan

Hap Hogan and Charlie Graham, both catchers of similar ages from the same town, were polar opposites in terms of style as managers. Born Wallace Louis Bray on a farm near Santa Clara, Hap Hogan developed into a manager who was part motivator and part sideshow. Whereas Graham had a detached, impersonal business-like approach to the game, Hap was all emotion. If his team lost, he felt that they had conspired against him. Raised on a farm in a family well known for its proficiency raising grapes and fruit, Hap's father didn't allow him to play baseball. So Hap played under the assumed name Hogan. Because of his cheery disposition, people started calling him "Hap," and the name stuck his entire life. When he married, his wife went by the name Bray. And he used two names throughout his life. But he would be well known as Hap Hogan.

Unbeknownst to his father, Hap started playing as Hogan in the 1890s with Charlie Graham at Santa Clara. He transferred to the University of Southern California for one year. The school didn't have a baseball coach, so Hap filled in. His team won the Southern California Championship. He played briefly in Arizona and managed a town ball team in Phoenix while working at a retail store. He attempted to make a living in Arizona as a professional gambler, but soon returned home having developed an aversion to gambling; he would later ban gambling in the clubhouse on the teams he would manage.

He returned from Arizona to Santa Clara in 1902, and one day walked to San Jose to try out for the club there. That was the beginning of his professional career. Santa Clara ballplayer Winnie Cutter, who was coached by Hogan, remembered that Hogan was called "Swats" when he was with the San Jose club. Santa Clara was in need of a catcher, and there was some talk of enrolling Hogan in the school. Always a smart aleck, when asked what course he intended on taking, Hogan responded, "Eloquence and shower baths" with "a twinkle in his eye and a comical smile."[3] He soon signed with Sacramento instead of playing for Santa Clara, although he coached at the school and took over from his best friend Graham when Charlie stepped down in 1904.

On his way to Sacramento, Hogan stopped to play in a game for Oakland for $5 because manager Cal Ewing needed a catcher to give Pete Lohman a break. Hap caught a nineteen-inning tie game. Cutter recalled that during the game, umpire Jim McDonald called Hogan out looking on a 3-2 pitch. McDonald never tolerated any backtalk, particularly from a rookie. McDonald was a tough guy. He defeated Jim Corbett in an unofficial bare-knuckle fight back when Corbett was a second baseman in San Francisco. But as soon as Happy was called out by the menacing McDonald, Happy shouted "Oh, Jim, I couldn't-a reached that one with a fish pole." Young Winnie Cutter wrote, "It was the way Happy said it ... the umpire turned around to hide a smile."[4]

Hogan's personality was universally disarming. Cutter recalled, "There was something about Hogan's personality which was bound to make him liked by all who had ever been closely associated with him."[5]

As a manager, Hogan was respected for being clever, smart, tricky, and tactical. And as one of the game's most clutch contact hitters, he was known for inserting himself into the game in key situations in the final inning, even when his team's best hitter was slated. Unlike Graham, whose posture would reflect the burden and responsibility he felt in such a situation, Hogan was lighthearted, with a flair for the dramatic; he would bound energetically to the plate, part conqueror and part entertainer, holding his bat like a wand, or brandishing it like a sword, waving it at the pitcher in jest before digging his spikes into the batter's box. His critics would say, however, that while he was great on the field, he had no control over his players off the field, particularly the youngsters. He was considered too good a fellow, far too easy. Unlike Graham, who was good with the younger players, Hogan's style was better suited for veterans who didn't suffer slumps in discipline because of his good nature.

In 1897, at a ball game between Alviso and Newark, Hap Hogan discovered a young talent named Hal Chase.

Hal Chase

Ed Chase, arguably the best athlete in the large family, organized a baseball game with top players from the Santa Clara Valley and completed his roster with his fourteen-year old brother Hal. Hap Hogan witnessed that game and remembered the young Hal Chase for his ability. Chase played in the outfield. By his conduct, he was shy among the other players who ranged in age from eighteen to thirty. Hal was still in knickerbockers when he was pressed into service, and according to Hogan, "the way he ate them up was a caution. Even then he displayed the indefinable something that stamps the natural player."[6]

Hal grew up in Los Gatos, a few miles west of Santa Clara on the grade up the Santa Cruz Mountains on the way to the coast. His family ran a lumber mill along Summit Road that his grandfather had started called S.H. Chase Company. His father Edgar ran the mill in Alviso, just east of Santa Clara on the southern edge of the San Francisco Bay. Chase attended Los Gatos High School where he starred in baseball. He played on various town ball teams, including Alviso and Soquel, in addition to his high school team. If you asked someone back then the "dope" on the young Hal Chase, they would have told you in the jargon of the day that he was a "real deadhead," a "baseball bum," or "ringer." He'd go wherever someone would pay him to play ball. He was always in demand. He played for a team called Mayer Brothers in San Jose, owned by Amy Mayer who would later own the San Jose team that Chase would play for. He traveled with friend Elmer Emerson, a pitcher at Stanford, to British Columbia during the summer where he starred and was implored to stay. Ultimately, Charlie Graham lured him to Santa Clara to play for his squad.

His consistent status as "ringer" not only shaped his career, but also his personality. If Chase learned nothing else in his life, he learned that he had something special that others wanted, and he was willing to comply. He wasn't just after the money. He wanted what he deserved. Often whatever he earned or won he shared with others. He basked in his good fortune; to receive acceptance, adulation, and atonement he needed only to play the game that he loved. And little came between him and a ballgame for the next three decades. In the simplest terms, Chase was a great ballplayer. And he just wanted to play. He had little tolerance for the other details. Over the next two decades, he would battle management for the simple right to play baseball whenever and wherever he wanted for fans that wanted to see him in uniform.

Chase was a defensive wizard with an above-average IQ both on the ball field and on the streets. Opponents took notice of his superior judgment, his all-around physical tools, and the grace and style with which he utilized them. Charlie Graham commented on his star first baseman,

> *Chase actually caught pop foul flies BEHIND the catcher, not once but many times. With a runner on second and the batter laying down a perfect bunt, Chase was fast enough to come in on the ball, field it perfectly and tag the hitter out on the way to first, then throw the runner out at third. His uncanny foresight in smelling out a play defied imagination. He was always at least one jump ahead of the batter. Invariably, he outguessed the batter. He always played exactly where he should have been playing. I never saw him make a bad guess on the diamond.[7]*

Chase was also an expert inside baseball player. A contact hitter, he would become one of the greatest hit-and-run batters and one of the fastest base runners in the game. The daring he displayed as a fielder he also demonstrated on the bases, always sliding headfirst. Managers warned that sliding headlong into a bag could cause injury, but Chase's bad habit could never be curbed.

While bold on the field, Chase was unassuming out of uniform. His calm, gentle manner served him well meeting challenges in the pool hall or at the card table. He was kind-hearted, not exploitative. Not the type to initiate, orchestrate, or instigate a hustle or take advantage of someone by capitalizing on an edge, he did however revel in opportunities to challenge the brazen and cocky. If Chase was ever within earshot of the words "Anyone else in here think they can beat me?" in a gaming establishment, one could be sure that Chase would take the challenge. And more often than not, he prevailed as the victor. He was generally a quiet observer, but when opportunity fell into his lap, a fiercely competitive fire would ignite. His skills became legendary, surely a product of time spent at an early age in Los Gatos, perhaps with older brothers, playing pool and poker. The wise soon learned not to enter into contests of skill or wit with Chase.

Hal was docile, charming, upbeat, soft-spoken, and not noticeably arrogant. He was confident without being brash. He was a man's man, popular among his teammates both young and old. He exhibited tremendous generosity toward other players and family members; ex-wives would later suffer from and complain about that generosity.

Christy Mathewson wrote a book in 1910 loosely based on Chase as a character. The story included a shy young boy from California named Harold Case. Mathewson accurately described him as follows:

> *He was a well built fellow, but modest and somewhat backward about pushing himself forward. His hair was brown and his features were good although no one would call him handsome. His eyes were light blue and clear, his mouth was firm, and if the other fellows only knew if, he was as quick as a flash in any game he was familiar with, and he was as graceful as a deer in motion. He could run almost as fast as a deer,*

too. ... He is a quiet chap and unassuming.[8]

When Chase joined the Santa Clara baseball squad, the team didn't have a need at first base, the likely position for the left-handed Chase. So Chase played second base and catcher. An enigma in many ways, Chase preferred second base to first base, even as a southpaw. He wasn't the only left-handed second baseman in the game. Kid Mohler, nine years older than Chase, started his pro career as a pitcher for the Washington Senators in 1894. But the 5' 4" Mohler injured his right arm after only a few games. He learned to use his left hand, and succeeded in playing over 2,800 games in the minors as a second baseman. But outside of Mohler, few left-handers played any infield position other than first. Chase played all of them.

Oddly, Chase was also a left-handed hitter who taught himself to bat right-handed while emulating his heroes as a child. Whereas most batters favored hitting from the left side, closer to first base, Chase belied reason when he switched to the more distant right side, particularly in the deadball era where speed was a mantle.[A]

The local press soon took notice of Chase as a youngster. They called him "crack," meaning a "cracker jack player." The San Francisco Chronicle noted,

> *Santa Clara has always been represented by strong nines, yet Santa Clara considers Hal Chase the greatest player her school has ever known ... Hal is possessed of every requisite that goes to make up an ideal first baseman. He is quick, sure of eye and of arm, ambitious, energetic, chock full of confidence in himself and his teammates, a strong batter and a hard worker ... no one who has watched him play the game can doubt that before long his reputation will be national and he will be known as one of the country's greatest exponents of the national game.*[9]

In 1903, Chase confided in assistant coach Hap Hogan that he wanted to break into the professional game. Hogan had played for the Sacramento squad and recommended Chase. When the team came to Oakland for a game, Chase went for a tryout. Still not twenty years of age, Sacramento passed on him. "Chase returned home without so much as getting a uniform."[10] In 1904, The Santa Clara squad traveled to Los Angeles to play Coach Frank Haggerty's St. Vincent's team.[B]

[A] Chase shares the distinction of being a left-handed fielding and right-handed batting first baseman with President George H.W. Bush, who captained his Yale baseball team to two consecutive national championship finals the first two years the championships were held in 1947 and 1948.

[B] St. Vincent's College became Loyola High School and Loyola Marymount University.

Haggerty had coached the football team to success, and had strung together a nineteen game winning streak in the baseball team's first season. The game's umpire the day Chase took the field in Los Angeles was James Morley, former player for the Los Angeles Tuft Lyons team, owner of a billiard hall, and the President of the Los Angeles Angels minor league baseball team, one of the strongest minor league squads in California.

Santa Clara defeated St. Vincent's in the three game series and Chase stood out. The Southern California newspapers said that Chase was the fastest they had ever seen in an amateur game in Los Angeles. Chase's good friend William (Bill) Benson introduced Chase to Morley. The next season, Chase played professionally for Morley and the Angels.

Upon signing the contract with Morley, the unselfish Chase purchased a home for his parents in San Jose at 239 Race Street between Park and San Carlos Avenues.[11]

Charles Strub

Santa Clara ballplayer Charles Strub remembered Chase as a "left-handed shortstop, bare-footed, wearing tattered overalls."[12] The observation contained a patronizing tinge that reveals as much about Strub as it does about Chase. A year younger than Chase, Strub's comment didn't exhibit a sense of respect, or even camaraderie due a player of a similar age. An older person, such as Chase's coach Hap Hogan, could point out in an endearing manner that he recalled Chase as a young man in knickerbockers. But as a peer, Strub's selection of words reflected that from an early age, he possessed a snobbish, superior socio-economic view of himself relative to Chase and others. Perhaps he was simply aware of the fact that his family had achieved a relatively high level of social status. During his career, his abilities in social networking, country club dealing, and raising capital would serve his relentless pursuit of entrepreneurial success and status.

Teammates Winnie Cutter and Charles Strub with Santa Clara College 1901-1903. Courtesy Santa Clara University Archives

Originally from Hollister, south of San Jose, Strub moved with his family to San Francisco and attended St. Ignatius High School before attending Santa Clara. For him to remember Chase in overalls, Strub likely played against him as a teenager in the mid 1890s in the San Jose area. They also played together at Santa Clara under Graham. Strub played at the college in 1901 and 1902. He was a slight-of-build, baby-faced second baseman. He didn't graduate from the school; he transferred to University of California Berkeley to complete his studies where he also captained the baseball team. At Berkeley, he became a teammate of legendary pitcher Orval Overall, who pitched the Cubs to victory the last time the squad won the Worlds Series in 1908. Strub went on to obtain a degree in dentistry, and became known for the rest of his life as "Doc" Strub.

It was not uncommon for players of the day to have the moniker "Doc" whether or not they practiced medicine. "Doc" Moskiman did become a doctor. But other ballplayers in the West over the next few decades, including Docs Crandall, White, Hall, and Newton may or may not have practiced medicine while still answering to the name. Strub likely was proud of the label and wore it as an emblem of prestige, even though he didn't practice dentistry throughout his life.

While at Berkeley, Strub, one of the many young men who at times digressed from their studies, grew fond of horse racing. He frequented the nearby Emeryville track where accounts say he "developed knowledge" of horse racing. In most circles, his activity would amount to missing class to bet on the ponies.

But like Hogan and Chase, Strub enjoyed gambling in an era where gambling and sport were intertwined and pervasive. Gambling was a rite of passage for many young men. Those who didn't gamble were more the exception. Strub was not the exception, and similar to Graham, Chase, and Hogan who dabbled in gambling at some point in their careers, he became interested in horse racing. He also eventually became a great poker player. During time spent at the track in Emeryville, the intelligent and observant Strub likely inculcated himself on the business of the sport. In time, he would bring that experience to bear professionally.

Strub was generally introverted, not particularly personable, and didn't make friends quickly. The friends he did make served him both socially and politically. Strub ultimately married a woman, Vera Wood, a dedicated Catholic from a wealthy San Francisco family. She maintained a casual understanding of her husband's business dealings. She likely took care of the house and home while her husband persevered as an entrepreneur determined to provide her with the standard of living she had been accustomed to growing up. Vera Wood Strub would be one of the only women that Strub would "tolerate," according to a long-time female associate. He admitted once to her that, other than Strub's wife, she was the only woman who didn't get on his nerves.[13]

What he lacked in social graces, he made up for in determination and intellect. Many believed him to be a genius. He had a propensity to plan, organize, take risks, and attend to details. In essence, he had the ego, ambition, aptitude, and resiliency that suited him as an entrepreneur.

Harry Wolter

Harry Wolter grew up in Monterey, the original capital of California. Steadfast on graduating from Santa Clara, he passed up all offers to play baseball until after he completed his studies. He worked for the Wells Fargo Express in Monterey to earn money to put himself through college. Initially a star pitcher, scouts came around in 1904 and tried to sign him professionally. Jack Gleason from the San Francisco squad was one of the first to approach him. But he refused to sign.

Wolter was athletic and handsome. He could pitch, hit, run, and play defense. He possessed the entire package. His strong, silent personality likely appealed to women. Reserved, he kept to himself and preferred to be an observer. At times he could be a bit surly or gruff, although always well mannered. And some claimed he was as obstinate as they come. A man of principle, once he decided on something, he became set in his ways. Sportswriter Dick Hyland, who played for Wolter at Stanford, said, "Never has he seen Harry Wolter talked out of anything. He is obstinate. If he makes up his mind to something, that is what is going to happen."[14]

Frank Arellanes, Elmer Stricklett, and Art "Tillie" Shafer

Elmer Stricklett and Frank Arellanes would become local minor league stars before and after careers in the majors. Stricklett was two years older than Charlie Graham. He pitched for Santa Clara and for local teams before signing a contract with the Chicago White Sox in 1904. He played most of his major league career with the Brooklyn Superbas, one of the worst teams in the majors at the time. He was one of the team's best pitchers, but few stories were told of the matchups he had with the greatest of the day, including Mordecai Brown and Christy Mathewson. Even with a good earned run average, Stricklett lost many one-run games and posted losing records every year of his career.

Frank Arellanes was much younger than Stricklett. His brother Abe starred as a second baseman for the Santa Cruz team for many years; he had been one of the top players in California around the turn of the century. The younger Arellanes was a year older than Chase. He likely pitched at Santa Clara around 1900. He would later sign with the Boston Red Sox, but primarily starred in the California minor leagues for much of the next fifteen years. Some claim that he was the first Mexican American player in the majors.

Art "Tillie" Shafer attended Los Angeles High School and St. Vincent's College with Fred Snodgrass, both future New York Giants stars.[15] He then transferred to Santa Clara and played beside Harry Wolter. He became a standout third baseman even though he was just seventeen when he arrived. He didn't graduate from Santa Clara. He also played for Stanford, Notre Dame, and perhaps St. Mary's. He was born into a wealthy family, and was considered by some fans and teammates to be spoiled and snobbish. He inherited a significant fortune at a young age, and in the prime of his career, retired from the New York Giants at the age of twenty-three. His manager John McGraw complained about his not being serious enough about the game. Nevertheless, McGraw pursued Shafer for almost a decade before giving up on him.

Considered a "pretty boy," Shafer attracted the attention of both female admirers as well as harassing teammates. He developed a reputation for having women pass him perfumed notes. He became known as "Pink Notes Kid," or "Perfumed Note Man." When he was with the Giants, Mrs. John McGraw remembered being introduced to the shy, good-looking Shafer in the clubhouse. The players all jumped in and started calling Art by the name "Tillie" in jest, giving him a woman's name to make fun of his pretty features. Although Art hated the name, it stuck. And to this day, Shafer is known as "Tillie" in baseball records.[16]

[1]   Turkey Mike Donlin, The Baseball Research Journal, January 1, 2000. Betzold, Michael.
[2]   Graham Gets Boost From Old-Time Rival, Ed R. Hughes, SF Chronicle, Dec 10, 1918, 10.
[3]   Sport Shrapnel, Harry A. Williams, LA Times, Feb 26, 1922, Pg 18 Sport Shrapnel, Harry A. Williams, LA Times, Feb 26, 1922, Pg 18

[4] Sport Shrapnel. Harry A. Williams. LA Times. Feb 26, 1922. Pg 18

[5] Hap Hogan's Busher Days. May 23,1915. LA Times. pg. VII7

[6] Hogan Tells How Chase Was Turned Down by Sacramento. Jan 1, 1914. Hap Hogan. Pg. H12

[7] Sep 18, 1941. The Sporting News.

[8] Christy Mathewson. Won in the Ninth. R.J. Bodmer Company, 1910

[9] Chase Is Best Young Player. SF Chronicle. Sep 25, 1904. pg. 36

[10] Hogan Tells How Chase Was Turned Down by Sacramento. Jan 1, 1914. Hap Hogan. Pg. H12

[11] The Black Prince of Baseball. Hal Chase and the Mythology of the Game. Donald Dewey and Nicholas Acocella. pg. 14.

[12] New York Journal. Oct 22, 1955. Joe Williams

[13] "Anita of Santa Anita. Miss Weil's 32 Years on Job Packed with Vivid Memories", Bob Hebert. Los Angeles Times.

[14] Behind the Lines with Dick Hyland. Los Angeles Times. May 8, 1941. Pg. A17

[15] Death Lurks For Those People Who Ignore Sane Speed Laws. Owen R. Bird. Oct 5, 1913. Pg VII1

[16] James K. Skipper, Jr.. Baseball Nicknames: A Dictionary of Origins and Meanings. McFarland, Jefferson. NC 1992. 252

Chapter 3

1903 Season: The Formation of the Pacific Coast League

On March 26, 1903, four teams played opening day games at Recreation Park in San Francisco; the other two teams opened at Oak Park in Sacramento.[A] Before the games in San Francisco, a parade of open-air automobiles rolled through town carrying the players dressed in their uniforms. Crowds assembled, a brass band played, and Governor George Pardee threw out the first pitch. The formation of the Pacific Coast league temporarily ended the California League. But Stockton, San Jose, Vallejo, and Petaluma eventually created their own new Cal State League.

While turmoil and change rattled baseball from coast to coast, Graham and his friends simply played baseball, unburdened by political events that transpired outside of the baselines, able to focus on competition, camaraderie, and play.

Perhaps the youngsters thought about getting their big break while still young, strong, and full of promise. If their aspirations to play in the major leagues didn't get fulfilled soon, then perhaps that recurring dream of playing with the best would remain with them until the aches in their bones and soreness in their muscles brought reason even to the subconscious.

One local had already received his break and ascended to stardom before suddenly falling from grace. Turkey Mike Donlin showed he could hit in the major leagues. For St. Louis and Baltimore he hit .323, .326, and .340 from 1899 to 1901. His defense was suspect, but teammate and manager John McGraw liked Donlin's fiery attitude, and his hitting placed him second in the league in 1901 behind Nap Lajoie.[B] But in 1902, Donlin was arrested for actions related to public drunkenness. He was fined and sentenced to six months in jail. The Baltimore club released him. In 1903, he returned to baseball, joined Cincinnati, and nearly won the National League batting title by hitting .351 to Honus Wagner's .355.

Charlie Graham, Hap Hogan, and Elmer Stricklett played the 1902 and 1903 seasons in Sacramento under owner Mike Fisher. Graham managed the team along with Fisher. George Hildebrand, former San Francisco player with Will and Fincks, anchored the outfield. During the prior year, Hildebrand discovered the movement he could put on a ball when it was wet. He said that he discovered the secret of the "wet delivery" largely by accident. Not being a

---

[A] Los Angeles faced Seattle and San Francisco took on Portland in San Francisco. Oakland contested Sacramento in the state capital.

[B] Donlin was a distant second behind future Hall of Famer Napoleon Lajoie's .426.

pitcher, he imparted the secret to his friend and teammate Elmer Stricklett.[1] Stricklett has since been credited with inventing the spitball pitch. He did go on to throw it in the major leagues, and he taught it to future Hall of Famers and legendary spitball pitchers Jack Chesbro and Ed Walsh. But the exact origins were debated.

In 1920, Hildebrand, a major league umpire at the time, wrote a letter with his explanation of the origins of the spitball to sportswriter and historian Ernest Lanigan.

San Francisco, Feb. 20th 1920

My dear Mr. Lanigan,

Yours received, very glad to hear from you. In regard to the spit ball only to (sic) pleased to tell you what I know of the discovery of same.

While at Providence, in 1902: One day I was warming up with a young pitcher named Frank Corridon. I notice him throwing a slow ball with quite a break. He did this by wetting the tips of his fingers before pitching.

I noticed him pitch several of these all of which broke with a downward drop. After awhile I told Corridon I would show him a real drop. While Corridon only dampened his fingers, I, in the parlance of the diamond, slobbered all over the ball, just as some of the masters of the spit ball do nowadays when the ball is breaking well. I held the ball the same as Corridon, only wetting it a great deal more. The ball I threw broke a good deal more than Corridon's and hit Aubrey(?) who was catching in the knee.

Corridon noticed this quick break and started experimenting with a wet ball, later getting this ball under control. This I think was the birth of the spit ball. Corridon later on joined the Philadelphia club, Nat. League.

In the fall of 1902 I returned to Pac. Coast. This long season had a couple of months more to go so I finished with the Sacramento club. Here I met Stricklet (sic) who was about to be released on account of a sore arm. I showed him this spit ball. Stricklet (sic) with an arm that was almost gone mastered this spit ball and went out & won eleven straight games. Late in 1902 the All Americans and All Nationals came to the Coast. Jack Chesbro who was one of the pitchers with the N. Y. Americans was with this crowd.

He studied this delivery under Stricklet (sic) & used same in 1903 quite a bit but it wasn't until 1904 that he had it down right. This was the year he pitched in more than fifty games and lost the pennant for N. Y. in the last game of the season with a wild pitch.

Hoping this will help you some,

I am - Most Sincerely,

Ger. Hildebrand [2]

Even at the age of twenty-eight, Stricklett's career was vitalized because of the new spitball pitch. Capitalizing on his newly found success, he signed with the Chicago White Sox for the 1904 season. When batters and managers got their first look at the spitball, they said it would revolutionize the game.

The Chicago White Sox manager suggested that baseball legislate against it. The pitcher already had too great an advantage over the batter, he felt. He said that nobody was able to judge the pitch; there was no way to know which way it would break. "It looks as big as a house, then drops out of sight."[A]

Sacramento wasn't a great team in 1902. The days of the town's great Gilt Edge teams had passed, and Graham's squad struggled near the cellar. In addition to Stricklett, Hildebrand, and Hogan, Graham had star players Truck Eagan and Tommy Sheehan. But that wasn't enough against the likes of teams such as the Oakland Oaks who had Kid Mohler, Walter McCredie, Brick Devereaux, Julie Streib, Doc Moskiman, Buck Franks and manager Pete Lohman. Pete Lohman was an outstanding manager and catcher whose career as a player was limited due to head injuries suffered while playing the dangerous position. Lohman and Mohler were two peas in a pod. For many years, wherever Mohler went, one would find Lohman. Buck Franks was from Los Angeles, where he starred for the Tuft Lyons team that won the Examiner Tournament in 1896. That year, Buck won the championship game with a three run home run. After the game, he was carried down Market Street in San Francisco on the shoulders of the fans from Los Angeles.[3] Walter McCredie was a devoted outfielder. Bill Lange would contact friend Ned Hanlon of the Brooklyn Superbas in 1903 to get McCredie a shot in the majors. Unlike other parents of that era, Walt's father John was proud. "He got $300 spot cash for signing the contract," the elder McCredie boasted, "and his salary for the season is to be $1,000 for three months' work."[4] Walter batted .324 before being released. But McCredie's lasting impact on baseball would come as an owner and manager of one of the most successful minor league franchises in history, the Portland Beavers. McCredie would also become a vociferous and active proponent for the rights of the African American

---

[A] The spitball would become banned in the winter of 1919-1920 for purposes of safety and to increase the advantage for the hitter. However, existing spitballers were allowed to continue using it throughout their careers.

baseball player thirty-five years before Jackie Robinson would break the color barrier.

In 1903, Graham improved his pitching staff over the prior year by adding two Santa Clara hurlers, Winnie Cutter and Bobby Keefe. Sacramento challenged the powerful Los Angeles team for the title in an increasingly competitive league. Winnie Cutter remembered how determined the team was to win that season, led by Charlie Graham. He recalled pitching in a big game. Hogan was catching, the game was tied, and a man was on third. Cutter threw a wild pitch and the runner was certain to score the winning run if the ball reached the backstop. To prevent a passed ball, Hogan reached for the ball with his bare hand. The ball split his hand wide open between the fingers. Blood was everywhere. But Hogan managed to keep the ball in front of him, and the runner didn't score. The cut was very deep, but Hogan wanted to tape the two fingers together and finish the game. But fortunately Charlie Graham wouldn't allow that.[5]

Graham would offset the win that Hogan's heroics had notched in the standings by throwing a game later in the season, although Hogan was indirectly to blame. Hogan, pulled from obscurity by Graham in 1902, had become one of the standout catchers in Pacific Coast League in 1903. He then fell in love with Laura Curtis of Sacramento. They planned to wed in the summer, and Hap asked Charlie Graham to be his best man at the wedding. But on June 28th, the date of the ceremony, Sacramento had a game. Hogan didn't report to the ball game so that he could prepare. His absence forced Graham to catch the game. The score was tied in the ninth inning... then in the eleventh... then twelfth.

Graham was swearing in 57 languages as the sweat poured off him in streams thinking he'd hold up the wedding. The sun was dropping and the courthouse was two miles away. In the twelfth, the first man singled. Another beat out a bunt. The next was walked to load the bases. The next batter hit a grounder to short, who threw to the plate for a force out. To complete the double play, Graham turned to throw to first base. One of the quickest and most accurate throwers in the game, Graham threw the ball over the first baseman's head and the winning run scored. Graham then raced to the courthouse.[6]

Later that year, on November 26, Charlie Graham would also wed, marrying Miss Black at St. Vincent de Paul Church in San Francisco. He dispelled rumors in the media that he would retire as a result.[7]

Frank Arellanes helped pitch San Francisco to a fourth place finish in 1903. But the dominant team in the league was Jim Morley's Los Angeles Angels, which posted a record 133 victories. The league's teams played over two hundred games in those days.[A] The Angels would not discover Hal Chase until just before the next season. And he didn't come as a savior, but a fill-in for their all-star first baseman Pop Dillon. In 1903, Dillon set the Coast record for most hits in a season with 275 in the 188 games he played. A cousin of major leaguer Clark Griffith, at twenty-nine Dillon also served as the team's manager. In the field, the team featured Dummy Hoy, who was coming off a 14-year career in the majors. A deaf mute, Hoy preferred the nickname Dummy, and was the reason umpires signal balls and strikes with their hands.[B] Gavvy Cravath was another talented position player on the team, although still at the beginning of his career.[C]

The strength of the team, however, was its pitching staff, perhaps the greatest in minor league history. Left-hander Eustace "Doc" Newton won nearly seventy-five percent of the games he pitched, posting a 34-12 record with a 2.43 ERA. Rusty Hall was 32-19 with a 2.31 average. He was 25-9 at one point in the season before becoming mortal. Joe Corbett went 23-16 and led the league with 196 strikeouts and eight shutouts. Dolly Gray completed the rotation with a 23-20 record. Newton was the best of the squad. He pitched the league's first no hitter against Oakland before 5,000 at Chutes Park in Los Angeles on November 8, 1903.

Chutes Park would become the central baseball establishment in Los Angeles for the next twenty years. Initially, the park seated 5,000,[D] was located on Washington Street and was also referred to in later years as Washington Gardens. Poolroom owner James Morley was given a franchise for Los Angeles, which played at Chutes, in the four-team California League in 1901. He named the team the Angels, but it became known widely and affectionately as the "Loo Loos."

Grand Avenue bordered the park on the West, Main Street on the East, Washington Boulevard on the North, and 21st Street on the South. David V. Waldron bought the thirty-five acres in 1887 to develop the property. At first it was a trolley park; he used a horse-drawn rail line to connect to the city streetcar

---

[A] Los Angeles Angels played 211 games and finished 133-78. Sacramento was a distant second at 105-105. The games were played every day except Monday, which was the travel day. The teams would play a weeklong series together from Tuesday through Sunday, with doubleheaders on the weekends. The season ran from late March to late November.

[B] Hoy raised nephew Paul Hoy Helms, the founder of the Helms Athletic Foundation, a Los Angeles-based organization that selected collegiate national champions and All-American teams for decades until the 1980s. The records maintained by the Helms Athletic Foundation were used as a source for this book.

[C] In 1914 Cravath would hit .341 with 19 home runs and 128 RBI for Philadelphia. In 1915, he would hit 24 home runs, the single season record in the modern era of baseball until Babe Ruth hit 29 in 1919.

[D] In November of 1904, the seating would be increased to hold 10,000.

lines. He transformed the land into an amusement park with varied attractions to draw people on the weekends.[8] Waldron began weekly variety shows in a small pavilion, brought in animals for display, and planted an orange grove. Unfortunately, the park declined by the late 1890s and was seldom used. In 1899, however, the property was sold to new owners that comprised the Los Angeles County Improvement Co., headed by the owner of Maier Brewery, Fred Maier. The Improvement Company built a new theater, baseball park, and brought in new rides. The highlight was to be Paul Boynton's "Shoot the Chutes Ride," named for an inventor and diver who had built similar attractions on the East Coast. Boynton's toboggan-like boats began their ride from a 75-foot tower and descended down a 300-foot ramp into a 50-by-150-foot lake. There was also a Japanese teahouse, shooting gallery, bowling alleys, children's playground with pony- and goat-drawn carts, a zoological building, picnic grounds, and a restaurant.[9] In 1901, sea lions, including one labeled as a "monster sea lion," became a star attraction at the park. The same year, the Catalina Marine Band attracted thousands to concerts.

The park was expanded during 1901. It added three lions. Down the main street, it featured a fishing pond, Flying Venus who did aerial stunts under the influence of hypnotic suggestion, and an expanded theater that seated 1,400 and featured vaudeville, comics, burlesque, acrobats, contortionists, jugglers, and singers. In 1903, the park added a steel-framed figure-eight roller coaster. Other attractions included a small railroad around the perimeter, a small circus, a den of serpents, hot air balloon rides, the House of Trouble, and the Cave of the Winds.

Chutes Park amusement rides, ca 1900

For the 1903 season, the previously "skinned" baseball field was covered with sod. The center field fence was just around 350 feet and the left and right field fences were just 330 and 312 feet respectively.[10] The park became known as a good home run park. Nevertheless, the twenty-nine home runs hit over more than one hundred games played in 1903 pale in comparison to the rate balls are hit out of the park in today's game.

The city and its most influential and active citizens spearheaded the park's improvement project. Many of those citizens, including Fred Maier, were members of social groups including the Jonathan Club, IOOF, Masons, Elks, Recreation Gun Club, Germania Club, as well as various country clubs including the Los Angeles Country Club, Pasadena Country Club, and San Gabriel Valley Country Club. Due to civic pride, they sought to bring all aspects of society enjoyed by the Eastern cities to Los Angeles, including opera, symphony, transportation systems, museums, amusement parks, and competitive baseball. Many, including Henry E. Huntington, also participated in the Improvement Company to increase the value of their most significant holding – land in Southern California. By enhancing the city, they increased their wealth.[A]

When those in cities throughout the country lobbied for taxpayer funds to create large amusement parks such as Chutes, they crafted a moral appeal. They would argue that the park acted "as a counter-irritant to the saloon and other demoralizing influences that afford diversion to the body politic in its frivolous moments." Chutes Parks existed in other cities, including London, Antwerp, Milan, Boston, Baltimore, Atlanta, Coney Island, Atlantic City, Chicago, and San Francisco. Los Angeles wanted a Chutes Park of its own.[11]

Chutes Park opened for business as Los Angeles' new baseball park on October 21, 1900 for Winter Challenge Baseball. The title of the event was surely aimed to attract Easterners, the major leaguers tempted by the region's warm weather; although called a "Winter Challenge," the temperature for the game was likely in the 80's in October. The Chicago Cubs sent Californians Frank Chance and Sam Mertes along with Clark Griffith and Charlie Decker. Jesse Tannehill, Jimmy Williams, and Bones Ely represented the Pittsburgh Pirates. Other major leaguers also participated as Chutes Park sold out for the game. In the coming years, Chutes Park organizers would draw the stars from the East to fill the stands for weekend baseball in Los Angeles throughout each winter.

James Morley secured Chutes Park as the home field for the Los Angeles Angels, fulfilling his responsibility to provide a venue essential for his franchise. Indeed, the owner also financed the ball club, paying for salaries, uniforms, transportation, umpires, and equipment. But most owners of the day weren't well capitalized. If they were fortunate to have a franchise in a good location, they risked that gate receipts would pay the overhead on a daily basis. There was not much room for failure. Securing an attractive venue was critical. There would be many great ballparks in the future of West Coast baseball. Some would become the jewels of franchises. Others would cause their demises.

In the earliest years, the parks did not provide luxurious amenities. The Helms Athletic Foundation wrote, "To make a comparison, there were still a few high-heel booted cowboys operating in the Golden West when the Pacific Coast League first blossomed in the spring of 1903 . . . skinned diamonds and weed outfields."[12]

[A] Huntington would later own a portion of the Angels squad. He would also mastermind the creation of a world class transportation system throughout the greater Los Angeles area. Not only would the trolley lines enhance the city and his holdings, they would carry baseball fans to parks throughout the region at a reasonable price to attend and participate in baseball games.

At the end of the 1903 season, Hal Chase still starred for Santa Clara, months away from his trip to Los Angeles where he would meet James Morley and eventually star at Chutes Park. He had already developed a taste for the popularity that he would find playing the game of baseball. Perhaps young Hal felt that he had it all figured out. Life could be so simple. Wherever he went, people wanted him to play for their team. Fans would love him and owners would pay him. So simple, it seemed. Or so it should have been.

[1] Is Original Spit Ball Man. Los Angeles Times, June 4, 1905 Pg. III2
[2] Letter courtesy of the Bradshaw Hall Swales Baseball Collection, 1871-1930. Manuscripts and Archives Division. The New York Public Library, Astor, Lenox, and Tilden Foundations
[3] History of Baseball in California and Pacific Coast Leagues 1847 - 1938. Memories and Musings of an Old Time Baseball Player. Fred W. Lange. Oakland, CA. 1938
[4] Baseball Records, Pacific Coast League, From 1903 to 1940 Inclusive, Published in Conjunction with Helms Athletic Foundation, pg. 4
[5] Hap Hogan's Busher Days, May 23,1915, Los Angeles Times, pg. VII7
[6] Did Graham Chuck It Up! Grey Oliver, Los Angeles Times, Aug 25, 1911, pg. III2
[7] Hodson's Forte is Fog Pitching, SF Chronicle, Nov 25, 1903, pg. 4
[8] Berman, Jay and Sesar Carreno. The Short Life of a Downtown Amusement Park. Los Angeles Downtown News, 9/4/2006.
[9] Berman, Jay and Sesar Carreno. The Short Life of a Downtown Amusement Park. Los Angeles Downtown News, 9/4/2006.
[10] The Stage is Set For An Historic Season, Carlos Bauer, April 23, 2003
[11] Shooting the Chutes, Los Angeles Times, August 25, 1900, Pg. I13
[12] Baseball Records, Pacific Coast League, From 1903 to 1940 Inclusive, Published in conjunction with Helms Athletic Foundation, pg. 4

Chapter 4

Urban Sports In America 1904

When Hal Chase prepared to leave the secure confines of the Mission Campus in 1904, the prevailing influences of gamblers, political corruption, and unfair treatment of ballplayers were deeply rooted in urban sports and baseball. Chase would soon be cast into a world with lessons not taught in school. Gambling and corruption were rampant in baseball throughout the major urban centers of the country; the highest levels of local government perpetrated criminal acts. And in industry, where baseball owners attempted to turn a pastime into a business, they would emulate their robber baron role models and collude, exploit, and blacklist. The issues of the ballplayer would parallel those of U.S. laborers that led to growing discord and the evolution of labor movements and anti-trust legislation. The ballplayer, previously concerned with hitting with men on base, or defending the bunt, would soon have to concern themselves with the details of the nefarious world that was baseball in the early 1900s.

The main Los Angeles baseball field was situated beside an amusement park. Conversely, San Francisco's Recreation Park at 8th and Harrison[A] was positioned next to Henry Harris' cigar stand, a convenient locale to place a bet if one couldn't be had within the ballpark, the center of bookmaking in San Francisco. Harris and Ted Goodman owned the San Francisco team and enjoyed the commerce afforded by the gambling. The San Francisco Examiner wrote:

> *So open was the bookmaking that the women in the grandstand took a hand in it. These women had their betting patronage solicited by boys who went through the stands announcing the odds and who carried the money of the fair ones to the bookmakers, who held forth in a sort of mezzanine section below the grandstand and to the right of the entrance. It has become notorious that many women are regular patrons of the betting ring at the ballpark.*

> *And the policemen are there all the time. Those policemen are supposed to enforce the law. There is a law against bookmaking in the city and county of San Francisco. There is no effort to disguise the breaking of the law.*

[A] The original Recreation Park was on Sacramento between E and F, 15th and 16th Streets in San Francisco and was built in 1885. The Recreation Park built in 1897 at 8th & Harrison lasted until it burned in the San Francisco earthquake in 1906. It was re-built on 15th and Valencia in 1907.

And now see to what this sort of thing leads. Already the 'national game' has become so smirched with suspicion on this Coast that comparatively few people patronize it. There is a rather more than a suspicion that many of the games are "fixed," and that the bookmakers and their friends know just what the result of the so-called contest is to be ... the game results just as the bookmakers knew it would. They and their friends reap their harvest accordingly.

But no matter whether the bribery of players is merely suspicion, or whether it is morally certain, there is no question that Harris and Goodman, with the connivance of the police, permit open bookmaking on the ball games played at Eighth and Harrison streets ...

The main gambling in the park went on in the upper grandstand along the first base line. The bar was also a prominent feature in the park. When the park was re-built after the 1906 earthquake, it contained a field-level bar behind home plate known as the Booze Cage where gambling was rampant. Fans paid a premium to get into the Cage. For the extra money, they received a shot of whiskey, beer, or a ham and cheese sandwich. Most chose the booze. All could hear the loud drunks in the Cage right behind home plate. Women didn't dare enter.

Similar to Chutes Park, Recreation Park sported a grass infield for the first time in 1903. The dimensions were oddly shaped. Right field was just 265 feet down the line, and then jutted out to buildings that encroached on the field at 330 feet into center field. Left field was the deepest part of the park at 385 feet.

The gambling that transpired at Recreation Park was common to any ballpark in any big city in America. And the influence of corruption in sports would often reach the offices of local politicians. San Francisco was no different.

Abe Ruef was an influential politician and labor movement leader in San Francisco after the turn of the century. Ruef selected Eugene Schmitz to front his party in a run for the mayor's office. Schmitz won the election and became mayor in 1902. Subsequently, Ruef used his power for personal gain. Among other things, Ruef ran a monopoly on all prizefighting around the city. At the time, San Francisco was the boxing capital of the West. Heavyweight champion Jim Corbett hailed from San Francisco. Great boxers including Jack Johnson, Joe Walcott, and Joe Choynski trained and boxed in and around San Francisco. At various times, boxing had been illegal in California and San Francisco. But Ruef authorized boxing in San Francisco as long as promoters paid him a fee.[A]

[A] After the 1906 Earthquake, charges were brought against Schmitz and Ruef for corruption related to telephone systems, trolleys, and gas rate deals, as well as the prize fight monopoly. Ruef was indicted on sixty-five counts, plead guilty in an arrangement,

Baseball, boxing, and horse racing, the three major professional sports in America, were dominated from their inception by political bosses and their cronies. The sports and related gambling contributed to urban development, politics, and organized crime. The unsavory elements staged a war with reformers - religious factions within the cities that appealed to the public and fought to engender change. The appeals extended beyond simply banning baseball on Sundays; the reformers challenged the crime bosses and their political machines.

In the early 1880s, New York City was the center of boxing. Like Ruef twenty years later in San Francisco, Tammany Hall arranged boxing exhibitions. By bribing police, they had little resistance to conducting popular, yet illegal four-round bouts. By the middle of the decade, however, reformers successfully pressured police to enforce the laws that banned boxing. Promoters moved to other, more hospitable locations.

Poster promoting "Grand Glove Contest" between John L. Sullivan and Jas. J. Corbett in New Orleans in 1892. The first "gloved" heavyweight title bout.

New Orleans then drew the focus of boxing promoters who worked with local politicians to circumvent the laws. At the time, the laws prohibited bare knuckle fighting. For that reason, the legendary heavyweight bout between Jim Corbett and John L. Sullivan in New Orleans in 1892 became the first heavyweight title bout fought with gloves. When a new law passed forbidding gloved matches, the city, spoiled by the tax revenues, continued to grant permits in exchange for a fee.

By the early 1900's, boxing was banned in many cities. San Francisco became the center of the sport during that period. It was the scene of more championship fights than any other city.

The scandal caused by Ruef in San Francisco during the era eventually fostered public disdain that forced boxing out of the state. By 1910 when Jack Johnson fought Jim Jeffries for the fight of the century, it was held in Reno, Nevada rather than in California.

Political machines and mobsters also dominated horse racing. In New York, some powerful and wealthy individuals including William C. Whitney, a Tammany attorney and former Secretary of the Navy, Thomas Fortune Ryan, one of the nation's wealthiest capitalists, and August Belmont II, for whom the Belmont Stakes was named, sponsored the sport. Combined with Tammany's political machine headed by Richard Croker and Tim Sullivan, horse racing was legal in various locations throughout the state within reasonable proximity to New

and incriminated Mayor Schmitz who was dismissed from office in June of 1907. Ruef was convicted of bribery and sentenced to fourteen years.

York. Gambling was organized in a syndicate run by the Tammany machine. Tammany protected gambling in town, so betting on the various races became commonplace through bookies in establishments such as billiard parlors, barber shops, newsstands, and saloons. Throughout the country, proprietary tracks had difficulty operating without strong ties to local political bosses.[1]

Tammany power broker Tim Sullivan managed the syndicate of poolrooms in New York in the 1890s. He received protection from police by paying them from the sixty to three hundred dollars per week that he collected from the poolrooms. Frank Farrell, who also owned the city's most luxurious legal gambling establishment, ran much of the syndicate. The syndicate's inside man in the police department was William F. Devery. Devery rose up quickly within the police ranks by requesting duty in the most crime-ridden precincts. Within each, he took bribes in exchange for protection. With the money raised, he bribed his way to more senior roles in the police force.

Frank Farrell and Bill Devery

The poster child for political corruption in city government in America was the notorious William M. "Boss" Tweed. In the mid 1800s, Tweed was the head of Tammany Hall, the Democratic Party political machine that shaped politics in New York in the 19th century. Tweed was eventually convicted for stealing from New York taxpayers an amount that may have exceeded $250 million. After his reign, Tammany Hall continued to control Democratic politics in the city behind John Kelly, Richard Croker, Charles Murphy, and Timothy Sullivan.

Like Tammany predecessor Boss Tweed, Frank Farrell possessed the girth of a man who lavishly indulged his gastronomical cravings. Boss Tweed had been known for devouring extra servings of food, as was Farrell's friend and businessman Diamond Jim Brady. Short, and with an anguished countenance that appeared to unsuccessfully harbor years of worry and concern, Farrell had eyes inset and suspended upon darkened bags. His hair was oily and parted down the center.

Involved in gambling and pool halls, Farrel partnered with Bill Devery of the New York Police in various operations including the "House with the Bronze Door," an elegant townhouse on West 33rd Street that catered to high end New York gamblers. The operation thrived, appealing to the city's interest in gambling. Devery provided protection for Farrell's nearly three hundred poolrooms that also operated as horse-betting parlors. Farrell owned more than half of the gambling operations throughout New York, and was also involved in horse racing.

Bill Devery rose up through the police department to become Tammany Hall leader Richard Croker's right hand man. Croker organized a network that took bribes from the owners of brothels, saloons, and illegal gambling dens. He succeeded in electing a front man, Robert A. Van Wyck, to the office of the mayor of New York. During Van Wyck's administration, Croker controlled the government of the city.

Devery was a round man with an endearing and jovial appearance. He sported a bushy mustache and carried himself with a bold confidence. He was well liked by his fellow policemen and took pride, as many Tammany members did, in proclaiming his working class roots and strong work ethic. He said he preferred working among the working class. He even chose to move out of the upper west end and back to his roots. He once said of the Upper West Side of Manhattan:

> 'There is one thing I have noticed about this neighborhood that is different from my old camp down in Twenty-eight Street,' he continued. 'Most of the people were poor in money, but they were rich in kids. It was a stingy wife that didn't present her husband with half a dozen. Up around here there are not so many children and a whole lot more dogs. I never knew there were so many breeds of dogs as you can see along West End Avenue and on Riverside Drive.' The former Chief then told of how they dressed the dogs in that neighborhood and declared that it made him "sore" to see a dog with seal skin pants on and to think of some boys he knew down on the west side who wouldn't have any pants at all if their father hadn't thrown a pair into the discard once in a while because the seat was worn out.[2]

With the protection from Tammany, Devery was never convicted of any crimes, although he was charged on many occasions. In 1894, he was indicted for extortion. Ill at the time, he couldn't stand trial. So his case was heard at the police headquarters and he was removed from the force. He appealed to the Supreme Court and was reinstated because his constitutional rights had been violated because he was tried without being present. In March 1896, he was again tried in criminal courts and acquitted. In October 1896, a reform Police Board brought new charges, but Devery obtained a writ of prohibition that restrained the board from trying him on the grounds that the board was not bi-partisan. In August 1897 he was commanded to suppress disorderly houses in his Eldridge Street Station in the precinct know as the "Red Light District." He denied their existence even when fifty were identified. He was indicted for failure to proceed, but was acquitted.[3]

The reform Police Board that attempted to bring charges against Devery in 1896 was headed by reformer Charles Henry Parkhurst, a clergyman and social reformer who was determined to bring down Tammany. In response to Parkhurt's attempts to corral Devery, Tammany quickly moved their star into the role of Chief of Police over a period of just nineteen months, during which time he worked in Brooklyn, was promoted to the Bronx, then to Manhattan, in each case overseeing crime-laden precincts and taking money in exchange for protection.

During Devery's ascension, Parkhurst's police board was disbanded. The power and influence of Tammany was apparent.

In 1898, Theodore Roosevelt, former New York Police Commissioner and newly christened war hero, only months after leading the Rough Riders up San Juan Hill in the Spanish American War, won the gubernatorial election in New York. He defeated Tammany Judge Augustus Van Wyck, brother of New York Mayor and puppet of Tammany leader Richard Croker. A war hero was needed to defeat the Tammany stronghold. Roosevelt, in his biography, said that in challenging Van Wyck "his objective during the campaign was to make the people understand that it was Croker ... who was the real opponent; the choice lay between Crokerism and myself." Roosevelt won by a close margin of just 18,000 votes.[4]

Roosevelt took on the New York machine in a manner only a war hero and descendant from New York old money and power could. Just three years away from the presidency, interest in Roosevelt emerged at the Republican National Convention in Philadelphia in June of 1900. Tammany and others were eager to get him out of the Governorship. Many Republicans wanted Roosevelt to take advantage of his popularity and seek the Vice Presidency by running with William McKinley. Roosevelt preferred the Governor role to the position of Vice President. Roosevelt turned down the role. Under pressure from Tammany Hall personnel, he held firm and wouldn't succumb to their challenges. His strong posture backfired, as his exhibition of might against the powerful political machine appealed to the Republicans. He was nominated without opposition.

Roosevelt found himself a lame duck in New York. The Legislature had adjourned. But Roosevelt still had the power to remove the Mayor, Sheriff, and the District Attorney for malfeasance. He wrote,

> *Such power had not been exercised by any previous Governor, as far as I knew; but it existed, and if the malfeasance ... warranted it, and if the Governor possessed the requisite determination, the power could be, and ought to be, exercised.*[5]

The Governor learned that Bill Devery, the Chief of Police, was working to defraud the upcoming elections. So Roosevelt created a State Bureau of Elections and appointed a Superintendent of Elections, Mr. John McCullagh. Roosevelt would write:

> *...Devery represented in the Police Department all that I had warred against while [NY Police] Commissioner. On November 4, Devery directed his subordinates in the Police Department to disregard the orders which McCullagh had given his deputies, orders which were essential if we were to secure an honest election in the city... I had no direct power over Devery; but the Mayor had; and I had power over the Mayor. Accordingly, I at once wrote to the Mayor of New York...*

State of New York

Oyster Bay, November 5, 1900

To the Mayor of the City of New York.

Sir: My attention has been called to the official order issued by Chief of Police Devery, in which he directs his subordinates to disregard the Chief of the State Election Bureau, John McCullagh, and his deputies. Unless you have already taken steps to secure the recall of this order, it is necessary for me to point out that I shall be obliged to hold you responsible as head of the city government for the action of the Chief of Police, if it should result in any breach of the peace and intimidation or any crime whatever against the election laws. The State and city authorities should work together. I will not fail to call to summary account either State or city authority in the event of either being guilty of intimidation or connivance at fraud or failure to protect every legal voter in his rights. I therefore hereby notify you that in the event of any wrongdoing following upon the failure immediately to recall Chief Devery's order, or upon any action or inaction on the part of Chief Devery, I must necessarily call you to account.

Yours, etc.,

Theodore Roosevelt.

Roosevelt sent similar letters to the Sheriff and the District Attorney of the County of New York. The letters prompted the mayor to require Chief Devery to rescind the order to disrupt elections, which transpired honestly and orderly.

Within months, in February of 1901, Mayor Van Wyck called Devery "the best Chief of Police New York ever had." Twenty days later Devery was removed from office by a legislative act initiated by Roosevelt that overruled the Mayor's veto. The act abolished the position of Chief of Police. On Sept 17 of that year Devery was arrested on charges of neglect of duty and oppression. He was found not guilty and discharged at the end of 1901.

The battle between future president Theodore Roosevelt and Tammany Hall's Chief of police Bill Devery demonstrated the pervasive corruption perpetrated by Devery in New York politics. With his protection, Frank Farrell's gambling establishments thrived throughout New York. And with the protection, the gambling was out in the open, public, commonplace. The young boy in the late nineteenth century grew up in a culture where a bookie was as familiar as a barber.

Frank Farrell and Bill Devery's influence would soon extend into baseball. About a year after Devery was discharged from the New York Police Department, he and partner Frank Farrell purchased the Baltimore Orioles.

Baseball in Urban America

Sports franchises, including boxing clubs, racetracks, poolrooms, and baseball teams created monopolies for the machine politicians in many big cities. It was not uncommon for concerns from transportation systems, breweries, and pool halls to be strongly represented in urban sports, as was the case in Los Angeles with Henry Huntington, Joseph Maier, and Jim Morley, respectively. The control of the venues, served by the expansion of electric rail at the turn of the century, created the monopoly. If no other team could find a place to play that could seat enough fans and provide access via affordable public transportation, they could not compete. The synergy between electric rail and baseball in urban centers was akin to that of the horse stable and the blacksmith; each served the other. Electric rail grew from 1,260 miles of track in 1890 to 22,000 miles in 1902. In 1897, Boston built the first subway. New York completed is subway in 1904. By the early 1900s, most social classes could afford travel to sporting events for about a nickel by using transfers. Over fifty transit firms also operated amusement parks, like Chutes Park, along their routes to encourage ridership. The urban amusement park often contained baseball parks.[6]

In New York prior to the turn of the century, Manhattan had one major ball team, the New York Giants. Businessman Andrew Freedman owned the team. Freedman was a life-long friend and advisor to Richard Croker. At times, Freedman was considered "a power behind the thrown" in New York politics, particularly during Mayor Van Wyck's administration.[7] Freedman had no plans to share the most lucrative baseball market in America. It was said that baseball owners needed to be aligned politically or they would find a railroad built through their ballpark. In New York, this threat was real. Freedman was active in the politics of building New York's subway system. In 1900, he was influential in creating the Interborough Rapid Transit Subway Construction Company that would complete the initial subway system in 1904. If anyone placed a competing franchise in New York, Freedman could literally build a subway through its ballpark. Freedman enjoyed his baseball monopoly in New York City from 1894, when he purchased the New York Nationals at the age of thirty-four, until just after the turn of the century.

The country had experienced economic depressions in the 1850s, 1870s, and the 1890s. As a result, capitalists were wary to invest without an edge. Most found their edge in political alignment. The burgeoning cities sought tax revenues to support their ever-growing needs, particularly following the severe depression of 1893. They partnered with businessmen to generate commerce that would raise revenues for the cities. The partnerships increased investment, generated tax revenues, and provided businessmen with assurances. The assurances could come in many forms, including justly awarded government contracts, legally questionable attempts to create monopolies, and the outright illegal activities of the most corrupt. Baseball mirrored society at large in that it attracted all of the above.

The Sherman Antitrust Act passed in July of 1890. It ruled that any form of a contract, trust, or conspiracy in restraint of, or to monopolize trade or commerce among the several States, or within foreign nations, was a felony. Over the next few decades, the enforcing parties in government would take both an aggressive "trust-busting" posture, as well as an accommodative stance, depending on the prevailing national sentiment and presidential leadership.

All of the National League enjoyed a monopoly during the late 1800s. It had prevailed as the sole league after a series of "baseball wars" that transpired in recent years. In 1876, the National League of Professional Base Ball Clubs was originally formed. In 1879, to ensure financial stability, the league's teams agreed to secretly reserve five players at the end of each season. By the early 1880s, the "reserve clause" would apply to all players and would become one of the most profound influences on baseball over the next century. As a result of the reserve clause, the first baseball war resulted in 1884. A league called the Union Association was organized to recruit players away from the existing National League and American Association. The teams in the Union Association went broke within a year.

The second baseball war against the reserve clause occurred in 1890 when the Brotherhood, or Players' League, came into existence.[A] The league had strong backing and appealed to the best players in the country because it didn't limit salaries to an arbitrary $2,000 as the other leagues had. The cream of the crop jumped to the league, including Charles Comiskey, John Montgomery Ward, Charlie Radbourn, Dan Brouthers, King Kelly, George Van Haltren, Buck Ewing, Jake Beckley, Ned Hanlon, Pud Galvin, Connie Mack, Ed Delahanty, Dummy Hoy, and John Tener. San Francisco Bay Area products in the league, in addition to Van Haltren, included Hank O'Day, Jim Fogarty, Phil Knell, Fred Carroll, and Ed Morris.

The owners had agreed in 1887 to remove the $2,000 salary limit to prevent the players from striking or leaving to play in another league. But the owners never removed the salary cap, and by 1890, the players had had enough. At the time, John Montgomery Ward was both a great ballplayer and an active proponent of a labor union for players. His involvement in the Brotherhood of Professional Base-Ball Players, the sport's first players' union, led to the creation of the Player's League in 1890. Ward was outspoken against the unfairness of the reserve clause. He stated the following about the oppressive impact of the reserve clause on the player:

[A] The league was called "The Players' League", "The Brotherhood League", and "The Brotherhood of Baseball Players."

Like a fugitive slave law, the reserve rule denies him a harbor or a livelihood, and carries him back, bound and shackled, to the club from which he attempted to escape. He goes where he is sent, takes what is given to him, and thanks the Lord for life.

On November 6, 1889, the Brotherhood wrote a manifesto explaining their motivation:

By a combination among ourselves, stronger than the strongest trust, the owners were able to enforce the most arbitrary measures, and the player had either to submit or get out of the profession in which he had spent years attaining proficiency.

The new league was organized based on profit sharing, and it had no reserve clause. And even though there was no overt socialist agenda, the league was criticized for being filled with anarchists. Anarchist was a derogatory term in 1890. The country was in the midst of a "red scare." Citizens feared an imminent violent revolution at the hands of socialist anarchists discouraged by their attempts to invoke change through peaceful, political means. It was true that a faction of the growing labor movement in America, advanced by a socialist agenda, did engage in strikes, protests, and sometimes-terrorist acts. Those in labor who took a position against management, such as the John Montgomery Ward and the Brotherhood of Professional Base-Ball Players, were perceived by some as troublemakers akin to the radical factions of the era.

The competing war between the Players' League, the National League, and the American Association strained each league financially. The teams competed directly within the same cities and markets. The Players' League competed well with the other leagues in attendance. But no team made money in 1890. In the end, the backers of the Players' league didn't have the stomach for the war of attrition. The National League asked for an "unconditional surrender," and the Players' League's backers accepted. Like the Union Association in 1884, the new league folded from financial strain after one season.

The third baseball war occurred in 1891. In the peace agreement following the demise of the Players' League, the two remaining leagues, the American Association and National League, agreed not to blacklist the players from the competing league, but to allow them back to the teams on which they played in 1889. Additionally, all teams reserved their players as had been done for many years, and allowed the other players to populate other teams. Two players, Louis Bierbauer and Harry Stovey, would return to the American Association's Philadelphia A's squad where they had played in 1889.[A] But Philadelphia failed to reserve the two players. Both would defect to National League squads – Bierbauer to Pittsburgh and Stovey to Boston. When Bierbauer

---

[A] Both were stars. In 1888, Stovey had stolen 156 bases in one season which is still a major league single season record.

signed with Pittsburgh, the American Association called the National League team "Pirates!" The Pittsburgh franchise has been known as the Pirates ever since.[8] Philadelphia appealed the technicality, feeling that the two players belonged to their team. But a commission decided in favor of the National League. The two leagues fought, but in the end, suffering from the financial crisis of 1890 caused by the competing Player's League, and contending with rising player salaries, the two leagues agreed to a truce. The two leagues combined to create one National League with eight original National League teams and four American Association teams. The sum of the parts was worth more than the two separate leagues; the combined league could better control player salaries, protect owners' property rights over players, and blacklist rogue players.

Andrew Freedman purchased the New York Nationals in 1894. Freedman enjoyed the monopoly afforded by the National League and his political influence in New York as a leader within the Tammany Hall political machine. In time, however, the National League's monopoly would be challenged and New York would welcome another baseball team.

[1] City Games, The Evolution of American Urban Socieity and the Rise of Sports, Steven A. Reiss, p. 181
[2] New York Times, June 21, 1919
[3] New York Times, June 21, 1919
[4] Theodore Roosevelt, An Autobiography
[5] Theodore Roosevelt, An Autobiography
[6] City Games, The Evolution of American Urban Society and the Rise of Sports, Steven A. Riess, pg. 209
[7] Andrew Freedman Dies of Apoplexy, New York Times, December 5, 1915, pg. 19
[8] Baseball, Benjamin G. Rader, pg. 70

Chapter 5

The Formation of the American League and "Clean Baseball"

In 1894, Ban Johnson, a sports reporter in Cincinnati, was named the President of the Western League, a minor league comprised of teams in Indianapolis, Minneapolis, Milwaukee, Detroit, Kansas City, Toledo, Grand Rapids, and Sioux City. While in Cincinnati, Johnson befriended Reds manager Charles Comiskey and owner John T. Brush, who recommended Johnson for the post.[A] Ban Johnson was instrumental in introducing "clean baseball" to professional baseball. While baseball had already appealed to fans as America's game, which contained an ideal of wholesome cleanliness, the reality was quite the contrary. "Dirty baseball," branded in the National League, was on display in the 1890s. Johnson and the Western League intended for baseball to be a gentleman's game. Johnson gave umpires unquestioned authority and didn't tolerate rowdiness from players or fans. Johnson was quoted from Chicago, where he took office:

> *Clean baseball has always been the American League's platform, ... and it is too valuable a trademark to be lost. Unless some of these managers and players curb their tempers and resort to less kicking they will find themselves on the bench for an indefinite period and will stay there until they learn our style of playing ... I have instructed the club owners there must be no profanity from the players on the field, and if they do not enforce the rules I will punish the offending players.[1]*

In 1895, Johnson began putting the pieces together for a new league. That year, Charles Comiskey retired as an active player and purchased Johnson's Sioux City franchise and moved it to St. Paul. In 1897, Connie Mack became manager of the Western League's Milwaukee team. The triumvirate of Ban Johnson, Charles Comiskey, and Connie Mack began formulating the American League, which Johnson pledged in 1899 he would create. That year, Johnson moved St. Paul to Chicago where Charles Comiskey became owner of the Chicago White Sox. Connie Mack's team found a home as the Philadelphia A's with Mack owning a minority interest with Ben Shibe. In 1900, the National League dropped franchises in Baltimore, Cleveland, Louisville, and Washington D.C. Johnson acquired the teams that the National League shed. Johnson then

---

[A] National League owner John T. Brush would soon despise Johnson for his efforts to set up a league to compete with the National League. Comiskey would remain a close ally to Johnson for many years until their relationship would also become acrimonious. Johnson's professional career is best understood through the battles he fought and the enemies he created as a result.

moved his Grand Rapids team to Cleveland, and Louisville to Boston, both owned by Charles Somers, a wealthy Ohioan in the coal industry who helped finance Ban Johnson's American League. Johnson kept the Milwaukee and Detroit teams from the Western League intact.[A]

While Johnson formed the league, the National League initiated a salary cap, which displeased the league's players. Johnson exploited the opportunity. He recruited Clark Griffith, who would later star for Comiskey's Chicago White Sox, to recruit disgruntled National Leaguers. Griffith was successful recruiting most of the players he approached.[2] The war between the National and American Leagues had been declared.

In January of 1901, Johnson announced the opening of the American League with eight inaugural teams – Philadelphia, Baltimore, Cleveland, Boston, Washington, Chicago, Detroit, and Milwaukee. Johnson's American League differentiated itself culturally from its competitor. He wanted to operate in a more civil manner, both on the field and toward the players. His ideal contrasted with the National League, whose owners, including the Giants' Freedman, encouraged rowdy play, yelling at umpires, and bullying players and other teams. Johnson declared that he would ban gambling in all American League ballparks, one of many principles that Johnson would eventually concede out of practicality. He also implemented the following rules out of fairness to the players:

1) No suspension of players for more than 10 days.
2) Clubs would pay doctor bills for injuries sustained in ball games.
3) If a club abandoned players, the players would become free agents after 10 days.
4) No farming out or selling players without the player's written consent.
5) The Reserve Clause would be in effect for no more than three years, nor would a player be forced to sign for less salary than the current season.
6) No binding arbitration for disputes.

While the more humane rules in the American League helped recruit National League players, Johnson would backpedal during subsequent negotiations with the National League. Throughout his career, Johnson would continually strive to create an ideal, but would undermine himself through compromise and concession. Later in his career, he adopted an unwavering posture, perhaps out of frustration caused by his past compromises and their ill effects. His righteous rigidity and crusading, although appropriate and well intentioned, was too little too late and ultimately alienated him from baseball and made him into a victim of the powerful politics within.

[A] As a result, Detroit is the oldest continuous franchise in the American League dating back to 1894 in the Western League.

Johnson's attempts at creating "clean baseball" in the American league found opposition in his Baltimore owner and manager, John McGraw. The two were often at odds over McGraw's rowdy behavior. In the 1890s when McGraw starred for the Baltimore Orioles, most owners in the National League believed that fans preferred a rough style, which they referred to as "scrappy." McGraw's manager Ned Hanlon said, "Patrons like to see a little scrappiness in the game." Hanlon's Baltimore Orioles won three consecutive National League pennants from 1894 to 1896 behind Dan Brouthers, Joe Kelley, John McGraw, and Willie Keeler. They were perhaps the dirtiest team in the history of baseball. They "hid balls in the tall outfield grass…spiked players as they rounded bases, and grabbed runners' long shirts or belts as they ran the bases."[3] Turkey Mike Donlin's "scrappy" attitude fit with McGraw's style. Donlin played at St. Louis with McGraw for Manager Patsy Tebeau, who perhaps surpassed McGraw with his rambunctious behavior.[A] Baseball pioneer Henry Chadwick once said of Tebeau "he degraded the game more than any other player of the previous quarter century." Tebeau and others on his bench teased, cursed, and distracted opponents, umpires, and visiting fans with profanity. Cut from a similar mold, McGraw embodied the bold, aggressive, and often indecent style of that era for decades, becoming a symbol of "dirty baseball."

Freedman capitalized on McGraw's dissatisfaction with Johnson, and seized the opportunity to undermine his impertinent nemesis. He and John T. Brush invited McGraw to New York and convinced him to raid ballplayers from the Baltimore Americans for the New York Nationals, and then defect to become manager of the Giants. McGraw rationalized his actions by admitting that, without a home in Johnson's league, and anticipating that the two leagues would imminently merge, he was creating a home for himself. Ban Johnson, however, would call McGraw "a traitor and an ingrate."[4]

Another adversary in Ban Johnson's attempts to create "clean baseball" in the American League was George Stallings in Detroit. Stallings, an outfielder and former player for Stockton and San Jose town clubs in the San Francisco Bay Area, owned a minority interest with Jim Burns. Like McGraw, Stallings liked to win at any cost, and yelled and screamed at umpires and players. As Johnson attempted to tolerate Stallings' antics, Stallings began discussions with the National League about defecting the next season. Enraged by Stallings disloyalty, Johnson forced Stallings and Burns to sell their interests to S.F. Angus and Ed Doyle in November 1901.[5] Detroit would remain in the American League. And Johnson would forever hold a grudge against Stallings, who would never be welcome in Johnson's league.

Johnson also devised a plan to deal with Freedman's attempts to lure away McGraw. One of Johnson's priorities was to secure a franchise in New

---

[A] Donlin would be one of McGraw's favorite players throughout his career.

York. He had successfully scouted and secured a ballpark in New York for the new American League team. Johnson's maneuvers, known to Freedman, fueled his adversary's motivation to raid the Baltimore Americans. Johnson wanted more than anything to have a franchise in Manhattan. For years he would play an active role in the success of an American League franchise in New York, the largest market in the United States. But he knew that if he put a team in Manhattan, Giant's owner Andrew Freedman would build a railroad through his ballpark. Freedman's Tammany Hall connections made the New York market seem impenetrable. But on January 9, 1903, Ban Johnson arranged for the purchase of the Baltimore Orioles by none other than Bill Devery and Frank Farrell. With political clout in New York equal to Andrew Freedman, the two moved the team to Manhattan.[A] On March 12, the New York franchise was approved as a member of the American League. Farrell and Devery hastily constructed a ballpark at 168th and Broadway, with no political opposition, on one of the highest spots in Manhattan; the team nickname would be the "Highlanders" and their home field would be known as "Hilltop Park." In his efforts to create "clean baseball," Johnson compromised and partnered with Devery and Farrell in order realize his dream – an American League team in New York City. And to ensure its success, he inserted trusted colleague Clark Griffith, who had been instrumental in the league's formation, as the manager and baseball man for Farrell and Devery.

McGraw managed the Giants for decades as an ambassador for "dirty baseball" in the National League where he believed that "it ain't cheating unless you get caught." Connie Mack would represent the "clean baseball" of the American League and Ban Johnson's hope for a virtuous game.

Mack's Philadelphia Americans were fortunate in 1902 when Philadelphia National's star Nap Lajoie refused to play because he found out that teammate Ed Delahanty made more money than he did. Lajoie ignored his contract, crossed town, and played for Connie Mack instead. He won the Triple Crown, batting .422 with 125 RBI. The Philadelphia Nationals took Lajoie to court to prevent him from playing with the cross-town team. The reserve clause could not force a player to play, but it could be used to enjoin a player from playing for another club. In April 1902, in one of the first challenges to the reserve clause, Pennsylvania Supreme Court Justice William P. Potter granted the injunction prohibiting Lajoie from playing for Connie Mack.[B] Ban Johnson didn't

---

[A] In 1902, Freedman had sold some of his ownership in the Giants to John T. Brush so that he could concentrate on implementing the New York subway system. However, many felt that Freedman remained involved for many more years while Brush operated as the front person. Brush, who had recommended Johnson to the presidency of the Western League, would now confront Johnson as an adversary.

[B] In an earlier challenge, in 1896, Freedman fined star pitcher Amos Rusie for poor effort. Upset, Rusie sat out the season. In 1897, he threatened to challenge Organized Baseball

70

appeal; rather, since the ruling was enforceable only in Pennsylvania, Johnson moved Lajoie to the Cleveland team and made sure he never played when games were in Philadelphia. The Philadelphia Nationals sought an Ohio court to hear the case, but no Ohio court would comply and lose their star player.

That same year, players from the Saint Louis squad contested the reserve clause in the court of Judge John A. Talty. They were the first to challenge and defeat the injunction. They argued that the contract provided the owners with a ten-day release clause, but that same right was not afforded the player. The lack of mutuality in the contract was a point of contention. Additionally, Judge Talty cited the Fourteenth Amendment[A] to the Constitution that prohibited involuntary servitude.[6]

The competition between the leagues, the player movement, impact on salaries, and the legal expenses once again created a condition whereby neither league prospered.

Prior to the 1903 season, in both the major leagues and the minor leagues in California, the leagues, cities, teams, and players changed constantly. But the leagues, teams, and cities in place in the major leagues in 1903 would remain unchanged for many years. Most are recognizable to this day, as the nation's population centers have embraced and supported baseball without interruption for more than a century.

The constant franchise changes in the 1800s were even confusing at that time. Teams were most commonly referred to in the papers as a combination of the city name and the league in which they played. For example, the Cubs would be the Chicago Nationals. The Browns were the St. Louis Americans.

based on the Sherman Anti-Trust Act that was passed in 1890. The owners of the league couldn't change the unpopular Freedman, but they paid Rusies 1896 salary to keep him from going to court. When he returned in 1897, he went 29-8 for the Giants. – Superstars and Monopoly Wars, Nineteenth Century Major League Baseball, Thomas Gilbert. (Rusie and Bob Gibson hold the distinction of the only two pitchers who were so good they changed the rules. Rusie threw so hard, the mound was moved to sixty feet six inches from the fifty-five feet. Gibson was so dominant in 1968 that the mound was lowered).

[A] One of the players in the suit, George Harper, later hit Cubs manager and part owner Frank Chance in the head. It would be one of many balls that would hit Chance, leading to deafness in his ear. Chance was so upset that he had Cubs' owner Murphy trade for Harper, then he cut his salary and sat him on the bench. Harper appealed to the National Commission, but soon quit. (Baseball, Harold Seymour)

NATIONAL LEAGUE		AMERICAN LEAGUE	
Pittsburgh Pirates	Same	Boston Americans	Boston Red Sox
New York Giants	SF Giants	Philadelphia A's	Oakland A's
Chicago Cubs	Same	Cleveland Naps	Cleveland Indians
Cincinnati Reds	Same	New York Highlanders	New York Yankees
Brooklyn Superbas	Brooklyn Dodgers became the Los Angeles Dodgers	Detroit Tigers	Same
Boston Beaneaters	Boston Braves became the Atlanta Braves	St. Louis Browns	Baltimore Orioles
Philadelphia Phillies	Same	Chicago White Sox	Same
St. Louis Cardinals	Same	Washington Senators	Minnesota Twins

The formation of the National and American Leagues was no small feat. For years, the owners and prospective owners struggled to balance the risk of financing a team and losing its star players to other teams. Over a period of decades, the owners learned that fighting amongst each other created too much turmoil and uncertainty to be consistently profitable. So they decided to collude, create a monopoly containing franchises, and agree to protect the rights that each franchise had to players.

On January 10, 1903, the leagues agreed to a peace compact. The Presidents of the American and National Leagues would be Ban Johnson and Harry Pulliam, respectively. At a meeting attended by Charles Comiskey (Chicago Americans), Charles Somers (Cleveland Americans), Henry Killilea (Boston Americans), August Herrmann (Cincinnati Nationals), James Hart (Chicago Nationals), and trolley-car magnate Frank de Haas Robinson (St. Louis Nationals) the leagues created the National Commission that would enforce "The National Agreement."[A] August Garry Herrmann, a personable front man to Cincinnati political boss George Cox, became the Chairman of the National Commission.[7] Over the next two decades, the National Commission would exert an absolute and oppressive force over major league and amateur baseball, and would be the source of conflict, animosity, legal proceedings, and sweeping negative repercussions. It would, however, bring stability to the ever-changing revolving door of baseball teams, cities, leagues, and players.

The peace accord didn't resolve the deep-seated animosity erupting from the preceding year's wars. The leagues would agree on the first World Series between the champions of the two leagues. The Boston Americans won the first

---

[A] Ban Johnson managed to ban gambling from within all ballparks as part of the accord. However, no teams enforced the ban, as gambling was pervasive throughout the game and contributed significantly to attendance.

Series over the Pittsburgh Pirates. But in 1904, when the Boston Americans repeated as the champions of the American League, John McGraw's National League Champion New York Giants refused to play because of McGraw's animosity toward Ban Johnson. In disgust, McGraw called Johnson's American League the "junior" league and claimed to be the world champion because he had won the "only real major league." Spite also persisted between Ban Johnson and George Stallings. Ban Johnson would forever hold a grudge against the traitor. As the American League formed, it created allies and adversaries that would shape baseball politics over the next two decades. The allies included Comiskey, Mack, Johnson, and Griffith. The adversaries would be Brush, McGraw, and Stallings.

Animosity aside, the two leagues did agree on creating the National Agreement, whose importance was so paramount to baseball in America, excerpts are reproduced here. The principles and charters leave no ambiguity about the intentions of major league baseball owners.

National Agreement 1903 (excerpted)

Protection of the property rights of those engaged in baseball as a business without sacrificing the spirit of competition in the conduct of the clubs.

Article VI

SECTION 1. All parties to this instrument pledge themselves to recognize the right of reservation and respect contracts between players and clubs under its protection.

SECTION. 2. Any club or league which harbors a player who refuses to observe his contract with a club member of any party to this Agreement, or to abide by its reservation, shall be considered an outlaw organization, and its claim to contractual and territorial rights ignored.

SECTION. 3. The right and title of a major league club to its players shall be absolute, and can be only terminated by release or failure to reserve under the terms of this Agreement by the club to which a player has been under contract. When a major league club serves notice of release on one of its players, he shall be ineligible to contract with a club of another league if, during ten days after the service of such notice of release, a club in the league in which he has been playing shall demand his services.

SECTION. 5. The National Association shall have the classification of its leagues, and the adoption of a salary limit for its clubs, according to such classification, and it agrees to withdraw protection from any league that allows any of its clubs to exceed the salary limit prescribed for leagues of its classification.

SECTION. 6. The right of a minor league club to its players shall be absolute, except that from September 1 to October 15 of each year, major league clubs shall have the privilege of selecting players from the National Association clubs for the following season, upon payment of $750 for each player so selected from clubs in Class "A" leagues; $500 for each player so selected from clubs in Class "B" leagues; $300 for each player so selected from clubs in Class "C" leagues, and $200 for each player so selected from clubs of a lower class...

SECTION. 7. Any club entitled to make selection of a player, and desiring to do so, shall notify the Secretary of the National Commission, stating the name of the player and of the club to which he is under contract and reservation, and enclosing the amount specified in the preceding section to be paid for such release or draft. The Secretary shall thereupon notify the Secretary of the National Association, who shall thereupon immediately notify the club and league from which such selection shall be made, and shall order the transfer of the player to the selecting club at the close of the current season.

Article VII

SECTION 1. On or before the 25th day of September in each year the Secretary of each party to this Agreement shall transmit to the Secretary of the Commission a list of players then under contract with each of its several club members for the current season and in addition thereto a list of such players reserved in any prior annual reserve list who have refused to contract with such clubs. Failure of a club to tender a contract to a player by March 1 shall operate as a release.[8]

The National Commission could be perceived as a portentous, foreboding authority. When players became "banned," the consortium could appear to the fan, particularly the fan in the West, to be lacking a heart or soul. Yet the rules of the National Agreement reveal the rather black and white, mundane, and administrative role of the Commission. The Commission had no grudge; it had no vendetta toward players. Rather, those bound by the National Agreement submitted the names of players in violation of their contracts. The National Commission mechanically enforced the Agreement. It didn't prowl the territory to catch barnstorming major leaguers in the act of sedition. It merely responded to the submissions of the owners of Organized Baseball. If an owner submitted that a player was under contract, and that player played with another team, the Commission acted to enforce the rules at the request of the owner. Whether a player was "banned" was often a function of an owner's desire to pursue the ban. In the end, the good players were often given a leniency that others with diminishing skills did not receive.

However, the objective of the Commission was clear – it created and preserved a monopoly for the owners, protected the property rights of the owners, and enforced a "blacklist" of those who acted in opposition to the objectives of the Commission and Organized Baseball. It created what the anti-trust legislation of the day intended to prevent.[A] But Organized Baseball's unfair practices, etched in stone in the National Agreement, would continue for decades with the vigor and collective power of baseball owners. All challenges to create a competing league based on more just terms for the player had failed in the past. Challenging the status quo in the future would be even more formidable.

And how would the Californians receive the National Commission? How would owners react to their inability to sign star players during the major league's off-season? How would star players react to being told that they could only play for one owner and only during the regular season? What would Jim Morley in Los Angeles, Henry Harris in San Francisco, or the teams that formulated the new California State League feel about the broad-reaching control of major league baseball's monopoly? The issue would tear apart the Pacific Coast League. And for many years, many baseball people in California would react to Organized Baseball with disgust, distrust, disregard, and disdain.

---

[1] Chicago Tribune, May 10, 1901

[2] The Imperfect Diamond, A History of Baseball's Labor Wars, Lee Lowenfish & Robert W. Creamer, Da Capo Press, 1991

[3] Superstars and Monopoly Wars, Nineteenth Century Major League Baseball, Thomas Gilbert

[4] Major League Managers, Los Angeles Times, Oct. 2, 1913

[5] New Detroit Baseball Club, The New York Times, November 15, 1901

[6] The Imperfect Diamond, A History of Baseball's Labor Wars, Lee Lowenfish & Robert W. Creamer, Da Capo Press, 1991

[7] This is the Fifth Baseball War, Los Angeles Times, February 8, 1914, pg. VII7

[8] Reach Guide, 1904 pages 115-123

[A] In 1903, President Theodore Roosevelt set up the Bureau of Corporations to enforce the Sherman Anti- Trust Act. While in office, the Bureau filed charges against forty companies.

Chapter 6

The Pacific Coast League Joins Organized Baseball

Throughout the 1800s and up until 1904, baseball on the Coast operated independently from baseball in the East. Whatever Ban Johnson and others did in their respective markets had no impact on baseball in the West and its popularity. In 1904, however, sandlot baseball had to choose between independence and conformity with the National Association. Impartiality was no longer an option. Leagues either sided with Organized Baseball or squared off in competition against it. The Pacific Coast and the California State Leagues would soon have to choose.

In 1904, the Pacific Coast league opened with teams in Seattle, San Francisco, Oakland, Tacoma, Portland, and Los Angeles. Mike Fisher claimed to have lost money in Sacramento, but was willing to sell the team to the city's Chamber of Commerce for $5,000 if they demanded that the team remain. They refused his offer, so he moved the team that finished second to Los Angeles the prior season to Tacoma.[1] Hap Hogan and Charlie Graham, two of his players, followed Fisher to Washington. Fisher also improved his pitching staff by acquiring superstar Orval Overall from the University of California at Berkeley.

In February, Brooklyn Superba owner Ned Hanlon complained to the National Commission that the Pacific Coast League had lured players from the major leagues to the Coast. Hanlon expressed concern about Walter McCredie, who had left his team to join Portland. Oscar Jones also entered talks with San Francisco. Hanlon was also in a battle with Jim Morley because the Brooklyn owner tried to sign the Los Angeles Angels star Pop Dillon. More significant than the players who actually signed with independent leagues was the threat that many additional players would also consider jumping. Organized Baseball had to act. Ned Hanlon, Jim Hart, Ban Johnson and Harry Pulliam traveled to San Francisco to convince the Pacific Coast League to join Organized Baseball. The major league officials promised to give the league a Class A designation, the highest level at the time, equal to the American Association, Eastern, and Western Leagues. The classification later became AAA. They also agreed to allow all players under contract in the Pacific Coast League to remain with their teams.

PCL President Eugene Bert, Los Angeles' James Morley, and San Francisco Seals owner Henry Harris met with the representatives who were sent to "reign in the PCL." Morley disputed with Hanlon over Pop Dillon, and showed reluctance to align with Organized Ball. Submitting to the governance of the National Commission would dictate that Morley's Angels and the other teams would make their players available to an annual draft. In the draft, they would receive compensation for players far below their value. The rules of the draft also limited independent minor league owners the ability to feature ex-major leaguers who had left the major leagues but were still property of a major league club. The other owners, particularly the Oakland Oaks' Cal Ewing, favored the partnership with Organized Baseball. But Morley feared that his concession would result in his losing his star Pop Dillon to Hanlon's Superbas.

Then Morley received news that made him irate. Without obtaining agreement from Morley, the other PCL owners chose to become part of the National Association.[2] Morley became furious. President Bert ordered umpire Jack O'Connell to prevent Dillon from playing in any more games for the Angels. Morley found himself swimming against the current when opposing the other owners as well as Organized Baseball. Ultimately, he had to relinquish his star to Brooklyn.

Unhappy, Morley decided to search for a silver lining. Knowing that the Pacific Coast League's annual draft was to be held in November of each year, he decided that for the next year, he would outsmart everyone and auction his best players to the highest bidders before the draft and receive fair compensation rather than the $750 that the major league teams were required to pay.

But for the upcoming season, he would need a first baseman. Just as Dillon prepared to head East, Morley found himself umpiring a game at St. Vincent's College. The first baseman in the game was Hal Chase. Morley liked Chase, but Dillon recommended Cy Townsend, who played the previous season for Sacramento, as his replacement. Dillon preferred Townsend's size and power as a hitter, and felt he was superior at first base. But Morley disregarded Dillon and signed Chase. Chase was an instant success. Cy Townsend's brief and uneventful minor league career had already peaked. He even eventually failed as an umpire.

Dillon's scouting foibles would soon become legendary. Other leagues had been forming near Los Angeles, most still playing on bald diamonds and weed-filled outfields in small population centers created by the oil boom. The railroad and the new electric railway systems connected the cities spread throughout the greater Los Angeles area enabling teams and fans to travel conveniently to neighboring towns for games. In 1904, the California Winter League was formed. At first, teams from Santa Barbara, Ventura, Oxnard, and San Louis Obispo formed a four-team league. They played games on Saturdays and Sundays in the fall and winter. By 1905, the team from Olinda, now Fullerton, featured a tall high school pitcher with a lively fastball by the name of Walter Johnson. Morley sent Pop Dillon, who traveled with former pitcher Rusty Hall, to scout the fireballer. Dillon and Hall signed two other players from the game, but didn't think the greatest pitcher the game would ever know was worthy of consideration. After the game, Dillon said of Johnson, "He won't do yet. He telegraphs everything he throws."[3]

Fortunately for Hal Chase, Morley disregarded Dillon's misguided advice in his case. Morley signed Hal as his regular first baseman to replace Dillon. He debuted on March 24, 1904 at Chutes Park with a 4-3 victory over Oakland behind the pitching of Spider Baum, who also played his first game for the defending champions that day. A description of the game read,

> *Baum, a youngster from San Francisco, pitched his first game and did excellent work. Hal Chase, an amateur from Santa Clara, played first base for the home team and made a big hit with the 5,000 fans who saw the game.*

The same season, Frank Arellanes played for San Jose in the California State League, considered an outlaw league because it competed professionally outside of Organized Baseball. That spring, Charles Strub graduated from Berkeley on his way to setting up a dentistry practice. And Elmer Stricklett took his spitball to Charles Comiskey's Chicago White Sox.

Mike Donlin played sixty games for the Cincinnati Reds in 1904 and batted .356 before being acquired by McGraw's Giants. Off the field, he consistently found trouble, or trouble found him. While with Cincy, Donlin irritated a customer at a bar in Georgia with his singing. The customer pulled a revolver on Turkey Mike before Manager Joe Kelley pulled Donlin from the trouble.

Charlie Graham and Hap Hogan's Tacoma squad had little trouble picking up where they left off from the previous season. Graham managed the team for the second consecutive season, this time seizing the championship from defending champion Los Angeles. The team featured catcher Hap Hogan and pitcher Orval Overall, considered the best battery in Pacific Coast League. In the off-season, Hogan continued to manage at Santa Clara College, where young Harry Wolter starred.

Even with the reformer Ban Johnson attempting to clean up Organized Baseball, gambling persisted as a common element in the national game. Newspaper reporters continually referred to how baseball was tainted. In time, evidence would surface that gamblers had attempted to fix even the first World Series in 1903 between the Boston Americans and the Pittsburgh Pirates. Lou Criger, the famous catcher for Boston, eventually admitted that he was offered $12,000 to throw games in the series. He was told to approach star pitcher Cy Young to participate. Pittsburgh owner Barney Dreyfuss allegedly bet heavily on his team leading to speculation that he advocated a World Series to create a venue on which to place bets. When the gambler first approached Criger in 1902, Criger later reported to Ban Johnson that John McGraw of the Giants accompanied him.[4] Criger refused to accept the bribe, and Boston won the series.

In 1904, a Washington Post reporter wrote how fixing games was a practice of a bygone era. Either the reporter turned a blind eye to the practice, took an active role in the promotion of the game, or "didn't yet have the dope on what was really going on in the game." Nevertheless, the topic of gambling was an ever-present part of the dialogue surrounding the sport.

Occasionally, one hears the accusation made against a player ... that he is 'trying to throw a game,' in other words, trying to make his side lose. There was a time when such a thing was possible in baseball, but it can't be practiced now ... Soon as a manager sees that one of his men is not working up to standard he immediately supplants him with another, this being especially true of pitchers. [5]

Chase performed well enough in 1904 to attract the attention of Clark Griffith, Pop Dillon's cousin and the manager of the New York Highlanders. Griffith planned to draft Chase and compensate Morley the required $750. Morley had another idea. He planned to auction Chase and star pitcher Doc Newton to the highest bidders, and expected to get three to four times the compensation offered by the National Agreement through the draft process. In the Agreement, the date of the annual draft was to fall between September and October 30. But because the Pacific Coast League season lasted longer than other leagues, the draft was scheduled for November. However, in an effort to create a uniform draft season nationally, the Secretary of the minor leagues, J.H. Farrell, wrote to the minor league presidents, including the Coast League's Eugene Bert, requesting that the draft be moved from November 1 to September 15. Bert, unaware of Morley's plans and remiss in communicating with league owners, agreed. Morley was already at odds with Bert and the other owners in the league because they had agreed to enter Organized Baseball without notifying him. They would also agree to change the draft without notifying him, a move that would cost him thousands of dollars. Morley already had offers of $2,500 for Newton. And an attractive bonus was expected for Chase, coined as Morley's "boy wonder."

The draft took place on September 15 without Morley's knowledge. The Highlanders drafted both Chase and Doc Newton. Frank Farrell paid Morley only the $750 apiece owed to him by New York.[6] One consolation was that Pop Dillon bombed in Brooklyn; he returned to manage the Angels and replace Hal Chase, who ironically had replaced Dillon just one year before. Dillon would manage the Angels for most of the next decade.

Understandably, Morley was livid with his PCL counterparts. He became determined to challenge Organized Baseball. He appealed to Chase in the off-season, and felt he could attract him away from the Highlanders by offering an option for Hal to play closer to home. Morley would need, however, to rally the other league presidents to renounce the National Agreement and become an independent league.

During the winter, Chase played for San Jose, which played in the independent Cal States League. At the end of the season, the San Jose Prune Pickers trailed the Stockton Millers in the standings by one game with one remaining. San Jose fortified themselves with Elmer Stricklett, back for the winter from his first year in the majors, and Hal Chase. On December 3, Stricklett surrendered only three hits against Stockton, but lost 2-0. At the end of the game that was played in San Jose, a miniature riot broke out on the field caused by the upset San Jose fans.

During this era, Stockton remained nearly unbeatable in the independent league. But San Jose behind Stricklett, Arellanes, Chase, and Wolter would challenge them in the coming years.

At the end of January, Hal Chase's brother Ed died suddenly of appendicitis. Soon thereafter, Chase indicated to the press that in spite of the National Agreement, he preferred playing closer to home, if not with the independent San Jose team, which was not beholden to the Agreement, then with Morley and the Angels.[7]

The Angels were scheduled to report March 1 at Chutes Park. The Chicago Cubs and Chicago White Sox were coming to California for spring training and scheduled games against the Angels and the San Francisco Seals. When the powerhouse Cubs took the field against Los Angeles with Frank Chance,[A] Joe Tinker, Johnny Evers, Johnny Kling, and Mordecai Brown, Los Angeles countered with Roy Brashear, Pop Dillon, Gavvy Cravath, Dolly Gray, and ... Hal Chase at first base. Chase would say that although he was under contract with New York (and had accepted signing money), he would wait to make a decision until Morley had resolved outstanding issues with the PCL owners, Organized Baseball, and the Highlanders. In the meantime, he intended on playing.

Manager Morley of the Angels rushed to Northern California to rally the Pacific Coast League teams together against major league baseball. Some of his star players, fearful of the repercussions of operating outside of the National Association, refused to sign for the next season until the owners resolved the issue. Even before Chase began his first full major league season, he was steeped in controversy over contract issues. The controversy, however, was external to Chase. He just wanted to play, but technicalities interfered. Certainly Chase favored playing in California. Nearly every season of his career, Chase would threaten to jump his contract to play among family, friends, the good climate, and

[A] Frank Chance actually finished the season with the Los Angeles Angels after the season ended with the Cubs. Technically, he played in violation of the National Agreement. But only if the major league ownership complained would the National Commission get involved. Since Chance was the manager and part owner of the Cubs, nobody protested his playing in the off-season with the Angels. Many major league players would play in California in the off-season for many more years, just as they had for many years prior. At different times, the National Commission would take a firmer stance against the practice, such as in the winter of 1908-09 when the practice was getting out of hand on a national level.

appreciative fans. He loved playing in the West. Bill Robertson grew up in Los Gatos with Chase and recalled Chase's local popularity, particularly with the idolizing young boys. "The younger boys all knew him, for after playing a Sunday, he would line us up under the old incandescent arc light on the corner of Main and Santa Cruz by the hotel and play catch."[8] Chase wanted a simple, unfettered life where he could toss the ball with the kids and play for his hometown. When things got tough for him in his career, he frequently sought the comfortable, capitalizing on his popularity and friendship with the California teams that provided an alternative to the shackles of the reserve clause and the major leagues. The current episode, where Chase's fate hung in the balance between the major league squad and the outlaw Californians, was the first in many chapters that would over time cast the guileless Chase as one of baseball's biggest "outlaws."

On March 11, Hal played shortstop for the Angels against the visiting White Sox, and then sent a letter to Clark Griffith explaining that he was in discussions with Morley about playing in Los Angeles the next season. He expressed his sentiment about wanting to remain closer to family. He also indicated that he was delayed in reporting due to the death of his brother. However, Chase's mourning now involved daily exhibition games against the barnstorming major league squads. Griffith immediately demanded that Ban Johnson take action against Morley.

Newspapers reported Chase committing to New York on one day, and remaining in California the next. Losing patience, Griffith commented that Chase was "keeping a lot of people guessing." Griffith sent Chase funds for a train ticket. Not wanting to feel under obligation, Chase sent the money back. Chase wasn't being a smart aleck or wise guy; he was stalling until Morley could play his hand. If Morley convinced the other teams to secede from Organized Ball, Chase would likely remain on the Coast.

The national press vilified Morley, which helped him to gain sympathy from the other PCL owners. They empathized with his predicament, having witnessed his opposition to joining Organized Baseball, the loss of Pop Dillon, then his misfortune with the current draft with Newton and Chase. Since the PCL owners had turned their back on Morley in the Pop Dillon case, they agreed to stand by him in the Chase controversy. The Pacific Coast League agreed to secede from Organized Baseball. In response, Clark Griffith threatened that Chase would play for the Highlanders or he would play nowhere. If he played in Los Angeles, Griffith promised a declaration of war. Griffith told reporters on March 22:

> *Chase got our advance money, and now it is the New York Americans or nowhere for him. This nonsense has gone far enough, and I am tired of it… If Chase plays with Los Angeles, it shall be under open war conditions, and I guess the big clubs, which are making money hand over fist, can stand such a war better and longer than one little minor affair*

out in California. It is generally felt that if Chase doesn't report, the bitterest baseball war in the history of the game will shortly be precipitated.[9]

The same day the papers reported the challenge from Griffith, Chase and Morley announced they had come to terms on a contract for 1905. For the next week, tensions ran high throughout the PCL. League administrators argued, commiserated, and pondered the future of the league. At the same time in Switzerland, Albert Einstein wrote the first of four papers that revolutionized science and pioneered quantum physics. The teams of the Pacific Coast League had a much less daunting task to consider. Still struggling financially, they could ill-afford a battle with Organized Baseball, no matter how noble their mission. In a sense, the league sold its soul in order to hold onto its wallet.[A]

Less than a week after Chase signed with Morley, the PCL owners instructed him to join the Highlanders. Chase avoided becoming an outlaw for the time being. But Chase and California Baseball would remain loyal to each other, often in opposition to Organized Baseball, for the next fifteen years.

[1] Sacramentans Dicker to Buy the S.F. Seals, SF Chronicle, Feb 24, 1918, Pg. N7
[2] Baseball Records, Pacific Coast League, From 1903 to 1940 Inclusive, Published in Conjunction with Helms Athletic Foundation, pg. 7
[3] How I Discovered Walt Johnson, The Pitcher, Joseph C. Burke, 9/21/1913, Los Angeles Times, pg. VII7
[4] Ban Johnson Digs Up Scandal of 1903 World Series, Washington Post, October 4, 1924.
[5] Washington Post, August 28, 1904
[6] More Trouble For Mr. Morley, Los Angeles Times, Jan 17, 1905, pg. II3
[7] Few New Men In His Team, Los Angeles Times, 2/9/1905, pg. II3
[8] Hal Chase, The Defiant Life and Turbulent Times of Baseball's Biggest Crook, Martin Kohout, pg. 47
[9] Will Make Chase Play, Direct Wire to the Times (New Orleans), Mar 23, 1905, II3

[A] Winnie Cutter, former Santa Clara College, Sacramento Solon pitcher and future sports editor of the Sacramento Union, recalled that when he decided not to pitch anymore for the San Francisco Seals, he was arrested and released on bail for $50. When the newspapers reported that players were arrested for jumping contracts, public opinion was often against the player – but players ignored the rules that declared they were the property of the teams. Because of the National Agreement, what innocence and virtue the game had previously possessed was compromised.

Chapter 7

Ain't No Stopping California Baseball: Before the National Commission Spoiled the Party

In 1905, when Harry Wolter made his first start as a pitcher for Santa Clara against Stanford, a child could enter a sporting goods store in San Francisco, Los Angeles, Sacramento, or Stockton and purchase a baseball for 5 cents or a glove for two bits. The fielders behind Wolter, however, didn't need their gloves against Stanford; Wolter pitched a 5-0 shutout and struck out fifteen Indians. Wolter always played well against Stanford. That season, he defeated them six times.

Another local hurler, Elmer Stricklett, went 9-18 in Brooklyn. On May 29, he defeated the New York Giants at the Polo Grounds using what the newspapers reported as a "mystery pitch."[1] Another reporter noted that at times Stricklett was "standing big league batsmen upon their heads in a thus far vain effort to solve its spinless shoots and sudden sidewise dodges... the saliva-smeared sphere is a never ending subject of interest wherever the American national game is a popular sport today."

Charles Strub was completing his education at Berkeley.[2] As someone skilled at connecting with the rich and powerful, Strub likely made the acquaintance of fellow student Ed Maier, the son of Los Angeles brewery owner Joseph Maier. The Maier family lived at the corner of Figueroa and Sixteenth Streets near downtown Los Angeles. Ed had an older brother, Fred Maier, who had attended the Wahl & Henius Brewery Academy in Chicago, and then joined his father's business. In July of 1905, the brothers' father, Joseph, owner of Maier Brewery, died. The two sons assumed ownership of their father's brewery business, one of the largest in the West. Fred would run the firm until Ed graduated from Berkeley. Fred also assumed from his father the role of heading the Los Angeles County Improvement Company, which among other projects managed Chutes Park, the center of baseball in Los Angeles.

In 1905, Los Angeles once again dominated the Pacific Coast League. With the loss of hurler Overall to the Chicago Cubs, Mike Fisher's Tacoma team, managed by Charlie Graham, dropped to the cellar in spite of Hap Hogan's strong efforts. The San Francisco and Oakland teams improved themselves. San Francisco finished three games back behind Kid Mohler, Tubby Spencer, San Francisco fixture George Hildebrand, Joe Nealon, and Jim Whalen. Oakland beefed up and finished a close third by recruiting Van Haltren from Seattle to take over for Lohman as player manager. He attracted former Santa Cruz stars Devereaux and Strieb, former Angelino Buck Franks, current Santa Clara College coach Jimmy Byrnes, Ham Iburg, and Doc Moskiman. Financially, the league struggled. It cut back on the teams' roster size to thirteen to cut expenses.[3] The small roster size contributed to the prevalence of the player/manager and the pitcher who could also hit and field.

One of those multi-tasking products of the West, Mike Donlin, had a standout season for McGraw's New York Giants. He was named team captain and batted .356 with a league-leading 124 runs scored. The Giants won the World Series behind Donlin's hitting and the pitching of Christy Mathewson. Within New York, Donlin and Mathewson were heroic.

Across town, Frank Farrell hoped that Hal Chase would be the draw for the New York Highlanders to counter the popular Giants' duo. In one of his first games, Chase dispelled any doubts with three hits including a game-winner with the bases loaded. He knocked star pitcher Bill Dinneen out of the box.[A] The league and its fans immediately embraced Chase and the skills that were readily apparent. The Sporting News wrote in April:

> *I took a look at Hal Chase, the American's new first baseman, today and was impressed with his style. He is a natural ball player, as fast as greased lightning, easy, confident and brainy. He is the counterpart of Fred Tenney in the way he goes after grounders, widely thrown balls and bunts. Better still, he seems to know what is meant by inside ball. As he is only a boy he will improve steadily from year to year and will always be a star. Chase will be a great drawing card all over the American League circuit. He has already made the fans forget all about Long John Ganzel.[4]*

In June, Chase sprained his ankle. If given the choice, Chase would have played baseball every day of the year. Two things that ever came between Chase and a ballgame were Organized Baseball and injuries. Injuries, particularly ankle injuries, plagued Chase throughout his career and prevented him from consistently producing league-leading statistics. When he wasn't on top of his game, the many New York critics sometimes questioned his effort. But the recurring injuries best explained the gaps in Chase's performance.

By August, at the age of twenty-two, Chase had established himself as the team's star. Observers began to notice his critical contributions to the team's success.

> *Without exaggeration and just a statement of plain truth, Chase is already responsible for the brilliant victories by his team, and today he is the pet of all fandom. His fielding has been of the sensational order. Nothing has been too hard for Hal to attempt, and some of his catches have brought thousands to their fee, baseball mad. Monday, in the*

[A] Perhaps due to this game's painful memories, Dinneen would state that Chase was the greatest first basemen of all time.

closing game of the Cleveland series, he reached over a fence and took a foul that nobody ever thought he would even attempt. Wednesday he ran fifty feet back into right field, jumped higher in the air and nabbed a Texas leaguer with his left hand, with two on bases and one run to tie and two to win. The papers called it Chase's spiral catch. Better than all this, his hitting saved no less than three games, and two of them in the ninth inning... Baseball experts here say that Chase is the best emergency hitter in the game.[5]

After a slow start the Highlanders climbed in the standings behind Chase, passing Boston and Detroit, and rose to within striking distance of first place. They won six in a row to begin the month of August.

Growing up, Chase played every infield position, even though he was left handed. He actually preferred second base to first base, and played there at times while at Santa Clara. Others remember him as the quickest catcher they ever saw. During his career, Chase played other infield positions in the majors. At times, he did so in an earnest attempt to use his defensive skills in spite of his lefty liability. In October, however, he needed to fill in at shortstop due to injury to other players. On September 30, shortstop Kid Elberfeld collided with outfielder Dave Fultz while chasing a fly. The collision was horrific. Fultz broke his nose and jaw and would never play in the major leagues again.[A] Elberfeld required stitches and sat out the remainder of the season. Manager Clark Griffith turned to Chase to fill in at shortstop for one game until he could sign another player to take Elberfeld's place.[6]

The Highlanders faded down the stretch and finished sixth, perhaps due to the loss of their shortstop and outfielder. The fickle owner Frank Farrell used thirty-four players during the season trying to find the best combination. The team had some strong core players, namely Jack Chesbro and Willie Keeler. But the team batting average was just .248, almost the same as Chase's that year. And the on base percentage was under .300.[B] The team had some success behind pitchers Chesbro and Al Orth, but could not consistently manufacture enough runs to win more games than they lost. Farrell's capriciousness with players and managers continued as long as he remained the owner, with Chase the only constant in the lineup for many years.

In 1906, San Francisco Seals' Charlie Gleason traveled to Sacramento where Charlie Graham had been involved in an automobile business and tried to sign him for the next season.[7] Instead, the Boston Americans drafted and signed Graham to a major league contract. Graham's close association with the Boston

---

[A] He would later become the head of the Players' Union.

[B] Chase's on base percentage was a dismal .277.

franchise[A] and its owner John I. Taylor[B] would remain intact for years as a result. Mike Fisher, hopeful for a better market than he experienced in Tacoma, moved his squad within the Pacific Coast League to Fresno. Hap Hogan relocated with Fisher to Fresno where he managed the team. Harry Wolter would join the Fresno squad the following year, but during the team's first year in the Central Valley, Wolter played for and coached the Santa Clara team.[8] He would play a role as a coach at Santa Clara for the next decade, although the head coaching duties would change. Wolter relished the opportunity to work out with the college players to get into shape for the professional season. In 1906, he played and coached Art Shafer, a speedy infielder.[C]

Coming off an all-star season and after promising New York Giants management that he would remain sober for the following season, Michael Donlin was arrested in February of 1906 for disorderly conduct on a train. In Albany, en route to an exhibition indoor baseball game, which was popular in the northeast in the winters, Donlin was charged with drawing a loaded revolver on a porter. His sometimes-volatile behavior, however, didn't prevent him from becoming intimately involved with a female New York celebrity. Two months after the incident on the train, Donlin and Mabel Hite, a Broadway musical comedy star, were married. Some have expressed that his poor performance in 1906 resulted from his falling off the wagon, as evidenced by his conduct on the train in Albany. Others speculated that the marriage to Mabel Hite kindled a desire to perform in theater, diminishing his drive as a ballplayer. But the real cause of Donlin's downfall in 1906 was a broken ankle, suffered after only thirty-seven games, which ended his season after he had batted a respectable .314.

A few months before Donlin broke his ankle, Doctor Charles Strub, who would forever be known as "Doc," opened his first dental office.[9]

For the 1906 season, the Highlanders offered Chase a $500 per year raise. Chase appeared pleased, and indicated that he liked playing for Clark Griffith and Frank Farrell. 1906 would be one of the only seasons in Chase's career where he would return to his team without threatening to jump to another club. Chase took up residence near West 155th Street and Amsterdam Avenue in Manhattan. John McGraw and his wife Blanche were neighbors.

On April 18, 1906 at 5:13 in the morning, an earthquake with a magnitude of 8.3 on the Richter scale pummeled San Francisco. Buildings

---

[A] At the time, the Boston Americans were named the Pilgrims, but Taylor would rename them the Red Sox in 1907. Taylor would also build the legendary Fenway Park.

[B] Taylor's father, Boston Globe owner General Charles Henry Taylor (General from the Civil War) purchased the team for his son in 1904. The Taylor family has run the Boston Globe to this day.

[C] He inherited at a young age a successful auto repair business and vast real estate holdings in Los Angeles.

collapsed throughout the city. Fires that followed the quake spread quickly destroying the Pacific Coast League offices and all of its records and files. San Francisco's main baseball venue, Recreation Park was destroyed.[A] All business in San Francisco shut down. Bread lines formed in Golden Gate Park to feed the city, with relief coming from throughout the country. Santa Clara and San Jose also received severe damage. The California State League and the Pacific Coast League suspended play. Opening day for the Pacific Coast league had been just two weeks away. Jim Morley, the Los Angeles owner, considered disbanding his club, knowing he would not meet his financial commitments. Many players fled from the Coast to play in the East.

Cal Ewing, who had assumed ownership of the Oakland Oaks from Fred Lange a few years before, had just purchased the San Francisco Seals squad weeks before the earthquake. Fortunate for the league, Mr. Cal Ewing had money. The major leagues also sent financial support. Pacific Coast League President Eugene Bert sent Jim Morley a message that funds were coming from Organized Ball to keep the league going and to have his team report as scheduled to their next game in Fresno. The city of Oakland fared better than San Francisco in the earthquake. Thus, the PCL moved its office to 1007 Broadway Street in Oakland.[10] And the League played the games scheduled for San Francisco in Oakland's new Idora Park at 56th and Telegraph. Severely injured, the league cobbled together the finances to limp forward.

On April 27, Clark Griffith's New York Highlanders and Connie Mack's Philadephia Athletics played an exhibition game in Manhattan with proceeds directed to a San Francisco Earthquake relief fund. The game was played on a Sunday even though Sunday Baseball in Manhattan was illegal at the time. Certainly the worthy cause appealed to even the most conservative religious reformers who had opposed Sunday baseball games. Other sporting events were held to raise money for San Francisco. Boxer Jack Johnson donated the gate from a fight with Sam Langford. Between the two events, $11,000 was raised to provide relief. The good nature of the athletes, owners, and promoters was indicative of the outpouring from throughout the country.

Play resumed throughout the Coast five weeks after the earthquake. The financial outlook for the leagues, however, remained grave. Fortunately, the Pacific Coast League received the support of wealthy individuals who saved the league.

Cal Ewing was born east of Oakland, where he spent most of his life. Although not a great baseball player, he loved the game in which he remained prominent for decades. An advocate for aligning with Organized Baseball, as financier for both the Oakland Oaks and San Francisco Seals, Ewing carried

---

[A] Another Recreation Park, ironically known as "Old Rec" would open in 1907 at a
   different location on 15th and Valencia Streets.

significant clout among the league owners. Ewing also financed and built many of the significant ballparks in and around San Francisco, including Recreation Park at 8th and Harrison, Freeman's Park in North Oakland, its successor Idora Park in Oakland, and later ball fields at Lake Meritt, "Old Rec" on Valencia street, Ewing Field on Masonic Avenue, and a field in Emeryville used by the Oakland Oaks.[11] His cool head and cold cash helped the league survive the aftermath of the earthquake.

Another wealthy figure played a role in the future of the Pacific Coast League, particularly in Los Angeles. Henry Berry had spent much of the past eight years in the Klondike, Ester Creek, and Circle City Alaska successfully mining some of the world's most plentiful gold claims. After brother Clarence "C.J." Berry rushed to the legendary Bonanza and El Dorado Creek strikes, Hen followed and netted $7,000 with a sluice box on his first day. He was hooked. He then purchased his own claims.

> ... *five years in the Klondike netted the Berry brothers a fortune. Hen Berry often boasted that he cleaned up the biggest pile of gold ever accumulated in a single day, $63,000 in the yellow metal. He also claimed the record of the biggest pan of gold ever washed by one man, $1,563 in one pan.*[12]

He returned to California after the turn of the century and purchased two billiard halls in Los Angeles. He and his brothers had always played baseball up in Selma, just outside of Fresno. And he had played in the Klondike. Fond of the game, with money in his pocket, and the world at his feet, Hen Berry chose to spend his time promoting baseball games. At the end of 1906, he organized exhibition baseball games at Chutes Park during the winter that he not only financed, but umpired as well.

After the 1906 earthquake, Charlie Graham excused himself from the Boston organization to return home to care for his family. He remained on good terms with Boston, which felt no significant loss, as Graham was not headed to the Hall of Fame. Good defensive catchers were handy, but expendable. Graham returned to Sacramento and became owner and manager of the Sacramento Solons in the California State League. In an independent league, Graham and his Sacramento squad technically operated as "outlaws." But Boston would never submit Graham's name to the National Commission for blacklisting purposes. And Graham would never be banned from the game for participating in the Sacramento venture. In fact, Graham maintained a good relationship with Boston and operated as a scout, sending them many prospects over the ensuing years. Labelling Graham an outlaw was like labeling Teddy Roosevelt an anarchist.

As the owner, general manager, and manager, Graham's role was complicated. At the time, most managers were also "general managers," responsible for finding the personnel to complete their teams. They administered budgetary, developmental, contractual, logistical, and marketing matters for their respective teams in addition to the tactics, strategies, and managerial responsibilities of the games. Being an owner didn't necessarily require capital. Graham acquired the Sacramento franchise for nothing. He found a field and players and hoped that attendance would pay the bills. Having played in Sacramento, Graham was welcomed by an accommodative chamber of commerce that helped him to secure a field. And Graham knew players. And as a baseball man, Graham knew that if there were people in Sacramento who wanted to watch good baseball, he could provide it for them.

Hap Hogan sought to create a winner in Fresno. Owner Mike Fisher, at Hogan's request, recruited Santa Clara star Harry Wolter to the Raisin Eaters. In November, Wolter shut out the Portland Beavers in ten innings. He also batted third and went 2 for 4. The lighter-hitting Hogan filled in at right field, batted ninth, and contributed a hit and a sacrifice.

Doc Strub also played professionally that season. He had just opened his first dental office weeks before the earthquake. In the fire, he lost everything. Distraught and uncertain about his future, Doc approached his good friend Charles Graham. Heavily in debt and out of work, Strub accepted Graham's offer to join the Sacramento Solons until he could get back on his feet financially.[13]

Hal Chase was not one to worry about finances in 1906. He had blossomed into a legitimate star. The Highlanders were playing well behind their first baseman. Then on July 22, in a game against Detroit, Chase fell awkwardly when pursuing a foul pop fly. He remained on the ground writhing in pain. Spectators thought he had broken a leg. He finally rose, having sprained his ankle, a condition that would plague him throughout his career.[14]

In August, the Highlanders took over first place from the White Sox by winning nineteen of twenty games. They held the lead until September 15, but the Chisox, known as the "Hitless Wonders," won the pennant on October 3. New York finished with a respectable record of 90-61, just three games back. Chase hit .323 for the third best mark in the league, just ahead of Ty Cobb's .316. In the field, Hal was considered the class of all major league first basemen.

In September, Chase announced his engagement to Nellie Heffernan who hailed from nearby Bayonne, New Jersey. With no date announced for the wedding, however, Chase returned to his first love, California baseball. In November, Chase returned for the final games of the California State League. Once again, the San Jose Prune Pickers battled Stockton Millers for the title. The two teams agreed to play a best of five playoff series that would surely fill the seats. Chase arrived just in time to participate. Chase was not the only major leaguer to join the contest. On November 19, Chase joined the San Jose team along with ringers Tub Spencer, George Hildebrand, Kitty Brashear, Harry Wolter, Elmer Stricklett, Charlie Graham, and Frank Arellanes. Stockton lined up Lefty Leifeld, Danny Shay, Kid Mohler, Frank Chance, Danny Sheehan, and Doc Moskiman. San Jose claimed two big leaguers; Stockton's lineup contained five.

But San Jose had Arellanes, who struck out Frank Chance, the Cub's captain, all four times he came to bat. If Casey at the Bat hadn't already been written about a mighty Stockton player who had struck out, perhaps there would have been speculation that Chance was the Mighty Casey.

The teams won two games each. Hen Berry convinced Chance and Chase to play the final game in Los Angeles at Chutes Park on December 9. Even though most players, with the exception of Frank Chance, were from Northern California and played for Northern California towns, Berry courted the players to

"Hen" Berry

the Southland. Certainly he knew that strong rosters and the appeal of a championship would put spectators in the stands, even in Los Angeles. But Berry had another agenda. He knew there was resistance among Coast League teams to travel down to Los Angeles for games. Both distance and cost were concerns. Part of his mission was as an ambassador of goodwill. He also wanted to attract the California State League into a broader Pacific Coast League. And Berry also loved hanging out with ballplayers. When one of the wealthiest men in the West called the ballplayers and offered to host them for the championship, the Northern California teams gladly complied.

The two teams boarded trains for Los Angeles on Thursday, December 6 in order to spend the weekend in Los Angeles, guests of businessman Mr. Henry Berry, before Monday's game. Recent rain had turned the rolling hills of central California a deep green. A few of the ballplayers enjoyed a game of cards. Chase, reading the San Francisco Chronicle, noticed an article about a Graham, San Francisco Superior Court Judge Thomas F. Graham, who was named to head a grand jury investigation into corruption in San Francisco city government allegedly perpetrated by Mayor Schmitz after the earthquake. The sun warmed his cheek through the glass window. The consistent clackety clack and shimmy of the railroad car mesmerized the young star as he gazed drowsily at the landscape sliding past the window.

"Oxnard! Oxnard Station Coming Up!" shouted the conductor, startling Chase from a stupor. Hal felt wetness on his cheek, which he wiped as he nonchalantly glanced around the car, wondering whether he had made any embarrassing grunts, groans, or snores.

"Next stop, Los Angeles Union Station. Union Station Next Stop!"

- - - - - - - - - -

The game scheduled for December 9 was cancelled on account of rain. The northerners remained in town, and Hen Berry arranged for an exhibition game labeled the "North – South Challenge" between Chase's San Jose squad and a

"Santa Barbara winter league squad" on December 15. The following day, San Jose would play for the California State League championship against Stockton.

When thousands of fans filed into Chutes Park past Tony Ryder's Monkey Circus, Sheik Hadji Tahar's Famous Arabian Horsemen, Billikin's Temple of Mirth, and a reenactment of the Civil War sea battle between the Monitor and Merrimac,[15] they witnessed a Santa Barbara squad that was loaded with Los Angeles Angels players. The contest represented Berry's ploy to create a championship between the Cal State League and the Pacific Coast League. His team included major league journeyman pitcher Rube Vickers, who led the Pacific Coast League the past year with 39 wins and 409 strikeouts. At game time, the wealthy Hen Berry rolled his shirt sleeves over his large arms, stood behind the pitcher, and yelled "play ball." Santa Barbara battled San Jose until Berry called the game due to darkness with the score still deadlocked at 0-0 in the ninth. Arellanes and Vickers fought to a stalemate. Chase entertained the crowd with spectacular play at first base. And the gamesmanship was generally civil with the exception of wrangling over Henry Berry's questionable calls. Spectators attributed his poor decisions to a lack of ability rather than to malicious intent or favoritism. Noticing weakness and insecurity from Berry, both teams attempted to take advantage of the floundering magnate. Yet neither could bring a player across the plate.

Four thousand were in attendance for the next day's championship game between Cy Moreing's Stockton team and Amy Mayer's San Jose squad. The more than 5,000 spectators weren't as intrigued with a "championship" as they were the stars. The fans didn't know the "State League" from a gathering at the Elks Lodge. The locals were enthusiastic to see up close Hal Chase, Frank Chance, Tommy Sheehan, Elmer Stricklett, Doc Moskiman, and Spike Shannon.

Lefty Leifeld, the ace hurler for Stockton, was yet unknown to the Los Angeles crowd. Some compared his style to Joe Corbett, a former San Francisco Seal and Los Angeles Angels star, only Leifeld threw with his left.

Against Leifeld, over the final six innings, San Jose struck out eight times and reached base just once when Lefty plunked a batter in the ribs. But the Pruners got to him early. Chase drove in Spencer in the first on a liner to left field that moved Hildebrand to third. Hildebrand scored on a wild throw. Chase ran to third on the errant throw and quickly scored on a sacrifice squeeze bunt. The third inning was more of the same, with Spencer once again drawing a walk, advancing to third on a wild pitch and subsequent sacrifice bunt by Hildebrand, then driven in by Chase on a fielder's choice. San Jose was out to an early 4-0 lead. Meanwhile, Stricklett's spitter baffled the Stockton nine.

Spike Shannon wasn't going to let the Pruners off easy. Having played centerfield for the New York Giants the past season, Shannon cast a unique profile on the field; as broad sideways as he was tall, his large neck and head perched on a body shaped like a barrel. When he first hit the ball, it appeared that his girth would prevent him from moving. But when dirt flew off his spikes, he thundered rapidly down the first base line. He scored two runs to help his team tie the game at 4-4 by the eighth inning.

Shannon led off the bottom half with a base on balls. When he inched too far off first, Charley Graham thew the ball wildly past Chase. On second base, Shannon then began shouting at Stricklett in an attempt to distract. His aggravating banter caused Elmer to throw wildly over Graham's head, sending Shannon to third. The crowd edged forward on their seats, wondering if Stricklett could get out of the jam. Kid Mohler struck out attempting to bunt a third strike. Frank Chance then hit an easy grounder back to Stricklett who caught Shannon off third base. The newspaper reported that "the fat fire plug" laughed and bounded back and forth in a pickle along the third base line with the game hinging on the outcome. The fielders, inefficient and careless, tossed the ball far too many times to satisfy the baseball purist. Yet even the most disciplined player, Charlie Graham, was one of the guilty parties. His excessive exchanges led to a muffed catch that gave Shannon the opportunity to slide back safely into third base. Hildebrand adeptly ran in from left field to cover the bag just in time to slap a tag on the sliding Shannon.

"SAFE!" yelled major league umpire Jack Sheridan.

The Pruners had squandered a chance to get out of the inning. During the hot box, Chance took second. With first base open, Stricklett walked the next batter, bringing to the plate big leaguer Tommy Sheehan with the bags full. The Pruners were looking for a ground ball double play. They didn't fear the squeeze play. With Chase's quickness at first and Stricklett covering the third base line, Shannon had no chance of scoring on a bunt. Chase was known to cover bunts all the way to the third base line. Stricklett was looking to induce the grounder, something likely from the slight Sheehan.

As Stricklett delivered his pitch, he saw Sheehan square around to bunt. What was he doing? Elmer covered the third base line. Chase charged. The third baseman covered third, shortstop to second, and second baseman to first. But the Pruners didn't expect a fake bunt; Sheehan slapped the ball firmly to the second base slot vacated by the infielder dashing to first base. Chase dove to his right, his body parallel to the ground, his glove outstretched. Sheehan made sufficient contact to push the ball just past Chase. But the once on the ground, the ball rolled feebly to its resting place only 75 feet from the plate. Shannon scored his third run of the game and Stockton claimed another title 5-4.

The crowd was ecstatic. Hen Berry was thrilled by the excitement of the game, the success at the gate, and the camaraderie with the players. Infatuated by the games played by the western all stars, Berry dreamed of greater involvement in baseball in Los Angeles. After the game, Berry sat down with Frank Chance and Hal Chase.

"Frank, I feel like managing me a baseball team," confessed Berry to the fellow Fresno native. Excited and with the capital to pursue a lifelong dream, Berry considered managing a professional baseball team as big a thrill as pulling gold nuggets out of a Yukon Creek. "What do you think Hal?"

"If you can pay the players, there's talent," offered Chase simply and practically. "But the reserve clause..." Chase paused. "Go independent and you can get good players."

"Oh, I don't know. That really necessary?" thought Berry, who was more interested in creating entertainment for Los Angeles than fighting with Organized Baseball. "Just wanna play good ball and put folks in the stands. Waddya say? Maybe we can play more Sunday baseball here at Chutes?"

"What d'ya have in mind?" asked Chance, the Chicago Cub first baseman.

"That series between Stockton and San Jose was something. We got the best players in the State battling. Let's play more games. Who can we get?" asked Hen.

"You willing to consider a small wager?" proposed Chance to the suddenly engaged Chase.

"What you got?" replied Chase, never one to back down from any challenge, particularly on the baseball field.

"I'll put up $500 against any team you can assemble from the State. Best two out of three," challenged Chance.

Berry held up one of his large hands. "How about playing one game Saturday and another on Sunday," thought Berry. "If we need a deciding game, we'll play the next weekend." Hen hesitated once again as the wheels turned in his head. "The final could be a bigger draw than the other two games combined! Who can we get?"

"I'll tell you after we shake," negotiated Chance, extending his hand to Hal. "Deal?"

The series offered two things that Hal Chase loved more than anything – a good, old-fashioned contest and the opportunity to play baseball as a celebrity in his home state. And playing against Chance stoked Chase's competitive fire. The California match was to pit North versus South, a rivalry that had begun in the 1890s and, like the lingering sentiment between the Union and the Confederacy, continues many decades later.

"The Pruners can handle anyone you bring." Chase shook Frank

Chance's hand to seal the agreement.

"Well fine, then," With an agreement in hand, Chance was willing to show his hand. "Just so happens some New York Giants will be in town next week. How's that sound, Hen? Muggsy McGraw at third?"

Berry's eyebrows rose sharply into the wrinkled baldness of his forehead.

Unfazed, Hal walked away, "Doesn't matter. Get John McGraw at third. Why not go for Comiskey and put together an old timer's team?"

"Just saying that McGraw will be in town," muttered Chance. "He's scheduling games for spring training. He might want to lace 'em up."[A]

"Don't matter who you bring," replied Chase. "See you then."

"I'll tell the papers," agreed Berry, revealing an uncharacteristic giddiness accompanied by a childlike grin.

The Chase versus Chance challenge match didn't turn into the North-South rivalry as planned. Rather, competition took a backseat to exhibition. Both teams recruited from among the local players, many splitting up the Los Angeles Angels squad and supplementing with a couple of other ringers. Most of the San Jose and Stockton players had returned home after the championship game. It was rumored that a number of New York big league stars were going to be in town.[16] John McGraw was slated at third base on Chance's team, although he hadn't been off the bench in a few years in the majors. He had played in an exhibition game the previous week in Los Angeles between baseball stars and actors, which fueled rumors of a repeat performance. But the following week McGraw was in San Francisco on business and didn't return to Los Angeles until the day after the final game. Reporters discounted the odds of his arriving in time when he wasn't seen around town. They reported, "no one had seen him around the usual haunts last night."[17] Those haunts would have included one of Hen Berry's or Jim Morley's billiard parlors, or the Lankershim Hotel[B] at 7th and Spring Street in downtown Los Angeles where most visiting ballplayers, including McGraw, stayed when they were in town.

Chance recruited Cubs' teammate Orval Overall as a pitcher.[C] Future Hall of Famer Jake Beckley also joined Chance's team, along with Kid Mohler

---

[A] During the trip, McGraw signed Fred Snodgrass after scouting him at St. Vincent's College.

[B] The building was torn down in the 1980s after it sustained damage in an earthquake. There was a hotel of the same name and similar construction at 5th and Market in San Francisco.

[C] The following season Overall would win 23 games for the Cubs, second most behind Mathewson's 24. In 1908, he would throw a shutout in game five to seal the Cubs' world from the North. Beckley was the standout player. He reportedly provided "all of the ginger" in the game. At thirty-nine years of age, and having played since 1888, he would be entering his final season in the majors. Regardless of his age, reporters wrote that he played "as frisky as a high school girl." Chase fielded ace Angel pitcher Rube Vickers on the mound. He also landed Angels players Kitty Brashear and Walter Carlisle.

Instead of playing on back-to-back days in one weekend, the teams agreed to play three games over three Sundays. The plan proved successful as Chutes Park swelled for the three games to nearly ten thousand fans that paid double the standard Pacific Coast League ticket price. They played the first game on December 23, which was won by Chance. On December 30, Frank Chance's team again defeated Chase 3-1 behind Orval Overall's pitching. The box score in the newspaper identified the teams by the names of their star managers:

Score by innings ---
Chance ……... 3 0 0 0 0 0 0 00- 3
Hits …………………………………….4 1 1 1 0 0 1 1 0- 9

Chase …………………..……………. 0 1 0 0 0 0 0 00- 1
Hits ………………………………….. 1 1 0 2 0 1 1 00- 6

On January 7, 1907, the teams played the third game, which Chase's team finally won by the score of 6-3. The following day, John McGraw finally arrived in town for spring training.[18]

Chase enjoyed the stardom and the attention he received from Hen Berry, who would be named the new manager of the Angels on January 11. Angel's owner James Morley was on his way out. Berry would soon also assume ownership. And Berry certainly planted a seed in Chase's head about coming back to the Coast. Courted by a man with the wealth to match that of Farrell and Devery, Chase felt good about his prospects. He leaked to Farrell through reporters that he wouldn't return to the Highlanders unless they doubled his salary.[19]

Chase continued to play winter baseball in California. He joined a team of St. Mary's college players and other Northern California ringers on a team called "The Phoenix" in both the California Winter Baseball League[A] and the

---

series title, the last the franchise would win. He was an All American at Cal in football. He played in the majors from 1905 to 1913 and has the eighth lowest career ERA in major league history at 2.23. He had ERAs of 1.68, 1.92, and 1.42 in 1907, 1908, and 1909 respectively. Arguably, when Overall played, he was the most dominant pitcher in all of baseball.

[A] The California Winter League, which produced Walter Johnson, was comprised of eleven teams around Los Angeles, including the Hoegee's Flags, Anaheim, Santa Barbara, LA. Pacifics, L.A. Morans, San Diego, Tufts-Lyons, Hamburgers, Pasadena,

Mid-winter Intercollegiate Baseball League. That season, he accepted the position as coach of the St. Mary's College squad, which featured future Hall of Famer Harry Hooper, who had yet to develop into a superstar. Conversely, Chase was in his prime. One reporter commented on Chase's unequaled abilities on the field:

> *... there is a magnetism and unrestrained grace in Chase's play that no other player quite possesses.*

The still immature Hooper didn't share the same opinion of Chase as a bench coach. Later in his career, perhaps jumping on the bandwagon filled with people looking for blemishes in Chase's past to cast him as an inherently flawed character, Hooper commented that as a coach Chase "wasn't all there." Coming from Hooper, who as a major leaguer had a squeaky clean reputation and four World Series rings, the comments were considered damaging by some. But when Hooper observed Chase, Harry was a snot-nosed kid still learning the game. Meanwhile Chase was one of the most accomplished players in the game, in the midst of stressful salary negotiations, planning his wedding, and finding time to coach a college team before hurrying back to celebrity in the nation's largest metropolis. In spite of the many demands, Chase led St. Mary's to a 29 - 0 - 1 record. Chase actually played in games. The team's sole blemish was a tie game against Pacific Coast League All Stars. They won the Mid-winter Intercollegiate League and the Nevada-California College League Championship. They defeated St. Vincent's college, featuring future New York Giant Fred Snodgrass, in the championship. That same weekend, St. Mary's also defeated the Los Angeles Angels 4-2 with Chase at first and Frank Arellanes pitching. Hap Hogan, who signed with Los Angeles for the 1907 season, caught for the Angels, which also featured their usual stars Walter Carlisle, Kitty Brashear, Pop Dillon, and Gavvy Cravath.

Because Chase enjoyed his experience managing at St. Mary's, he envisioned one day managing in the major leagues. At twenty-four, his goal was ambitious. But Chase would not have to wait long for the opportunity he sought.

During the winters, when the California ballplayers continued to play, the owners met in annual winter meetings and hashed out the issues of the day. In certain years, with 1906 as no exception, conflict resulting from the National Agreement created hostile enemies both on the national and local level. At the annual meeting of major league owners, Harry Pulliam was re-elected as National League President with a nearly unanimous vote. The sole opposing vote came from the New York Giants' John T. Brush who claimed Pulliam as his biggest enemy. Brush never approved of Pulliam; he wanted the chosen National League President to continue to fight with the American League and Ban Johnson.

Olinda, and San Bernardino. Players from the Angels and college squads would join the teams, or play against the teams in exhibitions. (Los Angeles Team Wins, Dec. 13, 1906, pg. 17)

Instead, owners selected Pulliam because he worked harmoniously with Johnson in pursuit of a more powerful unified National Association. At the meetings, the owners also agreed that visiting teams would be granted hot- and cold-water showers and lockers.[20] And they considered using numbers on uniforms to correspond to numbers in the scorecard. But the most significant development was the continuation of animosity between Brush and Pulliam, which perhaps contributed to Pulliam's untimely demise three years later.

When the Pacific Coast League met in the winter, Morley understandably had a short fuse. He had had enough of President Bert. With the league financially weakened by the earthquake and fire during the past season, Morley showed little tolerance for the man who had twice cost Morley because of poor communication. The first time he lost Pop Dillon when the PCL agreed to the National Agreement without conferring with Morley. The second time Bert allowed the draft date to be moved up without notifying Morley, which cost him proper compensation for Chase and Newton. Morley vowed that if Eugene Bert were reelected, he would quit the PCL and join or form an outlaw league. With one of the league's best franchises hanging in the balance, the threat to the league was substantive. The league had not only suffered financially the past year, it suffered in terms of prestige. And Seattle's Russ Hall also threatened to leave the league due to financial difficulties. The Fresno club had already folded. The loss of Los Angeles and Seattle would be damaging. So how did the owners react to Morley's threats? Not only did the PCL owners elect Bert, they roasted Morley for his comments about becoming an outlaw.[21] Unrelated to the decision on Bert, Russ Hall abandoned the Seattle team to start a team in Butte, Idaho. Backed into a corner without any partners, Morley deserted the Los Angeles Club.

Three Pacific Coast League pioneers led the league through the challenging year. Walt McCredie, who had taken over the Portland team and carried them to the championship in 1906, was committed to the franchise and the league. The Portland Beavers became the most dominant team in the league over the next seven years. It won the championship in 1906, would finish second in 1908 and 1909, and finish first in 1910, 1911, 1913, and 1914. McCredie was instrumental to restoring the Pacific Coast league's status as a premier minor league. Cal Ewing anchored the Bay Area teams and would not let the league suffer. Many referred to him as the father of the Pacific Coast League. And former gold miner Henry Berry would form a consortium to purchase the Los Angeles Angels squad from Morley. McCredie, Ewing, and Berry saved the Pacific Coast League following the financial difficulties after the San Francisco Earthquake. In 1907, The Pacific Coast league operated with the four teams that would be the league's core for many years - Los Angeles, Portland, Oakland, and San Francisco.

Berry paid $20,000 for a majority ownership share of the Los Angeles club. His partners included Frank Chance, the recent heir to Maier Brewery Fred Maier, Tom Darmody, "Comey" Pendleton, J.W. Brooks, Tom Stevens, and

Henry E. Huntington. While the owners didn't disregard financial concern, as civic leaders, they had a larger agenda - to enhance the city of Los Angeles. They wanted Los Angeles, which was fast becoming the West's largest city, to become a modern metropolis equal to the great cities of the world. Having a great baseball team for its citizens was one of the priorities. Additionally, sports entertainment often complemented the respective businesses of the owners, such as billiard parlors, breweries, transportation systems, and concessions. But the small investment that the men made relative to their wealth signified a civic pride and love for the game more than merely a business venture. Henry Huntington was the largest landowner in Los Angeles. He likely viewed his relatively small investment in the Angels as the equivalent to club dues. The 'A' list crowd in Southern California congregated around sports entertainment and baseball. The owners used the game to provide entertainment for the city as well as for them. And the game became particularly endearing for the fan when they saw owners create fun without exhibiting an obsession with profit.

Berry embodied the unselfish owner. Berry had no office. He didn't run the team like a normal business. He set up his office wherever he happened to find himself. Reporter Harry A. Williams remembered his first interview with Berry "in the Hoffman billiard hall on South Spring Street over Polaski's place." The first couple of years, Berry walked around with his pockets filled with tickets that he handed out to people on the street to promote the game. He didn't take over the club to make a profit.[22] And he treated his players fairly. One player worked for Berry for years with no contract. Nevertheless, the honest and dependable Berry gave him a raise each year. When a new club formed in Los Angeles, known as the Vernon Tigers, they recruited Berry's catcher Hap Hogan to be their manager. Berry never made a fuss. In fact, Berry joked for years that he always had an option on Hogan. Harry Williams reported:

> It is a standing joke that Hap Hogan technically belongs to the Los Angeles club. Berry bases his claim to Hogan on the fact that although he sold Hap to Venice four years ago, he has not yet received the money. Berry doesn't want the money, or he would get it. He would rather have the fun of reminding Hogan about once a year that he is his property. 'I see that you are goin to retire,' said Berry yesterday. 'Yes, when I grow false teeth,' replied Hap, a merry twinkle in his glass eye. 'Well, when you do, I'm going to make you catch for me: you know you are the property of the Los Angeles club.' "That'll suit me fine,' retored Hap. 'I want to wind up my career catching for you. And I'll tell you why: I want to be an angel when I die."[23]

Minority owner Henry Huntington made sufficient profits outside of baseball. In 1907, citizens of Los Angeles could ride the Pacific Electric Railway, which Huntington built, for twenty miles for a nickel. Henry's uncle, Collis

Huntington, one of the founders of the Southern Pacific Railroad, bequeathed Henry a fortune upon his death.[A] Henry owned many companies and much land. But his crowning achievement was the creation of one of the greatest interurban railway systems in the world. He bought all the competing lines until he was the sole owner of the street system throughout the Greater Los Angeles region. His lines carried passengers to beach cities, entertainment destinations such as Chutes Park, and to major valleys and towns in all directions.[B]

Having spent the winter in Los Angeles befriending the influential and wealthy new owners of the Los Angeles Angels, Hal Chase surely felt like his star had risen. Some limited discussions transpired about his joining the Angels. Chase held out hope, aware of the means behind Hen Berry and the other Angels owners. In the past, major league owners had commented that the limited financial capabilities of Coast baseball owners couldn't stand up to a challenge from Organized Baseball. But newcomers such as Hen Berry and Henry Huntington could meet any financial challenge Organized Baseball could bring down the pike. And Chase had surmised that he benefited from any competition between the Coast leagues and Organized Baseball.

But Angels owners Frank Chance and Henry Berry were not about to challenge Organized Baseball. Berry and Chance weren't about to undermine Organized Baseball while it accommodated the Angels and the PCL when enforcing the reserve clause. They enjoyed the winter exhibition baseball with teams filled with major leaguers. So far, those games hadn't come under the scrutiny of the National Commission. In addition, Chance was part of Organized Baseball as a player and owner of the Chicago Cubs. On January 7, the National Commission released its list of banned players. The list included Doc Moskiman who had jumped to the Stockton Millers from the Pacific Coast League.[C] No players who played in Berry and Chance's Los Angeles exhibition games appeared on the list.

Chase, however, didn't fear the ban from the National Commission. He dreamed of playing in San Jose, and knew that a double standard existed; if a player could play, the major league owners would come courting – ban or no ban. The newspaper reports from the day confirmed the prevailing sentiment:

[A] Upon his death, Collis Huntington also left behind a wife, Arabella, many years his junior. Henry Huntington married her.

[B] In the 1940's, a consortium of automobile companies purchased the lines in nearly fifty cities. They shut them all down in order to build transportation systems based on roads and automobiles.

[C] Other banned players included Spider Baum, Dolly Gray, and more than 100 less notable players on the Coast. Baum chose to marry Miss Hazel Root of Grass Valley and remain on the Coast than play major league baseball.

...if any of the men under the cloud turn out to be real big leaguers there will be plenty of offers to buy them and the big league "maggots" forget many things in one season.[24]

The reporter's colorful comments revealed the contempt that westerners had for the National Commission and major league baseball. The reporter identified the main principle in player relations that would apply to Chase and others for decades – a player could get away with much if they were a draw at the gate. When one's appeal declined, however, the National Commission and the owners proved unforgiving. The banned players became examples for whomever considered challenging the Commission's authority.

Because Hen Berry or any other Pacific Coast League team would not oppose the National Commission by courting Chase in 1907, to cultivate a bid to compete with the offer from the Highlanders, Hal had to approach a team in the outlaw California State League. He approached the owner of the San Jose Prune Pickers, Amy Mayer, who Chase had played for during the past two seasons, and offered his services. Mayer was interested. Chase sought an increase to his salary from $1,500 to over $3,000.

The Highlanders had already conceded an increase to Chase's previous salary, and they expected him to report for spring training. But when it was time for Chase to report in April, he was still in San Jose stalling while Mayer arranged a deal for Chase with local businessmen to get Chase $4,000 for the next season. In the meantime, Chase attended a banquet with his former Santa Clara teammates, played games with the Prune Pickers, and joined his St. Mary's squad when they played John McGraw's Giants during their spring training.

McGraw had a holdout of his own in Mike Donlin. Donlin joined the team on their trip West, but Mike refused to sign a contract because of dissatisfaction with the terms. Unwilling to accept whatever the Giants offered, Donlin approached minor league teams to offer his services. Donlin also sought nearly $4,000 for the next year, allegedly $3,300 plus a $600 bonus if he remained sober. Donlin continued to play for the Giants during spring. They played a series of games with the Los Angeles Angels, Portland Beavers, San Francisco Seals, and Santa Clara College in March. During the Giants trip to California, Hen Berry and John McGraw developed a friendship.

Harry Williams, long-time sports editor for the Los Angeles Times and future President of the Pacific Coast League, remembered the first time he met John McGraw and Hen Berry, who became his best friend, in March of 1907. Berry hosted a banquet at Al Levy's old café at Third and Main. Berry invited Williams, who had never before covered sports for the paper. He remembered that many luminaries of the city were invited, in addition to McGraw and other local sports figures, including John Brink, Barney Oldfield, Pete Lohman, Freddie Maier, Pop Dillon, and Hap Hogan. The next day, the Los Angeles Times sent Williams to cover his first ball game at Chutes Park between the Angels and

Giants, which the Angels won. Three days later he became the paper's sports editor.[25]

> *I didn't know how to keep score my first game. It was a wonder the fans of Los Angeles received a fair report of the game… In those days the newspapers did not devote a great deal of money to the sports page, and in addition to serving as sports editor I 'covered' railroads, hotels and Federal courts as well as acting as my own head-writer and make-up man.*

When the Giants were in town, Hen Berry displayed a bias against Donlin's contract negotiations in favor of the position of his new friend John McGraw. Berry commented that Donlin shouldn't complain. He said that Mike had made enough money and should count his blessings, particularly because he was nursing a bum leg. But he admitted that the Giants would miss his hitting if he didn't play. Giants' owner John Brush would not concede to Donlin's contract demands, so Mike signed with Nixey Callahan's Logan Squares for the 1907 season.

An enterprising promoter, the former White Sox star and manager assembled arguably the best baseball team outside of Organized Baseball. Callahan wanted to become a mogul like Charles Comiskey, owner of the Chisox. Callahan's Chicago squad had just defeated both World Series teams at the end of 1906. His team played most days during the season, often in front of large crowds. They played teams from the minor leagues, major leagues, black leagues, colleges, and towns surrounding Chicago. Their games against the black club, the Leland Giants managed by Rube Foster, consistently attracted a significant following.

Donlin's departure for the Logan Squares did not sit lightly with the National Commission. And Chase's simultaneous holdout with the Highlanders put the two Californians, as well as all competitive outlaw leagues, under a microscope. Because of the Logan Squares, Ban Johnson would eventually create yet another mortal enemy in Nixey Callahan.[A] And the pressures from the Commission on outlaws would mount over the next two seasons. As could be expected, Prince Hal Chase would play a leading role in the mayhem.

While Donlin arranged to jump from the New York Giants to the Logan Squares, Amy Mayer put together a deal for Chase. A prospective outlaw team in Los Angeles that planned to join the California State League also allegedly approached Chase offering $4,000 plus a half interest in a café.[B] Chase continued to plan for a wedding in April in New Jersey, but the Highlanders were becoming

---

[A] Ban Johnson enemies now include Nixey Callahan, George Stallings, John McGraw, Andrew Freedman, and John T. Brush.

[B] Perhaps the outlaw owner was Morley, but the entity wasn't disclosed.

less certain about his arrival. Clark Griffith did comment, however, that he doubted the claim about the outlaw club in Los Angeles. He said, "… it is farcical to think … that an outlaw club in Los Angeles can afford to pay $4,000 salaries."[26] The press in New York admitted that the loss of Chase would be a blow to the team's hopes for a pennant "for Chase is one player in a hundred in skill and an easy man to handle."[27] When Chase didn't report, the city of New York expected that George Moriarity would take over for Chase at first base.

The arrangements made by outlaw San Jose owner Amy Mayer to land Chase put pressure on Farrell and Devery. They finally agreed to increase Chase's salary to $4,000 for the next season. By mid-April, Chase had postponed his wedding, but he agreed to tie the knot once again with Farrell and Devery. By the time Chase reported, the season had begun.

[1] The Dugout Rail; San Antonio Express-News. San Antonio, Tex.: May 26, 2002.
[2] The Sports Parade, Braven Dyer, LA Times, Dec 15, 1943, pg. A7
[3] History of Baseball in California and Pacific Coast Leagues 1847-1938, Memories and Musings of an Old Time Baseball Player, Fred W. Lange, pg. 91.
[4] Sporting News, 4/15/1905
[5] Direct wire to the Times, Highlanders Climbing Up, August 6, 1905, pg. IV10
[6] Hal Chase, The Defiant Life and Turbulent Times of Baseball's Biggest Crook, Martin Kohout.
[7] Tonight's fight at Colma, Direct Wire to the Times, San Francisco, Jan 30, 1906. Los Angeles Times, Pg II3
[8] Stanford Baseball Coach Retires, Frank Finch, Apr 24, 1949, pg. 37
[9] Art Rosenbaum. San Francisco Chronicle (pre-1997 Fulltext). San Francisco, Calif.: Mar 8, 1985. p. 80
[10] History of Baseball in California and Pacific Coast Leagues 1847-1938, Memories and Musings of an Old Time Baseball Player, Fred W. Lange, pg. 98.
[11] History of Baseball in California and Pacific Coast Leagues 1847-1938, Memories and Musings of an Old Time Baseball Player, Fred W. Lange, pg. 149-150.
[12] News of San Joaquin Valley, Los Angeles Times, Mar 15, 1920, pg. 11
[13] Art Rosenbaum. San Francisco Chronicle (pre-1997 Fulltext). San Francisco, Calif.: Mar 8, 1985. p. 80
[14] New York Times, July 26, 1906
[15] Berman, Jay and Sesar Carreno. The Short Life of a Downtown Amusement Park, Los Angeles Downtown News, Sep 4. 2006.
[16] More Sunday Baseball, Los Angeles Times, Dec 19, 1906, Pg. I6
[17] Sunday Baseball, Los Angeles Times, Dec 30,1906, pg. III3
[18] Muggsy M'Graw in Los Angeles, Los Angeles Times, Jan. 8, 1907, pg. I6
[19] Minor baseball, Dec 31, 1906, Los Angeles Times, pg II3
[20] Harry Pulliam Retains Power, Los Angeles Times, Dec 14, 1906, pg. I7
[21] Gossip About Ball Players, Dec 17, 1906, pg. I6
[22] Williams Tells of "Hen" Berry, Harry A. Williams, Los Angeles Times, Mar 17, 1920, A5.
[23] Tigers Trying Hard to Dispose of O'Rourke, Harry A. Williams, Los Angeles Times, Nov 21, 1913, pg. III3
[24] Bad Business for Outlaws, Los Angeles Times, Jan 10, 1907. Pg I6
[25] Williams Tells of "Hen" Berry, Harry A. Williams, Mar 17, 1920, pg. A5
[26] New York Times, March 2, 1907
[27] New York Times, March 7, 1907

Chapter 8

The Best Thing to Do is Obey the Commission, Not!

Hap Hogan and Harry Wolter were cast adrift after the Fresno Raisin Eaters folded in the Pacific Coast League. Hogan and the Fresno franchise sold Wolter to the Cincinnati Reds.[1] Then Hogan joined the California Angels when Hen Berry acquired him as a catcher for 1907. Even though Hogan introduced Wolter to the Cincinnati Reds,[2] Wolter wasn't happy with his former Santa Clara coach or the Fresno management; when the team folded, they had failed to pay Harry. After sending letters to Hogan asking for payment, Wolter decided to turn in his pal and appeal to the club President August Herrmann – all over $40. The circumstances highlighted that players, managers, and owners had very little money in those days. Hogan certainly had nothing. And Fresno had gone broke.

At first Wolter sent letters to Hogan, who did respond. But by the time Hogan had written his response, he had already signed a contract with Hen Berry in Los Angeles and was packing up to move. He wrote his letter of February 2 on the Fresno Baseball Club stationery:

> *Friend Harry,*
>
> *Your letter received and I can assure you that you will get every cent that is coming to you. We attest to settle all differences soon and your case especially. I tried hard to make a little visit to Santa Clara but was too busy. Regards to Jimmy Byrnes[A] and all the boys.*
>
> > *I Remain*
> >
> > *Your friend, Hap[3]*

Wolter responded with an appeal February 25 to August Herrmann, President of the Cincinnati Reds and the National Commission, with a copy of the letter from Hap Hogan:

[A] Jimmy Byrnes was the Santa Clara coach for 1907. Wolter was an assistant coach.

Mr. Aug Herrmann

Dear Sir,

I am having a little trouble getting Forty ($40) Dollars from the Fresno Club for my services while with them. I wrote manager Hogan a couple of times. Also notified Mr. Evan[A]s of the same club but they do not seem to notice my letters. Enclosed find a letter from Hogan.

Respectfully,

Harry Wolter[4]

Fresno did eventually field a team in the California States League in 1907. The outlaw league featured teams from Oakland, San Francisco, Stockton, Sacramento, Fresno, Alameda, San Jose, and Santa Cruz. Many of Northern California's best players migrated to the league, many as outlaws, including Tub Hackett, Doc Moskiman, Ben Henderson, Phil Knell, Ping Bodie, Joe Nealon, Jimmy Whalen, Bull Croll, Cliff Blankenship, Duffy Lewis, Elmer Stricklett, Jimmie Shinn, Brick Devereaux, and youngster Harry Hooper. Stricklett joined the league after jumping his contract with Brooklyn because his wife didn't approve him playing for the National League; the league's "dirty baseball" was not only unrefined, but represented a moral dilemma for her and Elmer.

In 1907, Coach Frank Haggerty of St. Vincent's college retired to pursue a career as a lawyer. He had spent the last three years coaching the baseball team and overseeing all athletics on campus. He organized the football squad that played USC, Pomona College, Occidental, Cal, Stanford, the Sherman Indians, Los Angeles High School, and University of Arizona. He established the track team and basketball team for the first time while at the school. But his major accomplishment was the advancement of baseball at the school.

He had developed the preeminent college baseball team in Southern California in recent years. In his first year his team won the college championship, defeating all teams. This past year they lost a championship to St. Mary's, a team that unfairly featured many major league ballplayers. In the thirteenth inning, catcher Fred Snodgrass, who later starred in the outfield for John McGraw's Giants, attempted to throw behind St. Mary's Thacher at first base, but sent the ball sailing into right field allowing Thacher to score from first to win the championship. After realizing that he had blown the game, Snodgrass's face depicted misery as he stared dejectedly down at home plate.

Fred sat right down in the dust and dirt around the rubber and sobbed. Coach Haggerty came over to the boy and though the tears were

---

[A] Evans is President of the Fresno County Athletic Association, proprietors of the Fresno Baseball Club *streaming down his face, he led the shaken lad off the field. Thus did Fred Snodgrass go through his first big championship.*[5]

The game did not deter McGraw from signing Snodgrass to a contract.[A] After St. Vincent's played the Giants during the season, McGraw commented on St. Vincent's program[B], "'...the St. Vincent's boys stood up to the bat better than any college team he had ever seen. The Giants won 9-2, 8-1, and 7-1, but the hits were nearly even."

McGraw went on to comment that St. Vincent's squad lost to St. Mary's, but was at a disadvantage. "On that team were seven professionals, including Hal Chase, who played professional Sunday baseball for San Jose."[6]

In the major leagues, Chase had a mediocre year at the plate. He batted .287 for tenth highest in the league, and the Highlanders finished in 5th with a record of 70-78. But Hal continued to receive rave reviews for his fielding. In one commentary, Chase, described as an idol, was compared to Christy Mathewson, Honus Wagner, and Nap Lajoie.

> [Hal Chase] *is not only an idol because he can play ball well, but because he plays it with a physical grace which commands the admiration of every person who has a touch of the artistic in his nature... he can skip around the diamond with the polish of a French dancing master.*
>
> *... no first baseman ever has been his equal in ability to take a hop, skip, and jump from first base to the plate, pick up a bunt hit on the way and throw out some unfortunate runner who is trying to get to second base.*[7]
>
> *'Highlanders' First Baseman Is Perhaps the Most Graceful Man Playing Baseball. ... Four players stand out above all the others in the possession of this quality of style. They are Napoleon Lajoie, of the Clevelands; Hal Chase of the New York Americans; Jimmy Collins, of the Philadelphia Americans, and John (Honus) Wagner, of the Pittsburgs..... [Chase} is as lithe and unstudied in his movements as a panther. He combines naturalness, gracefulness, and a certain boyish unrestrainedness. There is a magnetism about him that brings people out to the ball park "just to see Chase play." This aside from his skill as a player. He is a big drawing card as are Wagner and Lajoie..... The young first baseman of*

[A] Irony exists in the story about Snodgrass blowing the championship at St. Vincent's. Fred would become infamous in baseball history for dropping a fly ball in the tenth inning of the deciding eighth game of the 1912 World Series that the Giants would lose to the Boston Red Sox. The error would be known throughout history as the "Snodgrass' Muff." Two of the Red Sox players in the Series were ex-St. Mary's players Harry Hooper and Duffy Lewis.

[B] McGraw also signed his teammate Art Shafer.

the Highlanders is as quick as a flash, and, inclined to be restless and fidgety on the field, never makes a false move. There is no quicker thinker in baseball than he, so that his mind is in keeping with his body. Whether he is smothering a fly ball, sliding to a base, fielding a bunt, or standing at the plate ready to hit, he is the embodiment of unconscious buoyancy and grace. He is natural as a child, care free but vigilant - never tense or set... as natural as for a squirrel to climb a tree ... poetry in motion. [8]

Stricklett had a decent season with a 2.27 ERA even though his anemic Brooklyn squad couldn't score runs for him. On July 18, he played against Harry Wolter. Stricklett didn't pitch, but Wolter threw and lost to Doc Scanlan 3-2. Ten days later, Stricklett pitched against Wolter's Cardinals and lost 1-0, although Wolter was on the bench throughout the game. In September, Elmer lost to Pittsburgh 2-1 behind twenty-year old Nick Maddox, who recorded the first no hitter in Pittsburgh history.[A] Stricklett didn't surrender any earned runs against Honus Wagner and the rest of the Pirates, but still took the loss. The Superbas never gave him the support he needed to be successful in the league.

Frank Arellanes continued to pitch well for the San Jose club in the Cal State League. His consistency didn't go unnoticed. Hen Berry signed Frank to join the Angels as of July 25, 1907. However, two days later, even though Arellanes had already agreed to play in Los Angeles for Berry who had offered more money than San Jose's Amy Mayer, Arellanes backed out and continued to play for his home team.

The National Commission continued to exert its power over baseball nationally. But political winds in America during 1907 blew in the direction of breaking up monopolies. "Trust Busting" President Theodore Roosevelt appealed to the national sentiment favoring competition and fair trade by aggressively enforcing the Sherman Anti-Trust Law. Many of the wealthiest individuals in the history of the world, including John D. Rockefeller (oil), Andrew Carnegie (steel), William Vanderbilt (railroad), Andrew Mellon (oil), and Henry Ford (automobiles) were products of recent industrialism in the United States. Even though Roosevelt spared Organized Baseball from scrutiny, he excused few others in efforts to curb corporate power in America. In 1905, Roosevelt appointed Kenesaw Mountain Landis as a District Judge in Illinois. In 1907, Landis presided over an anti-trust case against one of the nation's most prominent businesses, Standard Oil. Landis subpoenaed the world's wealthiest capitalist, John D. Rockefeller, and fined him nearly $30 million. The judgment was later overturned, but by taking on Rockefeller, Judge Landis demonstrated uncompromising perseverance to advance the current political agenda.

[A] Stricklett's bad luck is highlighted by the fact that Pittsburgh wouldn't throw another no hitter until 1951.

In spite of the trust busting activity, the power of the National Commission continued to grow. But the consortium faced surmounting competition from independent teams and leagues, including the California State League. Toward the end of 1907, the Pacific Coast League no longer boasted the best talent on the Coast. Teams that became increasingly more competitive in towns such as Alameda, Oakland, San Francisco, Stockton, San Jose, Santa Cruz, and Fresno directly competed against the Oakland and San Francisco Pacific Coast League teams and threatened PCL owners. And as an outlaw league, the Cal State League gained popularity when the major leaguers arrived after September and October to bolster rosters. The PCL owners became concerned about the growing popularity of the League. Cal Ewing appealed to the National Commission to curb the major leaguers' participation in the competing league.

San Francisco owner Cal Ewing attended the National Association meetings in October 1907 and vehemently protested the practice of major leaguers participating in late seasons California State League games. Through regular interaction with the top brass in Organized Baseball in the East, Ewing became influential, well connected, and well respected at the national level. His concerns were promptly addressed. The National Commission immediately issued an order forbidding all National Agreement players from joining the outlaw California State League during the winter. At the meetings, the Commission officially named the California State League an outlaw league. The Commission warned that any violations would result in a fine, suspension, or ban from Organized Baseball.

"Was that a challenge?" thought Hal Chase. "Do they really think they can stop me from playing?"

Hal Chase would not stop playing in California without a fight. Throughout his career, Chase was forever in motion throughout the year playing in baseball games. Few things would prevent him from playing – certainly not East Coast Baseball. A simple law of physics could easily predict the effect of the threat on Chase – it would create an equal and opposite reaction from the Northern California star.

In spite of the ban, Chase joined the San Jose team and played in October during and after the National Association meetings. Aware of the ruling and the threat of being banned from Major League baseball, Chase, reporters, fans, and the Cal State league had a laugh at the expense of Organized Baseball. Chase knew he could not play for San Jose without everyone associated with baseball hearing about it. Teammates, opponents, reporters, and fans all knew Hal Chase by sight. And from a distance, they recognized his unparalleled play on the field. Playing anonymously was not an option for Chase. But in a playful form of protest, and as a practical joke targeted at the National Commission, the PCL and Cal Ewing, Chase played for San Jose under the assumed name "Shultz" on October 30. And West Coast baseball outside of the Pacific Coast League, including the media, went along with the prank. Cal Ewing became enraged by the orchestrated irreverence. He insisted that the National Commission act at once.

> *Under the assumed name Shultz, Hal Chase, first baseman for the New York Americans, played shortstop for the team in a game that took place in SF for the SF State League team. He did so because he was afraid he would get into trouble with the American League and tried to dodge the situation by working under an alias. He violated a ruling by the National Commission and the mandate of his club. Obviously by playing under an alias, he understood the gravity of his actions. Kid Mohler has entered into negotiations with Chase to play first base if organized baseball takes action against Chase. Hal will accompany the San Jose team to Sacramento Friday night.[9]*

Chase wasn't the only major leaguer playing winter ball in California. Hen Berry once again organized winter exhibition games at Chutes Park. He scheduled games with Eastern stars every Saturday and Sunday.[10] As he had done in previous years, the Cubs' Frank Chance became a regular in the games.

And the California Winter League continued to grow in popularity with teams including the Santa Ana, LA Hoegees, Meeks, McCormicks, Christopher-Levy, Edisons, Santa Monica, Pasadena, Santa Barbara, Dolgeville, and Morans. Santa Ana Yellow Sox featured twenty-year-old celebrity Walter Johnson, who created a buzz wherever he played.[11] He had just completed his first season with the Washington Senators where he played in fourteen games.[A]

Other future stars were yet unknown and on the rise that winter. On November 18, 1907, Sacramento defeated Alameda behind great pitching by Spider Baum. But what caught Charlie Graham's eye was a fleet-footed outfielder for Alameda who played for nearby St. Mary's College. Harry Hooper made "a sensational catch of a fly deep in center," which made Graham take note and later attempt to purchase Hooper from Alameda.

Chase continued to play for San Jose in spite of the threat of being banned. He knew he was in good favor with the Highlanders, and no complaints from Cal Ewing or the Pacific Coast League would prevent him from playing for Frank Farrell in New York the next year. But by November 21, after playing through the Cal State season, Chase agreed to conform to the National Commission. The Sporting Life quoted Chase on November 21, 1907 that he played to earn some extra money to purchase his parents a home, but that he would now conform:

> *Yes, I will observe the rule. There is nothing else to do. The ruling is an unjust one and it is hard for the men in the big leagues, for it deprives*

[A] Not until 1910 would he win 25 or more games every year for 8 consecutive seasons on his way to 417 career victories for a team that had a losing overall record.

them of an opportunity to make some money after their contracts with the Eastern clubs have expired. Still, the Commission is powerful enough to enforce the penalties, and the best thing we can do is to obey the rule.

The response was classic Hal Chase. Throughout his career, his public comments were diplomatic, but duplicitous. When he responded to interview questions from the press, his true feelings were often the opposite of his comments. In the response above, Chase likely believed:

No, I won't observe the rule. There is more that I will do to oppose the Commission. The ruling is an unjust one and it is hard for the men in the big leagues, for it deprives them of an opportunity to make some money after their contracts with the Eastern clubs have expired. The Commission can go ahead and try to enforce the penalties, and I'll just play somewhere else.

On January 1, 1908, Hal Chase finally married Nellie Heffernan at St. Joseph's Church in San Jose, California. His best man was William J. Benson, a friend from San Jose who introduced Chase to James Morley, and who subsequently became a scout for the New York Highlanders. Based on Chase's comments to the press in late November about the respect he had for the power of the Commission, he didn't act fearful. One might have reasoned that Chase would want to return to the Highlanders, since his wife's family lived in nearby New Jersey. But soon after the wedding, Chase indicated, just as he did nearly every season, that the next year he intended to play in California.

Chase played in twelve games for San Jose at the end of 1907, nine games after the Commission warned him not to. His batting average was .800 in the twelve games. Chase was feeling pretty good about himself. He also felt good about the California State League. He claimed that the league played better ball than the Pacific Coast League and that it created an opportunity for major leaguers to remain in California and play. He reported that Stricklett might abandon Brooklyn to join San Jose. Jimmy Whalen signed with Sacramento, and Spider Baum and Bobbie Keefe were looking to land on a Cal League team.

But Frank Farrell undeniably understood Chase and didn't expect him to miss any Highlander games in 1908. He understood that while in California, Chase had many friends and was easily steered. A nice guy, Chase hated to say no to people. Much in demand, he postponed any decision to return while in front of family and friends. Farrell did not worry; he astutely and patiently waited for the return of his star. Farrell was correct. In March 1908, Hal Chase was the first of the Highlanders to report for spring training.

---

[1] These Boys Move Up To The Majors, San Francisco Chronicle, Sep 15, 1916, p. 8

[2] Harry Wolter to Quit Ball, Los Angeles Times, July 14, 1919, pg. 15

[3]   Santa Clara University Historical Archives, Small Alpha Box 18. Harry M. Wolter biographical material.

[4]   Santa Clara University Historical Archives, Small Alpha Box 18. Harry M. Wolter biographical material.

[5]   Death Lurks for Those Who Ignore San Speed Laws, Owen R. Bird, Los Angeles Times, Oct 5, 1913, p. VII1

[6]   Coach Haggerty Has Had Much Success, Los Angeles Times, May 19, 1907, VIII7

[7]   Ball Players Who Are Idolized By Fans Throughout the Country, The Washington Post, June 9, 1907, Pg. SP2

[8]   Style Among Players, The Washington Post, September 15, 1907, p. S4

[9]   Hal Chase, first baseman for the New York Americans Chase Violates Baseball Law, Direct Wire to the Times, Oct 31, 1907, LA Times, pg. I7

[10] Berry Plans Winter Ball, Los Angeles Times, Nov 13, 1907

[11] The California Winter League, William F. McNeil

Chapter 9

The 1908 Season: End of Innocence in Independent California Baseball

In April of 1908, the National Commission fined Mike Donlin $100 for playing with Logan Squares and other teams outside of Organized Baseball the prior season. The fine was a formality; the Commission required that Donlin pay penance before returning to the New York Giants, who wanted their star back. The fine was a pittance, but the Commission had to impose some punishment. The Giants likely paid the fine for Donlin. Since 1908 was an even year, Donlin was due for a great season. And he didn't disappoint. He finished second in the league in batting and RBI. He also won the award for the most popular athlete in New York City, an honor previously won by California's Van Haltren twenty years before. Donlin and the equally popular Christy Mathewson led the Giants to an unforgettable showdown at the end of the season with the Chicago Cubs for the national league pennant.

Chase and the Highlanders fared much worse. At the end of June, Manager Clark Griffith, upset with the capricious tinkering of owner Frank Farrell had had enough. He resigned on June 24 with the Highlanders in seventh place. Griffith felt that a change was needed. He reasoned diplomatically in the press that he had been bad luck for the team. But not only did the Highlanders need a change; so did Griffith. Frank Farrell named shortstop Kid Elberfeld as replacement for Griffith. The envious Chase did not take the news well. Over the next four months, he failed to disguise his disenchantment.

Back in California, Charlie Graham's friend Doc Strub no longer played for Graham's ballclub in Sacramento. But because Graham helped Strub by providing a job on the team after the 1906 earthquake, Strub established business connections that enabled him to get back on his feet financially and return to dentistry. Still a fan of baseball, Doc opened a chain of "painless" dental offices. Capitalizing on the widespread popularity of the automobile, Strub advertised his offices on roadside billboards. He became well known as "the billboard dentist." His involvement in baseball and California sports, however, was far from over.

General Manager Charlie Graham did not miss Strub's contribution, as he remained confident that his Sacramento Capitals could win the California League title the coming season. He signed ace hurler Jimmy Whalen, Ed Raymer at second, and Big Joe Nealon at first base. Nealon led the National League in RBI his

Fresno Raisin Eaters Team Logo

rookie season in 1906. The defending champion Stockton Millers, managed by Cy Moreing, had a solid team returning two strong pitchers, the league's best twirler in Ben Henderson, and a solid backup in Doc Moskiman. Both pitchers also hit well, and were supported well in the field. The Millers had won the California League championship every year since 1903. San Jose posed a formidable foe with three top pitchers – Elmer Stricklett, Frank Arellanes, and Harry Wolter. Santa Cruz behind Brick Devereaux, and Fresno led by Spider Baum, would compete strongly from the middle of the pack. The league began the season with eight teams – Graham's Sacramento Capitals, Moreing's Stockton Millers, San Jose Prune Pickers, Santa Cruz Sand Crabs, Alameda Encinals managed by Fred Lange, Fresno Raisin Eaters, Oakland Oaks, and San Francisco Seals.

The previous year, St. Mary's player Harry Hooper had caught Graham's eye with a great catch at a game between Hooper's Alameda Encinals and Sacramento. Hooper, born in Bell Station at the southern edge of Santa Clara County along what is now the Pacheco Pass, grew up in the San Joaquin Valley. As a little boy, he rode a horse to school six miles each way while carrying a rifle and his baseball, bat, and glove. Hooper was set to graduate in June with a degree in Civil Engineering in 1908. The Alameda owner, Mr. McMinnamen, asked Hooper to play on the team for a few months until graduation, at which time, he would be free to pursue his engineering career.

Doc Strub remembered the first time he saw Harry Hooper play in 1907. Strub was playing for Sacramento. Hooper was playing for Alameda. Strub was playing second base when Hooper bounced a ball to him. Strub went after it, but even before he got his hands on the ball, Hooper was over first base. Strub said that never in his life did he see a man streak down to first as fast as Hooper. He admitted that Hooper was not a good fielder in those days, but he could hit and run and throw. He recalled Graham signing him for $50. [1] Strub's memory faded a bit between the game in 1907 and the comments made more than a decade later - As the season of 1908 would show, Hooper still wasn't yet much of a hitter. And throughout his career, he was known as a solid fielder. And last, Graham would not pay $50 for him; he would pay just $25.

Graham liked Hooper and asked McMinnamen if he could purchase him for the Capitals, not knowing that he was to be released from his contract within the week. McMinnamen didn't want to disclose to Graham that Hooper's contract would soon terminate. In spite of the Alameda owner's wishes, Hooper told Graham that he planned to quit baseball as soon as he got an engineering job, which would be at the end of the summer. Graham knew he could get Hooper an engineering job as well as have him play baseball for Sacramento. Figuring that he could steal Hooper, Graham asked McMinnamen how much he wanted for the player.

"Oh, how about $200?" asked McMinnamen.

"How about $10?" Charlie countered, knowing he could drive a hard bargain.

"Make it $50."

"I'll make it $20"

They settled on $25.

Hooper claimed it was a blow to his ego to be sold for only $25.

Later, Graham confessed to Hooper he smelled a rat the minute the McMinnamen asked for $200 when he should have asked for $500. So he went as low as he could to test the situation, and it worked. Graham got Hooper a job working for the Western Pacific Railroad where he received $75 per month for surveying. Graham paid him $85 per month to play baseball.[2]

Hooper was a project. At first, he batted sixth in the lineup, just ahead of Graham. The team relied primarily on production from Joe Nealon, the league's best hitter. Initially, Hooper rarely got a hit, surpassed in mediocrity only by his manager Graham. At the plate, Charlie didn't get a hit for more than ten games. The San Francisco Chronicle empathized:

> *Charlie Graham of the Capitols has not yet broken into the hit column, but expects to climb the ladder speedily when he gets on the first rung.[3]*

The San Francisco and Oakland squads were terrible. The only bright spot for San Francisco was pitcher Frank Bodie. Bodie, the nephew and younger brother of two other Bodie players for San Francisco over the years, used an alias to conceal his Italian ancestry. The Bodie family's last name was actually Pezzolo, and they were from San Francisco's Little Italy. They were the first of the many Italian ballplayers from San Francisco, including Tony Lazzeri and the DiMaggio brothers. Frank Bodie was born Francisco Stefano Pezzolo. In 1910, he would become known as "Ping" Bodie, one of the best power hitters of the deadball era.

Oakland had no bright spots. They could not win a ballgame, both from lack of ability and an absence of karma. They lost twenty-seven consecutive games to start the season and were on a path to set an all-time baseball record for losses. After Elmer Stricklett defeated them 5-1, a headline read:

Great Record of Defeats for Oakland

McMenomy's bunch appears to be hopeless and helpless, but the manager says the tide will turn some day. Perhaps he intends to win a game before long.[4]

Even when they played well enough to win, they lost. In a game against Alameda, they out-hit the opponent seven to one, but lost 2-1. In a rematch,

Alameda no-hit the Oaks, but the game was still tied at 0-0 with a chance for Oakland to win until a fluke play decided the game. The San Francisco Chronicle reported:

> *In the fifth inning, Nelson hit to right field, the ball sank in the marsh and he was able to get home before it was recovered. The run proved to be the difference in the game.[5]*

The Chronicle reported that the all-time record for losses was twenty-nine held by Louisville in the American Association in 1889. A report in Sacramento errantly reported that Oakland already had the record. But the Chronicle pointed out that Oakland was still only the third worst of all time. Fortunately for Oakland, they won a game before breaking the record.

> *Louisville lost twenty-nine in a row and Oakland will have to stop claiming for a couple of weeks. That the team will eventually break the record is a foregone conclusion. If it is any consolation to Oakland, it might be stated that the team is in second place, so far as a losing record is concerned, for the Pittsburgh Nationals lost twenty-eight consecutive games in 1901.[6]*

By the time Oakland won its first game, Stockton, San Jose, Fresno and Sacramento were pulling ahead of the other teams. The rivalry between Stockton and San Jose continued after Stockton defeated the Prune Pickers by narrow margins the past two seasons. In May, the two teams paired up in one of the season's great match-ups to date. Frank Arellanes pitched nine innings of the greatest ball ever seen on the local diamond, allowing a single hit through regulation. Arellanes opened the thirteenth inning by hitting Joyce in the ribs. Three hits and three runs followed with Stockton outscoring San Jose 4 to 1 in extra innings.

By the end of May, the top four teams were tightly packed atop the league.

Stockton	13-4
Fresno	13-4
San Jose	13-4
Sacramento	12-5

During the same month, Amy Mayer sold the San Jose franchise to A.L. Jarman, a prominent attorney in San Jose, for $2,300.[7] Part of the incentive for Jarman was that he'd have Hal Chase down the stretch after the major league season ended. Chase had played for San Jose each of the last two years and was under contract to the club to return in September. Having Chase would not only be lucrative down the stretch, but would give San Jose a great shot at a championship against the formidable Stockton club.[A]   Upon purchasing the franchise, Jarman immediately arranged for a double car track system to take fans to and from the ball grounds.

By early June, Harry Wolter developed into a star in San Jose. Formerly a pitcher, Wolter was heating up at the plate as well as on the mound. In an 8-1 victory over San Francisco on June 7, won by Arellanes, Wolter had two triples and a double. By mid June, Harry Wolter led the Prune Pickers with an average of .367.

On June 13, former Santa Clara ballplayers Graham, Wolter, and Stricklett reunited in a game San Jose won 1-0 over Sacramento at San Jose's Luna Park, on the city's northern edge between N. 13th Street and N. 17th Street. As had been the case all season against Stricklett, Hooper went a hitless 0 for 4. With the victory, San Jose tied Sacramento for second place with an 18-6 record. In a rematch two days later, San Jose won again 1-0 behind Arellanes' two hitter. As was customary at that point in the season, Harry Hooper was again a hitless 0 for 3.

The Chronicle reported:

> *Arellanes pitched one of the most remarkable games of the year here, allowing the visitors but two hits, both lucky. Graham hit safely in the fifth inning, getting a short pop fly just out of the reach of the infielders. The other hit was even weaker.[8]*

In the pennant race, Sacramento stayed within striking distance of Stockton, which was led by Ben Henderson on the mound. He pitched a two-hitter over Santa Cruz for a shutout, and was also 2-4 at the plate, driving in Moriarity for the game's only run. Sacramento fell further behind June 28th following a close 3-2 loss to the Millers. Hitless Hooper, not yet playing like a major league All Star, was labeled the goat. The paper noted, "Hooper dropped a high one to right and the game was over."

At the end of June, Fresno traveled to San Jose for a heated series in which Fresno got the better of the hometown team, much to the locals' disgust. During one of the losses on June 29, a riot nearly occurred. Following the game, headlines read,

Kennedy Starts a Riot in San Jose

> *First Baseman Kennedy of the Fresno club barely escaped a richly deserved drubbing at the hands of a thousand angry fans in the game with Fresno today, when he purposely collided with, punched, and booted Bobby Eager, the local catcher, who was ready to put the ball on him as he attempted to make a foolhardy steal from third base. Eager*

[A]   At the same time, the Santa Cruz Beach Company purchased Santa Cruz franchise.

was knocked unconscious and for ten minutes the players and a doctor worked over him in the dressing room to restore him to consciousness. In the meantime, a score of angry fans had chased Kennedy headlong into the dressing room. There he was reinforced by Harry Spencer, who joined Fresno Saturday, and with a couple of bats they waited for the local people to start hostilities. Al Jarman, the manager of the local club, saved the day by throwing himself in the open doorway and preventing the entry of the fans.[9]

Luna Park was the scene of some more drama on July 12, when San Jose played the visiting Stockton team. Wolter and Henderson faced off on the mound. Wolter allowed only one hit, but walked eight batters, in winning 3-1. Henderson took the loss, touched for ten hits. The news, however, centered on Stockton's catcher "Tub" Hackett. The San Francisco Chronicle reported:

Hackett Swings on Umpire with Bat
Victory of San Jose Team is Too Much for Fat Catcher

A most regrettable affair occurred in the ninth inning when Hackett lost his head on Umpire McCarthy's mistake in calling a strike on a wild ball. Hackett strenuously objected and swung his bat at the umpire, who was behind the plate, but stopped it before it caused any serious injury. Manager Moreing... ordered Hackett to the dugout while McCarthy was trying to get to him. Hackett will be put out of the game for a time.[10]

In the next game of the series, Harry Wolter shut out Stockton. The Chronicle cited:

Wolter was in great form and scattered the four hits he allowed the visitors through nine innings and allowed them to become at no time dangerous. Nine men were struck out.[11]

At the same time that Wolter proved victorious over rival Stockton, Fresno swept a series from Santa Cruz at the beach. In a 7-5 victory for Fresno, Baum got into a little trouble with the umpires.

Police Escort Baum off the Diamond

Although the Santa Cruz fans had to see their team lose the fifth game of the series, they got their money's worth in fighting and excitement. Fresno had the game 5 to 1 in the eighth, when, after walking two men, Baum assaulted Umpire Moore and was taken from the lot by the police.[12]

There was some tension the same day between Sacramento and Alameda, where Sacramento won 10-1 behind 17 hits. Jimmy Whalen won the game for the Capitals, but was redressed by the umpire.

Jim Whalen spouted once too often and was assessed a five spot.[13]

Other colorful or interesting proceedings were reported during the eventful 1908 season in the Cal State League. The San Francisco Chronicle noted the following novelties.

During the course of a game, Doyle of Sacramento, who was on third, took the ball from third baseman Hallinan's hands, rolled it out into the field and came home without umpire Flynn getting wise to the truth.

On May 18, Sacramento and Stockton met. Graham wasn't slated to play, as Byrnes was in the catcher's slot. But Byrnes created a sensation by throwing a bucketful of water on umpire Moore because of a rank decision. The act was met with wild jeers and hooting. It was reported that Byrnes would either be suspended two weeks or ruled out of the league.[14]

Those Capital City fans are real candy when the Grahams are playing good ball. It was a treat to hear the rooting in the last series.[15]

Arellanes is getting Stricklett's habit of throwing men out at first base. He is nearly as crafty as his instructor and before long, he will be as proficient.[16]

There are few more popular players in the State than Charlie Graham, the manager of the Sacramento team.[17]

Bull Croll has been falling off badly in his hitting and has been ordered to do his practicing in Fresno in the future.[18]

To determine more fully the superiority of the rival teams [Sacramento and Santa Cruz] a $200 purse was raised for the best of three this week.[19]

Though Fresno is in fourth place, the fans of that city appreciate the efforts of the team to go higher up. When Baum and his nine returned from Santa Cruz, they were met by a brass band and a large gathering of fans.

Silent Loucks, the mainstay of the Santa Cruz team who pitched a shutout against Alameda last week, has handed in his resignation to the management, which has been accepted. He was a good pitcher, but a trouble maker.[20]

Umpire Jack McCarthy and Tub Hackett are the best of friends and there is nothing to account for the catcher's unprovoked assault last week.[21]

Everyone endorses President Hermann's prompt action in the case of Hackett. "Tub" promises to be very good in the future. He is lucky to have a future.[22]

Dashwood does not seem to be wanted anywhere. He has now been released by Coalinga for alleged throwing of games.[23]

Phil Knell thought he had a peach in Delaney, the new twirler from San Luis Obispo, but he turned out to be a lemon.

The Stockton fans are making up a purse to pay Hackett's fine. It is not a kindly act, as he is liable to forget his offense too easily.[24]

By the end of July, Charlie Graham's pet project, Harry Hooper, started hitting. Graham moved Hooper to the fourth position in the Sacramento lineup with good results. In a 7-1 win over Alameda, Harry went 2-4 and was beginning to be gain confidence at the plate. The paper reported,

Harry Hooper's batting was worth notice last week. He hit safely eight times and returned home with his average considerably augmented.[25]

In August, Sacramento closed in on Stockton with a 3-1 victory over the league leader. 3,500 fans turned out for the big game. Sacramento manufactured runs as only Graham could.

Inside ball and daring base running brought home the bacon for the locals. Hooper scored in the fourth without the aid of a hit, he stealing two bags and coming over on Shay's error. A neat squeeze play by Graham brought in Nealon in the sixth.[26]

In a rematch, Sacramento won again by a 3-1 margin, although Umpire McCarthy threw Whalen out of the game.

Umpire McCarthy put Whalen out in the first for slamming his glove on the ground when Shay was passed. Burns was sent to the bench in the next frame, when he called McCarthy a robber. After Whalen was ejected, forced to go into the box before he recovered from a recent illness, Fred Brown twirled a brand of ball today against Stockton that at all times was puzzling to the champions. He had not even warmed up for work when called upon, but aside from the second inning, pitched shut out ball. Sacramento won by a score of 3-1.

Graham became known for calling the squeeze play with a man on third. Often, the game hinged on the result.

On Saturday Graham and Jansing worked the squeeze play to a nicety, and on Sunday the Capitals robbed themselves of a game by an abortive attempt to work it.

The following were some batting averages and pitcher statistics through July:

Nealon	.427	Sacramento
Wolter	.362	San Jose
Bodie, F. (7 games 18 Abs)	.357	San Francisco
Blankenship	.342	Fresno
Shinn	.324	Santa Cruz
Collins	.318	Santa Cruz
Hooper	.250	Sacramento
Graham	.239	Sacramento
Stricklett	.207	San Jose
Wolter	8-1	San Jose
Henderson	19-3	Stockton
Whalen	17-5	Sacramento
T Hoag	11-4	Santa Cruz
Baum	15-6	Fresno
Arellanes	10-4	San Jose
Brown	13-6	Sacramento
Miller	13-6	Fresno
Stricklett	11-8	San Jose
Moskiman	9-7	Stockton

Toward the end of August, Stockton and Sacramento were neck and neck, with San Jose close behind. Fresno and Santa Cruz began to fall back from the main pack.

August 24

Sacramento	37-11
Stockton	38-12
San Jose	37-12
Fresno	30-18
Santa Cruz	42-34
Alameda	19-30
San Francisco	5-44
Oakland	3-50

San Jose won a big game 1-0 against Fresno on August 24 when Stricklett had his stuff working, avenging the sweep at home from earlier in the season.

Stricklett Hero of San Jose Game

Stricklett was the hero of today's game with Fresno. He allowed the visitors but three hits, one of them an infield scratch, and had them swinging two feet from the ball when hits meant runs. Poor support kept Fresno runners on the bases, crossing a man over the plate. Two catches in center field, one by Harry Wolter and another by Harry Spencer, were the big features of the game.[27]

Stockton beat Alameda 2-0 to keep pace, and Sacramento surpassed the Seals by the Bay 6-4. By the beginning of August, the race was a dead heat between Graham's Sacramento Solons, Jarman's San Jose Prune Pickers, and Moreing's Stockton Millers. Stockton would soon get a boost that would create the first baseball war in the California State League.

------- -------- ---------

Two days after Frank Farrell hired Elberfeld to manage the New York Highlanders, Hal Chase badly sprained his ankle. He missed ten games. The team continued to lose under Elberfeld. 1908 just wasn't a good year for the New York Americans. Even when Chase returned, he never played well. New York fans and media criticized him for "laying down," a term given to someone who didn't give their best effort. The term also possessed negative properties; it could imply that a player threw games to profit from gambling. Many historians have scrutinized Chase for his intermittent lack of effort. They have built cases for impropriety because of Chase's alleged indiscretions later in his career. However, Chase's performance in 1908 was negatively impacted by his objection to the selection of Elberfeld as manager, his ankle injury, and disgruntlement from an article claiming he played selfishly and without passion. Farrell often leaked his feelings to the press to send a message to players. Chase suspected that Farrell was behind the derogatory article. The betrayal and the questioning of his integrity tore at Chase. Feeling cornered and under stress, Chase lost thirty pounds.

Hal Chase couldn't stomach playing for the ineffective, stop-gap manager Elberfeld or the Highlanders. Like the immature boy that he still was, Chase reacted by "taking his ball and going home;" Chase called his friends in California to see if he could play there to finish out the season.

In August, Farrell began marketing Chase for a trade. Initially rumors surfaced that Chase was headed to play for Comiskey in Chicago.[28] One of the players to go to New York in an exchange was to be George Davis, who Farrell planned to hire as a manager. Another rumor had Chase being swapped to Connie Mack's Philadelphia squad for Harry Davis.[29] The trade rumors and Farrell's failure to consider Chase for the manager role were a last straw for Chase. Chase secretly contacted the owner of the Stockton Millers, Cy Moreing, about jumping to the Cal State League. Moreing agreed to pay Chase $1,000 to finish the last twenty-three games with Stockton. Chase remained with New York through August, a month in which he was criticized for not giving full effort, in order to get his final paycheck. He gave the following statement to the press:

I am not satisfied to play under a management that sees fit to give out a story detrimental to my character and questions my integrity and honesty. Such a story appeared in a New York Sunday paper August 23rd. I feel that I could not do myself justice under such conditions, and therefore I have decided to quit. I never had managerial ideas. I am giving you this exclusive signed statement because I do not want to leave New York without making my position clear to my friends. I am sure that I still have many friends here and in some ways I honestly regret the conditions that compel me to leave the New York club, but as things stand at present I have no other course to pursue. I cannot and will not play ball for Norman Elberfeld. There are other players on the team who feel as I do, but some of them are not in a position financially to take the independent stand that I have taken.

I am a young man, it is true, but not a child, and I am able to think for myself. I have threshed this matter all out and I want to say to you and your readers that I would beg on the streets before I could ever bring myself to play ball for Frank Farrell again.

… if any attempt is made by the management of the club to roast me, I will tell a story which will rip the baseball world wide open.[30]

Chase's comments were revealing. Young and sensitive, he disliked Elberfeld, was envious of the manager, and was hurt by Farrell's comments in the press. His grudge was as much with Farrell as it was with Elberfeld. Chase's final comments revealed the nature of negotiation during that era. The reserve clause gave the player few tools with which to bargain. One option was to threaten to leave the game or sign with an independent league. Organized Baseball's leverage came from its ability to blacklist and malign the reputation of a player in the press, potentially causing financial ruin. Not to be shortchanged in his toolbox of tactics, Chase countered with a threat of his own toward Farrell and Baseball – to reveal a story that would "rip the baseball world wide open."

Not many players used a threatening tactic successfully. The media worked too closely with management to enable a player to gain an upper hand in public opinion. And without a trial to prove any claims, a player's threats ultimately became idle conjecture. Additionally the cost of a trial to prove any claims would exceed the financial limits and the spirit of any ballplayer. One player did eventually have the spirit and financial means to challenge Organized Baseball with such a tactic - Ty Cobb would stage that battle twenty years in the future. He became the rare case of a player who could successfully threaten to reveal the underbelly of Organized Baseball and win.

Not just any story would "rip the baseball world wide open." Baseball had a legacy of impropriety that had been known to the public. Revelation about scurrilous activity would hardly raise an eyebrow. For a story to have a rippling effect, Chase would have had to name names and demonstrate that unsavory conditions pervaded into all ranks. Nobody would ever know the substance behind Chase's threats. But as a youngster plucked from obscurity in California to star for the corrupt Frank Farrell and Bill Devery for three years, Chase likely witnessed much that lacked virtue. Chase's comments signaled that a gap existed between the product that Organized Baseball marketed to America and the activities of the owners. In a few months, National League President Harry Pulliam would confront the paradox in a drama that would threaten his life.

Chase left the shady world of the major leagues and returned to California to play for Stockton businessman Cy Moreing. Moreing was one of five Moreing brothers all raised in the San Joaquin Valley. They grew up on a ranch on Waterloo Road outside of Stockton. Their father was a Stockton pioneer who arrived in the small inland town in 1862. He became a rancher and farmer and later established a construction business that landed him contracts to build many of the area's roads. A popular local citizen, he served as city councilman. The sons followed their father in his successful business and also played baseball growing up. Cy had a twin brother named Will who played outfield for the Stockton club. Cy was the manager and owner. Under Cy, Stockton became the class of the California League.

Hal Chase and Cy Moreing shared a long-term friendship. Along with Hen Berry, Al Jarman, Charlie Graham, and other owners and managers on the Coast, Chase could count on his connection with Moreing as an alternative to Eastern Baseball. Moreing always operated in Stockton, which represented one of the smallest markets in the league. Population determined franchise profitability in most towns. Yet Moreing created such a powerful club that fans would drive from one hundred miles in every direction to see his team play – from Sacramento in the North, San Francisco in the West, Fresno to the South, and the Gold Country in the Western Sierra Nevadas to the East. Having Hal Chase would be fortuitous for Moreing and his quest to make Stockton a financially viable baseball town in spite of its small size.

Soon after Chase left the Highlanders, the New York media uncovered and reported that tremendous discord had existed on the team under Elberfeld. A disaster as a manager, Elberfeld lost more games than his predecessor Clark Griffith - with or without Chase. Elberfeld won only twenty-seven of the last ninety-eight games. The players lacked confidence in him and the team suffered from internal strife, not just due to Chase. Initially, Chase's dispirited play and abandonment were criticized. But upon further review of conditions under Elberfeld, New Yorkers became sympathetic to Chase.

When Moreing signed Chase, San Jose owners Al Jarman and T.C. Barnett became outraged. They had purchased the San Jose squad expecting Hal Chase to be part of the package. Amy Mayer had promised that Chase would return at season's end to play for the Prune Pickers. Instead, Chase was slated to play for their rival. Moreing argued that Chase was a free agent as soon as he returned to play for the Highlanders the previous season. The disagreement led to war between Moreing and the San Jose owners. Hostilities eventually subsided because most league owners became ecstatic that Moreing had lured Chase to the league. Chase would increase revenues in all cities, including the currently very weak San Francisco and Oakland markets. The league awarded Chase to Moreing.

A few days later, Charlie Graham dialed John I. Taylor, owner of Boston. He told Taylor to get on a train to the Coast right away. He notified him that the California State League was rich with players that he could recommend. His list included Harry Wolter, who had transformed from a second-rate major league pitcher to a prodigious and speedy hitter. He also mentioned Frank Arellanes and the young Harry Hooper. Taylor agreed to make the trip. But the Boston owner wanted something else. He wanted Hal Chase. He asked Graham to use his friendship with Chase to talk him into joining the Boston Americans. Graham was told to offer Chase a raise and an option to be the team's manager. Taylor promised to arrange a trade or buy his contract outright from New York. For now, however, Chase was not considering any new offers – he was coming home to play.

A few days later, on September 13, Chase became a local attraction as Stockton shut out Oakland.

-------- --------- -----------

Mike Donlin's New York Giants and Frank Chance's Chicago Cubs were virtually tied down the stretch in 1908. On September 23, the two teams played a game that could have decided the National League pennant. At the Polo Grounds in Upper Manhattan, with two outs in the bottom of the ninth, Al Bridwell singled home Moose McCormick from third to break a tie. Fred Merkle was on first base. In those days, at the end of a game, a center field gate opened allowing fans to exit through the field. Players knew that when fans rushed on the field, they needed to run for the clubhouse to avoid being trampled. So when McCormick crossed the plate, fans mobbed the infield, and Merkle, rather than running to touch second, ran off the field. The Cubs appealed that the game did not end because Merkle was forced out at second. Umpire Hank O'Day would decide the outcome of the game that created the legendary "Merkle Boner." He ruled that Merkle was out at second and the game was a tie. The Giants' John T. Brush and John McGraw appealed to Hank Pulliam, National League President. Both Brush and McGraw were openly disdainful of Pulliam because he had been an accommodative partner to their enemy Ban Johnson. The animosity ran deep. The young Pulliam took several days to consider the appeal. He ultimately supported O'Day's decision and declared the game a tie. Brush and McGraw viewed Pulliam's decision as revenge and retribution for their having opposed him for so many years. They threatened a civil suit and harangued Pulliam in the press.

The greater controversy, however, had yet to occur.

On October 8, 1908, the Cubs and Giants played a makeup game to decide who would go to the World Series. Umpire Bill Klem claimed that he and fellow umpire Jim Johnstone were approached with a bribe to throw the game to the Giants. Later reports stated that New York Giants trainer Joseph Creamer offered Klem $2,500 and asked for favoritism toward the Giants. He also said that those who were behind him would make sure he had a job for life. The organizers could have been criminals, or they could have been from within the Giants organization. Regardless, Klem could not be bribed. Chicago subsequently won the game.

With his season over, Donlin joined his wife Mabel Hite in a show called "Stealing Home" that opened at the Hammerstein Theater on October 26. Ballplayers and athletes from various sports often capitalized on their acclaim by appearing in vaudeville shows. Tourists to New York would pay for a ticket to see the likes of John McGraw, Christy Mathewson, and Chief Meyers on stage. Donlin, however, had more than a fleeting interest in the stage. His show opened to critical acclaim behind Hite's considerable talent. Donlin soon contemplated giving up baseball to focus on a Broadway career.

Unlike Donlin, Pulliam could not run from his obligations in baseball. He would need to investigate the bribery claims stemming from the rematch between the Cubs and Giants. He created a committee to investigate, and oddly, assigned John T. Brush to head it along with Garry Herrmann and Charles Ebbetts. The public would never completely know the findings, but the New York Giants organization fell within the realm of suspicion. Complicity by the Giants would come as no surprise to many. For years insiders commented how John McGraw "owned" the umpires to receive favorable treatment. The investigation into the bribery would be conducted over a period of months. And like so many other matters surrounding baseball since 1908, the truth would be kept a secret from the public so as not to sully the brand. The truth and the subsequent cover-up, however, would have a devastating impact on the life of Harry Pulliam.

Pulliam was under tremendous stress. His counterpart in the American League, Ban Johnson, felt stress for different reasons. At a bar in Chicago during the World Series, Johnson cracked under pressure and entered into a brawl with Logan Squares owner Nixey Callahan. A thorn in Callahan's side, Johnson had fined Callahan and banned his players from Organized Baseball. Callahan, upset because Johnson and his Commission interfered with his franchise after he had recruited talent from the major leagues, including Mike Donlin the prior year, knocked the American League President to the ground. The Washington Post wrote that Callahan beat Johnson. The bar fight renewed Johnson's conviction to fervently enforce the National Agreement against all outlaw players and leagues.[A]

The next day, on October 14, Orval Overall won game five of the World Series for the Chicago Cubs over the Detroit Tigers. Overall threw a three hitter and fanned ten in a 2-0 shutout over Sam Crawford and Ty Cobb. It was the last World Series victory for the Cubs.

Even as Detroit competed in the World Series, it contacted Hal Chase in California about joining their squad for the next season. They were willing to trade five players including a top pitcher and three of their four starting infielders from a pennant-winning team for Chase. With all of the demand for Prince Hal, it seemed that Organized Baseball needed Hal Chase more than Hal Chase needed Organized Baseball.

Organized Baseball had nothing to do with a game on October 18, 1908 in the California Winter League. The Los Angeles Black Giants had begun to establish itself as a premier baseball team in California. The Los Angeles Herald described the team as the "champion colored team." On October 18, they faced the Santa Ana Yellow Sox. The pitcher for Santa Ana was Walter Johnson. Johnson struck out twenty of the Black Giants. But he lost 6-5. The game was the first game on the Pacific Coast, and one of the first nationally, where a colored team received recognition for competing against a white opponent. Capitalizing on the enthusiasm created by the game, the progressive and enterprising Hen Berry scheduled challenge matches through the winter between the Los Angeles Angels and the LA Black Giants. Thousands of people, both black and white, attended the games.[31] That winter, notable players George Stovall, Fred Snodgrass, Rube Ellis, Walter Johnson, and Dolly Gray played in the Winter League for at least one game.[B] Walter Johnson pitched in four games.

On November 1, the Los Angeles Angels played the first of their games at Joy Park. The Colored Giants were considered the best amateur team in the city or vicinity. Prior to 1908, all black teams competed as amateurs, drawing from the local labor market. In spite of the disadvantage, the Giants won almost every game they played, posting a 34 and 1 record. The Los Angeles Angels fielded Dolly Gray, Hap Hogan, Pop Dillon, and Kitty Brashear. The Black Giants fielded Clark, Hunt, Slater, Bronson, Boggs, McLain, Lane, Hunt, Battles, and Brock. Five thousand attended the first game, split evenly between black and white. The Angels won the game 14-2. The success of the Los Angeles Giants in

---

[A] Nixey Callahan's altercation with Ban Johnson did not deter the enterprising sports promoter. In 1909, Callahan turned instead to boxing from baseball and became the promoter for heavyweight boxer Jim Jeffries national tour. He gained valuable experience that served him promoting baseball barnstorming tours.

[B] Stovall played for Edison for a game, Snodgrass played 3 games for Hoegees, rube Ellis played 4 games for San Pedro, Walter Johnson played 4 games for Santa Ana, and Gray Dolly played 1 game with the Hoegees.

1908 inspired Rube Foster and his Chicago-based Leland Giants, considered one of the best black teams of all time, to play in the Winter League in 1910. The California Winter League would soon make history among professional leagues due to the seeds planted by the Los Angeles Black Giants and the game against Walter Johnson in 1908.

-------- --------- ----------

Based on Charlie Graham's urging, Boston American's owner John I. Taylor arrived in California to observe the end of the California States League in September 1908. Taylor recruited extensively from the West. His current lineup featured Gavvy Cravath and Walter Carlisle from the Los Angeles Angels.[A] He would also soon sign former St. Mary's player Duffy Lewis. Graham was still unsuccessful convincing Chase to play for Boston, but had other prospects in mind for Taylor. In 1908, Graham began to establish a legendary reputation for both identifying and developing young talent for the major leagues. Graham wasn't one to horde players for the Cal State League. He approached baseball as a business. The purpose served by his knowledge, dedication, and hard work was in the financial reward earned from attracting spectators, selling players to major league teams, and receiving finder's fees for scouting.

Hooper had been hitting well for Sacramento in recent weeks. Graham approached the young player and asked him, "Well, how would you like to play with the Boston Red Sox?"

"Well, I don't know," Hooper said, "I'm not a ballplayer. I'm an engineer."

Graham informed Hooper, "John Taylor, the owner of the Red Sox, is coming to town next week and I think he's interested in you. Why not give it a whirl? What have you got to lose? You're only twenty-one, and even if you played ball another two years, you could still take up engineering at twenty-three."

Graham penciled Hooper in the fourth position in the lineup in a game against the Seals from San Francisco. Hooper went 3-4 in front of the Red Sox owner. He later met with Taylor at a bar for a glass of beer at the corner of 8th Street and J Streets in Sacramento. Graham had tipped off Hooper to ask for $3,000. Graham said that although he was probably worth $2,500, he should start out asking for more so he would not seem like a chump. With that in mind, Hooper met with the owner and negotiated to play with the Red Sox for $2,800.[B]

[A] He also had a young star by the name of Tris Speaker, future hall of famer who had played in Arkansas for former San Francisco and San Jose player and manager Mike Finn.

[B] Harry Hooper won four World Series titles with the Red Sox from 1912 to 1918 and has been enshrined in the Baseball Hall of Fame.

Hooper remained with the Sacramento club through the end of the season. Taylor then passed through San Jose and met with Harry Wolter, recommended by Charlie Graham. Taylor had already signed Wolter's San Jose teammate Frank Arellanes, who played respectably in eleven games in Boston posting a 1.82 ERA before returning to finish the Cal State League in October and November. Arellanes became the third highest paid player on Boston behind stars Lou Criger and Cy Young. When Arellanes left the San Jose squad, Wolter filled the void on the mound, splitting time with Elmer Stricklett. Wolter had originally broken into the major leagues as a pitcher. He bounced around his first year until he was sold to a minor league squad in St. Paul, Minnesota. Never reporting to St. Paul, he jumped to become an outlaw for San Jose. Wolter pitched extremely well, but more important, he established himself as a premier hitter. John Taylor wanted Harry Wolter for his outfield. To acquire Wolter, Taylor had to purchase him from St. Paul, which technically still owned him. Taylor gladly paid the $50 fine.[32]

Wolter remained with San Jose to finish the season. By the end of October, with the season approaching completion, Sacramento faced off for the championship in a series against perennial favorite Stockton. On October 19, they played a double header in front of 6,000 people, the largest crowd to ever attend a game at Oak Park. Featured for Stockton was major leaguer and New York Highlander first baseman, Hal Chase, who played using his own name. Stockton won the first game 4-3.

Chase batted third for Stockton and went 2-4 with 2 runs scored. Graham moved Hooper to the leadoff spot for the first time for Sacramento, a slot in which he would later thrive as a player for the Red Sox. He went 3 for 4 with 1 run scored, but it wasn't enough to notch the victory.

In the second contest, the crowd witnessed a great game. Sacramento's Whalen outperformed Stockton's Moskiman, allowing the Millers but three hits. Big Joe Nealon won the game in the first inning when he slammed a double to left field, bringing in the only tally of the game. Squeeze plays were tried twice, once by each team, but in both cases the runner was caught at the plate.

The competition between Sacramento and Stockton was fierce. In one game, the two teams cleared the benches in a heated brawl. Hal Chase collided with pitcher Charlie Doyle who attempted to tag Chase who was running down the first base line. In an aggressive attempt to dislodge the ball, Chase hit Doyle with an uppercut to the mouth. When the benches cleared, the much larger Joe Nealon raced after Chase. Chase wisely ran, but was tackled by Charlie Enwright who had played for Chase at St. Mary's. The Sacramento team held Chase until police arrived and took him into custody.[33] Graham's plans to convince Chase to play for Boston and John Taylor became increasingly more difficult after his team violently subdued the prospect and had him arrested.

Once out of jail, Chase continued to show off at the plate through the end

1908 Sacramento Senators
Top: Jimmy Whalen, Charles Doyle, Bobbie McHale, Fred Raymer, Harry Hooper
Bottom: Jimmy Byrnes, Fred Brown, Charlie Graham, Joe Nealon, Charlie Enwright, Iverson. Mascot is Cal Creston. Right is young Charlie Graham. Santa Clara University Archives and Special Collections.

of the season in the field and on the mound, as he assured Stockton another championship. He hit .385 and scored twenty-one runs in twenty-one games. More spectacular was his defense, which was a major draw at the gate. In one of the final games he went 3 for 5 with 2 runs scored and pitched in relief.

> *Moskiman had an easy time for seven innings, when he gave way to Chase, who tossed them over and let two men complete the circuit in the final innings to keep them from being blanked. Chase made an unassisted at first that looked impossible.*

In the final game of the season, in which Stockton clinched the title, the Chronicle noted Chase's defensive ability at first base.

> *Chase's work around first base was the feature and the fans closely followed every move.*

San Jose swept Alameda in a double header to nip Sacramento for second place behind victories by Stricklett and Wolter.

But the season wasn't a disappointment for Graham. He had sold Harry Hooper to the Red Sox. And Hooper agreed to keep Graham on as his personal advisor for the remainder of his illustrious major league career.

---

[1]   Port Talk, Ed R. Hughes, San Francisco Chronicle, Febuary 26, 1918, Pg. 10

2   The Glory of Their Times: The Story of Baseball Told By the Men Who Played It, Lawrence S. Ritter

3   San Francisco Chronicle, Apr 26, 1908

4   San Francisco Chronicle, May 24, 1908

5   San Francisco Chronicle, June 15, 1908

6   San Francisco Chronicle, June 22, 1908

7   San Francisco Chronicle, May 8, 1908

8   San Francisco Chronicle, June 15, 1908

9   San Francisco Chronicle, June 29, 1908

10   San Francisco Chronicle, July 13, 1908

11   San Francisco Chronicle, June 30, 1908

12   San Francisco Chronicle, July 27, 1908

13   San Francisco Chronicle, July 12, 1908

14   San Francisco Chronicle, May 18, 1908

15   San Francisco Chronicle, June 14, 1908

16   San Francisco Chronicle, June 14, 1908

17   San Francisco Chronicle, June 14, 1908

18   San Francisco Chronicle, July 19, 1908

19   San Francisco Chronicle, July 21, 1908

20   San Francisco Chronicle, July 19, 1908

21   San Francisco Chronicle, July 19, 1908

22   San Francisco Chronicle, July 19, 1908

23   San Francisco Chronicle, July 19, 1908

24   San Francisco Chronicle, July 26, 1908

25   San Francisco Chronicle, July 26, 1908

26   San Francisco Chronicle, August 2, 1908

27   San Francisco Chronicle, August 24, 1908

28   Hal Chase Slated for White Sox, Los Angeles Times, Aug 2, 1908, pg. 16

29   Chase is Traded, Direct Wire to the Times, LA Times, 9/6/1908, pg VI4

30   New York Journal, Sept 3, 1908

31   The California Winter League, America's First Integrated Professonal Baseball League, William F. McNeil.

32   Harry Wolter Is Weak From Operation, Special dispatch to The Call, Feb 15, 1911

33   Sacramento Union, October 18, 1908

Chapter 10

The California Baseball War

In November 1908, Frank Farrell named a replacement for Kid Elberfeld as manager of the New York Highlanders. For many years, Ban Johnson took an active role in making sure Farrell's squad would thrive in New York. After a string of losing seasons, and a team in turmoil, Johnson viewed the next appointment as critical. In the franchise's initial years, Johnson had planted personal friend Clark Griffith in the role. But the revolving door that was, and would continue to be, a hallmark in New York Yankee baseball for many years, swept in one of Ban Johnson's enemies, George Stallings. As minority owner of the Detroit Tigers when the American League was formed, Stallings negotiated to defect to the National League. Johnson removed the traitor Stallings (and Burns) as owners, but he continued to hold a grudge. Johnson vowed that Stallings would never return to the American League. Somebody either forgot to "send the memo" to Farrell. Or Farrell simply didn't care.

At the same time, a baseball war developed throughout the country as openly defiant minor leagues threatened to operate as "outlaws" throughout the country in direct competition with Organized Baseball. In the West, Pacific Coast League owners wanted to merge the PCL and Cal States League. The PCL had been running a four-team league spanning from Los Angeles to Portland, and admittedly had dropped in quality when compared to the resurgent California State League with Graham's Sacramento, Moreing's Stockton, and Jarman's San Jose squads. PCL President Cal Ewing approached the Cal State League, which agreed to comply with the rules of Organized Baseball. But the league wanted to keep all "contract jumpers" that were currently on their rosters. The Pacific Coast League had offered the same deal to Organized Baseball when it joined the National Association in 1904. At that time, Organized Baseball had agreed to the demand.

Cy Moreing, however, adamantly opposed becoming part of Organized Baseball. He would tap his reserves and resources to keep Stockton independent and financially viable. He even "passed the hat" among local merchants to keep independent baseball in his city. Cy Moreing became the consummate outlaw. Determined to defy Organized Baseball, he had the financial strength and the will to attempt independence. His strategy would admittedly never make him wealthy. His life-long support of the Stockton club was driven purely out of love for baseball and the community.

Cal State League owners were willing to conform, including Herman, Evans, and Toomey in Fresno, Swanton and Linde in Santa Cruz, E.J. McMenomy in Oakland, Louis Schroeder in San Francisco, and Jarman and

Barnett in San Jose. Charlie Graham and Bill Curtin in Sacramento were publically uncommitted. Hen Berry of the Angels said he didn't mind if Graham and Sacramento didn't join. He threatened to blacklist Graham and his players if they remained outlaws. Graham was not one to cower from a threat. But Berry did appeal to Graham's conservative, pragmatic, and logical nature; perhaps remaining an outlaw wasn't financially feasible.

On December 2, the league owners of both leagues met in San Francisco at the St. Francis Hotel. At the same time, Cy Moreing asked Chase to remain with the Stockton team for the next season.[1] In the meetings, Chase represented a bargaining chip for Moreing. And if his team remained as an outlaw, perhaps it would need Chase for survival. The Cal State League teams agreed that they would collectively opt in, or all would remain out of the PCL. If they all did stay out, Moreing requested that Chase become property of Stockton. If any discussions were to occur to discuss Chase as property of Stockton and not the New York Americans, major league baseball was to be represented. On December 14, Ban Johnson and Harry Pulliam boarded a train from the East to join the meeting.

In addition to the PCL controversy, the National and American League Presidents had other pressing matters on their plates. On December 11, the National Commission began hearing charges from Umpires Bill Klem and Jim Johnstone about the attempted bribe to fix the playoff game of October 8 the prior year in favor of the New York Giants. The next day, Pittsburgh Pirate owner Barney Dreyfuss publicly blasted Pulliam and blamed John T. Brush for the attempted bribe and the seedy characters that continuously hung around the Giants and the Polo Grounds.

In California, Johnson and Pulliam planned to discuss merging the California State League into Organized Baseball. Their mission failed. The California League owners agreed to remain independent. During the trip, however, Johnson and Pulliam met with Hal Chase in San Francisco. Johnson told Chase that the Commission would look kindly upon his situation with New York; it understood that he had abandoned his team the prior year because of a feud with Elberfeld. Besides, Highlander owner Frank Farrell didn't file a grievance with Johnson and was still hopeful that Chase would return. Ban Johnson also wanted Chase in New York. He wanted the franchise to be successful and wasn't keen on the new manager, Stallings. Chase agreed to work with Johnson and Farrell as long as they didn't "try to make an example of him" for having negotiated with an outlaw team. Perhaps not so ironic, Chase's concern was justified. In time, "making an example of players" was exactly what Organized Baseball did, as Hal Chase would learn.

Cy Moreing counted on Chase to return to Stockton. Moreing quickly surmised that he needed to move his team, the strongest in the State, into a larger market in order to survive future challenges from the PCL. In January of 1909, he announced plans to move his Stockton Millers and Hal Chase to San Francisco.

And in response to threats by Henry Berry in Los Angeles, he claimed to have lined up an outlaw team in Los Angeles that would compete directly against Berry. Moreing had a lot of fight in him, and he was willing to take on Organized Baseball, the PCL, Cal Ewing, and Hen Berry.

The vote to merge with the PCL was not clear-cut. At first, all owners, with the exception of Moreing, wanted to join the League. Then the momentum shifted toward remaining independent. Al Jarman stood up in favor of the outlaws. Then Moreing unveiled his idea of moving his squad to San Francisco with Chase, which rallied sentiment back towards independence.

Charlie Graham, however, had determined that he wanted to join the PCL. He had yet to make his decision public. When he stated his case, the outlaw owners challenged that if he took his team to the PCL, they'd have an outlaw team in Sacramento immediately. Graham's partner Curtin didn't mind remaining since the franchise made money the prior year as an independent. The league finances were in good shape, and the owners felt they could attract the likes of Chase and Christy Mathewson to the league. But Graham, with his connections with Boston and other teams, was partial to an alliance with Organized Baseball.

As of January 2, 1909, Charlie Graham was no longer an outlaw. When the Cal State League owners voted, Graham decided to abandon the California State League to join the Pacific Coast League for 1909.

Perhaps Graham's conformity rubbed off on Chase. On January 5, Hal Chase applied for reinstatement to Organized Baseball. Only a few weeks before, Chase said he would not seek reinstatement, and instead would transact business with Cy Moreing. But the conference with Ban Johnson steered the young first baseman back to New York. That meeting sparked an allegiance, if not a friendship, that would soon have important repercussions for Chase. Chase had chosen to align with the powerful Ban Johnson and Frank Farrell once again instead of friend Cy Moreing…. at least until next year.

With the Pacific Coast League fortified by Graham's Sacramento squad, Cal Ewing sought to create another baseball club in the Los Angeles market. At first he sought a franchise in San Pedro. In doing so, he publicly announced that he was "ready for a war" with the California League and said that the National Commission had $300,000 in the treasury ready for such an emergency."[2] Ewing's comments represented idle posturing. Any team could hire the best players in the world, including Mathewson, Chance, and Cobb for approximately $5,000 each. Resolving issues related to the PCL would never require that much money. And the major leagues didn't value the PCL to the point of spending $300,000 to fight battles with a competing league. But Ewing wanted to demonstrate the relative power and significance of the organization to which the PCL belonged, much bigger than any one of the teams or any independent league.

Los Angeles and Portland would certainly field excellent teams the coming year. But the surprise was the turnaround of the San Francisco Seals, which ran away with the championship behind Kid Mohler, Ping Bodie, Harry Melchoir, Duffy Lewis, and Claude Berry.

In Sacramento, Graham strengthened his squad by signing first baseman Chick Gandil, pitcher Spider Baum, and Jimmie Shinn at shortstop. Gandil had played for Fresno in the California State League, but now that Graham owned a PCL team, he made Gandil a better offer to move to Sacramento. When Gandil left the Fresno squad, the team claimed he took his uniform and advance money. Charges were filed and Gandil was arrested for stealing $225 in money and goods.[A] Charlie Graham paid restitution to Sacramento and bailed Gandil out of jail. Gandil would make the All Star squad that season, but Graham's team would struggle to approach .500 by year's end.[B]

The other new team in the PCL did not settle in San Pedro, but in a small area just outside of the Los Angeles City limits called Vernon. Young and wealthy brewery company executive Fred Maier was awarded the franchise for $1.[3] The league originally contacted Henry Berry's brother Clarence Berry to finance the new club. But Clarence declined so that he wouldn't compete against his brother.[4] As soon as Maier was notified that he received the franchise, he hired Hap Hogan from Hen Berry's Angels squad and made him the manager. Hap Hogan and the best man at his wedding, Charlie Graham, would face off in 1909 as the two new managers in the Pacific Coast League. Vernon, however, would understandably finish in the cellar, needing to assemble a team from scratch. Graham was able to rise to the middle of the pack with the foundation of returning players that challenged for the Cal State League championship the prior year.

Hogan immediately began recruiting for his new team the last week of January. The standard formula in the minor leagues was to balance the old and experienced with the young and unproven. He was quoted, "I want a few old heads to steady the team, and then we will have some youngsters." One of the steadying influences Hogan called upon immediately was veteran Brick

---

[A] This story comes up as an example of Gandil's early penchant for crime, whether justified or not. What is more interesting to the context of this story is that when the same Fresno owners didn't pay Harry Wolter $40, he had nowhere to turn to get compensation. Yet when Gandil allegedly stole $225 in value from Fresno, they had him arrested. Maybe Wolter should have had Fresno police arrest the Fresno owners until he was paid his $40. The double standard is apparent.

[B] Graham was able to sell Gandil during the season to the Chicago White Sox, but he negotiated that Gandil would complete the season with Sacramento. This practice, perhaps first negotiated by Graham with Gandil, would become an important and integral tactic used by Graham in the future. He sold many players to the majors, including Joe DiMaggio, but he negotiated for their services while marketing the players as "The next first baseman of the Chicago White Sox," or "Outfielder for the New York Yankees."

Devereaux. He also claimed to have an outfielder lined up, and "although he isn't Bill Lange, he is almost as well known." Hogan could have been referring to Jess Stovall, who played outfield for Vernon. He also landed vets Kitty Brashear and Truck Eagan. One of the youngsters he vowed to develop was ex-Santa Clara infielder Art Shafer.

At the time, little existed in the small town of Vernon. But all that would change … because Vernon was wet.

Temperance reformers pushed legislation that made Los Angeles nearly dry by 1907. Vernon was an exception. The Vernon Board of Trustees at first promoted Vernon by making it a center for professional boxing. Sportswriter James Kilty wrote,

> The enterprising little group, under the leadership of John B. Leonis, with James Furlong and his brother, Thomas Furlong, long established residents of the district, started a campaign to advertise the city through sports. That their venture was successful is attested by the fact that the city of Vernon was considered the boxing capital of the world from 1908 until the 1920s.[5]

James Kilty's account of Vernon in the early years best provides an understanding of the town and its conditions:

> Next to the pig farms and new factories a string of bars and brothels opened, where Angelenos clustered on Sundays for the hot night life. Shortly after the town was incorporated there were three saloons, the most popular of which was Jack Doyle's Central Saloon at the corner of Santa Fe Avenue and the well-named Joy Street. Soon Leonis himself founded an even bigger place at Santa Fe and 38th Street, and leased it to Jack Doyle, a former Southern Pacific engineer, who built Jack Doyle's Saloon into one of the most famous bars in the region.... the town undesirable for business by encouraging drinking and prostitution. One Los Angeles newspaper wrote: 'Sunday the town is wide open and drunken men stagger on the streets, toughs shout ribald remarks at passing women and crap games are played.''[6]

Jack Doyle spent his life's savings to lease land from Vernon's founder John Leonis and build his bar. Doyle built what was labeled as the largest saloon in the world. The straight-laced teetotaler built a 100-foot bar with thirty-seven bartenders, all imported from Ireland, and thirty-seven cash registers. Behind the bar he hung the sign "If your Children Need Shoes, Don't Buy Any Booze." He kept an office above the bar and drilled peepholes to keep an eye on his employees, patrons, and pickpockets.[7]

In 1908, Doyle built an outdoor boxing ring surrounded by wooden seats. It soon became the venue for some of the greatest fights in America. Doyle also used the boxing venue as a training site with its own handball court and swimming pool. Heavyweight champion Jim Jeffries also had an athletic club within blocks. The Vernon Country Club, an upscale bar and restaurant run by Baron Long, also soon became an attraction for the city's socialites. And although Doyle's Bar was the center of the town, the Vernon Tigers baseball squad soon became a draw as well. Fred Maier built Maier Park, a baseball field for his new entry in the Pacific Coast League, with the left field wall abutting into Doyle's Bar. The bar had a separate entrance directly into the park. Vernon's male amusement park was taking form. Suddenly, Vernon was the hot spot for baseball and boxing.

The town could be rowdy, but bar owner Doyle had a big heart and didn't tolerate a lack of restraint. During boxing matches, he didn't allow anyone to cheer so that the environment remained civil for women. And when individuals had a spat, he'd lace up the gloves and throw them in the ring and have them settle their differences. When they were done, he required them to shake hands. A local recalled that as a child, he and his friends regularly broke into Doyle's bar to steal candy. Later he learned that they weren't getting away with it; Doyle continually left the candy out for them.[8]

Hap Hogan would struggle to bring a championship to Vernon. But he became an icon in the city of Los Angeles and in West Coast baseball because of his colorful personality and fiery competitiveness. Quite simply, Hogan was an entertainer. Unbeknownst to him, he found himself in the city that was fast becoming the entertainment capital of the world. Well suited for the market, his popularity would soon become unrivaled among sport celebrities in the city.

Unfortunately, young Fred Maier died on April 11, 1909. His brother Ed, a recent graduate of Berkeley, took over the brewery, the Vernon Tigers, and the many other responsibilities of the family. Ed had played baseball growing up and was considered a good player.[A] He was a member of the Los Angeles Athletic Club, the Los Angeles Bowling Association, and a prominent member of the Masons and Elks.[9] He also assumed his brother's responsibilities overseeing the Vernon Athletic Club and the Los Angeles County Improvements Company. Ed Maier and Hap Hogan worked together splendidly. Ed loved to host a party, and Hap Hogan loved to be the master of ceremonies, both on and off the field. And Maier never questioned Hogan's judgment. Within reason, whatever Hogan wanted, Maier could and would provide to him.

The partnership between Harry Pulliam and the National League owners, in contrast, became disturbingly strained. Baseball's winter meetings were held in Chicago from February 15 to 19. Harry Pulliam very likely knew the facts surrounding the past year's bribery scandal by the time the meetings were held. And he had become perplexed about how to disclose the findings. The ensuing events suggest that the National League was consumed by a coverup and the need

---

[A] Ed was surprised when the population of Los Angeles exploded and many people began attending the games in Vernon.

for damage control. Pulliam seemed torn between the virtuous ideal that he diligently pursued and the reality that his earnest efforts had little effect; in fact, for the good of Organized Baseball, his duty would now be to cover up and thereby perpetuate the corruption that he intended to eradicate. To make matters worse, the National League owners, whose interests Pulliam promoted ardently for many years, now turned on him in ridicule.

At a dinner organized by White Sox owner Charles Comiskey, Pulliam took his turn addressing the owners in a speech. Once at the podium, the National League President lost control. He lambasted the owners who had pressured him not to release the names involved in the bribery. In the middle of his rant, the owners interrupted him and removed him from the hall. He had not revealed any names. The owners quickly announced to the press that Pulliam had a breakdown, informing them that he was given time off to recuperate. John Heydler assumed his duties.

With Pulliam on a leave of absence for months, the committee researching the bribery presented their findings to the National Commission. John T. Brush, owner of the Giants, headed the committee. It found Giants' trainer Dr. Joseph Creamer a convenient scapegoat. Two months later, the National Commission announced its findings to the public. It announced that an attempted bribe did occur, and that the perpetrator was forever banned from major league ballparks. Nobody knows for sure if Creamer's involvement was the tip of an iceberg involving the New York Giants franchise. Considering the history of the franchise (as well as the future), impropriety was a distinct possibility. Rumors abounded that Creamer took the fall for John McGraw. With baseball owners investigating themselves, the truth would likely never surface. Pulliam would remain anguished by the outcome and not return to work for months.

The major league ballplayers began the 1909 season unburdened and unconcerned by the strife among National League owners. Comiskey and his White Sox boarded the "Comiskey Special" on February 27 carrying the team to San Francisco for spring training. The next day, Hal Chase boarded a train out of Oakland with his wife Nellie on his way to Macon, Georgia to join the Highlanders. On the same train were Harry Hooper, Harry Wolter, and Frank Arellanes departing to join the Boston Americans.

When Chase arrived at spring training, new manager George Stallings welcomed him with open arms and called him "the greatest ballplayer he has ever seen." Elberfeld remained with the team at shortstop; Chase and Kid repaired their differences from the prior year. Then on April 1, Chase sprained his ankle once again. But worse, the next day, he contracted small pox. He was admitted to a local hospital in Augusta, Georgia where he remained for three weeks. The team began the season without Chase. On April 26, he announced he was returning to play and would be ready for the game on May 3. The day he returned, the Highlanders scheduled "Hal Chase Day" at the ballpark.[10] The San

Francisco Chronicle reported to West Coast fans that as Chase arrived on the field, he received a tremendous ovation from the crowd, which was large for Monday game.

> *Immense volumes of cheers began when the California player arose from the bench and went to bat in the first inning. Some one yelled "everyone up," and everybody stood up and roared for Chase. All the New York players gathered at home plate and presented Chase with a big silver loving cup.*[11]

The same day, the New York Globe featured a poem by George Moriarity about his popular teammate:

> *Old New York is a cheery place*
> *Most everyone seems glad*
> *The heavy hearts are happy now*
> *Where once they were sad*
> *It's not because Jim Jeffries said*
> *He'd fight that smoke next year*[A]
> *We're soused with joy and bliss because*
> *Our old friend Hal is here!*[12]

The tribute to Chase served as an olive branch to their star, sponsored by Frank Farrell, supported by fans, and carried out by the players and manager. Ever since Chase suited up as a Yankee just four years before, the team had gone through nearly one hundred different players. Through all of the change, Chase had been a constant – a star. And as the team rebuilt, it wanted to build around Hal Chase.

In 1909, Chase still hit below his career averages, hitting .283 with twenty-five stolen bases and sixty-three RBI. In August, he once again sprained his ankle and was out for most of the month. Whenever Chase had an injury, which occurred most often to his ankle, the impatient New York management and media quickly forgot about the silver cup they extended to Chase just months before and started riding him for slacking off.

On August 23, sportswriter Ernest Lanigan wrote an article maligning Chase. Like many sportswriters of the era, Lanigan befriended baseball owners and management, working in concert with them to both promote an agenda as well as leak sentiment. Many sportswriters were like the current day White House press contingent, relying on the convenience of leaks and premeditated releases from the press secretary rather than reporting. Reporting didn't serve a market or constituency; there wasn't sufficient demand for reporting to warrant extensive

---

[A] The "smoke" is a derogatory term referring to the African American Heavyweight champion of the world Jack Johnson would face retired champion and "Great White Hope" Jim Jeffries in the fight of the century the next year.

investigation. The media found that with deadlines and papers to sell, fast and easy stories served their needs. And owners such as Farrell gave them what they required. Truths have been concealed throughout baseball history because of the media's complicity with management.

In his article, Lanigan pointed out that Chase had indicated that he could do a better job than Stallings as manager. Ever since his success at St. Mary's, Chase had aspirations to be a major league manager. Between Chase's rumblings about wanting to be a manager, which demonstrated dissension with Stallings still at the helm, and his weakened play due to his ankle injury, Lanigan felt justified to criticize the star. He warned Chase to shape up and not to be too smart with management. And he advised management not to coddle the stars. The article would mark one of the initial chapters in the ensuing battle between Stallings and Chase.

> *... the manner in which baseball players found out how wrong they were was by allowing them to follow an unwisely chosen course to its end. 'Don't try to humor your topliners ... or you'll rue the day.'.... If Chase should be compelled to play for Charley Comiskey or Hughie Jennings, he would find out how much harder his labors would be. ... The outlaw bugaboo is a thing of the past, and Chase in order to retain his standing as a star ought to get over the grouch he is carrying around because he wasn't selected as manager of the Highlanders and play the game which he is capable.[13]*

The team finished fifth under Stallings. Chase continued to be the team's best player and most popular draw. For the 1910 season, he was given a raise to $5,500, which placed him towards the top of the league in compensation.

In July of 1909, Charlie Graham's Sacramento squad challenged Hap Hogan's Vernon team in Los Angeles.[14] Both managers were well out of the running for the championship. Hogan's squad was deep in the cellar. Vernon still needed more talent. But perhaps Hogan's easy manner with the players also contributed to their weakness. For example, left fielder Jess Stovall was known to run into Doyle's Bar beyond the left field fence between innings for a pint of beer.

A few weeks later, in a demonstration of renewed conviction against the outlaw players in California, particularly the California State League that fielded a team in Sacramento, Ban Johnson fined Charlie Graham for playing on the same grounds as the outlaw team. Graham received a pardon because the street railway owned the ballpark in Sacramento and rented it to the outlaws when Graham wasn't using it.

Ban Johnson's partner, Harry Pulliam, had other concerns in September 1909. Pulliam was still only forty-four. The past year had been stressful and had taken a toll on his physical and mental health. He had been on leave from his role as the Commissioner of the National League since February, where his outburst at the Winter Meetings resulted in a leave of absence. Pulliam's outburst was prompted by his disgust with the owners who pressured him not to reveal the facts surrounding the previous year's bribery scandal. During Pulliam's absence, the National Commission released its findings. Subsequently, Pulliam took residence in New York at the New York Athletic Club, and according to many, was getting himself back into shape.

On the 28th at 9:30 in the morning, Pulliam arrived at his office and opened his mail. Witnesses said he then stopped working and just stared out the window. He left the office at one in the afternoon claiming he was feeling ill. Nobody saw him for the rest of the day. Around 9:30 pm, a telephone boy noticed that the switchboard light in Pulliam's room was lit, meaning that the phone was off the hook. At ten, a hall boy went to Pulliam's room. He found the door unlocked. He opened the door and found Pulliam on the floor in the corner of the room with a bullet wound to the head. He was still alive, moaning. The gunshot had entered the left temple and exited through the right. The shot was fired from close range, his face badly burned. His right eye was missing. When the doctor and coroner arrived, Pulliam was still alive. When asked how he was shot, Pulliam uttered before passing out, "I am not shot." He never regained consciousness and died the next morning.

Nobody knew conclusively the cause of death. The coroner reported suicide. If Pulliam did commit suicide, the owners within baseball perhaps summoned the demons that haunted him. Pulliam was conflicted by his quest for an honorable and purposeful life, but found he had become the advocate for contemptuous owners. The conflict, however, wouldn't necessarily explain the suicide. Pulliam could have left baseball and started anew. Either Pulliam was predisposed to mental illness that was exacerbated by his conflicts with Organized Baseball, he was pushed into choosing suicide because he was blackmailed, or he was murdered. The circumstances surrounding Pulliam's death signal that all was not well in Baseball. Perhaps his death was simply a tragedy caused by sickness. Or the death of Harry Pulliam, whose record was without reproach, could have been the manifestation of malignant maladies within the national game.

1   All the Latest Sports, Local and Telegraphic, Los Angeles Times, Dec 2, 1908 Pg 16
2   Ewing is Ready for Baseball Fight, SF Chronicle, Jan 19, 1909, pg. 9
3   Sacramento and Vernon Voted Franchises, SF Chronicle, 1/23/1909, pg. 9
4   Clarence Berry and Hen Berry would later jointly finance teams
5   Leonis of Vernon, James Kilty, 1963
6   Leonis of Vernon, James Kilty, 1963
7   A Teetotaler's Bar and Boxing Mecca:[Home Edition], Cecilia Rasmussen, Los Angeles Times, Los Angeles, Calif.:Jun 22, 1997. p. B, 3:3
8   City of Vernon: a collection of oral histories, Marianne Dissard, California State University Fullerton Oral History Program, 1995, Personal interview with Clyde "Tiger" Brown, child in Vernon before 1920
9   Notables of the Southwest, Press Reference Library, Los Angeles Examiner, 1912
10   Hal Chase is Back, LA Times, Apr 26, 1909, Pg. I11
11   Hal Chase Is Cheered by a Mob of Fans, SF Chronicle, May 4, 1909, pg. 7

[12] New York Globe and Commercial Advertiser, May 3, 1909
[13] New York Press, August 23, 1909
[14] Sporting News, Local and Telegraphic, Los Angeles Times, July 27, 1909.

Chapter 11

Judge Graham Ushers In Temporary Peace in Coast Baseball

The darkness cast on Eastern Baseball by the death of Harry Pulliam couldn't disturb the brightness that shone down on California's winter baseball. The Winter League teams found homes in the growing medium-sized towns in Southern California, including San Diego, Santa Barbara, San Bernardino, Pasadena, and Orange. It even added a team in Salt Lake City, Utah. And a league sprouted in the arid Imperial Valley east of San Diego. Similar to the Winter League, the Imperial Valley league attracted players, including Kitty Brashear, Oscar Jones, and Jim Scott interested in playing year round. The league featured teams from El Centro, Imperial, Hotville, Yuma, and Brawley.[1]

As usual, Hen Berry promoted winter baseball at Chutes Field. On November 11, he hosted "Johnson Day" at the ballpark to feature a match-up between Walter Johnson and an all-star team against Berry's locals comprised mostly of his Angels players. Johnson had won thirty-two games over the past three years for the Washington Senators, and was on the verge of greatness.

On the same day, the National Association passed a resolution to "advance the welfare of players." Players were required to be under contract before playing with any minor league club. The Association wanted better controls to punish "reserve jumpers," and threatened suspensions of up to five years for breaking a contract and three years for violating a reserve.

Within a week of the announcement, Elmer Stricklett was given a three-year ban from major league baseball for not returning to Brooklyn. He had abandoned Brooklyn during the 1907 season because his wife didn't approve of the immoral climate within the National League. At thirty-three years of age, and not having pitched in the majors since 1906, Stricklett's ban was more of an administrative formality than an impediment to Stricklett's career. Elmer would continue to throw his spitball in the California League as long as he was able. No major league squads were likely to come calling.

Stricklett's ban highlighted the reality of the National Commission enforcement. Hundreds of mediocre players who were not in demand by the major league teams were banned. Players with star credentials didn't remain on the "blacklist" of banned players for very long.

On November 15, 1909, at the winter meetings for the Pacific Coast League, the owners voted on a replacement for the President's role after Cal Ewing stepped down. Superior Court Judge Thomas F. Graham was selected.[2] Within a few days, President Graham announced an end to the "War on the Coast" posed by Cal Ewing the prior year between the PCL and the California State

League. Graham, who in court specialized in the divorces, was known as "The Great Reconciler." Surely the owners of the two leagues would be easier for Graham to handle than two bitter spouses. President Graham wanted to create a culture that would capitalize on the recent financial weakness of the California State League and ultimately encourage it to merge into the Pacific Coast League. Under the contentious former President Cal Ewing, reconciliation had not been likely.

Graham knew baseball. He rarely missed a game. A former player, he once heard a court case presented by Mrs. Doretta Yoell, a mother who sought to use $150 from an inheritance fund to pay a doctor's bill incurred by her son Laurence, who had broken his arm three times playing ball. Mrs. Yoell received little sympathy from Judge Graham. He said,

> *The trouble with Laurence is that he slides hands first for the home plate. You want to instruct him to slide feet first and then there won't be any doctor bills.*[3]

Judge Graham helped the Pacific Coast League prosper. In hindsight, from a financial perspective, Sacramento's Charlie Graham had chosen the better league to join the prior season when he defected with his squad to the Pacific Coast League. The outlaw California State League suffered through the 1909 season. They considered reducing the roster to twelve players and capping salaries at $1,600. That was a long way from the days a year ago when Moreing aspired to sign Christy Mathewson and Hal Chase. Many teams floundered. The Fresno team was kept afloat by the other teams in the league. The Sporting Life reported on December 4, 1909 the following:

> *Practically every fan around the circuit will admit that the California League failed because of the "war" salaries of last season. More money went out than was taken in at the gate... the inevitable arrived and the league crashed onto the rocks.*

Harry Wolter returned home to Castroville in the off-season, uncertain about his future with Boston. He hit only .240 in a backup role in 1909, and in 1910 the Red Sox outfield would start Tris Speaker, Harry Hooper, and Duffy Lewis. The three outfielders would comprise the greatest outfield in the history of baseball to date, and one of the greatest defensive outfields ever.

While at Boston, Wolter befriended Hooper and former Portland player Babe Danzig. In his personal photo album submitted to the Santa Clara University Archives & Special Collection, Wolter kept a picture of Hooper and Danzig in their Boston uniforms, the still child-like Hooper approaching the plate. The album features other photos of family and friends, including a solo shot of Cincinnati player Hans Lobert, who Wolter played with in Cincinnati, under a palm tree in California. Lobert, a jokester and one of the fastest players in baseball, commonly traveled to California in the winter to play in games and meet up with best friend and Cubs hurler Orval Overall, who had played with Lobert in Cincinnati.

Boston placed Wolter on waivers. Seizing upon an opportunity, Hal Chase immediately contacted Frank Farrell and recommended that the Yankees[A] pick him up. Based on Chase's recommendation, Farrell immediately sent Wolter a blank contract for three years and asked him to name his price.

On January 8, 1910, the Yankees claimed Harry Wolter off waivers for $1,500. A few months later, manager Stallings named Hal Chase the first captain in the history of the New York Yankees. On April 6, Hal Chase's good fortune continued when Nellie gave birth to son Harold Jr.[B] Even another ankle sprain, suffered on March 20, could not deter Chase from a breakout season.

In California, the sporting scene continued to blossom, particularly in the entertainment capital. Hen Berry vowed to be the first to bring a major league team to California. Berry would underestimate the logistical difficulties that such an endeavor represented. The distance between Los Angeles and the westernmost city in major league baseball, St. Louis, was nearly twice the distance from St. Louis to New York City. Not until commercial aircraft became a viable and cost-effective means of transportation would a major league team locate in California. In spite of Berry's proclamation, major league baseball would not arrive in California for nearly fifty more years.[C]

But California became a boxing center in the early part of the century. Both San Francisco and Los Angeles featured championship bouts. Jim Jeffries' ran a facility in Vernon on the southwest corner of thirty-eight and Santa Fe Avenue up until his fight with Jack Johnson in 1910. He then sold it to Tom McCarey, who renamed it Uncle Tom McCarey's Vernon Arena.[4]

Ed Maier, the owner of the Pacific Coast League's Vernon Tigers, also knew how to promote sports in Los Angeles, which he did as a hobby while running the Maier Brewing Company on 440 Aliso Street.[D] The brewery was one of the largest on the Pacific Coast and had a dozen buildings two to six stories high close to downtown. Maier lived nearby at the family home on the corner of Figueroa and Sixteenth Streets. Vernon was equally close, located on the southwestern border of the city.

[A] The Highlanders were also referred to as the Yankees in prior years, but in 1910, the team was more uniformly referred to in the press as the Yankees.

[B] Hal and Nellie lost their first child as an infant. (San Jose Mercury, Feb 7, 1997)

[C] The Brooklyn Dodgers and New York Giants moved to California in 1958. Ironically, their arrival ended the reign of highly competitive and popular minor league baseball in California's major cities.

[D] Aliso Street now runs along the 101 Freeway between N. Main and N. Los Angeles near the current courthouse and the Federal Building and across the freeway from Union Station.

For recreation, Maier aspired to be a rancher. He purchased a ranch in Ventura County that he named Rancho Selecto, which he used to host large parties to promote his business ventures and sporting interests. The ranch was located in what is now Simi Valley in a large canyon at the southern end.[A] At the time, the ranch was referred to as "in the mountains" due to its remote location and natural setting. However, the mountains were more like hills, and the elevation of the ranch was actually only a few hundred feet over sea level. The peaks of the local hills topped out at only 2,000 feet. Yet those who attempted to drive a car rather than arrive by train, considered the roads mountainous, hazardous, windy, and treacherous. Now, the valley's population exceeds 100,000, and freeways carry commuters to and from the region daily to neighboring San Fernando Valley and downtown Los Angeles, only forty miles away.

In May of each year, Maier hosted the Elks Club at Rancho Selecto. Each year, a baseball game was played, followed by a lavish Spanish-style barbecue. He scheduled games for the guests, "officially announced" by racecar driver Barney Oldfield, whose exploits on the track Maier sponsored. There was jig dancing, acrobatics, boxing matches, fencing, wrestling matches, a derby race, sack race, and three-legged race. Oldfield finished fifth in the "fat man's race." Amateur champion gymnasts also demonstrated roman rings. The event would become a tradition, each year attracting more and more local notables including politicians and sports celebrities.

One local sportsman who was making good during 1910 was Fred Snodgrass who hailed from Oxnard, California, which was just forty miles west of Simi Valley on the way to Ventura. Playing for the New York Giants' McGraw, Fred started the season hitting over .400. He was aggressive, hit every pitch hard, and had the fans in awe. Then according to Christy Mathewson in his book Pitching in a Pinch, the Chalmers Automobile Company ruined everything. They offered an automobile to the batter in either league who finished the season with the highest batting average. In later years, this offer led to bribes of pitchers to go easy on a hitter so he would win the car. But for Snodgrass, the prize represented a jinx. Mathewson said that Snodgrass admitted to him,

> 'They got me worrying about myself. I began to think how close I was to the car and had a moving picture of myself driving it. That settled it.' According to Matty, 'His batting fell off miserably until, in the post season series with the Yankees, he gave one of the worst exhibitions of any man on the team.'

Hal Chase also enjoyed a good season. In July, the Yankees were in second place behind Connie Mack's Philadelphia Athletics. Then Hal allegedly

[A] The entrance was a few blocks west of what is now Los Angeles Avenue, less than two miles west from the historic train station that is still in use. Visitors would arrive at the train station, and then take horse and buggies to the ranch.

contracted malaria on July 20 and missed two series at the end of July. Chase later revealed that doctors did not find malaria, but suggested that he rest. In truth, Chase left the team because of a feud with manager Stallings. He traveled back to New York to appeal to Farrell in person and request that Stallings be replaced – with Hal Chase. It was very likely that Farrell heard Chase's appeal and agreed with him. Worse yet, Farrell likely promised Chase the manager role during their visit.

In effect, Stallings became a lame duck manager. And he vented his frustration by lashing out at Chase. Stallings began criticizing Chase in the media as a malingerer. Stallings had a grudge with Hal for going to Farrell, saw the writing on the wall, and engaged in a petty public battle with the first baseman for the favor of Farrell and the public. Rumors that Chase would replace Stallings only heightened Stallings's contention. But Stallings could never win his fight. Ban Johnson would make sure of that.

Ban Johnson despised Stallings ever since Stallings attempted to move the American League Detroit franchise to the National League. Meanwhile, the American League President and Hal Chase had befriended each other, initiated during Johnson's trip to San Francisco when he convinced Hal to return to the Yankees. Since Hal returned, the franchise improved, and Chase was their star. Chase was considered the answer, not the problem.

Additionally Ban Johnson had been investigating Stallings for stealing signs. Cheating may have been tolerated in the National League. But Johnson was not going to allow cheating in the American League, particularly from his enemy George Stallings. If he found the claims to be true, he would insist Farrell remove Stallings as the manager. Hal Chase later described how Stallings allegedly stole signs. He was using a "Black Hand" signal. In center field, a black bar (or "black hand") was fastened to the fence. A man outside of the park controlled the bar with a handle.[5] An assistant with field glasses stole pitch signs from the catcher, which were communicated to the batter by the positioning of the black bar.[A] Chase claimed that during a game in Detroit, some Detroit players suspected that Stallings was using the "Black Hand." They walked outside the park and caught his operators red-handed. Some claim that Chase's accounts were untrue and that Chase spoke out to discredit Stallings. No matter, Johnson favored Chase in this episode. The American League President would find a way to eliminate Stallings.

The newspapers of the day indicated that Farrell and Johnson supported Chase. Yet historians since then painted Chase as a malcontent, as Stallings

---

[A] The manipulator signaled to the batter at the plate in the following code: 1. Bar slanted at a right angle to the left meant curve. 2. Bar slanted at a right angle to the right meant spit ball. 3. Bar pointed straight up equaled a fast ball. 4. Bar wiggling in all directions signaled a pitch-out.

claimed, because it supported their theses that Chase was inherently corrupt. While dramatic, that explanation masked the truth. Indeed Chase had aspirations to manage. Perhaps Chase undermined Stallings to get the manager's job. But it was time for Stallings to go and for Chase to take over. Everything else was just details.

On August 1, Chase missed a game due to a neck injury suffered in a train crash. The train accident occurred toward the end of July when Chase was "recuperating" from malaria. The accident was severe. The conductor and another passenger were killed. Chase sat out the game on August 1 against Detroit to rest his neck. Surely his missing the prior two series and the game against Detroit angered Stallings and prompted his comments about Chase as a malingerer. Throughout August and September, the feud between the two festered. Chase missed games. And Stallings, who felt that Chase used as an excuse the false medical maladies, continued to claim that Chase played with a "willful indifference." Some reported that in spite of missing games for the Yankees, Chase played in other games around the New York region. The papers reported on the discord:

> Chase's absence from the New York team is not due to illness, as reported, but to a severe case of sulks.... Chase has practically been promised the management of the club for next year and he probably wants it now.... Stallings' contract does not expire until next fall.... Without Chase the Yankees will be a weak club, and with Chase it seems impossible for Stallings, who is under contract, but be around.[6]

Any conflict that occurred was exacerbated by Farrell's mismanagement. With Stallings still under contract, he promised Chase the manager role. Chaos ensued. Farrell would go through good managers with regularity. In six years he would go through six managers. Two are in the Hall of Fame and another won the World Series in 1914 (Stallings). And in some instances, Farrell hired the incoming manager prior to notifying the incumbent. In the current situation, after coming to terms with Farrell in private, Chase was unable to remain discrete and go about his business. The relationship between Stallings and Chase became acrimonious. Farrell and Johnson waited patiently for Stallings' contract to expire. They wouldn't get rid of him before the end of his contract unless he gave them cause. By the middle of September, Stallings gave them cause.

In the papers, Stallings made a statement that Chase was "laying down," which implied that he accepted bribes to throw games. Farrell reported to the press:

> If Chase is guilty of Stalling's charges, there is no place on the New York American League team for him, or any other team, in my judgement. If he is not guilty, he should be promptly cleared of the charges, that he may stand vindicated before the public.

On September 19, Ban Johnson promptly summoned Stallings to his office during the team's road trip to Chicago. Disgusted by Stallings' accusations against Chase, one of the league's stars, Johnson promptly investigated Stallings' claims and made a decision. He discussed his verdict with Stallings, and then invited Farrell to his office the next day. In no uncertain terms, Johnson ordered Stallings out of the league and made his announcement to Farrell during their meeting. By September 21, reporters learned of Stallings' dismissal. The next day, the papers reported that Hal Chase was the new manager. All papers uniformly reported, "the writing had been on the wall." The San Francisco Chronicle reported that Ban Johnson was after Stallings' scalp ever since he was placed in charge of the club two years before.

Farrell was quoted as saying about Chase, ""No ball player can afford to have his reputation and the reputation of his club besmirched by such charges."[7] Ban Johnson released a similar statement:

> *Stallings has utterly failed in his accusations against Chase. He tried to besmirch the character of a sterling player. Anybody who knows Hal Chase knows that he is not guilty of the accusations made against him, and I am happy to say that the evidence of New York players given to Vice President Somers this morning showed Stallings up.*[8]

The aftermath revealed that the cantankerous Stallings had been immensely unpopular. Under his reign, the team became torn by discord and acrimony. In contrast, the team liked and respected Chase, the franchise's biggest star. Ban Johnson and Frank Farrell dismissed Stallings's spurious claims against Chase as a final salvo, a parting shot inspired by sour grapes. When Stallings was still at the helm, many players allegedly sided with Stallings. But once Chase became manager, all claimed that they were behind Chase because they preferred his good nature. In truth, the manager wielded significant influence on players' precarious careers. So they understandably aligned themselves with whomever might control their fate. So for now, everyone loved Hal Chase. The honeymoon had begun.

Chase managed his first game, which was against Detroit, on September 26. The Highlanders' got off to a good start under their young skipper. They won seven of their first nine games. They finished the season in second place, its best showing since 1906. Hal batted .290, tenth in the league. With the dual role of player and manager, his salary was raised to $6,000 per year.[9]

At the end of the season, Ban Johnson passed a new rule – in a parting shot to outgoing George Stallings, Johnson banned all "sign tipping" in the American League. He warned that those found guilty would be permanently banished from the game.

That season in Sacramento, Charlie Graham's squad set a Pacific Coast League record for the worst batting average by a team for a complete season at .203.[10] Graham needed to shake up his roster. Still associated with the Red Sox,

Graham agreed to take Frank Arellanes off the hands of John Taylor in exchange for prospect Ben Hunt. Graham also hired passionate manager Patsy O'Rourke to light a fire under the anemic team. Graham, always aware of his weaknesses, was willing to take a back seat if he felt that someone else would do a better job as manager. As owner and general manager, Graham focused on assembling the talent and maximizing profits. O'Rourke could be the general on the field.

O'Rourke was a young man whose volatile and sometimes violent disposition, coupled with a face worn beyond his years, indicated that he may have spent time in a bar as well as at home with his family. During 1910, while coaching in Albany in New York, O'Rourke claimed to discover Pete "Grover Cleveland" Alexander, who broke into the major leagues in 1911. The superstitious and confrontational O'Rourke prided himself on playing an aggressive style of baseball known only in the East. Graham hoped that O'Rourke would teach the squad how to avoid the jinx as well as play a more spirited brand of baseball the coming year.

At the conclusion of the regular season, the California Winter League resumed play. Only this year, the league would become the first integrated professional baseball league in the United States. Rube Foster felt that his Lincoln Giants, with future Hall of Famers Pop Lloyd and "Cyclone Joe" Williams, were the best team ever assembled. Foster brought his team to Los Angeles to play during the winter. As was the team's custom, they traveled on their own Pullman cars that they attached to standard commercial trains. That winter, the league featured stars Kid Mohler, Tom Seaton, and Walter Carlisle. And Foster's Giants not only played in exhibition games, they joined the league for the entire season. Foster would return each year, and the California Winter League would annually become the venue in which the greatest white and black players of the era competed against each other. Only in the California Winter League could one compare the likes of a Satchel Paige in competition against a Walter Johnson or Bob Feller. In 1910, Foster's Giants didn't field all of its regulars. Stars Pop Lloyd, Bruce Petway, and Pete Hill chose to play in Cuba instead.[11] Consequently, the Giants did not dominate the league; rather, they met competition of similar ability.

African American players were strictly forbidden from major league baseball during this era. John McGraw, Tris Speaker, and Ty Cobb were reported to refuse to take the field against an African American opponent. Yet in spite of the ban against American players of African descent, baseball would become an international phenomenon with mounting interest in Europe, Asia, Central America, and the Caribbean. The game was promoted abroad by barnstormers. Foreign teams visited the United States from places such as China, Japan, and Australia. Baseball leagues existed in Canada. Players of many nationalities played the game. Yet, only the African American was not allowed to play in Organized Baseball. The American Indian could play. Chief Bender, Chief Meyers, and Zack Wheat were notable players to date. Mexican Americans could play. Sandy Nava was the first, and Frank Arellanes was a more recent entrant. Latin Americans could play. Luis Castro played for the Philadelphia A's. And Jack Calvo, born in Cuba, would play in 1913. Strangely, before Calvo was allowed to play, the team's owner explained that Calvo was Cuban and not African American. Many men of color played in Organized Baseball, but specifically the black American could not play. In California, not all owners were agreeable to integrating the black American into professional baseball. But in the California Winter League, a glimmer of hope for racial equality in baseball existed.

That same year, the Los Angeles economy was in turmoil. Employers and workers clashed over labor's attempts to unionize in order to increase the hourly wage, obtain overtime pay, and improve general conditions. Los Angeles Times owner Harrison Gray Otis had successfully suppressed unionization in the past. He influenced public opinion against unions in his paper and established the Merchants and Manufacturers Association (M&M), a group of local businessmen who intimidated local businesses from hiring union labor. Because of Otis' concerted effort, labor costs in Los Angeles were far below the rest of the country. A national union for Iron Workers was determined to unionize workers in Los Angeles. The organization had a history of perpetrating violent acts, although the bombs they allegedly planted never resulted in deaths. The Iron Workers began striking on June 1 and grew in strength into the fall.

On October 1, 1910, a bomb exploded tearing off the corner of the Los Angeles Times building, setting off a fire, and killing at least twenty and injuring many more. The Los Angeles Times immediately printed a special edition with the headline:

Unionist Bombs Wreck the Times

A manhunt turned up two suspects, brothers John and Jim McNamara, labor activists with affiliations with the Iron Workers Union. The two men eventually submitted a guilty plea. Job Harriman, a socialist running mate to Eugene Debs in the 1900 presidential election, was the leading candidate in the mayoral election in Los Angeles at the time. He gained popularity opposing Otis and the M&M by representing the common man. He was assigned to the defense team on behalf of the McNamara brothers. But when the two alleged bombers surprised Harriman by submitting a guilty plea, Harriman's luster with the voters faded, and he lost the election. The bombing and the ensuing proceedings proved a severe blow to the socialist movement in Los Angeles and the United States, and continued to paint the anarchist as a violent and lawless individual.

The bomb exploded very close to the headquarters of the Maier Brewing Company. Just down the street, Hap Hogan had opened a billiard parlor on Spring Street. His pool hall became the headquarters for western baseball. Both ballplayers and common men congregated there. And the players, managers, owners, and scouts who came west to play, practice, or find talent all stopped by at Hogan's. Reporters looking for a story stopped in at Hogan's. Owners looking to cut a deal went to Hogan's. Regulars over the years included John McGraw, Mike Donlin, George Stovall, Frank Chance, Jake Stahl, Joe Tinker, Charles Comiskey, Christy Mathewson, Rube Marquard, Jim Scott, Nixey Callahan, Ed Walsh, Mordecai Brown, Doc White, Orval Overall, Ray Schalk, Harry Hooper, Duffy Lewis, Fred Snodgrass, and many more. Other sportsmen common to the Los Angeles sports scene, including Jim Jeffries, Jim Corbett, and Barney Oldfield mixed with both the regulars and the down and out.

> *Many big deals were put together at his pool hall,, and many times big baseball news broke there. Any time there was rain in Los Angeles, the ivory was clicking and the ballplayers were at Hogan's. The charm that was there was no exclusivity... it had a flavor of the old days... newspaper men flocked there in droves. His place was the single greatest source for sports news in the west.[12]*

Certainly bets were wagered at Hogan's. Bookies had hung out at billiard parlors for decades conducting pool betting. Before oddsmakers, the bookie served as a middleman mediating bets to avoid controversy. The term "pool room" did not originate in a billiard parlor, but in reference to where pool selling took place by bookies. In the nineteenth century, billiard parlors throughout America became popular centers for pool selling. Thus, the billiard parlor became known as a "pool hall."[13]

Over the past decade, the popularity of billiards exploded throughout America. In 1900, for example, one hundred forty Chicago taverns had billiard tables. By 1909, four thousand had them.[14] The urban working class male in his teens and twenties who enjoyed participating in sports used the billiard parlor and tavern as an outlet. Saloons became "workingmen's clubs." Billiard table games became popular because they provided males with an athletically competitive outlet where they could display skill, mingle, gamble, cajole, and meet friends in a collegial setting. Not verbal by nature, men often preferred a social atmosphere that didn't require them to converse. To that end, billiards was much like golf, but more accessible for the urban working class. Games were only a nickel a game, and the winner never paid. A good player could play at length without spending any money. And he likely had bets on the games as well, so he could actually leave the bar ahead financially.

Billiard halls had a propensity to develop a bad image because the public justifiably viewed them as hangouts where young men from the inner city loafed, gambled, plotted crimes, drank, and corrupted minors. The Broadway musical "The Music Man" memorialized the pool hall as "trouble" (with a capital "T," that rhymes with "P," and that stands for pool). Many establishments earned the seedy reputation. A small percentage of billiard halls in each city became known as denizens for troublemakers. They served not only as a home away from home and a place to meet friends, but a place to organize criminal activity or fix a ballgame.

These halls were often located in economically challenged sections of a town and had no windows and very few tables. But the majority of a city's billiard parlors were respectable establishments. And many baseball men also owned pool halls, an association that should not imply a stigma. The finest billiard halls were often located downtown and owned by the local businessmen. They often contained over a half dozen tables and had windows facing the city's most commercial thoroughfares to attract walk-in traffic. The nicest billiard parlors in America's cities existed on streets such as Spring Street and Broadway Avenue in Los Angeles, Madison Avenue and State Street in Chicago, Market Street and Van Ness in San Francisco, and 5th Avenue and 7th in Manhattan. One third of a city's billiard tables were located on the major streets in the urban centers, which was where Hap Hogan set up shop.

At the end of the 1910 season, Hal Chase didn't hang out at any billiard parlors until he had completed an exhibition tour in upstate New York and Canada with Christy Mathewson and other all stars. They played indoors in armories through a region that welcomed stars each year at the end of the major league baseball season. In December, he pitched a game and defeated Rube Waddell. The paper reported:

> *Chase was a star, striking out eleven batters and allowing just 6 hits. His support in the field was miserable, although he fielded his position brilliantly. He had one hit and scored one run. Waddell only allowed three hits -- one to Chase, one to Larry Doyle, and one to Dan Brouthers, Jr.* [15]

Chase, Nellie, and Harold, Jr. then hurried home to San Jose to be with Chase's family. On January 15, Hal was back out at Santa Clara College playing with the youngsters. In a baseball game in which Chase played, the Santa Clara pitchers, coached by Bobby McHale, baffled Chase. One of the pitchers named Ybarratelo "showed up from Rugby last fall." Another player was Chauncey Tramutolo, an infielder.[A] Chase also took notice of a young outfielder from San Mateo High School named Justin Fitzgerald. In fact, he was so impressed that he sent friend and scout William Benson to try and sign Fitzgerald to a contract with New York.[16]

The same month, Hal purchased an income-producing orange grove in Lindsay, California. He spent $5,000 on the grove[17], located in the San Joaquin Valley between Bakersfield and Fresno. The property was within close proximity to the southern Sierra Nevada foothills and gold country. He entrusted the property to his sister Jessie.

Chase also gave an interview at Christmas and dispelled rumors that Frank Farrell was considering releasing Harry Wolter. In the interview, Chase said that any story about Harry Wolter being cast adrift was a lie. He said that

---

[A] He would later be one of the pallbearers at Hal Chase's funeral.

Wolter would prove to be one of the most valuable outfielders in the American League the coming season.[18]

On February 12, owner Farrell called Chase back to New York hastily prior to spring training.[19]   Harry Wolter, however, went home to Castroville, where his parents lived, to recuperate from surgery to remove his tonsils. He had the surgery in Palo Alto a few days prior and was still weak. He expected to join Chase and his team shortly for spring training.[20]   Not until Wolter donned a Yankee uniform for the regular season, however, would his fate be known. Rumors surfaced that Farrell was still hesitant to sign Wolter. He had concerns that Wolter and Chase had a rift over the handling of the Stallings' episode the prior year; apparently Wolter sided with Stallings.[21]   The past season, Wolter only hit .267, but showed he could get on base, steal bases, and score runs. He was third in the league in walks, sixth in runs scored, and stole thirty-nine bases. Chase assured Farrell that the two Californians were on good terms and that Chase wanted Wolter on the squad. He also asked Farrell to approve signing Santa Clara prospect Justin Fitzgerald.

When spring training started, the Red Sox chose to prepare in California. Upon their arrival to Los Angeles, they were met by Henry Berry, Jim Jeffries, Eddie Maier, Pop Dillon, Happy Hogan, and the media. The White Sox readied themselves by signing Nixey Callahan.   Comiskey, impressed by Callahan's promotional skills, hired him as the team's President. But Callahan convinced Comiskey that he could also play in the outfield. Still able to perform, Callahan turned in two productive seasons before officially retiring as a player. In another transaction in Chicago, the Cubs announced the retirement of star pitcher Orval Overall.   The paper reported, "From what he showed last year no one is surprised."[22]

As Chase prepared for spring training, he sent William Benson a note to sign Fitzgerald.   Fitzgerald stood out while playing for San Mateo and Watsonville the past summer. He hit .410 and fielded well. At Santa Clara, he commonly punched out three hits per game. But when Benson approached him with the Yankees' offer, Fitzgerald turned him down claiming he wanted to finish his college courses. His relatives were dead set against a baseball career for him. But Justin promised that if he ever considered professional ball, he would give Benson and the Yankees first choice.[23]

Approaching his first season as manager of the Yankees, Chase's management style was described by sportswriter Mark Roth of the New York Globe and Commercial Advertiser:

> *Chase is easy-going and will not bully his men, and will get along with them. He has a pleasing personality, and will be patting the men on the back and getting the best there is from them.[24]*

Farrell agreed to sign Wolter for the 1911 season. As the season opened, Chase bragged about Harry:

Hal Chase and Harry Wolter appeared together on a Hassan Cigarettes Trading Card while playing together for the New York Americans.

I expect Wolter to do some grand ball playing this season. It was on my recommendation that Mr. Farrell secured him from Boston. His arm had gone bad on him a bit and he was forced to quit pitching. But I knew he had the makings of a great outfielder, and so when Boston asked waivers on him, the Yankees secured him ...

Chase was correct about Wolter. He steadily improved each season. In 1911, he had another solid season hitting .304, characteristically showcasing patience at the plate and speed on the bases.

[1] The California Winter League, William F. McNeil.

[2] The Sporting Life, December 4, 1909, pg. 7

[3] Judge Tells How to Slide, Los Angeles Times, Sep. 5, 1913, Pg. I1

[4] City of Vernon: a collection of oral histories, Marianne Dissard, California State University Fullerton Oral History Program, 1995

[5] The Sporting News, September 18, 1941, Lester Grant (Oakland Post Enquirer)

[6] Sporting Life, August 6, 1910

[7] Farrell Probing Scandal in New York Highlanders, September 23, 1910, Los Angeles Times, pg. 16

[8] Hal Chase Exonerated, New York Times, September 24, 1910

[9] Sporting Comment, The Melancholy Dane, Los Angeles Times, Mar 5, 1911, VII7

[10] The record stood as late as 1940. Baseball Records, Pacific Coast League, From 1903 to 1940 Inclusive, Published in Conjunction with Helms Athletic Foundation, p.50

[11] The California Winter League, William F. McNeil.

[12] Baseball World Misses Hap Hogan's Rendezvous, Harry A. Williams, LA Times, Nov 4, 1915, pg. III3

[13] The Dark Side of the Diamond, Gambling, Violence, Drugs, and Alcoholism in the National Pastime, Roger I. Abrams.

[14] City Games, The Evolution of American Urban Society and the Rise of Sports, Steven A. Riess, pg. 73

[15] New York Times, December 17, 1910

[16] Santa Clara College Ball Team Promises To Be Strong, San Francisco Chronicle, Jan 15, 1911, pg. 44

[17] The Black Prince of Baseball, Hal Chase and the Mythology of the Game, pg. 147, Don Dewey and Nick Acocella

[18] Balls and Strikes, Los Angeles Times, January 19, 1911, pg. III4

[19] Chase Goes East, Direct Wire to Times, Los Angeles Times, Feb 13, 1911, Pg, I10

[20] Special dispatch to The Call, Feb 15, 1911, "Harry Wolter Is Weak From Operation"

[21] Wolter to Coach Santa Clara Team, SF Chronicle, Dec 3, 1911, pg 59

[22] Baseball Chips Off the Diamond. LA Times Mar 9, 1911, Pg. III2

[23] Hal Chase Is After Santa Clara Player, San Francisco Chronicle, Mar 4, 1911, p. 11

[24] New York Globe and Commercial Advertiser, Feb. 24, 1911

Chapter 12

Fearful of the Jinx

In May, back on the Coast, Eddie Maier embraced the spring with his annual barbecue for the Elks Club at his Rancho Selecto. Meanwhile, Hal Chase opened the season hampered by a case of bronchitis that forced him to miss seventeen games as a manager at the beginning of the season. Certainly he wanted a better start. Upon his return, he received some good news - young Justin Fitzgerald had completed his studies for the year and finally agreed to sign with the Yankees.[A]

Veteran Mike Donlin's prospects were not much different from the youthful Fitzgerald. Both needed to prove themselves. Donlin had spent the past two years on the vaudeville circuit instead of playing baseball. A Hall of Fame-caliber player in even-numbered years, Donlin last played in 1908 and missed his next opportunity for an upswing in 1910. In 1911, there were few teams he could turn to other than the Giants. Manager John McGraw always loved Turkey Mike. On June 7, 1911, the National Commission reinstated Donlin for the second time in his career, and he joined the Giants. He was no longer a star, or even a starter, but McGraw knew Donlin's potential and was willing to see if he could return to form.

While Donlin played for the Giants, the team couldn't hit its stride. Perhaps Turkey Mike was a jinx to the team. If the origin of the team's bad luck could have been traced to Donlin, John McGraw would have sent him packing faster than a signal-stealing batboy.

Players didn't call themselves superstitious. Rather, they were "fearful of a jinx," or "in deadly fear of the jinx." The players almost uniformly avoided jinxes that could be brought on by any of the following:

Bad Luck
1. Seeing a cross-eyed man.
2. Number 13, particularly on a train car.
3. Saying to a pitcher in the 8th, "just six more," or in the 9th, "three more."
4. Black cat crossing one's path.
5. Crossing bats. (Batboys trained to make sure two bats didn't fall upon each other with one crossing the other, usually at the handle).

[A] He debuted on June 20. However, the twenty-year old offered little support. He played in only sixteen games during the year before being released. He then pitched for Charlie Graham in Sacramento.

6. Losing or changing from a reliable glove and having to use a new glove.
7. Gazing too long at full barrels.
8. Breaking a bat in the middle of a streak.
9. Outfielders passing inside of first base or third base when running into the dugout between innings.
10. Touching one's socks once one has slid in a game.

Good Luck

1. Hunchbacks.
2. Rubbing the head of an African American child.
3. A load of empty barrels.
4. Sitting with legs crossed. If luck seems to be shifting, cross with the other leg.
5. Going to church.
6. Touching second base when coming in from the outfield.
7. Finding hairpins.

Removing a Jinx

1. Taking off another person's hat and spitting into it.
2. In a batting slump, trying out every bat.

Baseballers in California had their own ways to defend themselves from the jinx. Sacramento's Patsy O'Rourke said it was unlucky to change brands of chewing tobacco during a game. Harry Wolter believed that if a player dressed incorrectly before a game (shirt inside out, socks backward), it was unlucky to correct the error before the game. And Hen Berry once wore the same pair of socks for two weeks during a winning streak.

On August 1, Donlin's fortunes changed for the worse. With the Giants playing poorly and in third place, McGraw dealt Donlin to the Boston Rustlers. Soon thereafter the Giants traveled to St. Louis for a series.

On the trip, a man named Charlie Faust entered the Planters Hotel and asked for McGraw. He said that he was from Kansas and that a fortuneteller had told him that he could be a great pitcher for the New York Giants. Faust suffered from a form of schizophrenia that caused delusions, hallucinations, and silly behavior. His exceptional good nature, however, was endearing to McGraw and the team. Faust went to the ballpark and playfully warmed up. He hung around on the bench through the game, which the Giants won. He returned for each game of the series, and the Giants swept the Cardinals. When the Giants boarded the train back, Faust appeared at the station expecting to go with the team. McGraw cruelly told him that he left his ticket at the hotel desk. The train left without Faust.

Once back in New York, Christy Mathewson reported:

Faust entered the clubhouse with several inches of dust and mud caked on him, for he had come all the way either by side door special or blind baggage. He said, 'I'm here all right,' as he began to climb into a uniform.[1]

The team won the next few games with Faust hanging around the dugout and clubhouse. McGraw decided to cut Faust loose. Charley broke down and cried when McGraw broke the news. The Giants lost that day. Fearful of the jinx, McGraw decided to bring Faust back. When Faust permanently joined the team as one of baseball's first mascots, the third place Giants posted a winning streak of 37 wins against only two losses to clinch the pennant. Faust became known as the "Kansas Jinx Killer." Before every game during that 1911 season, Charlie Faust suited up in uniform and warmed up for the game expecting to pitch. Every game. Fans began to arrive early to games to watch him in warm-ups. Technically he was not on the team, but Faust did not let on if he was aware of that fact. He put on a pre-game show of pitching, fielding, and running the bases that entertained the crowd. He also led the brass band. Before one game, he struck out the great Honus Wagner, who played along for show. The crowd loved him.

When the Giants were behind, McGraw would send Faust to the bullpen to warm up; every time the hurler believed he was actually going into the game. Seeing Faust warming up with his bizarre windup provided comic relief for the players and kept the team loose.

On October 7, in a game with the Donlin's Boston Rustlers, the Giants had already sewn up the pennant. The game had no significance and the attendance peaked at a meager 1,000 fans. When the few in attendance shouted for Faust, Donlin and McGraw decided to have some fun. McGraw sent Faust in to pitch. Charley allowed a hit and a run. Batters had difficulty hitting him because his pitch lacked any speed. At the top of the next inning, Faust readied himself on the on-deck circle when Boston recorded the third out. But Donlin and the Rustlers remained in the field to give the Giants a fourth out. The Rustlers then allowed Faust to run out his hit for a home run. He did so by sliding into second, third, and then home.

Faust showed up the next year for spring training in 1912. The Giants began the season an amazing 54-11, and the legend of Charlie Faust was cemented. The Giants repeated as national league champs. During the season, however, his illness and general ill health prevented him from continuing on with the team. Ultimately, Faust's condition became too much of a distraction; McGraw felt compelled to end Faust's contract, at which time Charlie moved to Seattle to live with relatives.

With Faust as an example, baseball owners embraced the appeal that playful entertainment had on the fan. In Los Angeles, the dedication to entertainment at Chutes Park rose to a new level. The amusement park re-opened as Luna Park. The park shared its name with a similar park in San Jose where the

Prune Pickers played their games, as well as with other locations around the country, including the hugely successful Coney Island. It opened with new attractions including Nemo's Trip to Slumberland named for a popular comic strip of the time. The opening attracted 16,000 who saw Stanley and Hoxiel's Congress of Rough Riders and Wild West Show and Madame Schell's Ferocious Lions. A diorama depicting the sinking of the USS Main in Havana Harbor to start the Spanish-American War replaced the previous mural of the Monitor and Merrimac. The attempt was to create an amusement park that appealed to children.[2] When Luna Park was built, the baseball field then became known as Washington Park.

The Vernon Tigers also knew how to entertain the Los Angeles fan. A master at providing fans with a show at each game, Hap Hogan took note of the mood in the stands as the innings progressed. And if interest appeared to wane, he'd run on the field to protest a call with an umpire, creating as much of a spectacle as possible. As he ran back to the dugout, the crowd often cheered their fiery manager for his passionate performance. And in critical situations with men on base, Hogan, who had one glass eye, would enter the game, stride to the plate dramatically, and punch out a base hit for the locals. He was loved because he knew how to combine a passionate pursuit of a championship with an entertaining product for the fan. A Los Angeles newspaper described Hogan and his popularity.

> *Hogan is smart enough to know that the baseball fan has a secret hankering for drama. They like to see the skipper wildly flailing their arms to yell at the umpire. They don't so much like the rough stuff as much as the dramatic stuff. Hap has always noted the importance of giving the fan a good time. 'In a way, I am the host, and it is up to me to see that they have a good time. They come out there to see something happen. I try to give them what they want.' Major league teams have shown an interest in Hap... but Hap is Vernon and Vernon is Hap.[3]*

Sacramento's Patsy O'Rourke also provided a spectacle for the fans, although the fans and the league didn't condone his virulent displays. He had an uncontrollable temper, and he often used vulgar language. He sometimes regretted his outbursts. At other times, he'd stand atop a proverbial soapbox and declare that he brought East Coast passion and aggression to the laid back Californians. In one game, George Hildebrand, who had made the transition from ballplayer to umpire,[A] reported O'Rourke to league President Thomas Graham. Manager Graham sided with the namesake league President; he would not tolerate vulgar and uncivil behavior. Hildebrand reported to the league president that O'Rourke's vile and profane language could be heard all over the grandstand. And he also reported that Patsy had made a couple attempts to hit the umpire

---

[A] He later became an umpire in the major leagues.

before he could be restrained. President Graham suspended O'Rourke for the second time that season.

Charlie Graham had been patient with O'Rourke. Patsy had played and managed well otherwise. The owner and manager worked well together for the most part. Just a month before, they had traveled together to Chico to see their former player Ben "High Pockets" Hunt who was suffering from pneumonia. The prior year, Graham had traded Hunt to the Boston Red Sox in exchange for Frank Arellanes. Hunt started for Boston, but preferred California and negotiated a return. He had played for Sacramento. But on June 26, Charlie Graham received word that Ben Hunt was dying.

> *Recognizing that death is near, Hunt begged this morning that Charlie Graham, manager of the team, be sent for. Graham and Capt O'Rourke left this afternoon for a farewell word with the big pitcher.[4]*

That Graham and O'Rourke would make the trip to see the pitcher revealed something about the men. And that Graham was whom Hunt sent for on his deathbed revealed even more about Graham.[A]

But in spite of Graham's caring nature, he wasn't about to tolerate O'Rourke's outbursts much longer. While suspended, O'Rourke contacted San Francisco and Los Angeles clubs about leaving Sacramento. He reported to the press that the other teams were courting him. Patsy made no efforts to conceal dissatisfaction. O'Rourke said that Hen Berry indicated that his manager Pop Dillon was getting old and that the Angels could utilize a good second baseman.[B] Contrary to O'Rourke's comments about Hen Berry courting him, Berry said that he had not approached O'Rourke, and that he didn't want or need him. Many agreed that O'Rourke had been a capable manager, but his outbursts had become unpopular with the fans; the fans pressured Graham to remove him as manager.

A week later, the impulsive O'Rourke calmed down and realized that he'd better conform to the program in Sacramento. He publicly gave a half-hearted apology. O'Rourke said that Hildebrand had provoked him and that he just couldn't take it any more. He said that anyone could ask the players if they doubted his story. He admitted that his temper got the best of him and promised that it would never happen again. Still only thirty years of age, O'Rourke acted like the youngest manager in the Pacific Coast League. Married and with a 6-year old boy, O'Rourke decided to reform. In the meantime, due to his suspension, he paid the 5 cents at the gate, sat in the stands, and managed from a distance.

[A] Ben Hunt survived to pitch again.

[B] It would have been completely out of character for Hen Berry to tell anyone, particularly O'Rourke, that Pop Dillon was getting too old and that he was dissatisfied with his current second baseman.

Hap Hogan's Vernon Tigers and McCredie's Portland Beavers were the class of the Pacific Coast League in 1911. President Graham felt that the league played the best minor league ball in the country, and wanted to prove it. He proposed to the National Commission that the class A league champions play in a national championship playoff at the end of the seasons out in California. Travel costs were a considerable deterrent to a playoff, but the biggest obstacle was that the various leagues ended their seasons at different times.[5] No agreement could be reached.

At the end of August, still only thirty-three years old, but already a California baseball veteran, Charlie Graham decided to formally retire as a baseball player and focus solely on ownership and general management. He announced his decision while on a road trip to play in Los Angeles. The reporter credited Graham with the success of the franchise. He reported that Graham wouldn't have received twenty dollars for his interest in Sacramento last year, but now wouldn't take ten thousand dollars. When asked the teams he liked in the league, Graham said,

> ... I like Vernon. It's a good team that Hap has. The pitchers are strong and if they hold up their present form and the team has luck, the combination may finish at the top. I like Vernon and Portland, one-two...[6]

Graham also credited Hogan as the "best pinch hitter in the state." Hogan responded by saying that his friend Graham was the best ever and is "up-to-date, a credit to baseball, heady catcher, wise player, and great handler of young pitchers." The reporter described Graham's veteran status by saying that "Graham was part of the Coast League before they began to grow grass on the playing field and had opera chairs in the grand stand..."[7]

O'Rourke continued to lead Graham's Senators, and although the team played well toward the end, they vied for fourth in the standings. In spite of the success toward the end of the season, O'Rourke criticized his team for being too nice. He vowed to replace all of his players the next season with players who would play his way.

> They will fight more between the lines... I don't wonder that many of the fans think the pro games are fixed. They ought to when they see the teams come on the field and mix it like it was a pink tea, instead of a real ball game where we are out to win.[8]

His comments didn't sit well with Graham, who certainly wasn't one to condone criticizing his team midseason. In another interview, the tactless O'Rourke told umpires that the next season he intended on making their lives miserable by crabbing. He said that baseball in the league was entirely too tame.

Graham had two problems to deal with. He had to tell O'Rourke to stop talking. And he needed to overcome the Sacramento fans' objection to the skipper. A mathematician by schooling, the calculating Graham considered how to solve for the condition while accounting for the simultaneous constraints.

Frank Arellanes pitched well for the Sacramento club, and was the highest paid player on the Coast. But he started to fatigue toward the end of the season. On a recent road trip, Hogan commented on the amount of innings Arellanes was pitching. He joked, "They're working you pretty hard today, aren't they, Handsome?" Arellanes found out that he had contracted malaria.[9] He took the final months of the season off and recuperated at home in Santa Cruz. Graham could have used Elmer Stricklett in the rotation to fill in for Arellanes. Stricklett was down the road playing for Moreing's Stockton team in the Cal State League. On September 4, he threw a no hitter against Modesto. The Chronicle reported that "he had everything that could be put on the horse-hide,"[10] referring to his spitball. But Graham's task at hand was to salvage O'Rourke.

On September 20, the Senators traveled to Vernon to play Hogan's Tigers. O'Rourke had the Senators playing well "... hitting like a wild fire, and there seems to be a winning spirit spread over the crowd." Graham wanted to keep Patsy. So he met with Hogan and devised a plan. He asked Hap to tell the press that he wanted O'Rourke on his team. On September 24, the press reported that Graham turned down an offer from Hogan for the purchase of Patsy O'Rourke, "the fighting leader of the Senators." The report said that Hogan offered one of his best infielders and cash. But Graham replied that he wouldn't let go of Patsy under any condition. When the Senators returned from their road trip, Graham's ploy succeeded; the Sacramento fans welcomed their hot commodity back with open arms. Graham demonstrated support for his manager and created an environment in which the manager could start anew.

The Senators would start anew in other ways as well. John I. Taylor, owner of the Red Sox also owned a portion of the Senators along with Charlie Graham.[11] In 1911, he decided to sell both franchises. He sold the Boston Red Sox to James McAleer,[A] former manager of the Washington Senators. With Taylor moving away from baseball, Graham would lose a close and trusted relationship in the Boston organization.

The 1911 season for Hal Chase was his best as a hitter. The San Francisco Chronicle reported that major league veteran player and manager Fielder Jones said that Hal Chase and Ty Cobb were the most valuable men in the game. "I consider Cobb and Chase two of the greatest assets both in attack and defense that any team ... could wish for."[12] Chase hit .315 with 82 RBI. He received accolades for his play. One reporter dubbed him the greatest first baseman to ever play the game.

[A] Taylor timed the sale badly. In 1912, the team that Taylor built won the World Series. It would also win in 1915, 1916, and 1918.

As a manager, Chase acknowledged his shortcomings. The team finished in sixth place, and Chase admitted he was more of a teammate and friend than the disciplinarian he needed to be. Once the season had begun, and he had not asserted himself as a disciplinarian, he couldn't put the genie back into the bottle. Chase offered to resign in October. He said that the "trials and tribulations of a manager were driving him to distraction." But at twenty-eight, the immature Chase probably had expectations that Farrell would give him support and encouragement to continue. Chase expected to return at the helm the next season.

But on October 31, Ban Johnson contacted San Francisco baseball man Bill Lange and asked him to recommend umpires. Lange referred George Hildebrand, who subsequently began a long and esteemed career in the major leagues. Lange also recommended the PCL's Oakland Oaks manager Harry Wolverton as a possible replacement for Chase.[13] Farrell acted upon Lange's recommendation and immediately began considering Wolverton. On November 4, the San Francisco Chronicle ran a headline that read "Harry Wolverton May Leave Oakland to Manage New York Americans." Even though Wolverton would not officially be named as Chase's replacement until December 11, certainly Chase knew his fate well in advance. After November 4, Chase conducted interviews with the press and made comments in an attempt to save face. In one instance, he said that Farrell offered him the job again in 1912, but he didn't want it, so Farrell hired Wolverton. In an interview conducted a week before Wolverton was named, Chase said the following even though he knew he was on his way out as manager:

> I am going to handle the team by a new method. When I assumed the management I concluded that the way to get winning ball out of the players was to smooth them over and treat them civilly. I believed that kindness and good nature would get results on those lines from the start. I didn't feel like slapping fines or suspending players without pay when they failed to deliver the goods, for I was new at the game of handling a team, and I was afraid of being too hasty... I began to realize the need of discipline ... I had been entirely too easy and ... some of the players had taken advantage of my leniency.[14]

The day after the interview was published, on November 20, Farrell named Wolverton as the new manager of the Yankees. Perhaps when Chase gave the interview, he held out hope that he would return as manager. Or perhaps he left a door open for an opportunity to manage again with another team. Not until December 11, did the American League officially announce the appointment. In the interim, Ban Johnson performed a background check on Wolverton. Still looking after his favorite franchise, Johnson wanted to make sure Wolverton would be a good replacement. All who knew him recommended him highly.

Chase felt regret and some amount of betrayal when Farrell replaced him with Wolverton. He also worried about his contract. He didn't want his salary cut due to a reduction in his responsibilities. He told Farrell that he would return as long as the Yankees paid him the same as he earned the prior season. But Farrell cut his salary to $6,000 from $8,000, which didn't set well with Chase.

In the end, Chase did go on record as resigning as manager, but probably because he preferred resigning to being fired. Clearly disgruntled by the replacement and the salary reduction, Chase couldn't conceal his emotions when quoted in public. He often said one thing, but believed another, particularly when he lacked leverage or felt backed into a corner. Often attempting diplomacy in the press, his actions contradicted his public statements. For example, he said,

I have been treated all right by the owner of the New York club, and will stick by him. There seems to be no doubt in my mind that we will fix up the matter satisfactorily.

Translated, Chase really meant,

I've been slighted by the New York management and I don't plan to stick by them. There is no doubt in my mind that the matter is beyond repair.

In time, part of Chase's difficulties could be explained by the same conditions that plagued Clark Griffith - the meddling and fickleness of Farrell. The Highlanders would go through Griffith, Elberfeld, Stallings, Chase, Wolverton, and later Chance and Roger Peckinpaugh in short succession. Only after Farrell sold the franchise in 1915 would the owners settle on a manager, Miller Huggins in 1918, who would remain for an extended period of time. Certainly the managers under Farrell would not be the first in a line of New York Yankee managers who faced pressure from the owner, the media, and the fans. Elberfeld and Wolverton would have tenures shorter than Chase. Stallings would last only months longer. Chase still harbored ambitions to manage in the major leagues, but not for the New York Yankees.

---

[1] Pitching in a Pinch, Christy Mathewson, pg. 248
[2] Berman, Jay and Sesar Carreno. The Short Life of a Downtown Amusement Park, Los Angeles Downtown News. 9/4/2006.
[3] Down the Pike, The Piker, Los Angeles Times. Sep 14, 1911, pg. III3
[4] Ben Hunt Dying of Pneumonia, Direct Wire to the Times, LA Times, Jun 27, 1911, pg. III1
[5] New York Times, August 6, 1911
[6] Old Timer Quits Game Forever, Grey Oliver, Los Angeles Times, Aug. 24, 1911, pg III2
[7] Old Timer Quits Game Forever, Grey Oliver, Los Angeles Times Aug 24, 1911, Pg III2
[8] Down the Pike, The Piker, Los Angeles Times, Sep 14, 1911, Pg. III3
[9] Arellanes, Groom, Is Ill In San Jose Home, San Francisco Chronicle, Jan 3, 1912, pg. 13
[10] Stricklett Pitches No-Hit, No-Run Game, San Frrancisco Chronicle, Sep 5, 1911, pg. 14
[11] Taylor May Sell Red Sox and Senators, FA Purner, SF Chronicle, Jul 30, 1911, pg. 55
[12] Chase and Cobb Ranked as Greatest, F A Purner, Jul 9, 1911, pg. 51
[13] Harry Wolverton May Leave Oakland To Manage New York Americans" F A Purner, SF Chronicle, Nov 4, 1911, pg. 11
[14] The Sporting Life, Nov. 20, 1911

Chapter 13

Players Show No Loyalty

Organized Baseball's mounting influence over professional baseball produced discord in unexpected places. Even Cal Ewing, the father of the Pacific Coast League and leading advocate for the PCL's adoption of the National Commission in 1904, suddenly turned against Eastern Baseball.

During 1910, Doc Moskiman played for the Boston Red Sox. He actually didn't play much, but occupied a position on the bench. Dissatisfied, Moskiman returned to the Pacific Coast in 1911. In 1912, Cal Ewing wanted him to play for San Francisco, but Moskiman had jumped his contract and was still Boston's property. Of all people, Cal Ewing threatened to convert the Pacific Coast League to an outlaw league if Moskiman wasn't allowed to play for San Francisco. The major leagues backed off, and Moskiman joined Ewing for 1912.[1]

In addition to owners, the players became increasingly disheartened by the grip that the reserve clause and the owners had on their conditions. Star pitcher Walter Johnson gave an interview entitled "Walter Johnson on Baseball Slavery; The Great American Principle of Dog Eat Dog." He was upset because he made $7,500 while players of equal or lesser value, namely Christy Mathewson and Ty Cobb, made $10,000 and $9,500 respectively. In the interview with Baseball Magazine, Johnson said:

> *I am not making any complaint. This is simply the direct application of the great intelligent business principle of dog eat dog.... The employer tries to starve out the laborer, and the laborer tries to ruin the employer's business. They quarrel over a bone and rend each other like coyotes.[2]*

The players had little loyalty to the owners. If someone showed up on the scene with a better offer, most players would have jumped their contracts. With conditions prime for a challenge to Organized Baseball's monopoly, a group of capitalists seized the perceived opportunity to establish another league. On May 1, 1912, the United States League played its first game with clubs in Pittsburgh, Richmond, Reading, Cincinnati, Washington, Chicago, Cleveland, and New York. The league struggled from the outset, but perhaps if it could have hung on, it could push the major leagues to a tipping point. In May, that tipping point seemed more probable.

In May of 1912, Ty Cobb instigated the first strike in Organized Baseball history. During batting practice, he heard a fan yelling profanities. His biography entitled <u>Cobb, A Biography</u> cited taunts included "Your sister screws niggers," and "Your mother is a whore." To Cobb, those were fighting words. Unable to tolerate the harassment, Cobb jumped into the stands and pounded the man with his fists and cleats. The fan was Claude Lueker, who Cobb would later learn had suffered an industrial accident and had no fingers on one hand and only two on the other. While the fan was still capable of defending himself, the media latched onto the story that Cobb went into the stands to attack a crippled man. Ban Johnson immediately suspended Cobb indefinitely.

Cobb's teammates wrote to President Ban Johnson attesting to the fan's foul language. But Johnson understandably felt that the protection of the public should be his highest priority. The Tiger players then telegraphed Johnson and threatened to strike until Cobb was reinstated. Reacting to the ban, Cobb had two comments:

We the men who make baseball must have some rights.

Let Johnson ban me and the hell with him.[3]

Baseball players took up the cause for Cobb's initial comment. During the 1912 season, they discussed the formation of a players' union. By September, the Base Ball Players's Fraternity formed to represent players' rights. Cobb had become the catalyst for a players' organization that became extremely unpopular with the owners.

During the strike, Johnson fined the Tigers $1,000 for each game they missed. For the next game against Philadelphia at Shibe Park, the team avoided a fine by fielding a team of locals, including prizefighter Billy Maharg, who played under the name Graham (Maharg spelled backwards).[4] There was some irony in Maharg's playing for Detroit that day. In seven more years, Maharg would allegedly help organize the fix of the World Series of 1919. That didn't necessarily mean that in 1912 he had any association with gambling. And Maharg had close ties with baseball and Philadelphia between 1912 and 1919, which explained his proximity to the incident. But it was possible, perhaps even likely, that he did have some involvement with gambling, having already "grown spots" in 1912 that would be evident in 1919. His involvement in the baseball game demonstrated the close proximity of gamblers to baseball during the era.

The dissatisfied fifteen thousand fans that watched the substitutes play protested violently. Ban Johnson threatened to ban the entire Tigers team, so Cobb convinced his teammates to return. Cobb served a light 10-day suspension and paid a fifty-dollar fine.[A] The strike did serve as a catalyst for the players' union,[B] but it didn't escalate into an exodus to the new United States League. Within a month, with teams having played roughly twenty games, the new league folded.

[A] The controversy didn't impact Cobb's performance . Through July, Cobb batted .521.

[B] Players' Union organizer Dave Fultz, Hal Chase's former teammate with the Highlanders who saw his playing career end following a severe collision with shortstop Kid Elberfeld, asked Cobb to serve as president of the union. Cobb accepted.

The players union pressed immediately for better conditions for the players. Issues included:

1. Limit harassment of players by fans
2. Require that fares be paid by the major league teams when players are sent to the minors
3. Pay players for spring training
4. Pay travel expenses to spring training
5. Disallow the suspension without pay of injured players
6. Require that a list of waived players be sent to all teams (league suppressed list of available players)
7. Making public a player's grievance against a club
8. Providing a 5-day notice prior to a release

Player representative Ty Cobb added:

> *Until now the cheap owners had made players pay their own travel expenses when traded. We got rid of that crap.*[5]

In 1912, Harry Wolter became a head coach at his alma mater Santa Clara. He remained with the team as long as possible, getting into shape on his own before reporting late to the New York Yankees. The Yankees still didn't pay a player for spring training, so Wolter felt no compulsion to report until the season started. Wolter's attitude revealed both his stubborn disposition as well as the options that he had as a coach and a businessman. Wolter always felt he could make a decent living outside of baseball near his new home in Redwood City. If baseball wanted him, they'd have to pay for him. The head coaching assignment for Wolter was his first.[6] He had previously coached every season in some capacity in the spring before reporting for the regular season.

As the season approached, Hal Chase reported that he would play second base the next season for the Yankees because they signed a player named Jack Knight, a top hitting prospect who couldn't play anywhere other than first base. After 1920, first base often became the position where teams hid a weak fielder who could hit. The defensive capabilities of the first baseman throughout the game diminished significantly after the deadball era. But in 1912, proficiency at first base, led by the unequaled Hal Chase, was expected with defensive specialists including Chick Gandil and Jake Daubert. Chase would not remain at second base.

> *Hal Chase, the Californian, known wherever baseball is played as the greatest first baseman the game has ever known, intends to switch from his favorite position and try his luck at second base next year.*[7]

Other off-season activities included the Frank Arellanes' recovery from malaria. He still found time to scout for Graham. He sent him a message in November about an outfield prospect he saw play in Santa Cruz. Three weeks later, on December 14, he married Miss Mabel Woolsey in San Jose. Miss

Woolsey[A] was a talented pianist and stepdaughter of a prominent hotel man. Father Valponi married them at Holy Family church at the corner of River and San Fernando Streets. Only immediate relatives and the closest friends attended, as the ceremony was called "an elopement." After the ceremony the bride's parents hosted a supper party at their home at 830 West San Fernando Street. The papers reported that the frugal Arellanes had saved considerable money playing baseball and was considering retirement to begin a business.[8] Arellanes had been the highest paid player in the West the prior year. But he had too much left in his arm, and he would return to the game.

But Frank never fully recovered from his illness. In January, the papers reported that he was ill with pneumonia in San Jose and was unable to leave his in-laws' house. He and his wife returned from their honeymoon prior to New Year's Eve, but he had since fallen ill. He thought he was fully recovered prior to the wedding.[9] He felt better after another ten days and appeared with Hal Chase in an exhibition game between Santa Cruz and a team called the Fraser Photos. Santa Cruz won 4-0. Chase played first and pitched a bit. He went 4-4 at the plate.[10] Arellanes didn't pitch, but played in the field.

During the winter, Hap Hogan traveled to San Antonio for an annual winter meeting between minor league owners and managers from throughout the country. He intended to make deals and network with other managers throughout the country. Hogan was full of confidence; his team had posted a 118-88 record to finish closely behind champion Portland. And he had the support of wealthy owner Ed Maier, pleasantly surprised by the overwhelming success of his team in Vernon. Hogan relished his new role as baseball magnate, and could not hide his exuberance during the trip. The papers reported that all of baseball took notice of Hogan's spectacle during the proceedings.

> *He was pronounced the funniest man to ever attend a meeting in San Antonio. Stepping off the train, he announced upon arrival to a crowd: 'I am a wild son of the mountains. I am from the Far West and a bad man. I'd just as soon drink a man's blood than look at him. I fight with knives, guns or fists, and I make it life against life. I am Happy Hogan from Vernon, and I don't care who knows it!' .... He conducted many trades, talked a lot, drank and danced. Happy was known to announce, "Come on, fellows, and let us have some wines." It was always 'wines.' 'I am a natural wine drinker; I have $50,000 to spend on this trip, and I am having trouble getting rid of it!' Hap was offering to send a case of wine up to all the magnates' rooms, and when one of them took him up he stepped over the hotel clerk's desk and ordered seven cases up to the rooms. It was a bluff, but everyone laughed.[11]*

[A]   Miss Woolsey graduated from Notre Dame in Belmont, just south of San Francisco.

A week later, Hogan joined the Pacific Coast League executives at meetings in San Francisco at the St. Francis Hotel and once again proved to be the life of the party. The other owners and managers gave him a hard time about reports from San Antonio that he intended to purchase a battle ship in Galveston that he and his friends would use as a pleasure craft. Regarding his comments, Hogan received two telegrams during the conference.

I expected to go on the cruise with you in your warship. Have positive information that you were bringing me.

Sweetie Cutie

--- ---- ----

You have proved yourself dishonest. Have heard from good authority that you never bought war ship at Galveston. It is a great disappointment, as I had bought silver service and liquids to stock same. Wire me immediately and let me know what I should do. On your return you shall be shot at sunrise, if you are able to stand.

Ed F. Maier[12]

At the meetings, President Graham stepped down as Pacific Coast League President and was replaced by Allen T. Baum, Spider Baum's brother. Unrelated to the change at the league's helm, Charlie Graham traded Spider to Hap Hogan in Vernon. Graham claimed that he feared that Baum's cigar store in Sacramento would take his interest away from playing baseball. But Baum would remain involved in baseball for many years to come, many of those with Charlie Graham.

In the off-season, Hap Hogan agreed to an indoor game with the local National Guard in Los Angeles. The National Guard team had won their championship, so Hogan agreed to give them a game against some professionals. They played to the largest crowd that ever attended an indoor game in Southern Cal. They made several hundred dollars at the gate, which Hogan donated to the soldiers. The soldiers never forgot Hap; they kept a photo of him in the locker room in their armory for years.

At the same time, Rube Foster returned to the California Winter League with his Chicago American Giants for the 1912 season. His squad continued to compete in the integrated league.

Elmer Stricklett was reinstated to Organized Ball after his three-year ban. Three years before he jumped his contract from Brooklyn because his wife objected to his playing in the National League. Stricklett agreed to return to the Brooklyn Nationals, who were expected to profit by selling him to Binghamton in the New York State League.[13] He ended up playing for Toronto of the International League

Elmer Stricklett

in 1912, his last season as a player. After the season, he returned to San Jose to enter the fruit business. He later moved to Santa Cruz and operated the Sherman Villa located at 209 Market Street where he rented cottages.

In February, the town of Vernon hosted one of boxing's premier matches on the 22nd. Johnny Kilbane defeated champion Abe Attell for the featherweight championship.[14]

In March, the Pacific Coast League attempted to strong arm the California League into Organized Baseball as a class C minor league that could potentially feed talent to the Pacific Coast League. Hen Berry recently took ownership in the San Jose franchise in an attempt to force a move. His actions were viewed by "the outlaw leader" Cy Moreing of Stockton as an unpleasant encroachment by the enemy. Other teams favored the move for financial reasons. But Moreing favored independence. No matter the decision of the other teams, Moreing was determined to remain independent. If he had to find another league to play in, he would. And the Stockton fans were behind him. Hap Hogan traveled to Fresno to meet with the owners he knew there to promote the Class C designation. Fresno fans favored the move. But Moreing and Stockton were determined to stay as far away from Angel's owner Hen Berry as possible. They said,

Hen Berry is about as welcome in Stockton as a yellow dog on the Fourth of July.

If Berry didn't succeed in separating teams from Stockton's hold, his San Jose team would surely fail in the California League, as his team would be boycotted for every game in Stockton. In the end, the Class C league formed, and Cy Moreing broke away to head a new outlaw league. He was joined by George Fraser of San Francisco, who had a Fraser Photo squad, Frank Baum of Sacramento, J.G. Leske of Modesto, Roy Garman of Fresno, George Whitaker of Galt, Walter McMenomy of Oakland, and Hal Chase's friend from his travels in British Columbia before turning pro, Elmer Emerson of San Jose. Emerson promised to play, as did retired Orval Overall from the Chicago Cubs.

At the beginning of the 1912 baseball season, Hal Chase and Nellie considered divorce. As one of the marquis players in New York, the drama of the proceedings played out in the papers like a soap opera. Hal and Nellie engaged in a public battle in an attempt to destroy each other's credibility. Chase lost custody of Harold, Jr.[A] The trial precipitated a nervous breakdown by Chase, who recovered in a sanitarium in Atlantic City for nearly a month in April and May.

[A] The prideful Chase also demonstrated delusional characteristics when he attempted to take custody of Harold, Jr. He had neither the skills nor the constitution to raise Harold. Chase's mother fortunately talked sense into Hal and told him to leave the baby with Nellie. Nellie moved to San Francisco and remained close to Hal's family for many years.

Chase had signed the divorce papers in March, but didn't have his attorney file them until late in May. When Hal took his leave, he was in the middle of filing his divorce decree. He would claim infidelity, as would she. The facts remained, however, that they both wanted a divorce, and the proceedings demonstrated pettiness on both sides. Eventually, each got their wish, but not before it put a strain on both. Chase would later say before his death that one of his biggest regrets and failures in life was not staying with Nellie. But in his youth, his pride and perhaps his habits prevented him from holding onto his one true love.

Chase remained with the team while it donned new uniforms that featured pinstripes on April 11.[A] A day later, the Titanic sunk in the Atlantic. The news devastated New York and reverberated throughout the world. On April 21, Chase and the Yankees played the Giants in a benefit for the survivors of the tragedy. A little more than a week later, Chase was taken to a hospital in Washington for an illness.[15] Two weeks later, he recuperated in a sanitarium. The paper reported he suffered from a stomach ailment.

On May 18, he returned to the lineup for the Yankees. Rumors surfaced that he'd be traded to the Boston Red Sox. In spite of rumors, his team's poor performance, his divorce, and a slump, Chase remained as easy-going and upbeat as possible, which was his general nature. Baseball Magazine wrote the following about Hal Chase's consistently good mannered, humble, and likeable personality:

> [Chase] had the easy, disingenuous air of the man who is perfectly at peace with his surroundings and with life in general, that attitude of the happy-go-lucky individual who takes things as he finds them and can find gilded linings to every cloud... without any tinge of affectation or egotism, which might be easily overlooked in the case of so young a man who has attained such prominence in his chosen profession. But Chase is as free and open in his dealings with other humans as the most critical person could wish and has a kindly considerateness in his make-up which is particularly reassuring ... [16]

By the end of June, Chase's constant infirmities, marital problems, and envy caused by Wolverton's hiring contributed to his slump. Most recently, he was hit in the chest by a bat that flew from the hands of a player. Nothing was going right for Chase. Sportswriters wrote how he needed a fresh start somewhere else, which was understandable. But in spite of trade rumors, Chase finished the season in New York. Hit hit a lackluster .274 and reached base less than thirty percent of at bats.

Chase completed the season. Harry Wolter wasn't as fortunate. Harry started the season on a tear. In the first twelve games, he had eleven hits, ten

---

[A] Official Web Site of the New York Yankees. That the Yankees added pinstripes to make Babe Ruth appear thinner is myth, as Ruth was not yet on the team when the pinstripes were added.

walks, eight runs scored, and five stolen bases. But on his way out to the field the next game, he noticed that he put his stirrup socks on backwards. Temporarily unconcerned about the possible jinx, Wolter returned to the clubhouse to fix the socks. During the game at Hilltop Park, Wolter slid awkwardly into second base and broke his left leg just above the ankle. He was out for the remainder of the season. Wolter, now forever afraid of the jinx, would never again change his uniform once outside of the clubhouse.

In the spring of 1912, Vernon owner Ed Maier hoped his Vernon Tigers would avoid a jinx during the upcoming season. For opening day, Hogan and Maier organized an automobile parade through downtown Los Angeles to kick off the campaign featuring a brass band, a speech by the mayor, and comments from other local politicians. The Los Angeles community embraced Maier's Vernon squad. They played Graham's Sacramento squad in the first game. Frank Arellanes, fully recovered from his winter illnesses, hurled for Sacramento in the first game. Hogan sent Spider Baum to the mound to challenge him.

A week later, the sportsman Maier sponsored racecar driver Barney Oldfield at the Santa Monica Gran Prix. The Los Angeles Times wrote, "Eddie Maier, of the Maier Brewing Company, purchased the "Select Kid," the big Fiat Barney Oldfield drove, and made it possible for the former world's speed king to be a drawing card for the big road battle."

A month later, as Maier customarily did each May, he opened up his Maier Ranch for a large social event for Los Angeles' leaders. He entertained 4,000 Shriners with his typical elaborate barbecue at a cost of $7,500. As usual, he organized games and other activities and chartered a special train to carry the passengers to and from the all-day event.[17]

In July, Sacramento and Patsy O'Rourke returned to Vernon to play the Tigers. Patsy stopped in at Hap Hogan's pool hall and played "fifty-hall straight pool." The newspaper reported that he wore a flaming red necktie. O'Rourke admitted that he got jinxed when he played at Hap's pool hall because he couldn't avoid getting angry when in town to play Hap. But O'Rourke's blood appeared to boil during most endeavors. While in Los Angeles, he reiterated comments from the previous year that the players in the PCL were too nice.

Not nice however, was the boxing match that Hogan and O'Rourke watched at Vernon the week of their series together on July 4. The match became one of the greatest in the history of Vernon boxing. Champion Ad Wolgast fought Mexican Joe Rivers for the title. Wolgast was 54-6-10 coming in. Rivers had a record of 15-1-2. Both fought furiously through regulation, without either showing dominance. As the match concluded, both delivered simultaneous blows that knocked each of them out. Referee Jack Welch counted to ten, but the bell went off at the count of four. Technically the round ended with the bell. But in a controversial decision, the referee awarded the match to Wolgast claiming he began to rise before the "ten count" concluded.

As the population of Los Angeles exploded, it became a center for sports and entertainment in the West. Some developers invested in ocean front amusement parks, particularly in Venice, the other wet city near Los Angeles. Ed Maier announced that he too intended to build a new amusement pier at Center Street, five blocks south of the current popular destination known as the Abbot Kinney Pier. He announced his plans prior to a terrible fire that hit the Ocean Park Pier, which made his plans more viable due to the elimination of a potential competitor. It was to be a 1,300-foot concrete pier featuring rides and parking. When his contractor partner disputed him over fees for construction, however, Maier simply walked away, and the pier was never built.[18]

But Maier was still enamored with the Venice party town. By the end of 1912, PCL President Allen Baum decided that having a bar attached to the outfield fence of a league ballpark was unacceptable. He felt that the town of Vernon was too rough for the league. The league owners voted to move the Tigers out of Vernon. So Maier moved his team to Venice. For the 1913 season, the team became the Venice Tigers.[A] Maier built a ballpark for $125,000 and promised to have it built by the time the Chicago White Sox arrived for spring training. He completed it in twenty-seven days. When the team moved back to Vernon two years later, Maier dismantled the entire ballpark and re-assembled it in Vernon. Even the grass was cut up and transplanted. The second move cost $75,000. So Maier paid $200,000 for ballparks over a two-year period. But he was never concerned with expense. According to the newspaper, "He was big time."[19]

Hap Hogan's popularity continued to grow. Even though PCL President Allen Baum warned Hogan about yelling at opposing players, Hogan knew the rebuke would have no impact on his popularity. He commented, "The statement by the president of the league that I will be fined every time I address a player of the opposing team will make no impression on the Vernon boys." The unabashed Hogan did whatever he felt was necessary to spark his team to victory. Hogan became so popular that he signed a contract to perform a baseball monologue at a local theater. He received $500 per week, much more than he received for playing baseball. The show was not only a testament to Hogan's appeal, but to the trend to sign athletes and other sports notables for vaudeville shows.

With the Sacramento team mired deeply in the cellar of the PCL, O'Rourke's spirited manner didn't earn him the popularity afforded the winning Hogan. The papers reported that he got off on the wrong foot with two or three players, and they insisted he depart. Considering the team's record and Patsy's volatile demeanor, Graham complied. Although Graham kept Patsy through

---

[A] On Sundays or holidays when alcohol could not be served in Venice, the team played its games in Los Angeles at Washington Park (formerly Chutes Park), the home of the Angels.

season's end, Oakland, San Franciso, and Vernon contacted Patsy about joining their clubs for the next season. O'Rourke agreed to join Hogan in Vernon.

Fortunately for Mike Donlin, recently dismissed from the New York Giants and Boston Rustlers, he found a home in July in Pittsburgh. He completed the season with reasonable results, hitting .316. But the Pirates still released him in the fall.

Released by the Pirates, Turkey Mike Donlin neared the end of his baseball career. Perhaps some felt that he would return to a life on Broadway or Vaudeville performing with his beloved wife Mabel Hite. But soon after Donlin received his release from Pittsburgh, Donlin's wife Mabel died from cancer.

The Yankees finished the 1912 season with a terrible record. Wolverton inherited a team in shambles. His winning percentage of .329 (50-102) remains the worst in franchise history. He was released at the end of the season. Charlie Graham quickly contacted Wolverton and hired him to replace Patsy O'Rourke. That transaction turned out to be one of Graham's most fortuitous exchanges – a seasoned leader for a volatile youngster. Wolverton turned the Sacramento franchise around and challenged Portland for the championship in 1913.

The Boston Red Sox, with new owner James McAleer, won the World Series in 1912. And like many World Series before and after this date, the results were plagued by rumors of a fix. Boston sportswriter Tim Murnane suspected that some poor performances by Boston pitchers were deliberate. Game 2 was played to a 2-2 tie and called due to darkness. The National Commission ruled that the players were not entitled to their regular share of the gate receipts due to the game not being played to a conclusion. So Murnane believed that players colluded to lose games throughout the series so that more games would be played to maximize their share of the receipts. There was no proof, as there rarely is, but the 1912 World Series represented one more episode of public suspicion regarding fixes that would haunt the Series throughout the decade.

---

[1] History of Baseball in California and Pacific Coast Leagues 1847-1938, Fred W. Lange, p.65

[2] Baseball Magazine, Walter Johnson On Baseball Slavery; "The Great American Principle of Dog Eat Dog" by Johnson, Walter, July, 1911 (Vol. 7, Issue 3) -- p. 75, 2 page(s)

[3] Cobb, A Biography, Al Stump

[4] Cobb, A Biography, Al Stump

[5] Cobb, A Biography, Al Stump

[6] Wolter to Coach Santa Clara Team, San Francisco Chronicle, Dec 3, 1911, pg 59

[7] Hal Chase Will Try Hand At Second Base, SF Chronicle, Oct 31, 1911, pg. 9

[8] Arellanes Married to Society Belle of San Jose, Dec 15, 1911, pg 10

[9] Arellanes, Groom, Is Ill In San Jose Home, San Francisco Chronicle, Jan 3, 1912, pg. 13

[10] Hal Chase Big Noise In Beating Fraser Photos, San Francisco Chronicle, Jan 12, 1914, p. 4

[11] Happy Hogan Was Real Card At Meeting, FA Purner, San Francisco Chronicle, Dec 2, 1911, pg. 11

[12] Happy Hogan of Vernon a Gay Deciever, San Francisco Chronicle, Dec. 8, 1911, pg. 10

[13] The Breeders' Race Meeting, San Francisco Chronicle, Mar 27, 1912, pg. 10

[14] City of Vernon, A Collection of City of Vernon: a collection of oral histories, Marianne Dissard, California State University Fullerton Oral History Program, 1995
[15] Hal Chase Seriously Ill in a New York Sanatorium, San Francisco Chronicle, May 8, 1912, pg. 10
[16] F.C. Lane, Baseball Magazine June, 1912.
[17] Four Thousand Going, Los Angeles Times, May 8, 1912 page 115
[18] Never Built Projects, Copyrighted 1998 by Jeffrey Stanton
[19] The Sports Parade, Braven Dyer, Los Angeles Times, Dec 15, 1943, pg. A7

Chapter 14

Chase And Chance Reunited in New York

With the New York Yankee franchise spiraling downward, Frank Farrell looked for a big name to turn around the squad. He needed someone whose stature rose above any political pettiness in the clubhouse, whose experience demonstrated an ability to win at the highest level, and whose toughness would not tolerate distraction or excuses. With Ban Johnson's recommendation and blessing, Frank Farrell contacted Frank Chance in Los Angeles. He offered Chance $20,000 to manage the team. Considering that stars of the day made closer to $10,000 per year, the offer was considerable. After some posturing customary in a negotiation, Frank Chance agreed to manage the New York Americans in 1913.

During the winter, the California exhibition season began. Hap Hogan lost to Frank Chance in an All-Star game for charity. Another All-Star team from Oxnard challenged a team assembled by Ed Maier. Giants' first baseman Fred Snodgrass, who hailed from Oxnard, recruited New York teammates Chief Meyers, Art Fromme, and Art Shafer to join Kid Mohler and Harry Hooper. Maier's team countered with Jack Bliss, Orval Overall, Roy Brashear, Rube Ellis, and Jake Stahl. Three thousand people attended and more than two hundred cars parked beyond the outfield fence.

Further south, Rube Foster's Giants returned once again to compete in the Winter League.

When the Chisox arrived for spring training, they took on Graham's Sacramento club. The Chisox would have lost if not for Arellanes giving up six runs in one inning. The Chisox then traveled down to Venice for the grand opening of the new ballpark. The game against the Tigers was preceded by a parade from downtown Los Angeles to the ballpark near the ocean. The school children of Venice were given a half-day off school and free admission to the game. They packed the grandstands and bleachers that held 4,000 that day. The White Sox prevailed 7-4.[1]

In spite of the loss, Hap Hogan was characteristically enthusiastic heading into the season. The reporters described him as "a fiery but lovable character." The Venice fans appreciated Hogan most for dedication to making Venice a winner. He loved baseball, and he loved the Venice Tigers. In the past, when Henry Berry joked that he still owned Hogan and would claim him after Hogan was through with the Tigers, Hogan joked about playing ball until his dying day, even if that meant dying as an Angel. A local reporter expressed similar sentiment about the passionate Hogan managing his entire life.

Hap will never quit. When he passes it will be in harness, and his shroud will be a baseball uniform.[2]

The Tigers and Angels opened the Pacific Coast League in a game at Venice on April 6, 1913. The Angels won 3 to 2 when the game was called so that the teams could catch a trolley to Washington Park to play the second half of the double header.[3]

As usual, a month later Venice owner Ed Maier treated seven hundred members of the Elks Club Lodge 99 to a barbecue at Maier Ranch. On May 4, he once again chartered a special train that carried athletes and Elks Club guests to the ranch at 7:30 in the morning. He had turned the ranch turned into an adult playground. Maier encouraged eating, smoking, drinking, and gambling. He gave a tour of the extensive acreage, and fed the guests roast beef, roast pork, roast veal, roast chicken, and other birds. Food was prepared as always "after the manner of the Mexicans." Maier also planned boxing matches and other athletic events including sack races and the like. Acclaimed athletes were present. And no Maier barbecue would be complete without the award for the fattest Elk.[4] Maier hosted a party in a manner only a wealthy owner of a brewery could.

Harry Wolter re-joined the Yankees for spring training in Bermuda after having broken his leg the prior year. He was in good physical shape, and the leg was nearly healed. Chase also arrived in Bermuda and began playing at second base with first baseman Frank Chance now on the team. Chance admitted that he could never be the first baseman that Chase was, but Chase could play other positions. For a few days, Chase played second base well, but on March 8, he severely injured his ankle. With a history of ankle problems, one might suspect that Chase twisted it once again. But a sliding player who struck his ankle on the way into the bag caused the injury.

In 1913, the New York Americans officially changed its name to the Yankees, although the press had been referring to the team as such increasingly for the past few years. The team also moved into the Polo Grounds, which they shared with the New York Giants. With the Yankees coming off their worst season ever, the Giants were not concerned about having to compete for fans within their park. The Giants were regularly one of the best teams in baseball and were undoubtedly the most popular team in New York.[A]

Whether the new Yankee manager was Frank Chance or anyone else, Hal Chase would have had an issue. Chase had been the only Yankee to remain with the franchise since 1905. After seven years as the organization's star, Chase would have harbored envy regarding any skipper. And ever since he challenged

---

[A] They won the pennant in 1904, 1905, 1911, 1912, and would again in 1913. They also won the World Series in 1905.

Chance to baseball games at Chutes Park many years before, Chase's competitive streak didn't allow him to easily accept Chance as his superior.

In terms of style, Chance had a temperament much like the fiery John McGraw. He was both feared and respected by his players. While demanding of them, he'd defend them when the errors were physical rather than mental if effort was sufficient. He was a driver. But unlike McGraw, Chance didn't have an endearing quality that made the players love him. But he did manage the Chicago Cubs to the pennant in 1906, 1907, 1908, and 1910. He also won two World Series for Chicago during that run.[5]

Chance's considerable contract didn't signify a change to his social class. Chance was already the second wealthiest player in the game. He owned a ranch in Glendora, California a few miles east of Los Angeles that he called CUB RANCH where he often spent time recovering from health conditions that plagued him throughout his life. He made his money as a player and an owner. When he played for and managed the Cubs, he held a minority stake in the club. The franchise consistently made over $1 million per year during that period, surpassed only by the New York Giants as a franchise. The value of his stock increased in value many times over. His net worth approached $200,000.[6]

But all the money in the world couldn't give Chance what he wanted most, which was a clean bill of health. In 1912, he had brain surgery to deal with the after effects of bean balls. He had lost all of his hearing in one ear and some in the other.

As a player, Chance was hard-nosed. Christy Mathewson described him in his book Pitching in a Pinch.

> *Chance is the sort of athlete who is likely to get injured. When he was a catcher he was always banged up because he never got out of the way of anything. He is that kind of player. If he has to choose between a pair of spikes in a vital part of his anatomy and getting a put-out, or dodging the spikes and losing the put-out, he always takes the put-out and usually the spikes.*[7]

Frank Chance had always been fond of Hal Chase. He didn't enter the 1913 season harboring any negative predisposition toward his associate from California.

On May 27, Chase married Anna Cherung in Jersey City, New Jersey.[8] Because of his previous divorce in New York to Nellie Heffernan, Hal and Anna weren't able to marry in the State. But the divorce proceedings with Nellie were resolved in April, enabling Hal and Anna to marry a month later. A few days after the wedding, however, the honeymoon between Hal Chase and Frank Chance would abruptly end.

Injuries that hampered his performance in the field continued to plague Chase. The team played poorly, which created frustration and anxiety that

Manager Chance directed toward Chase. Chance approached the press out of frustration and uncharacteristically complained about Chase's play. Farrell had to mediate to keep the issue from blowing up. Chase and Chance were off to a bad start, and Chance wasn't going anywhere. In an interview months later, Chance admitted that although the press accurately reported that he had used the term "laying down" to describe Chase's play, Chance never suspected that Chase was losing games on purpose or not giving his all. He just felt that injuries and age limited his ability to play; he called him "broken". He said,

> .. [Chase is] trying to do his level best, but he just cannot play the way he used to. His days as a star are over. Now he's trying to accomplish things, but it's too late.[9]

The first half of the season under Chance was difficult for Chase. He hit only .212. It appeared that Chance was right – Prince Hal had seen his better days. The slump affected Chase emotionally. Throughout his career, everyone had wanted Hal Chase on his or her team. He had been the star for the Highlanders for many years, extremely popular in New York City. Through all the changes in personnel through the years, Frank Farrell had stuck by his star. But for the first time, Chase no longer felt welcome. The media alienated him, his star had fallen, and the organization showed no particular allegiance to him. Frank Chance later said that Chase once hid in the clubhouse until all of the players had left so that they wouldn't see him crying. Chance was there late and saw Chase on his way out, visibly emotional. Chance claimed that the exchange was emotional for him as well. His claim that Chase was "broken" certainly appeared to have credence. What Chase needed was a change of scenery. He would not likely dig himself out of his condition while with the Yankees.

In fact, two days after his marriage to Anna, Prince Hal dug himself an even deeper hole. Frank Chance had been unaware that Chase enjoyed a practical joke with the other players at the manager's expense. Knowing that Chance was deaf in one ear, Chase used to sit on the side of Chance's bad ear and make fun of him without his knowledge. One day, another player who didn't appreciate Chase's irreverence, particularly since Chance's serious medical condition involved potential blood clots on the brain, told Chance that Chase had been mimicking him in front of the other players. Enraged, Chance immediately sent Chase to the clubhouse. Within days, Farrell traded Chase to the Chicago White Sox.

Rumors had surfaced the past year that the White Sox had been interested in a trade for Chase. Perhaps the teams had been discussing a transaction for some time. Or perhaps Chance traded him immediately after the game with little concern for what he received in exchange. New York received Babe Borton and Rollie Zeider from Charles Comiskey's Chicago White Sox. Comiskey felt that Chase would be good for their young shortstop Buck Weaver, a former San Francisco Seal, who had a tendency to throw balls in the dirt at first base.

Comiskey, a former standout first baseman himself, believed that Chase's unparalleled ability to scoop Weaver's wild throws would improve the team. Chase needed a fresh start, and Comiskey was pleased with his acquisition.

Chance received two players that the media felt were far inferior to Chase's potential. One reporter wrote about Chase:

> *... as a winning factor was through some time ago... That he can play first base as it never was and perhaps never again will be played is well-known truth. That he will is a different matter.*[10]

Taken out of context, some writers have interpreted the above quote to demonstrate that Chase had the ability to play superior first base, but would choose not to. They have implied that he would choose to "lay down" or lose games for betting purposes. However, in the context of the events, the comments reflect the question whether Chase was past his prime. Indeed Chase had potential. But the writer pondered whether Chase would overcome his physical maladies and return to his old form.

Charles Comiskey was a believer. Comiskey willfully conceded Rollie Zeider, who was known to have such a bad bunion condition that he required daily lancings. His nickname was appropriately "Bunion." After Zeider arrived, Chance complained to Chisox manager Nixey Callahan that the extent of Zeider's physical condition had not been fully disclosed. Comiskey also dealt Babe Borton, who many felt was an utter failure. Reporter Mark Roth wrote that Chance made a bad trade. He said, "Chance traded Chase for a bunion and an onion." But Chase would have had no value for Chance in New York. And Chance wouldn't tolerate his immaturity.

As soon as Chase left town, the New York media blasted him. Chase would not be the first New York athlete to be denigrated by the press. They called him "a loafer", "grandstander," "quitter," and a player who was "laying down." Historians have often referred to the articles written about Chase during this period as circumstantial evidence that Chase was taking money to throw games. But the articles mostly featured harsh words by an unforgiving media describing a player who was disenchanted, dispirited, distracted, and in need of a change.

Chase found vindication in Chicago. Over the second half of the season, Chase hit .286 for Chicago, the highest average on the team over that stretch.

---

[1] Venice Sports, Jeffrey Stanton, 1998
[2] Hap Hogan is Dean of Pacific Coast League, Harry A. Williams, Los Angeles Times, March 23, 1913. Pg. VIII6
[3] Venice Sports, Jeffrey Stanton, 1998
[4] Bathe Hoofs in Spring Verdure, Los Angeles Times, May 5, 1913 Page I17
[5] Is M'Graw A Better Manager Than Mack?, Los Angeles Times, Pg. III4, Feb 3, 1914
[6] Huge Profits of Baseball, Special Contribution, Apr 22, 1914, pg. III4
[7] Pitching in a Pinch, Christy Mathewson, pg. 297

[8]   Hal Chase's Wife Suing for Divorce, LA Times, Nov 23, 1920, pg. II11
[9]   Special Correspondence of the Times, Los Angeles Times, Jan 4, 1914, pg. VII4
[10]   The Sporting News, June 12, 1913, W.J. Macbeth

Chapter 15

The 1913 World Baseball Tour

On February 11, 1913, the Chicago White Sox and the New York Giants agreed to stage a World Baseball Tour very similar to the one organized in 1888 by Albert Spalding. They arranged to begin the tour barnstorming west across the United States beginning on October 18. Charles Comiskey and Nixey Callahan gathered a team of predominantly White Sox players that challenged a team of mostly Giants assembled by John McGraw. Callahan, with the support of Comiskey, agreed to finance and promote the tour.

By the time the regular season concluded in 1913, baseball was fast becoming a national and international sensation. During the 1913 World Series between the New York Giants and the Philadelphia Athletics, California fans intently followed each game on billboards that were positioned throughout the town on which regular updates were posted. The Los Angeles Times reported that in Los Angeles,

> ... youngsters and the graybeards, and all the men and some of the women between those two extreme periods of life, halt breathlessly before the bulletins of The Times, furnishing every detail of the game between the Giants and the Athletics just as fast as the wires can rush the information from the scene of action to The Times offices...Baseball ... deserves to be the national game: it represents the epitome of brain and brawn in a friendly contest... Almost within a generation the game has developed from an indifferent and rule-less sport played by boys on vacant lots to an institutional factor in the athletic life of this country... Never in the history of the world has sport that was harmless been so vital. The gladiatorial combats entertained their thousands; the pageant tournaments of chivalry thrilled the medieval multitudes; but the baseball games of this age enthuse practically ninety millions of people.

> All members of the human family love a contest, and when proficiency reduces chance to a minimum, when physical danger is eliminated, when the technical skill is developed to a science, and when the plays may be viewed and understood by even those who are not present, then that contest becomes the most vital that is conceivable in the realms of sport. Such is baseball. [1]

When idol Christy Mathewson shut out Philadelphia to win the second game, twenty thousand fans gladly endured in the rain:

> Lines of men and boys stood all night in the drizzle awaiting the opening

of the gates to the bleachers, and long before noon this section of the stands was crowded to the utmost capacity… Probably 4,000 more saw the game from the roofs of the brick buildings outside the park. The charge to watch from the roof is just thirty cents.[2]

Games at the Polo Grounds attracted a capacity 36,000 fans. But they could not motivate their Giants to victory. In game five, Eddie Plank defeated Christy Mathewson 3-1 on October 11. Mathewson then started packing his bags for the World Tour that started the next Saturday.

The Entertainers

The tour's objective was to entertain. The core rosters came from the Giants and the White Sox. Additional players were added based on the need for the position they played and their relationship with the respective managers. But each player's appeal as an attraction was paramount. Players were equally welcome to either star in the field or entertain on the sidelines.

The most qualified for the latter was Germany Schaefer. The clown prince of baseball, Schaefer was at the end of his career when the tour began. In spite of his diminishing skill, he remained a popular spectacle. He was baseball's current master of shadowball, exaggerated theatrical movements acted out on a baseball field without a ball, often in the form of "phantom" infield practice. Schaefer tickled the fans into hysterics with his shadowball, juggling, and wisecracks directed toward the opposing team's dugout.

Schaefer was a loveable clown, but he could also play baseball. Earlier in his career, he was called to pinch hit against the White Sox with his Tigers down by one run with two outs in the ninth and a runner on base. As Schaefer approached the plate, he announced to the crowd,

"Ladies and Gentleman, you are now looking at Herman Schaefer, better known as "Herman the Great," acknowledged by one and all to be the greatest pinch hitter in the world. I am now going to hit the ball into the left field bleachers. Thank you."

Schaefer during pre-game hijinx at the opposing team's dugout. He grabbed a camera and asked the Highlanders to pose for him. The man in the derby enjoys the show.

World Tour Lineups

GIANTS (NATIONAL LEAGUE)	WHITE SOX (AMERICAN LEAGUE)
Christy Mathewson, P – Domestic	Reb Russell, P – Domestic
Jeff Tesreau, P – Domestic	Jim Scott, P
Al Demaree, P	Red Faber, P – International
Art Fromme, P	Walter Leverenz, P (AL - Browns)
Hooks Wiltse, P	Joe Benz, P
Bunny Hearn, P	Doc White, P
Chief Meyers, C – Domestic	Ray Schalk, C - Domestic
Ivey Wingo, C (NL - Cardinals)	Tom Daly, C
Jack Bliss, C (NL - Cardinals)	
Fred Merkle, 1B	Hal Chase, 1B – Domestic
	Frank Isbell, 1B - Domestic (due to injury)
Larry Doyle, 2B	Germany Schaefer, 2B (AL - Senators)
Dick Egan, Infield (NL - Cardinals)	Morrie Rath, 2B - Domestic
	Joe Berger, 2B
Mickey Doolan, SS (NL - Phillies)	Buck Weaver, SS
Hans Lobert, 3B (NL - Phillies)	Don Rader, 3B
Mike Donlin, OF	Sam Crawford, OF (AL - Tigers)
Jim Thorpe, OF	Tris Speaker, OF (AL - Red Sox) – International
Fred Snodgrass, OF	Ping Bodie, OF - Domestic
Steve Evans, OF (NL - Cardinals)	Wally Mattick, OF
Lee Magee, OF (NL - Cardinals)	
Umpire Bill Klem	Umpire Jack Sheridan
	Walter Johnson, P (AL - Senators: 1 game)
John McGraw, Manager	Nixey Callahan, Manager (Financier)

Off of Chicago's Doc White, he hit the first pitch over the fence. As he circled the bases, he slid into first, second, third, and home. As he jogged around the horn, he announced his progress, as if he were a horse in a horse race. "And Schaefer rounds first base. He is ahead by a neck. Schaefer leads at the half. Around the turn, he is holding his lead. He scores and wins the game!" Following a dramatic and dusty hook slide into home plate, he popped up, doffed his cap to the crowd and announced,

Ladies and Gentlemen, this concludes this afternoon's performance. I thank you for your attention.

In another game, after Schaefer hit a home run off legendary Rube Waddell, he circled the bases holding his bat as if it were a gun, shooting at Waddell all the way around the diamond.

In a game played under rainy conditions, when it was Schaefer's turn to hit, he went to the plate wearing a yellow slicker and rain boots. At other times, he chose to wear a fake mustache when at the plate.

In the field, Schaefer persistently talked to the base runners, trying to throw them off their game. He used his reputation as a talker to his advantage, often engaging the runner in conversation, and then tagging him out with the "hidden ball" trick.

In recent years, Schaefer served both as a player and coach; when not playing, he manned the first base coach's box when his team was at bat. Between innings, he often had the crowd in stitches. One time, he brought a box of popcorn with him to the first base box and ate while the inning was played. Walking from the third base dugout to first base coach's box, he frequently walked up the first base line as if he were a tightrope walker in a death-defying high wire balancing act. At other times, he took two bats with him to the box, and while holding the knobs in his hands like oars, he'd pretend to row himself across the grass.

Perhaps the strangest thing that Schaefer did, however, was base running. He was a smart player who enjoyed the bunt, the steal, and the manufactured run. Whenever he was on first and a runner was on third, he forced a pick-off play so that the man on third could run home for the score. On one occasion, after he drew a walk, he jogged to first, and then started walking to second. The defensive team ignored him, conceding second base. Frustrated, on the next pitch Germany took off from second base backwards and slid in safely at first. He had stolen first base. It was the first recorded steal of first base. Schaefer repeated the steal of first base at other times in his career until the rules were changed disallowing it.

Other entertainers and jokesters were featured on the tour. The compassionate John McGraw offered Mike Donlin, recovering from his wife's death and still seeking an opportunity to return to baseball, a role in the tour. Donlin's experience as a formal entertainer exceeded that of many of the other players. His experience as a showman was perhaps as big as in the sports world. But as a showman, he always took a backseat to his wife's celebrity. Even though Mike had been a popular baseball player in New York, Donlin became known in New York as "Mabel's Mike."

Other players on the tour also performed in vaudeville. Pitcher Jim Scott dated Harriet "Hattie" Cook, one of the four Cook Sisters, who performed in a vaudeville act known as "The American Girl Quartet." Teammate and shortstop Buck Weaver, another player on the tour, dated another one of the Cook sisters, Helen. Scott and Weaver later became brothers-in-law when they married the sisters. Buck and Helen were married prior to leaving on the World Tour. Helen joined Buck on the tour, which became a honeymoon for them. Helen was also a popular silent movie actress who had roles with Will Rogers and William Fairbanks. The two ballplayers and the two beautiful and talented sisters formed their own vaudeville act and performed periodically.

Pitcher Christy Mathewson and his regular season and tour catcher, John "Chief" Meyers, had a vaudeville act that they performed at the Colonial Theater in New York called "Curves," written by sportswriter Bozeman Bulger, the ghost writer for Mathewson's famous "Matty Books" for children. For some shows, Matthewson received nearly $1,000 per week, compared to $10,000 per season for baseball (Matty claimed to have made more money outside of baseball; he specifically claimed to make more from poker than baseball). In the show, the players wore their uniforms while Mathewson demonstrated pitches and Meyers explained how to play catcher. They later joined a vaudeville act in which Matthewson dressed up as a cowboy, and came to the rescue of the forlorn maiden captured by the bad Indian, played by Meyers, by hitting him in the head with a baseball.

John McGraw also made $2,500 per week in 1912 for a monologue called "Inside Baseball." Frank "Ping" Bodie, another colorful character, was a fun-loving center of attention on a tour filled with attention-getters. With a contagious twinkle in his eye, all loved Ping, even though he was a relentless braggart. He'd brag about his minor league record 30 home runs in 1910 for the San Francisco Seals, or his victory over an ostrich in a spaghetti-eating contest (Percy the ostrich passed out after 11 plates of pasta). Ping Bodie was a better minor leaguer than a major league player. He swung a 52-inch bat and was nicknamed "Ping" for the sound the ball made when he connected. He began his career with the San Francisco Seals in 1908. When he arrived, the Seals were a relatively weak squad. But a year later his team edged Portland for the Pacific Coast League championship. He and Seals teammate Buck Weaver later signed with the Chisox.

When he first joined the Chisox, Bodie didn't see the field much. But Comiskey was unhappy about the lack of hitting on the team and said so publicly. So Ping approached the owner and said, "You want some hitting, put me in the lineup." Comiskey told manager Callahan to give Bodie a try. He became a regular, hitting .289 with 97 RBI his first year.

Other former vaudevillians on the tour included Larry Doyle and songwriter Doc White, who had sung in a quartet with pitching great Addie Joss before his early death. And often silly Hans Lobert and Steve Evans added comic relief along the way.

The Pitchers

Christy Mathewson was the pride of the tour's pitching staff. The teams featured marquis players of the times, but fans understandably wanted to see Mathewson pitch every game. The tour played a game every day for months, so the burden on the mound had to be shared by the entire staff of hurlers. Even though Mathewson was the dominant pitcher on the tour, he actually lost more games than he won during the trip.

The Giants and the White Sox each provided two twenty-game winners. The Giants supplied Mathewson and Jeff Tesreau. The White Sox sent Reb

Russell, a twenty-three game winner as a rookie, and "Death Valley" Jim Scott.

"Death Valley" Jim Scott had just won twenty games for the Chicago White Sox. A big hurler at 6'1" and 235 pounds, Scott derived his name from an iconic figure in the early 1900's, Walter Scott, who gained notoriety as "Death Valley Scotty." Scotty was a performer and con man who eventually built a castle in Death Valley known as "Scotty's Castle". He gained infamy by conning New York businessmen out of thousands of dollars by selling them the rights to fictitious gold mines. In 1905, he gained national acclaim with a promotional stunt to break the cross-country train speed record. Upon the train, the "Death Valley Coyote", Scotty broke the record for a trip from Los Angeles to Chicago. Since pitcher Jim Scott's middle name was Walter, even though he hailed from Deadwood South Dakota via San Francisco, teammates gave him the nickname "Death Valley" Scott.

Another pitcher named Urban "Red" Faber attempted to break into the major leagues via the tour. He had not yet pitched a season in the majors. In 1911, Faber threw out his arm in a long-distance throwing contest while playing for the Minneapolis Millers. His infirmity forced him to learn the spitball, which he used with sufficient success to attempt a comeback. In the closing weeks of the 1913 season, Comiskey saw Faber and signed him for the 1914 season. He was then added to the touring team.

Certainly the best pitcher on the tour was Christy Mathewson of the Giants. Mathewson was the most popular baseball player of the era. He was the best pitcher on the best team, the New York Giants. His persona grew legendary. He was the golden boy of the game. On one train trip that Mathewson took with his newlywed wife, the conductor posted a sign that read:

Christy Mathewson

From "Pitching in a Pinch"
by Christy Mathewson

> *Christy Mathewson and Newlywed Wife Are On This Train. Make Them Feel At Home. Note: He Will Be Easily Recognized By His Boyish Countenance and Apollo Like Form.*

In the foreword to Christy Mathewson's book <u>Pitching in a Pinch</u>, John Wheeler described "Big Six" in the following way:

> *Introducing a reader to Christy Mathewson seems a superfluous piece of writing and a waste of white paper. Schoolboys of the last ten years have been acquainted with the exact figures which have made up Matty's pitching record before they had ever heard of George Washington, because George didn't play in the same League.[3]*

Mathewson was best known for his control. The young journalist Ring Lardner once spun the following description of Christy's abilities:

... they ain't nobody else in the world that can stick a ball as near where they want to stick it as he can. I bet he could shave you if he wanted to if he had a razor to throw instead of a ball. . . . I an't tryin' to make you believe that he don't never fail to pitch where he's aimin' at. If he done that, he wouldn't be here; he'd be workin' agin the angels in St. Peter's League. But he's got ten to one better control than any guy I ever seen, and I've seen all the best o' them.

Mathewson amassed 373 career wins and a 2.13 lifetime earned run average. He became the first real baseball hero, an enigma playing in the National League and for John McGraw. In the past, few good players existed that the fans admired for their respectable character. Generally baseball players were considered rough - not the sort that parents wanted their children to emulate. That all changed with Mathewson.

The Star Fielders

The position players on the tour included two American Indians who drew Indian fans to games throughout the Midwest. John "Chief" Meyers, Mathewson's catcher for the New York Giants, had been one of the best players in the game the past three seasons. John Meyers was a Cahuilla Indian from Riverside, California. Between 1911 and 1913, when the Giants won three consecutive pennants, Meyers hit .332, .358, and .312 finishing among the top vote getters for MVP all three seasons.

Since his father died when he was seven, Meyers' mother raised him while working at the Mission Inn in Riverside. Meyers dropped out of high school and worked at a raisin packing plant. While playing ball in New Mexico, Meyers was spotted by a Dartmouth College player, Ralph Glaze, who convinced the school to recruit him. But Meyers had drawn the attention of a semi-pro team that offered him five times what he made packing raisins. He attended Dartmouth briefly, and then signed to play professional baseball.

Another American Indian on the tour was Jim Thorpe of the New York Giants. One of the country's greatest athletes, Thorpe had attended the Carlisle Indian Industrial School where the legendary football coach Glenn "Pop" Warner coached him. While Thorpe excelled most at football, where he led his Carlisle team to a national championship in 1912 and was named All American in 1911 and 1912, he gained fame in track and field. The prior year, at the 1912 Olympics, he won gold medals in the pentathlon and decathlon. Thorpe returned from the Olympics a national hero. He was honored with a ticker tape parade in New York City. Soon thereafter, he joined the Giants for thirty-eight at bats and then joined the World Tour. Wherever the team went on the tour, Thorpe was the center of attention, particularly overseas, where people continually yelled his name. Thorpe married wife Iva in 1913. They were one of the couples that seized the opportunity presented by the tour to honeymoon while traveling the world.

Thorpe's wife Iva was probably the second most recognizable person when the team went abroad since fans knew her from photos, standing next to Thorpe, in the papers during the Olympics.

Baseball superstars on the tour included Sam Crawford and Tris Speaker in the outfield, joined by Snodgrass. 1912 league MVP Larry Doyle played second. Speedy Hans Lobert, the game's fastest player, played the infield. "Good field, no hit" Mickey Doolan and Buck Weaver, not yet converted to third base, manned shortstop. Catcher Ray Schalk was behind the plate for the American Leaguers. Hal Chase and Fred Merkle covered first base.

The tour began in Cincinnati, Ohio. The team then traveled westward via train playing a game nearly each day in a different town. Six ballplayers and their newlyweds honeymooned on the tour, including Hal and Anna Chase, Hans Lobert, Jim Thorpe, Buck Weaver, Sam Crawford, and Larry Doyle. The tour also included reporters George Rice (Chicago Journal), I.E. "Cy" Sanborn (Chicago Tribune), George Robbing, Irving Vaughn (Chicago Tribune), Larry Woltz, and Malcolm McLean. During different legs, the tour was accompanied by Charles Comiskey and his parents, Frank Farrell and his parents, James McAleer, Mrs. John McGraw, Nixie Callahan's wife and children, and Eddie Maier, who "selected" 4,000 bottles of wine for the sixteen-day trip overseas.[4]

In addition to drinking, singing, and dancing, the players enjoyed a continuous card game. Buck Weaver reported being up $400 on a game after being behind $86 when he left Seattle.

The trip was filled with levity and fun, as the players understood their role as ambassadors. But on the field, the competitors removed their party hats and lampshades and battled one another as if each game was the World Series. And off the field, as the teams navigated the globe, another battled raged.

The 1913 World Tour - America

Just as the tour began, a new professional league formed that threatened to steal the best players from Organized Baseball. The new Federal League declared war on the major leagues. The war would be fought as the touring team circled the globe. The Fed league's president, Edward Krause said from his Indianapolis office:

> It will be war to the hilt with organized baseball from this time forth. We have the money and the ambition to succeed.[5]

US Barnstorming Schedule / Results

Date	Location		Winning Team	Winning Pitcher	Losing Pitcher
Oct 18	Cincinnatti, Ohio	11-2	Nationals	Mathewson (1-0)	Benz (0-1)
Oct 19	Chicago, Illinois	3-1	Nationals	Demaree (1-0)	Russell (0-1)
Oct 20	Sprinfield, Illinois	6-4	Nationals	Fromme (1-0)	Scott (0-1)
Oct 21	Peoria, Illinois	6-4	Chisox	Leverenz (2-0)	Wiltse (0-1)
Oct 22	Ottumma, Illinois	7-3	Chisox	Russell (1-1)	Tesreau (0-1)
Oct 23	Sioux City, Illinois	6-3	Nationals	Fromme (2-0)	Scott (0-2)
Oct 24	Blue Rapids, Kansas	8-5	Chisox	Benz (1-1)	Wiltse (0-2)
Oct 25	St. Joseph, Missouri	4-3	Chisox	Leverenz (2-0)	Mathewson (1-1)
Oct 26	Kansas City, Missouri	6-2	Nationals	Tesreau (1-1)	Faber (0-1)
Oct 27	Joplin, Missouri	13-12	Nationals	Fromme (3-0)	Benz (1-2)
Oct 28	Tulsa, Oklahoma	6-0	Chisox	Johnson (1-0)	Mathewson (1-2)
Oct 29	Muskogee, Oklahoma	7-1	Chisox	Scott (1-2)	Fromme (3-1)
Oct 30	Bonham, Texas	4-1	Nationals	Tesreau (2-1)	Russell (1-2)
Oct 31	Dallas, Texas	9-3	Chisox	Leverenz (3-0)	Mathewson (1-3)
Nov 1	Beaumont, Texas	3-2	Nationals	Wiltse (1-2)	Benz (1-3)
Nov 2	Houston, Texas	9-4	Chisox	Russell (3-2)	Fromme (3-2)
Nov 3	Marlin, Texas	11-1	Nationals	Tesreau (3-1)	Benz (1-4)
Nov 4	Abilene, Texas	Rain			
Nov 5	El Paso, Texas	10-7	Chisox	Scott (2-2)	Mathewson (1-4)
Nov 6	Douglas, Arizona	14-5	Nationals	Wiltse (2-2)	Leverenz (3-1)
Nov 7	Bisbee, Arizona	9-1	Nationals	Fromme (4-2)	Faber (0-2)
Nov 8	Los Angeles, CA	5-3	Chisox	Russell (3-2)	Mathewson (1-5)
Nov 9	Los Angeles, CA	7-7	Tie		
Nov 10	San Diego, California	4-3	Nationals	Hearn (1-0)	Scott (2-3)
Nov 11	Oxnard, California	3-2	Nationals	Mathewson (2-5)	Benz (1-5)
Nov 12	Sacramento, CA	Rain			
Nov 13	Oakland, California	5-2	Chisox	Russell (4-2)	Wiltse (2-3)
Nov 14	San Francisco, CA	3-2	Chisox	Benz (2-5)	Fromme (4-3)
Nov 15	San Francisco, CA	6-3	Nationals	Mathewson (3-5)	Scott (2-4)
Nov 16	Oakland, California	12-8	Chisox	Faber (1-2)	Hearn (1-1)
Nov 16	San Francisco, CA	4-2	Chisox	Russell (5-2)	Tesreau (3-2)
Nov 17	Medford, Oregon	3-0	Nationals	Wiltse (3-3)	Benz (2-6)
Nov 18	Portland, Oregon	2-0	Chisox	Scott (3-4)	Fromme (4-4)
Nov 19	Tacoma, WA	Rain			
Nov 20	Seattle, WA	Rain			

Ban Johnson surprised the owners when he didn't condemn nor counter-attack the Federal League. While Johnson acted in the interests of the owners, he also had become disgusted in recent years by their activities. He didn't explicitly name names or reveal the types of indiscretions he found reprehensible. But through the episode that led to the death of Pulliam, and the many other activities that Johnson uncovered over the years, it seemed likely that gambling and game fixes were on the list of unsavory activities. But he was most upset by owners who damaged their franchises and the competitiveness of the league by mismanaging players. He felt the competition from the Federal League would be good for the game.

> *...The Federal League ... will result in a general house cleaning...Elimination of undesirable persons who have been attracted to baseball by the apparently easy path to wealth offered by it, eradication of evils which have crept into the sport..., and the elevation of the game to a higher, cleaner, sporting plane... It may prove the proverbial broom. Mind you, I do not say the American League club owners will welcome a battle as a rule. I am speaking from the broader standpoint of baseball as a national sport. I hope the result will be ... the eradication of some of the methods that are anything but good for the sport. The fight is likely to be the hottest in Chicago.... the losers will have only themselves to blame.*[6]

Johnson pointed out that the main battleground would be fought in Chicago. Perhaps his comments were an indictment of his friend Comiskey, who owned the only team in Chicago in his American League. But more likely he referred to the Cubs owner Charles Murphy who had been a recent thorn in the side of National League President John Tener. Murphy was unpopular with players and the other owners. Because of a dispute with his managers, including Frank Chance, Murphy began disassembling his team. Murphy had also voted against hiring John Tener, being the sole dissenter because he felt Tener's salary was too high. With no love lost between them, Tener negotiated actively for new ownership in Chicago. He brokered a bid between Charles Taft, Charles Weeghman, and Harry Sinclair. Taft won the bid and purchased the club a little more than a month after Johnson made the comments above. Weeghman and Sinclair then directed their interests toward the Federal League, where they became significant financial backers. Johnson's conciliatory attitude toward soon-to-be rivals Weeghman and Sinclair was understandable, as they very nearly became part of Organized Baseball instead of the Feds.

At thirty-eight, Weeghman was a self-made millionaire. Son of a blacksmith, he arrived in Chicago with $5 in his pocket, took a job as a cook, and worked his way up until he purchased his own restaurant. He claimed to be accustomed to eighteen-hour workdays his entire life. By the time he purchased the Chicago entry into the Federal League, he owned ten restaurants, a theater, a billiard hall, and part of a coal company. When he assumed the Chicago club, he hired Joe Tinker from the Cubs to be his manager. [7] Weeghman soon signed a 99-year lease on property in the northern portion of the City where he began building a new park. Securing a ballpark would be critical for each city as it battled the major leagues. In St. Louis, the building commissioner condemned the grandstands erected for their new Federal League ballpark because it was not sufficiently fire proof.[8] It was not clear whether major league baseball influenced the decision. The impediment proved damaging considering the fragile circumstances facing the franchises as opening day approached.

The battle soon waged by Weeghman and his Federal League partners found its way to the courts. Weeghman stated his case:

> *The major leagues are infringing on the Sherman anti-trust law, and it is about time they stopped it. We have hired competent lawyers, who know how to handle a case of this importance, and before the war is over there will be some astonishing facts made known to the baseball public. They have been exercising an injunction restraining a player from competing in the Federal League, and we are going to force them into court to settle the dispute... The Federal League wants to clean out organized baseball... it is open to the star ball players, and intends to treat them like human beings. We will have no strings attached to the players.[9]*

Pennsylvania Governor Tener countered:

> *... the Federal League has officially announced that it will test the reserve clause in the courts... it will seek to have organized baseball investigated and dissolved as a trust...it is well known that the legality of the present form of the contract between the league and players was attacked, but its validity in law and equity was sustained by the Supreme Court in Pennsylvania in the Lajoie case.[10]*

The emergence of the Federal League provided an interesting backdrop for the World Tour. On October 23, when Art Fromme won his second consecutive game of the tour over Jim Scott in front of four thousand fans in Sioux City, Illinois behind Larry Doyle's three doubles and Sam Crawford's home run, manager John McGraw didn't know that Fromme was simultaneously negotiating with the Federal League. Nearly ever player would negotiate with the Feds over the course of the tour.

In the meantime, Charles Comiskey appeared like the proud and protective parent to his star first baseman Hal Chase. In a game in Kansas City, Chase once again sprained an ankle. The frustrated Comiskey, taking a chapter from his days as a player in the '80s, offered practical advice for baseball. With vehemence he advocated the abolition of the low shoe and recommended the adoption of the old-fashioned high shoe. The paper reported:

> *Comiskey's advocacy of the high shoe grew out of the accident of Hal Chase ... whose disability resulted in the addition of Frank Isbell... The crack first-sacker has been nursing a weak ankle for a whole season, and it interfered with his playing to a considerable extent. The recent sprain happened to the other ankle... When Comiskey played, he always laced up the shoes that supported the ankles.[11]*

The day Comiskey's comments became public, the All Stars played the most notable game of the tour in Tulsa, Oklahoma. Throughout the tour, every city wanted to see Christy Mathewson pitch. Yet only eight cities would experience Matty on the mound. On October 28, the city of Tulsa would not only see Matty, but also witness a showdown with the greatest pitcher in baseball history, Walter Johnson. Mathewson was the most popular player in America, having led his team to the World Series behind a record of 25-11 and a 2.06 ERA. But at thirty-one, his abilities would soon fade just as Johnson's career was taking off. The past year, at the age of twenty-five, Johnson had completed one of the most dominating seasons of any pitcher in baseball history, posting a record of 36-7 with a 1.14 ERA and 243 strikeouts. Naturally, the game was a sellout.

The bleachers in Tulsa had never before been filled to its 700-person capacity. The crowd huddled together to get a glimpse of their heroes on a cold day marked by a storm that dusted snow on the field. Before the game began, tragedy struck. The bleachers collapsed under the weight of the sell-out crowd. Two spectators were killed and dozens hospitalized.[A] In spite of the calamity, the game was played. The two stars battled through the storm, with Johnson chasing Mathewson in the fourth inning. John McGraw, Mathewson's manager, conceded after the game with the plain, uncultivated simplicity of a baseball lifer "Johnson is surely all that has been said about him."

The teams continued to play each day, as the tour progressed westward while swinging south to Texas. There was only one day, a rainout in Abilene, which offered a respite from play. Some of the players stopped in at a bar. One of the young players on the White Sox, catcher Ray Schalk, hung back at the hotel and told Hal Chase, Buck Weaver, Mike Donlin, and Jim Scott that he would catch up with them later.

The four friends preceded Schalk to the bar. Chase and Weaver were very much alike in that they both possessed upbeat dispositions and a passion to play baseball. It was said that Weaver came alive when he took to the field, always with that big grin on his face. All he wanted to do was play ball. He loved to suit up for one more season, for one more game, for one more at bat. Similarly, between major league baseball and winter ball, Chase clandestinely played year round, health permitting. The daily rigor of the World Tour suited the two perfectly, giving them opportunity to play nearly every day - with the approval of major league baseball.

Arriving later to the bar was the catcher Schalk. At just 145 pounds, the slight backstop physically resembled a young schoolboy.[B] The bartender stopped the diminutive major leaguer and said, "We don't serve no school kids in this joint." Schalk turned to his teammates for support, but they stayed quiet and asked the bartender to please remove the youth from the bar.

[A] This was the second game in Mathewson's career that filled grandstands collapsed killing fans.

[B] On the field, he made up for being a small target with energy, quickness, and speed. With his speed, he became the first catcher in baseball to regularly back up first base on grounders to the infield, and third base on throws from the outfield.

Since his ankle injury, Chase didn't play in any games until the teams arrived in Arizona November 5 for games in Douglass and Bisbee. During that era, mining was the largest industry in Arizona, and the two towns that had recently known the likes of Wyatt Earp and Doc Holliday, were home to prominent copper mines. For entertainment, the towns fielded baseball teams that played each other in "Copper Leagues."

Leaving Arizona, the tour headed to Los Angeles. John McGraw had sent a telegram to Henry Berry from the tour announcing that Mathewson would pitch in Los Angeles. But Mathewson refused because the game was played on Sunday. Berry then wired McGraw in Bisbee warning about the possibility of a riot if Matty failed to take the mound. The tour players wanted Mathewson to pitch; they shared 50% of the gate, which could be considerable with two games in Los Angeles.

When the Chicago squad arrived at Washington Park wearing red, white, and blue uniforms, the sell-out crowd stood and cheered. The crowd was filled with fans as well as local sports personalities including Henry Berry, Ed Maier, Hap Hogan, Jim Morley, and Frank Chance. Frank Chance posed for a photo shaking hands with John McGraw while the crowd enjoyed batting practice, infield practice, and a display of "shadow baseball." Then Jim Morley approached the plate with a megaphone to introduce the umpires Bill Klem and Jack Sheridan. Throughout the game, Klem was up to the task as umpire-turned-entertainer, as he bellowed the names of each player as they approached the plate. With a voice described as "lofty bellowing," Klem introduced each player, also offering commentary on why each was noteworthy.

> *[Klem announced about the players]… whether he votes the Republican or Democratic ticket, divulges certain secrets of his past, explains what part he plays in the general scheme of things, and unfurls other important data.*[12]

When Klem introduced Mathewson, the crowd became hysterical.

During the game, Chase doubled to left in the eighth inning and once again drew up lame on his way to second base. The crowd was disappointed to see the former local star leave the game to be replaced by "a comparative stranger from New England." Reb Russell defeated Mathewson 5-3. Harry Williams wrote coarsely of Russell:

> *Lefty can niether read nor write, it is said, and is by no means a fluent speaker, but, believe me, brethren and cistern, there is no impediment in his pitching.*

Williams' crude writing style reflected a rough, frank, and often-insensitive culture in sports coverage that appealed to the public. Williams' tactlessness indicative of the era sometimes included racial bias, including the following comment, intended as a joke, about Jim Thorpe who played for the

Giants squad.

> *... I have reason to suspect that some of Jim's forefathers scalped some of my forefathers, but as he is our guest, it would appear ill-bred of me to display any venom in the matter.*[13]

Harry Williams also reported on the fine play of Chicago shortstop Buck Weaver, former San Francisco standout. Still a question mark in the field, Williams playfully teased manager Nixey Callahan who had been bragging about the progress of his shortstop.

> *From a baseball standpoint, Buck Weaver's brilliant capers at short were the redeeming feature. Buck covered the port side of the place like a tarpaulin, and in other ways convinced the skeptical that the encomiums heaped on him by his busy little press agent were not all bunk.*[14]

When the tour left Los Angeles for San Diego, Hal and Anna Chase remained in Los Angeles to rest Hal's ankle. Anna was also feeling ill. They would re-join the team the next day when it passed through Los Angeles on the way north to Oxnard and the Bay Area. During the week, trade rumors circulated out of Hap Hogan's billiard hall that Nixey Callahan was looking for another outfielder and wanted someone of the caliber of Ty Cobb, Tris Speaker, or Sam Crawford. He indicated that he'd be willing to trade Hal Chase. But the talk was more wishful than substantial. With Chase continually coming up lame, Callahan and Comiskey certainly considered finding value in exchange for their damaged goods. But as the paper reported, if Detroit or Boston gave up on stars such as Crawford, Cobb, or Speaker, they might as well close up their box offices.

When the tour played in San Diego's Athletic Park, an overflow crowd attended to see hometown favorite Chief Meyers. And the next day, Oxnard turned out en masse to see their Fred Snodgrass. The teams arrived at about seven in the morning and were met at the train by ten stagecoaches that carried the players to a ranch for an elaborate barbecue. According to Hans Lobert, Oxnard was great cattle and lima bean country. A large ox had been roasting for two days; for breakfast, the teams ate the ox served with lima beans, onions, and beer.

After the meal, the mayor singled out Lobert, known as the fastest man in baseball, and asked if he would race a horse around the bases during the afternoon game. McGraw talked Hans into agreeing. The race with the horse was supposed to take place after the ball game. But even with Christy Mathewson pitching, the crowd had less interest in the game than they did in seeing Lobert race a horse. Five thousand people packed into rickety stands and lined the perimeter of the fence-less field. Several hundred cowboys on horseback watched from beyond the outfielders. Most had a wager on the outcome of the horse race and couldn't wait for the baseball game to end. The cowboys on horseback kept creeping in closer until they were well in the middle of the outfield.

In the seventh inning, McGraw went up to Lobert and said, "John, we can't finish the game. You might as well get ready to race the horse around the bases." McGraw motioned to the mayor, and the wall of cattlemen parted. A beautiful black horse with a Mexican cowboy dressed in chaps and spangles sauntered forward.

Lobert and the horse walked around the bases to practice. The crowd began to roar in anticipation, and the local news cameras readied to capture the spectacular event. When everything was set, umpire Bill Klem agreed to referee. A pistol was fired, and Lobert led down the first base line by at least five feet. By second base, he was at least ten feet ahead. He was gaining speed as he circled the bases. But between second and third, the horse crowded Lobert and threw him off stride. Hans had to dodge to avoid being knocked down. Still in the lead, Lobert sprinted for home plate. But the horse won. Referring to the size of his prodigious probiscus, Hans Lobert joked after the race, "Umpire Bill Klem announced that the horse won by a nose, but obviously that is impossible."[15]

Mathewson won the game 3-2. Some of Matty's success came from his first attempt to throw a spitball. Chief Meyers, his regular catcher, remained in San Diego after the tour's game there. So a replacement catcher worked with Matty in Oxnard on an experimental spitter. Mathewson had it working, and won only his second game against five losses on the tour. One reporter explained the irony that perhaps they'd soon witness the wholesome Mathewson convert his ways and begin sporting chewing tobacco in his jaw during games.

On the tour, the opponents with whom he shared accommodations didn't particularly like Mathewson. The White Sox admitted that they were cold toward Matty during the trip because they were annoyed that he didn't mix with other players. One reported to Harry Williams:

> When he met us on the street, he couldn't see us. ... I'm not saying he is swelled up. It may just have been his way. But if he couldn't see us on the street we decided to impress him with the fact that we could see him on the ball field.... he speaks to us now, all right.[16]

The teams were rained out in Sacramento, so they continued on for games in San Francisco and Oakland. Many players had played in the Bay Area during their careers, including Donlin, Chase, Weaver, and Bodie. The draw in San Francisco, however, on November 15, 1913 was Christy Mathewson. Ten thousand fans crammed into Recreation Park to watch Matty of the New York Giants face Jim Scott.

It was Christy's last outing on the trip, as he would not continue with the team overseas. Buck Weaver who transformed into a hitting star on the tour, had become Mathewson's nemesis. The San Francisco Chronicle wrote of his

appearance the previous day,

> *Buck Weaver looks like the same old happy-go-lucky kid who made his reputation with the Seals. He appears more finished, however, and certainly has a lot of boosters who claim that he is the coming shortstop of the country.*[A]

The Giants scored five runs in the first three innings. Mike Donlin doubled off Scott, Hans Lobert walked, and Larry Doyle singled. The following inning, Jim Thorpe hit a double and used his world-class speed to score on Chief Meyers' single. The next inning, Buck Weaver made a rare error. His overthrow at first put Mike Donlin on base. The speedy Lobert then beat out Weaver's throw to Hal Chase on a slow roller. Larry Doyle walked to fill the bases. Fred Merkle sacrificed Donlin in from third. Then the floodgates opened. Jim Scott threw a wild pitch. Lobert scored, and then Ray Schalk threw away the throw to the covering pitcher, allowing the second runner Doyle to score. Meanwhile, Matty shut out the Sox until the fifth. The fans yelled for Jim Scott's replacement. Matty cruised the rest of the way to a 6-3 victory. Mathewson pitched the entire game, then went over to the Giants dugout, picked up his six year old son Matty Jr., put him on his shoulders, and walked to the clubhouse to the cheers of the San Francisco fans.

Christy Mathewson with Christy, Jr.

From "Pitching in a Pinch" by Christy Mathewson

The team finished up in the Northwest in Portland and Seattle. In Seattle, Snodgrass was paid a visit by friend and former New York Giants's mascot Charles Victory Faust.

During the 1912 season, Faust's illness and general poor health prevented him from continuing on with the team. When John McGraw broke the news to Faust, Charlie moved to Seattle to live with relatives. In 1913, with McGraw and many of the Giants in Seattle for the World Tour, Faust excitedly contacted his former teammates for a reunion. He reached Snodgrass. "Snow", he said. "I'm not very well. But I think if you could prevail on Mr. McGraw to send me to Hot Springs a month before spring training, I could get into shape and help the Giants win another pennant."

[A] Later in his career, Weaver moved from shortstop to third base for the White Sox.

But Faust would never rejoin the Giants. Later that year, he was admitted to a sanitarium where he died soon thereafter of tuberculosis.

[1] Baseball, King of Sports, Los Angeles Times, Oct 9, 1913, pg II4

[2] Christy Mathewson Is The Scintillating Star, AP Wire to the Times, Oct 9, 1913, pg. III1

[3] <u>Pitching in a Pinch</u>, Christy Mathewson, pg. xiii

[4] Buzzin' Around Town, Gardner Breadford, Los Angeles Times, Feb 3, 1914, III3

[5] Federal League Will Start War On Majors, Los Angeles Times, Oct 16, 1913, III3

[6] Federals Will Be A Benefit? Los Angeles Times, Dec. 31, 1913, Pg. III1

[7] Federal League Boss Began on Nerve and $5, Mar 5, 1914, LA Times, pg. III4

[8] Federal Stands Are Condemned, LA Times, Jun 6, 1914, pg. III3

[9] The Big League War, Los Angeles Times, Jan 1, 1914, pg. III1

[10] National League Policy Clearly Outlined by President John K. Tener, The Sporting Life, January 17, 1914

[11] Comiskey Says Baseball Shoes Should Be Higher, Los Angeles Times, Oct 28,1913, pg III1

[12] Mathewson is Defeated by Chicago White Sox, Harry A. Williams, LA Times, Nov 9, 1913, p. VII1

[13] King Matty on Mound Today, Harry A. Williams, Los Angeles Times, Nov 8, 1913, pg. III1

[14] Mathewson is Defeated by Chicago White Sox, Harry Williams, LA Times, Nov 9, 1913, pg. VII1

[15] <u>The Glory of Their Times: The Story of Baseball Told By the Men Who Played It</u>, Lawrence S. Ritter

[16] White Sox Had Grudge Against C. Mathewson, 11/12/1913, Harry Williams, III3

Chapter 16

The Federal League Attempts to Sink the Majors

The success of the World Tour proved that Baseball had become a spectacle. And few could create a spectacle better than Venice's Ed Maier with the help of his sidekick, Hap Hogan. On June 30, 1913 Maier invited six hundred wholesale and retail liquor dealers to his ranch. He chartered ten coaches on a train out of Los Angeles to carry the men to the sports, baseball game, foot races, keg rolling, Spanish barbecue, and flag raising that Maier had hosted in recent years.

Maier staged a "battle royal" in a boxing ring with some of the greatest fighters of the day, including Joe Walcott, Kid Snowball, Charlie Snow, Jimmie White, and Chick Sunbeam. The last man in the ring would be declared the winner in a no-holds barred event. After five minutes Kid Snowball jumped to his feet after being knocked down and put the last adversary out.

At season's end, Maier had another party, this time for his Venice Tigers and its fans. On October 27, he opened up the ranch with another one of his famous "beef-steak feeds" that lasted for three days. The party also served as a housewarming for the $50,000 country home called "Las Delicias" just recently completed for him and his widowed mother. He hosted more than fifty guests who left for the ranch at 5 pm on a special railroad car. He offered a Castillian banquet, Spanish barbecue, and other epicurean offerings. And once again, he organized athletic events for all participants, including a turtle race between Barney Oldfield and Jim Jeffries, a diving exhibition by Hap Hogan, and three baseball games between two teams – the Selects and the Old Fashions managed by Ed Maier and Hap Hogan respectively. In addition to the Venice players were Tom Darmody, Jack Bliss, Jack Kipper, Art Krueger, Orvie Overall, Lefty Leifeld, Jack McCarthy, Garnet Bush, Jimmie Toman, Frank Chance, Cy Myrick, Jack Jeffries, and newspaper men.[1]

The team celebrated a great season, even though the Tigers finished closely behind Portland and Sacramento in the standings. With Harry Wolverton on board in Sacramento, Graham's Senators surged past the competitive Venice squad and challenged Portland for the championship. Frank Arellanes featured prominently for Graham, who awarded the pitcher a $500 bonus when he won his twelfth game in July. By September, Portland, Sacramento, and Venice were neck and neck headed toward season's end. In a game at Sacramento against Portland, the biggest crowd in the city's history exceeded 6,000.

The excitement of the race and the popularity of the league also attracted riff raff. On September 15, four men were charged with openly offering wagers at Washington Park in Los Angeles in defiance of the gambling law.

Frequent complaints to the police, charging open gambling at the ball parks, brought about the arrest of four men at the close of the game Saturday afternoon at Washington Park.... The betting was carried on openly. Several men stood in the reserved seat section and formed a pool to take all bets offered. These men wagered on the result of any single inning, on the length of time a pitcher would last, on whether or not any given batter would get a "hit", in fact, upon any phase of the game that appealed to the sporting blood of the spectators.... there was no indication of crooked work in connection with the betting. It is simply a plain proposition of betting. According to reports made to the police several prominent men have lost large sums recently at the Los Angeles and Venice ball grounds.[2]

As the off-season began, and the teams speculated about the coming season, the Los Angeles reporters reflected on the personalities of the local owners and management. As Hap prepared to head east for the winter meetings, the Los Angeles Times reported how he professed that Eddie Maier loved to part with his money.

[He was willing to]... loot the big leagues like a pirate boardin' one of them old Spanish galleons I used to read about in dime novels when I was a kid... Then in the spring, Hap comes creakin' out leadin' a bunch of respectable old parties, held together with bandages. Hap divides his time fifty-fifty during the winter. One half of the time he is snoopin' around the alleys behind the other baseball clubs to see what's been throwed out. The rest of the time he is tryin' to patch up what he's got with arnica.[A]

The banter fed to the media by Hap Hogan and Hen Berry in their downtown billiard halls on a rainy afternoon articulated the sentiment of every minor league baseball man across the country. General managers filled rosters with veterans and up-and-coming youngsters. Any success was short lived, as the major leagues scooped up any prospects. Each season represented hopeful re-building, a resurgence of an aging player and the emergence of a superstar. Most often, however, as the reporter described above, while good players passed through, each year ushered in more of the same with the general managers piecing together disparate parts to create an entertaining product for the fans.

The papers depicted Hap Hogan as someone who paraded like Rockefeller, but never quite spent the necessary money to ensure a championship. Instead, he was more like Ford, engineering strong performances through superior management. Hen Berry, on the other hand, was truly willing to spend money.

[A] Arnica: Flowers formerly used as an external application in sprains and bruises. Spark-Plug M'Closky Talks About Hen Berry, Los Angeles Times, Oct 21, 1913

But his manager Pop Dillon was criticized for not getting his team to perform up to expectations.

> *Hen pays real money and gits players and can't make them play. They lay down for him like Maggart done. Hap don't spend no money fer players, but he collects a lot of old parties and makes em play their heads off. Hap ain't got nothing and Hen can't do nothin' with what he's got.[3]*

The reporter also criticized the two general managers for not identifying good prospects, even though many grew up playing in the talent-laden California.

> *... these here green college boys ain't fast enough for Hap Hogan or Hen Berry; they're just good enough fer a few rotten second class teams like Connie Mack's Athletics and the New York Giants. When McGraw was out here in Los Angeles on vacation he seen a couple of kids playin' in a sand-lot game on the St. Vincent's College team, and when he went home he took Snodgrass and Artie Shafer wit him. They wasn't good enough fer Hap er Hen. This poor, miserable busher Walter Johnson wanted to git a job wit the Angels when he was playin' on a hick team in the oil wells, but Dillon looked him over and said he wouldn't do.[4]*

Referring to the veterans that came back from the major leagues, the reporter admitted that Berry's alliance with the Washington Americans was beneficial. But he said that by the time the big leagues were done with a vet, there wasn't much left. He said the players generally looked like "a parade of veterans of Gettysburg."[5]

Hap Hogan rested in Murrietta after the season ended to be at full strength for the winter ahead. Hogan prepared for the normal trades, discards, and acquisitions. What he didn't prepare for was the competition created by the war between the Federal League and Organized Baseball, or the civil war in the Pacific Coast League that nearly shifted the balance of power in Coast Baseball to the outlaw California League.

As the 1913 World Baseball Tour approached Los Angeles from Arizona, Hogan was already on his way to San Francisco to pick up Allen Baum, Cal Ewing, Del Howard, Walt McCredie, Harry Wolverton, Charlie Graham, and others on their way to wheel and deal at the minor leagues' annual meetings in Columbus, Ohio.[6] Because of the timing of the annual event, the league owners and managers missed the touring All-Star team. However, Hen Berry, Ed Maier, and Pop Dillon greeted the tour as it arrived in Los Angeles at the depot on November 8. Hen Berry had refused to attend Baseball's Winter Meetings, still fuming about a controversy during the season over rules that allowed major league teams to re-claim players released the prior year. The issue would be a point of contention at the meetings, but Berry was still too incensed to address it personally. The National Commission ruled that major league teams that waived players by September 15 each year could recall the player until August 15 the following year. The ruling had cost Berry one of his star players the past season. He was none too happy with the National Commission about the ruling.

At the meeting, Hogan hoped to dispose of Patsy O'Rourke, who continued to express dissatisfaction with the Coast and it's style of play, which he described as "too nice." Hogan would grant O'Rourke his wish and attempt a trade or sale that would send him where the game was played more roughly. Hogan received some offers – one for Patsy to manage in the Western League, and another for him to play in Montreal, and then Omaha. But O'Rourke had cost Hogan $750 to acquire from Sacramento, and he held out until he received a similar offer from the East. Hogan ultimately traded Patsy to Louisville, although it took him three months to do it. In Columbus, Hogan also announced the release of Roy Brashear, who relocated to Jerome, Arizona to play in the Copper Leagues.[A] During the trip, Wolverton proposed to Hogan a trade sending Arellanes to Venice in exchange for Walter Carlisle. Hogan and Maier were "sweet on Arellanes," who had a great season and had proved a nemesis to rival Venice. Arellanes faltered down the stretch, leading Wolverton to consider a deal. But Hogan expected that Frank would return to form and agreed to the exchange.[7] Hogan also picked up pitcher Doc White and Johnny Kane. And in one final deal, Hogan acquired Babe Borton, who very recently was sent to the Yankees for Hal Chase. Since the trade for Chase, Borton had been sent down to a New Jersey minor league team. In his excitement, Hogan fatefully stated, "Babe Borton will show much class."

Then in late November, the Pacific Coast League turned on its head.

When the executives returned from the meetings in Ohio, Orval Overall officially announced his retirement from major league baseball (for the second time). Overall had retired a few years earlier and subsequently played for the San Francisco Seals. But he returned to the Cubs for a portion of the 1913 season. With little success, he agreed to formally hang up the cleats. Immediately upon his retirement, Eddie Maier offered him a position with Venice. Maier's offer created a firestorm that at times threatened to splinter the Pacific Coast League into another "outlaw league."

Technically, Overall was the property of Cal Ewing and the San Francisco Seals. Ewing had an option on Overall if he left the Cubs. In spite of the rules, Orval negotiated a contract with Maier for better terms the moment he retired. On November 21, Cal Ewing declared war on Maier. Overall explained to the press that as an aging ballplayer with declining skills, it was necessary for him to make money while he could. On any day, if his season turned out to be a

---

[A] Hogan and Brashear had apparently been discussing Roy's future in late November when they were traveling together in Hogan's chauffeured automobile in Los Angeles when they hit a pedestrian. Driver Matthew Hammond ran into Edward Carpenter at 5th and Los Angeles. Carpenter's condition was not reported in the police report.

bad one, the owner would think nothing of cutting him loose entirely. So he felt that he needed to get what he could while he could.[8] But that wasn't how Organized Baseball operated. As long as Maier belonged to Organized Baseball, he needed to honor the property rights of the other owners.

Hogan, Maier, and Overall retreated to the seclusion of Maier's ranch for a "stag" party they had planned. Barney Oldfield set up at the ranch as well. Pacific Coast League President Allen T. Baum hurried to Los Angeles to mediate between Ewing and Maier. He stayed at the Hotel Van Nuys about twenty-five miles south and awaited a meeting with the Venice club. Rumors surfaced that Maier might be planning to leave the Pacific Coast League to form an outlaw league. James Morley, former owner of the Angels whose name surfaced whenever an outlaw league was mentioned in combination with a Los Angeles team, denied any connection with talks.

When Baum arrived in Van Nuys on the 21st, Hogan and Overall met with him. The pretentious Baum initially rebuffed the men, stating that he came to see Maier. During their meeting, Overall stated his case to the President. He said he had decided to retire and not play for San Francisco. Then Barney Oldfield, learning of Overall's desire to quit, volunteered to speak with Maier on his behalf. Maier made him a nice offer at double what he was making in San Francisco. Ewing, however, had $5,000 invested in Overall and had high expectations for him to be a star attraction.

Baum remained at the Van Nuys Hotel for three days while Maier and his friends completed their "party." There may have been a party. Or Maier may have initially responded to Ewing's challenge by scrambling to organize a rogue league. It was not in his nature or interest to do so. But once threatened, he certainly had the means to create havoc for the PCL. The media covered the events as if a rogue league was being planned.

Rounding up powerful and interested parties appeared possible. Upset with Organized Baseball over the rule that allowed for major league teams to have a one-year option on players sent to the minors, Berry perhaps would consent to a split. He already had an investment in the San Jose and Fresno teams in the California League. His consent and financial backing would certainly prove formidable to the Pacific Coast League. And in spite of his denial, Morley would consider any mention of an outlaw team in Los Angeles. Certainly Cy Moreing in Stockton was contacted about possible interest. And in addition to owners, the most important commodity, talented baseball players, were contacted to determine interest. Christy Mathewson, Hal Chase, and Fred Snodgrass were three players in town who had recently left the World Tour. All were likely in contact with Berry and Maier. They were known to have been in talks with the Federal League's main recruiter, George Stovall. It was likely that before the owners considered their next move relative to the Pacific Coast League and Organized Baseball in general, they contacted the local stars.

Ironically, the formation of a super outlaw league in California was likely undermined by the emergence of the Federal League. At the same time Maier and others considered a severance with Organized Baseball, Stovall and the Feds were courting the stars. The competition for minor league baseball posed by the Feds was too daunting to overlook. Maier and the others likely decided that banding together the Pacific Coast League and Organized Baseball against the Federal League would be more profitable to their respective organizations.[A] So that is what they did.

On November 23, Hap Hogan's wife received an urgent telegram at the Bray home near downtown Los Angeles. Hogan was still holed up with Maier and the others at the ranch. Nobody could reach Hap or Eddie Maier by phone. Mrs. Bray loved automobiles and enjoyed racing. The papers reported that when she was bored, she'd take apart her husband's car and put it back together. Nobody reported what the urgent message contained, but she had to deliver it within two hours, which she did by speeding over the winding mountain passes. Was it from Baum? Was it from the Federal League? Christy Mathewson? Cy Moreing? Hen Berry?

The next day, Maier agreed to meet with Baum. He announced that his "stag party" was a success, and agreed to reconcile with Ewing. He shunned the California League, and said he favored "organized ball" and had no intention of severing the relationship with it. Hogan claimed that the Overall incident was a misunderstanding and said that Maier had no malicious intent. A wealthy man with many business interests, Maier had not paid attention to baseball protocol. When Oldfield approached him and proposed he sign Overall, Maier simply acted upon what he thought was a good idea.

When Baum returned to San Francisco and presented his report, he placated Ewing. The matter would now be decided between Ewing and Overall. Overall would play for San Francisco. Baum summarized:

[A] The financial strain caused by competition from the Federal League likely caused Babe Ruth to be sold to the Boston Red Sox in July of 1914. Shortly after his 19th birthday, Ruth signed a contract with the Baltimore Orioles of the International League. Because Ruth was not yet a legal adult, Orioles owner Jack Dunn became his guardian. In spring training Ruth acquired the distinctive nickname Babe, a reference to his status as "Dunn's Baby." Because the Feds placed a team in Baltimore in direct competition with Dunn, the owner's finances suffered and he was forced to sell Ruth to Joe Lannin and the Boston Red Sox. Boston optioned Ruth to the Providence Grays of the International League to give him the opportunity to play every day and develop his talents. Ruth was called up to the majors late in 1914, and the following season he became a regular pitcher for the Red Sox. Led by Ruth, Boston won the World Series in 1915, 1916, and 1918. During Ruth's six-year stay in Boston, he won 89 regular-season games and three World Series contests for the Red Sox.

*After laying the facts as I found them in the Overall case before Mr.
Ewing, he stated that while he thinks Maier should have consulted with
him before dealing with any player belonging to the San Francisco club,
he is still satisfied that Mr. Maier did not intend any injury to him or the
Pacific Coast League. And that he holds Mr. Maier blameless.[9]*

In January, Eddie Maier threw another stag party, but this time he sent
his cronies with host Hap Hogan to Santa Maria in Central California for a
combined hunting and baseball trip. Maier couldn't host the friends at Maier
Ranch because he had joined the World Baseball Tour on the international leg.
Included in Santa Maria were baseball's Orval Overall and Roy Brashear, who
accompanied other sports figures such as Jim Jeffries, Jimmy Clabby, Larney
Lichtenstein, Barney Oldfield, and Venice publicist Gene Doyle. They played a
team put together by boxer Jimmy Clabby,[10] who had won the welterweight
championship in 1911. The pride of Hammond, Indiana, Clabby recounted his
experiences hobnobbing with the rich and famous during this exciting period:

> *Gee, it's tough to be broke, but, boy, when I think of the days I
> hobnobbed with the millionaires and spent money like a drunken sailor,
> it just makes me feel as though I were in a dream. But, on the level, I'm
> not sore about it and if I had to do it all over again, I guess I'd do the
> same thing.[11]*

Enamored with the weather and natural beauty of Santa Maria, Hogan
decided to train his squad there before the season began. He wanted to take them
away from the distractions of the city. Maier liked the idea of getting the team out
of the city. But he had a better idea. He announced that the Tigers would train the
following season at his ranch. He said he would build a top-notch training camp.
He promised to add a baseball diamond, handball, tennis courts, golf links, and
other attractions. But it wouldn't be complete until 1915.[12]

While on the trip to Santa Maria, the San Francisco media criticized
Hogan for welcoming an enemy into the Pacific Coast League. George Stovall,
brother of Jesse Stovall who had played for the Tigers, was the most active
recruiter for the Federal League in the country. And he hung out at Hogan's
billiard hall. Some said Hogan's pool hall was Stovall's headquarters. Hogan had
already been approached to manage in the new Federal League, so for a period of
time, Hap was understandably conciliatory to the league's ambassador. But critics
called for Hogan to bar Stovall from his poolroom. Cal Ewing feared he would
lose star pitcher Lefty Leifeld, who was rumored to be talking with the Feds. As a
result, Cal Ewing called for a war on the Federals while Hogan allegedly
fraternized with the enemy.[13]

Stovall recruited on behalf of the entire Federal League. The League was
organized like a syndicate. Players were hired by the league and were the
property of the consortium of clubs. Players could be moved around as the league
saw fit for the benefit of all. In the original plans, players were offered a contract

without a reserve clause. And the players were to be paid from the beginning of spring training, something that had not yet occurred in major league baseball.

The Federal League would have loved to land Christy Mathewson. Stovall was told to throw a lot of money at Matty. Matty admitted that the offer proposed was so large that he had to consider it.[14] But Mathewson had other plans. Matty decided to remain in California during the winter, where he met with Stovall, rather than join the World Tour on its international leg. He didn't leave the tour to negotiate with the Feds. Rather, he feared the high seas. His fears were justified. When the teams boarded the Empress of Japan in Seattle on November 19 en route to Japan via Vancouver, they felt secure in the graceful 6,000-ton clipper-bowed ship with three schooner-type masts and first class accommodations. But once at sea, the ship sailed through the worst typhoon in decades.

The storm began almost as soon as the team left Victoria and did not clear for three days. On Thanksgiving night the storm had become a typhoon, and conditions were made worse by a shortage of good coal. Most players became sea sick. In the midst of the storm, on Thanksgiving afternoon, a giant wave reported by Buck Weaver to be two hundred feet high hit the ship with such force that many on board were knocked down. Some sustained minor injuries.

> *Harry Sparrow, business manager of the tourists, was standing in one of the corridors when a monster wave struck the boat, and he fell on his right arm, spraining it. George Wiltse went down at the same time and a trunk fell on his right hand in such a way that it opened a good-sized cut. H.P. Burchell of the baseball party, who was in the library at the time, was knocked down and he sustained a cut head and a sprained shoulder. At one time it was thought that the ship would be forced to make for Northern Japan on account of the coal shortage, but the Captain decided to continue on to Yokohama. The steamer came into port slightly damaged from the storm.[15]*

In spite of the difficulties, the teams kept up their spirits and transmitted a greeting back to America on Thanksgiving that assured that all was well:

> *Baseball party all well owing to the special attention of Cap. Hopcraft and crew of Empress. Wish friends at home Happy Thanksgiving.*
>
> *Signed*
>
> *Giants-White Sox [16]*

When the ship finally landed, Mathewson's replacement, Red Faber, didn't leave the ship for days due to sickness. While the players and crew healed and recovered from the adventure, Mathewson sunned himself on the golf links at the Los Angeles Country Club, where he played with mining millionaire P.H. Smith. Mathewson had always said that he made more money outside of baseball than within baseball between his gambling, vaudeville shows, and series of children's books. Perhaps mixing with the wealthy in Los Angeles in the burgeoning metropolis planted ideas in Christy's head to consider retirement. Just a month earlier, the Los Angeles Aqueduct had been dedicated, bringing water from the Owens River to the city. The mantra for the project had been "whoever brings the water, brings the people." The slogan would prove prescient as the population of Los Angeles exploded over the next two decades.

When the media heard that Mathewson considered retirement, new National League President and Governor of Pennsylvania John Tener said that Mathewson simply had to remain in the National League. Tener understood Mathewson's value to the league, not only for his pitching, but also for his character. Tener said that when Matty was through pitching, if he wanted to pursue business, he should be fixed up with a franchise.

> *We cannot afford to let a man like that get out of the game… To keep baseball a success it must be represented by men of intelligence and dignity… The one great feature in the success of the American League is that President (Ban) Johnson has taken a personal hand in constructing the various parts so as to keep it on an even keel.[17]*

Tener also demonstrated significant insight and foresight when he stated his goal as National League President:

> *It will be my purpose to see that the game is kept sanitary and avoid the little things that, if left alone, might bring on disease.[18]*

Organized Baseball was far from sanitary. The symptoms of illness would quickly emerge through the winter as the Federal League raided major league baseball and signed players. The Empress of Japan carried some of baseball's most prized All Stars. Even under the close watch of many baseball executives on board, the Feds would infiltrate the tour to begin planting seeds of dissension.

Further unrest occurred when the National Commission passed an unfavorable ruling that banned "player writing." Christy Mathewson could no longer publish children's books. John McGraw, who had been writing an account of the tour, was notified by Ban Johnson to cease. The Giants' share of the World Series money was held pending an investigation of "player writers" offering accounts. Baseball didn't want players to profit from baseball outside from their contracts with their teams. The Commission threatened players with bans for violations. The National Commission also intended to control reports to the media. The relatively new Baseball Players' Fraternity opposed the ruling.

Dissatisfaction with Organized Baseball transcended the issue of "player-writing". If the Federal League could demonstrate financial stability, as well as pay the players better than Organized Baseball, every player would consider jumping leagues without hesitation. Few deep loyalties existed.

The World Tourists worked their way around the globe through Japan, China, Philippines, Australia, and Ceylon in the East. They entertained themselves with shuffleboard tournaments on board. On Christmas eve, Hans Lobert dressed up like Santa Claus for the children and young at heart on board. The ship enjoyed the 4,000 bottles of wine supplied by Eddie Maier. Some on board speculated whether it would be enough.

Reports back in the states revealed that the Feds approached tourists Buck Weaver and Jim Scott. Weaver indicated that he wasn't serious, but Scott listened. He had a poor season in 1911 that resulted in a wage cut. But he had a big season in 1912 and warned that if he didn't get more money, he would walk.[19] It wasn't much more complicated than that. Finally, the major leaguers had a competing bid.

On international soil, the spectators were largely unfamiliar with the stars on the team. They were attracted and entertained by the players' clowning. The most popular "clown" was Germany Schaefer. In Sri Lanka, the team played for one of the wealthiest men in the world, Sir Thomas Lipton. Lipton's empire, not limited to tea, made him a prominent figure throughout the country. He hosted the team, treated them to lavish accommodations, and befriended the comical Schaefer. After Sri Lanka, the team played two competitive and entertaining games in Cairo, Egypt. The intensity of the games was so high that the umpires had to eject McGraw from one of the games. The players met Abbas II, the last Khedive of Egypt, who they all found to be charming. He enjoyed the contests. Between games, the team visited the pyramids and hit baseballs onto the Sphynx.

Leaving Africa, the team sailed to Italy where they played two games in Rome. McGraw was humbled during a visit to the Vatican to meet Pope Pius X. In France, the team played a game in Nice. Fed representatives approached Mickey Doolan there.[20] Other players snuck away to nearby Monte Carlo where Germany Schaefer posed as a German prince during a night of decadence. The teams were rained out in Paris on the way to London, England where they played two games. When the tour was still in Paris, Venice owner Ed Maier sent a contract to catcher Jack Bliss to ensure that he wouldn't sign with the Feds. Bliss agreed to play for the Venice Tigers the next season. The Feds had an agent in Paris trying to sign the Red Sox Tris Speaker.[21] The Red Sox sent a cable to request that Nixey Callahan address Speaker on their behalf.[22] The Bosox were successful keeping Speaker, but had to double his salary to $18,000 per year.

The tour ended with an exhibition game in front of 30,000 people at Westminster Abbey with King George V of England in attendance in January of 1914.[23] Little did the King know that six months after the baseball game, World War I would begin, leading to the end of the European monarchies. The monarchies had ruled similarly to the National Commission, with absolute power over the working class. And similar to the imminent World War in Europe, a war was mounting between the National Commission and the Federal League that threatened to end the monarchy of Organized Baseball.

Appropriately, after completing the tour in England, the teams then crossed the Atlantic for New York City aboard the passenger ship Lusitania. But instead of sinking the ship to start their war, the two leagues chartered boats to combat each other with contracts that they offered to the arriving players. The tour was scheduled to arrive back in New York City On March 6.

Both the Federal League and Major Leagues rushed to greet the teams. Ironically, Ban Johnson and Federal League President James Gilmore not so coincidentally arrived in New York on the same train. Charles Comiskey's eighty closest friends chartered a cutter named Niagara to greet the tour's boat at sea. The Niagara was a government boat that allowed Comiskey's party access to the Lusitania prior to its arrival in quarantine. When the Federal League owners tried to charter their own boat, they could not find one that could access the Lusitania before Organized Baseball's boat. So Gilmore wired Speaker, Crawford, Magee, Egan, Leverenz, Doolan, and Evans about his interest in them and told them not to sign with organized ball.[24] He promised a reception committee when the team finally arrived in New York.

As the Lusitania surged across the ocean, rumors surfaced that the Feds had signed Hal Chase. Still in San Jose, Chase had not yet reported to the Chisox spring training in Paso Robles in Central California. Most of the team was still on the tour. So Chase remained visiting his parents and playing baseball at Santa Clara College with Harry Wolter. When the Chisox "B" team arrived for a game against Santa Clara in early March, Chase was there, but did not play. Ping Bodie batted fourth for the losing team; Santa Clara shut out the Sox 7-0 behind future major league star pitcher Dutch Leonard.[25] Chase commented that the rumors about him signing with the Federal League were untrue. He said would play for the Chisox and "intends to play the best game of his life in an effort to 'show up' Chance for releasing him from New York." In "Chase Speak" that translated to "I'm talking with the Feds."[26]

Reports from the Federal League indicated that they were most interested in signing Mathewson to a contract reported to be $65,000 for three years. By comparison, they claimed that Chase asked for $10,000 for one year plus a $10,000 advance. The Fed stated that they wired Chase and told him that they were not interested. At least not yet.[27]

Wolter once again helped coach the Santa Clara squad in the off-season to work himself into shape. The Yankees were rebuilding their team around youth, and sold Wolter to Hen Berry and the Los Angeles Angels so that Wolter wouldn't play for a competitor. Harry Wolverton told Berry that Wolter was one of the best outfielders in either of the major leagues.[28] Hen Berry told the Los Angeles Times that he would approach Wolter and stick a contract under his nose that would make him love Los Angeles for the rest of his natural life. However, the first contract he sent didn't possess the power of Aphrodite that Berry intended.

Wolter had reasonable expectations. But when he saw the first contract presented by Berry, a Bay Area paper reported that Wolter, residing in Redwood City, "flung the contract ... back in to the face of the Los Angeles man today." He said, "... if Los Angeles wants to deal with him further it will have to send a representative here to meet him." Wolter was upset that Yankee owner Frank Farrell never asked waivers, thus railroading Wolter away from competition and ending Wolter's major league career. Nonetheless, Wolter was willing to negotiate, but also threatened jumping to the Federal League.[A]

The prior season, Wolter made $4,500. Berry offered $2,400. Hen Berry asked him to go to Los Angeles to work out a deal. But Wolter, still busy with the Santa Clara team, sent Berry a message that he preferred the postal service as the medium to correspond. He denied any objection to playing for Los Angeles, a hint to Berry that all he needed was a sweeter deal. When Wolter hadn't signed by the beginning of spring practice, Berry had enough. If Wolter wouldn't come to him, he'd go to Wolter. Berry boarded a train to Redwood City, twenty miles north of San Jose. The paper reported:

> *Henry Berry will not be present at the opening spring training spasm of the Angels at San Bernardino next Monday. On that day he leaves for the north on a most important mission; that of inducing Harry Wolters (sic) to be a good boy and sign up.*[29]

Wolter and Berry came to an agreement. Wolter joined the Los Angeles Angels where he'd become their superstar. The signing was a coup for Berry, whose franchise was threatened by the invasion of the Federal League. Stovall had already stolen his second baseman Claire Goodwin, a University of California player in his second year. Stovall had claimed to be in Los Angeles duck hunting.[30] But any ballplayer in the State was what Stovall had in his sights.

The deals on the West Coast were only matched by the frantic dealing in the East. Just as the Lusitania steamed into port, the Federal League President announced that the Buffalo Federal League club had come into money that would be at their disposal[31] when approaching players came ashore. When the ship arrived, a player unfurled a large American flag and draped it over the side of the

---

[A] Now married and with a laundry business in Redwood City and coaching at Santa Clara, Wolter would prefer remaining in California, if not near Redwood City, then in Los Angeles.

boat to the delight of a cheering mob. Players dressed in their uniforms and waved small flags from on deck as the crowd watched as a light snow fell.[A]

San Francisco Seals Pitcher Lefty Leifeld was there when the Feds approached the players with fat contracts.

> *As soon as Steve Evans stepped off the boat from England, the Saint Louis outfielder was handed a cold $3,000 bonus. I saw the money.*

Leifeld considered an offer, but explained that for the average player, the financial inducement wasn't sufficient to overcome the threat of being banned from baseball if the new league folded. But he admitted that if enough money were put up, he would have taken it. He told the San Francisco Chronicle:

> *I am making no secret that their offer was better than the one I accepted from the Seals. The trouble is they would not put up the money for me. All they offered was a fat contract and only $500 advance money, and that did not suit me. I wanted to be guaranteed protection in case the outlaw organization fails. Then, again, if they succeed this season, it is a cinch that they will be taken into organized baseball, and what is to prevent them from going back on their fat contract? It is strictly business with me, and I did not think I could afford to take the chance.[32]*

In all of the excitement, the Federal League only lured two of the incoming tour players, Mickey Doolan and Steve Evans. But the competition they brought to the negotiations raised the salaries required to keep the other stars in their respective hometowns. Ty Cobb went from $10,000 per year to $15,000 in 1914 and $20,000 in 1915. Walter Johnson received the same kind of money after threatening to jump. Connie Mack tore up old contracts and offered his players more money to stay. And Tris Speaker doubled his salary from $9,000 to $18,000. Leifeld did return to the San Francisco Seals where he became one of the most reliable pitchers in the Pacific Coast League for years. But Cal Ewing lost one of his other pitching stars, Claude Berry, to the Pittsburgh Nationals. The Federal League represented a real threat to the Coast League. Financial uncertainty was a certainty the next few years in the league. But the Pacific Coast League would recover and soon boast a procession of superstars that would raise it to new heights.

[A] The tour was a success. Tours were planned for the next two years, but the outbreak of WWI would prove a setback to the internationalization of baseball, as the tour and many other tours were canceled or not scheduled.

1913 World Tour Player Highlights

Tour Player	Federal League Outcome	Ultimate Outcome
Hal Chase	Federal League	Allegedly participated in fixing the 1919 World Series
Mickey Doolan	Federal League	
Steve Evans	Federal League	
Sam Crawford	Re-Signed with Detroit	Hall of Fame
Tris Speaker	Bosox doubled salary to keep him from Federal League; ban from baseball overturned	Hall of Fame Allegedly participated in fixing baseball games
Red Faber	Returned to Chisox	Hall of Fame
Ray Schalk	Returned to Chisox	Hall of Fame
Christy Mathewson	Returned to NY Giants	Hall of Fame
Charlie Comiskey		Hall of Fame
John McGraw		Hall of Fame Allegedly participated in fixing baseball games
Bill Klem		Hall of Fame
Walter Johnson	Returned to Wash Senators	Hall of Fame
Buck Weaver	Returned to Chisox	Allegedly participated in fixing the 1919 World Series
Lee Magee	Banned from baseball	Allegedly participated in fixing baseball games
Morrie Rath	Sent to minor leagues	As first batter in the 1919 World Series, his being hit by a pitch thrown by White Sox Ed Cicotte signaled to gamblers that the series fix was on.
Jack Bliss	Signed with Pacific Coast League Venice Tigers	
Mike Donlin	Joined NY Giants	

[1] Oakland Club is After First Baseman Myers, Harry A. Williams, Los Angeles Times Oct 27, 1913
[2] Baseball Betters Nabbed, Los Angeles Times, Sep 15, 1913 pg II1
[3] Spark-Plug M'Closky Talks About Hen Berry, Los Angeles Times, Oct 21, 1913
[4] Spark-Plug M'Closky Talks About Hen Berry, Los Angeles Times, Oct 21, 1913
[5] Spark-Plug M'Closky Talks About Hen Berry, Los Angeles Times, Oct 21, 1913
[6] Scores of Players Are Swapped Or Purchased, Harry A. Williams, Nov 5,1913, pg. III3
[7] Arellanes May Come To The Venice Club, Harry A. Williams, Nov 6, 1913, LA Times, Pg. III3
[8] I Will Fight Back - Overall, Harry A. Williams, LA Times, 11/21/1913, Pg. III1
[9] Overall Matter All Blows Over, Los Angeles Times, Nov 26, 1913, Pg. III2
[10] Hogan Waxes Enthusiastic, 1/12/1914, Pg. III2
[11] Hammond High School web site, Hammond Indiana, Jimmy Clabby page, T.S. Andrews
[12] Wilson of Giants to Sign With Federals, Harry A. Williams, Feb 12, 1914, pg III3
[13] Hap Hogan Is Roasted By San Francisco Fans, Los Angeles Times, 1/16/1914, pg. III1
[14] Chance Off For Camp; Matty To Get Fortune, harry A. Williams, feb 28,1914, pg. III3
[15] New York Times, Dec 7, 1913
[16] Los Angeles Times, p. III4, Nov 27, 1913
[17] Los Angeles Times, Nov 23, 1913, Pg. VIi10

[18] Los Angeles Times, Nov 23, 1913, Pg. VIiio
[19] Federals After Buck Weaver and Jim Scott, Harry A. Williams, LA Times, Dec 29, 1913, p. III3
[20] Feds Will Tempt Giants and Sox, Feb 25, 1914, pg. III3
[21] Feds Will Tempt Giants and Sox, Feb 25, 1914, pg. III3
[22] Feds Send Agent to Meet Tourers, Los Angeles Times, 2/17/1914, pg. III4
[23] World Tour Ends in Fitting Climax, March 5, 1914, The Sporting News
[24] Big Gang to Meet Tourists, Los Angeles Times, Mar 6, 1914, Pg. III3
[25] Santa Clara Wallops Sox, Los Angeles Times, Mar 2, 1914, pg. III4
[26] The Federals Divide Loot, Los Angeles Times, Mar 1, 1914, Pg. VII3
[27] From the Baseball War, Los Angeles Times, 3/3/1914, pg. III4
[28] Hughes Signs, Wolter Says He'll Play Here, Harry A. Williams, Los Angeles Times 2/18/1914 pg. III2
[29] Chance Off For Camp; Matty To Get Fortune, Harry A. Williams, LA Times, Feb 28,1914, pg. III3
[30] Snodgrass Visits Stovall, Los Angeles Times, 1/24/1914, pg. III4
[31] Big Gang to Meet Tourists, Los Angeles Times, Mar 6, 1914, Pg. III3
[32] San Francisco Chronicle, Fred Purner, May 19, 1914

Chapter 17

McCredie and California Winter League Show Leadership on Racial Matters

The success of the World Tour demonstrated the interest that Organized Baseball inspired internationally. The National Commission contributed $1,000 to the tour to help promote baseball as a truly international game. International interest in America's game peaked in 1913 and 1914 with the tour. Teams and players from abroad visited the United States for exhibitions. Often the coverage by the press of the visiting teams revealed the racism predominant during the period.

Baseball had been played in China for years, and teams from China toured the United States for exhibition games. As the professionals in the United States prepared during spring training in 1914, a team from the Chinese University of Hawaii played games against college and winter baseball teams in California. The Los Angeles Times promoted one of the team's games against Occidental College with a cartoon depicting the Chinese players in stereotypical form. Under the cartoon, the paper attempted humor by fictitiously naming the players Ken Vin, Luck Yee Yaw, Lai Tin, Sing Hong, One Lung, Ping Pong, En Sue, Row Fong Long, Shang Hai, Sing, Skin-Ny, and Sink Poo. It wasn't the first time that Chinese were referred to in the Los Angeles sports pages derogatorily. A few months earlier, in an article commending Brooklyn pitcher Earl Yingling[A] for his hitting ability, the paper made it known that "Yingling is not a chink." But the papers were also respectful of the Chinese team's ability. It had come to the Coast the past two years and defeated many of the United States' best college teams, amassing a record of 70-11. They admittedly played as well as the best teams in the country, exhibiting good defense, base running, and singles hitting.

In 1914, Organized Baseball also expanded further into Canada. West Canada formed a minor league for the first time with teams in Calgary, Edmonton, Medicine Hat, Reginar, Moose Jaw, and Saskatoon.[1] In January, prospects for baseball expansion to Australia also seemed likely, as 8,000 spectators demonstrated an interest in watching their home team lose to the New York Giants 18-0 in a six inning game during the World Tour. They admitted, however, that the quality of play by the Americans was a revelation. France also boasted interest in baseball. In March, the President of the Vesinet Baseball Club, W.H. Burgess, arrived in New York and professed that France had taken up baseball with great enthusiasm.

[A] Yingling's nickname was "chink."

Major league scouts also descended upon Cuba for its rich talent. Hen Berry signed Cuban Jacinto del Calvo for the 1914 season. An article in the Los Angeles Times described the popularity of the Cuban baseball player, albeit with racist references:

> *Formerly, when the Cubans wanted to work off some of their surplus energy they would start a revolution. Fighting the Spaniards got to be a regular pastime with them. Finally, when the attendance dropped off at their daily revolutions they turned to baseball.... Baseball seemed to suit the Cuban temperament, the kids took to it handily, and the result has been the development of a number of teams which compare favorably with some of the best clubs in this country... Major league scouts got wisenheimer to the fact that Cuba was a rich recruiting ground, and finding that the color line did not bar the natives of that island from the organized game, began importing the pick of the Cuban players. There are now thirty Cubans playing professional baseball in the United States... Jacinto del Calvo ... has been the center of attention since joining Dillon's squad ... with the languor of his race when in repose, but so many pounds of dynamic energy when in action.[2]*

The paper also reported that the manager of Stockton, Jack Thomas, signed two Indians and a native of Guam for the coming season. He remarked that Henry Berry might have felt one-upped because he had signed only one foreigner, a Cuban named Calvo for the season. The reporter quipped, "Only by signing a Hottentot[A] can Henry hope to regain his lost prestige."[3]

Japanese players also visited the Coast during the same period. A team from the University of Keio in Tokyo, Japan played a series of games against Stanford, University of California, Santa Clara University, St. Mary's, and other college teams from Southern California, the Midwest, and the East. Stanford returned the favor by visiting the team in Japan the prior year.

Before signing with John McGraw and the New York Giants, Art Shafer played against the Keio All Stars in the West. One year, he also joined the Stanford team on a trip to Japan to play them. After joining the Giants, Shafer didn't initially get playing time, as was customary with McGraw and rookie players. Upset, he didn't report one year and instead went to Japan and coached a college team. In 1914, he officially retired from baseball at the age of twenty-three and again went to Japan to coach.[4] Shafer still had two years on his contract, but Shafer said that the Giants couldn't make him play. He had inherited a significant sum when his mother passed away, so Shafer never committed to playing baseball professionally. He played on and off when convenient. McGraw said of Shafter when he retired, "If Shafer had to play ball as a livelihood and not

---

[A] Hottentot is a race of indigenous people from Southern Africa.

as recreation, he would develop into one of the best players of the game."[5] He played a bit in 1914 for the Venice Tigers. John McGraw then pursued Shafer for six years after he left the Giants. Instead of playing, Shafer chose to become an international ambassador to the game. Like Bill Lange, who scouted and promoted baseball in Europe, Shafer promoted baseball in Japan. And from the seeds that he and others sowed, baseball continued to grow in popularity in Japan over the next century.

In June 1914, when World War I began, the advancement of international baseball stalled. And with World War II two decades later, the movement faced additional significant setbacks. But over time, the early ambassadors for the game laid the foundation that fostered great players from throughout the world.

An obvious irony during the era was that while baseball was promoted throughout the world, Organized Baseball didn't allow all U.S. citizens to play in its leagues. Rube Foster's Chicago American Giants returned to California for another season in the California Winter League, the only league in which they could play professionally with non-African Americans. As usual, Foster attached his Pullman cars to the backs of the commercial railroad trains when the team traveled. After the Winter League season ended, Foster planned to barnstorm his way north to San Francisco and Oakland to play exhibition games against the San Francisco Seals and the Oakland Oaks. But Pacific Coast League President Allen T. Baum wouldn't allow Foster's Giants to use the Pacific Coast League ballparks. San Francisco's Ewing and Oakland's McMenomy supported Baum's decision. The San Francisco Bay Area did not tolerate integrated baseball in 1914. Baum's decision was likely influenced by both racism and his attempt to conform to the policies of Organized Baseball.

Portland Beavers' owner Walt McCredie didn't care about Organized Baseball's rules. He spoke out against Baum and protested his ruling. In defiance of his league's President, McCredie asked Foster to continue north to Portland to play against his Beavers. Foster's team won four out of five exhibition games in Portland. Cyclone Joe Williams pitched a no hitter in one game. Pleased with the exhibition, McCredie agreed to play Foster's team on an annual basis. A true leader, McCredie acted swiftly and with conviction against what he perceived to be a tragedy and an injustice. And his actions preceded integration in Organized Baseball by more than three decades. He declared:

> *If I had my say, the Afro-Americans would be welcomed inside the fold. I would like to have two such ballplayers as Petway and Lloyd of the Chicago Colored Giants, who play out here every spring. I think Lloyd of the Chicago Colored Giants is another "Hans" Wagner around shortstop, and Petway is one of the greatest catchers in the world.*[6]

[1]   Pg. III4, LA Times, 12/27/1913
[2]   Harry A. Williams, Los Angeles Times, Mar 12, 1914, Cubans Are Invading Organized Baseball, pg. III3
[3]   Pg. III3, Los Angeles Times, Feb 12, 1914
[4]   Notre Dame Baseball Greats: From Anson to Yaz, Cappy Gagnon
[5]   Shafer Says He Is Out of Baseball, New York Times, Mar 10, 1914
[6]   The California Winter League, William F. McNeil.

Chapter 18

The Anarchist Hal Chase

Although involved in dentistry, Doc Strub's heart was never far from baseball. As the 1914 season approached, Strub capitalized on business opportunities that brought him closer to his destiny as a leader in urban sports in California. The "billboard dentist" had opened six successful "painless dental" offices, enabling the enterprising doctor to make additional investments in the prospering West. Strub soon mastered the use of financial leverage. He borrowed and invested in real estate in Sacramento and San Francisco with exceptional results. He remained close friends with Sacramento owner Charlie Graham, as his wealth grew.

In Los Angeles, Hap Hogan prepared for the opening of the 1914 season. The manager put his team through a three-hour practice that challenged the out-of-shape players. Shine Scott, the Tigers' trainer, was busy counteracting the damage caused by the practice. The papers said that Hogan, in particular, looked the worst for wear after an eventful winter.

Having taking criticism for being too conciliatory to the Federal League, Hogan and Dillon eventually banned Federal League players from Washington Park. Players who had previously worked out with the Tigers and Angels during the winter but signed with the Feds were quickly ostracized.

Players, however, were not in short supply. The Chicago White Sox spent the final weeks of March playing in Los Angeles against the Angels and Tigers. With the many ballplayers in Los Angeles at the same time, Stovall managed to corner Buck Weaver, Jim Scott, and Hal Chase for a "flirtatious meeting." Rumors circulated for months that Weaver would jump to the Feds. But Weaver informed Ed Maier that he had no intention of jumping. And he never did.

Hogan shared stories and strategies with the Chisox and its manager Nixey Callahan at his pool hall. Hogan was particularly proud of a new play he designed and hoped to use the coming season. Hogan announced:

> *With the bases loaded, a 3-2 count and two outs, send the runner from third as if stealing home ... the outcome at home has no bearing ... only the ball or strike. It is assumed that when the pitcher sees the runner coming from third that he will throw wide, which would force the run in.*[1]

When Hogan announced his play, newspapers reported it as a testament to the manager's genius. The media was not critical of the fact that Hogan had compromised any element of surprise by publicly disclosing his play. For Hogan, the discussion of the play in the pool hall among his cronies was as important as any unveiling on the field. Nonetheless, before Hogan retired from the game, he would get his chance to stage his play during a contest.

The opportunity did not arise during the four game series between the Tigers and Chisox played March 26-30 at Washington Park. While playing against the Sox, Hogan injured his side. Shine Scott attended to the immediate needs of the one-eyed player and manager, but the injury became acutely painful and required a physician's care.

After the series, Hal Chase and the Chisox barnstormed back to Chicago. They played games in Yuma and Mesa, Arizona at the beginning of April, and scheduled "bush league" teams across the Midwest during their return. They arrived home on April 13 in time to open the season against Cleveland.

The Federal League opened its season prior to the major leagues. Worries about whether the public would support the new league abated when 20,000 attended a game between Baltimore and Buffalo at Terrapin Park. The attendance set an all-time record for any game played in Baltimore. Most interesting, however, was that John McGraw's Giants played an international team at the same time at Oriole Park within view of the Fed's field. While crowds flocked to the Federal League game, only 1,500 showed up to watch the defending National League pennant winners.[2]

In California, Ed Maier prepared for opening day with another bash on his ranch. A week before the assembly of Elks arrived, two nests of yellow-billed magpies were spotted. The only bird found exclusively within California's borders, the relative to crows and jays shared traits with Hap Hogan; they were flashy, gregarious, and accustomed to drawing attention to themselves. And like the magpie, Hogan never left California; he was a founding participant in the Pacific Coast League and would remain a league fixture throughout his career. On May 4, the magpies' shrill call could not be heard over the shouts of the nine hundred Elks hosted by Maier. As was custom, a train left the Southern Pacific Station at Third and Olive at 7:30 AM for "Casa Delicias" carrying the participants.[A] Maier staged a baseball game between the "Mutts" and "Jeffs." Maier stated, "Gambling on this game will not be tolerated, but if you do gamble place your money on the "Mutts." A feast followed the usual track and field events, boxing contests, and fireworks, and prizes were awarded to the tallest, shortest, fattest, youngest, and oldest Elk.[3]

To the north, Cal Ewing opened the season at a new ballpark off Geary Boulevard on Masonic near Golden Gate Park. Ewing Field, with covered grandstands behind home plate, seated 18,000 and was to be a marked improvement over the Old Rec field. Ewing invested $100,000, but failed to scout

[A] This year, the contingent included city officials including ex mayor Jack Berdie, mayor L.L. Brodeen, Chief of Police Martin Berne, Chief of Fire A.M. Larsen, and Police commissioners H.P. Densel, Tom Abbott, E.H. Crippen, Deacon Pyle, and Fred Ussher.

the weather conditions in the afternoons at the new location. Much like Candlestick Park, built nearly fifty years later to house the San Francisco Giants, Ewing Field became inhospitable after three o'clock. The wind picked up, temperatures, dropped, and fog often rolled in. Fog was so thick at times that outfielders couldn't see the ball leave the bat. In one game, a mascot was ordered to run out to the outfield and notify a player that the side had been retired.

As the fans froze at Ewing Field, Hal Chase prepared for his first full season with the Chicago White Sox and Charles Comiskey. Comiskey appreciated Chase's defensive abilities. In the field, Chase resembled Comiskey. Many considered Chase the best defensive first baseman the game had ever known. But at one time, Comiskey held that distinction. Clark Griffith said of Comiskey,

> *... before his day, a first baseman was only a basket. He stood glued to the bag, received balls thrown to him, but never moved away ... discovered playing about ten feet back of the bag and about the same distance to the right... he finally forced the pitcher to do the unheard-of-thing of playing the first baseman's position when the first baseman was fielding the ball.*

Griffith equally praised Chase for his defense:

> *Until Hal Chase came, there were no great first basemen during the intervening years.*

Ban Johnson also held high expectations for Chase in Chicago. Chase had been a star in the American League nearly every year since Johnson and Comiskey started the league. Johnson had sided with Chase in the past during the Stallings episode in New York. And when Chase threatened to jump to the California League, Johnson convinced Chase to return to the Highlanders. They shared a long accommodative relationship. Johnson and Comiskey counted on Chase to remain loyal to the American League through the threat from the Feds. Papers reported that forty major leaguers, including Chase, were ready to jump. The vindictive Johnson publicly warned that any player who defected to the Feds would never again play in the American League as long as he was President. Amidst reports of impending defections to the Federal League, Chase met with Johnson and assured him that he would honor his contract with Chicago and remain with the White Sox through the season. He gave similar assurances to Comiskey.

Within a few hours of his meeting with the American League President, Chase sent a letter to Comiskey stating that he had signed with Buffalo of the Federal League. In an act unprecedented at the time, Chase gave Comiskey seventy-two hours to bargain with him. Most other owners had faced threats of defection and salary demands from their stars, ultimately conceding and signing the most popular players. But Comiskey ignored the letter.

Six days later, on June 21, Chase starred for Buffalo at a game in Chicago's Weeghman Park against Joe Tinker's Chicago Federals. Comiskey and Callahan did not know Hal was playing across town until Chase didn't show for their game against the Boston Red Sox. Chase had been to the White Sox clubhouse in the morning and packed his belongings. Then he went across town to report to the Buffalo team. Ten thousand appeared for the game with Chase and the Bisons. When newspapers reported after the game that Chase would return for the next game between the teams, Comiskey made plans to have him arrested.[4] Comiskey said that if he had known that Chase was going to play in the previous game on the 21st, he would have immediately taken action to stop him. Ban Johnson commented for the press:

> *I notice Chase played with the Federals on Sunday, in open disregard of his own statements to Mr. Comiskey. ... action will be taken to keep him from playing with the Buffalo team.*[5]

The newspapers also reported that the "sensational jump from the White Sox to the Buffalo Federals is the talk of the whole United States."

In Chicago, Chase selected a most appropriate stage for his labor uprising against Charles Comiskey. If one city in America were to lay claim to the origins of labor movement in America, it would be Chicago.

Chicago gained prominence as a center for the national labor movement and socialist party in the aftermath of the infamous Great Chicago Fire on October 8, 1871. Mrs. O'Leary's cow, a metaphor for the immigrant population, took the blame for that disaster during a period in which the divide between the classes was vast. Living and labor conditions for the working class were substandard. During the Railroad Strike of 1877, Albert Parsons, a white orphan raised by a former slave, became an outspoken advocate for better labor conditions and the ultimate ownership of business by labor. When he moved to Chicago, he witnessed abuse of power by the police toward organized labor; he was threatened at gunpoint and told to leave the city or be killed. He lost his job, was blacklisted, and threatened. In an attempt to combat the abuses of powerful monopolies, Parsons was willing to lose – lose battles and even his life in order to advance the cause for those much further into the future.

The "Great Strike" occurred during an economic depression and amidst lingering discontent. Over a hundred workmen were killed when police failed to maintain order. The strike, the first of its kind, was the top national story. It represented the first bloody protest over labor conditions in the country. The strike spread to the Pennsylvania, the Erie, and the New York Central railroads and paralyzed the transportation system. By July, the general strike had spread across the country to California. The entire country witnessed the mutiny by labor. Scab labor was brought in, and police sided with capital. When bloody altercations occurred, President Hayes called up federal units to prevent a national insurrection and to restore the national transportation system.

In the aftermath, the media printed inflammatory reports about the rebellious strikers. Throughout labor's struggles, management would resort to blacklisting and manipulation of public opinion through ridicule and smear campaigns. The New York Times referred to the strikers in terms that have been directed towards activists throughout history:

> ... *roughs, hoodlums, rioters, mobs, suspicious-looking individuals, bad characters, thieves, looters, communists, rabble, labor-reform agitators, dangerous class of people, gangs, tramps, drunken section-men, law-breakers, bummers, ruffians, loafers, bullies, vagabonds, cowardly mob, bands of worthless fellows, incendiaries, enemies of society, malcontents, wretched people, loud-mouthed orators, rapscallions, brigands, robber mob, riffraff, terrible fellows, felons, and idiots.*[6]

By December of 1877, the Socialist Party in Chicago had gained sufficient backing to invoke change through civil political means. The predecessor to the Socialist Party, named the Workingmen's Party, won many significant elections in Chicago. But local officials manipulated the tallying of votes. An anarchist movement grew out of the futile attempts to work within the system in a democratic and peaceful manner. Over time, anarchists resorted to violence, which became a defining characteristic of the movement in the imaginations of the American public.

In 1886, Chicago would permanently galvanize as the center of socialism in America. At the time, the city and nation were gripped in fear of the anarchists and the perceived unprecedented threats facing the country.

> *Panic ran deepest in Chicago. The city was seized with a fear and hatred unprecedented in its history.... Wild rumors filled the air: The anarchists were planning to wipe out the police, blow up public buildings, plunder stores and warehouses; there was a deeply laid conspiracy to destroy the whole city ... the entire country.*[7]

Albert Parsons and others formed labor unions in an attempt to create an eight-hour workday as of May 1, 1886. Nearly fifty separate strikes occurred throughout Chicago between April 24 and May 5 to support the initiative. On May 4, Parsons met for a rally with the striking workers in Haymarket Square in Chicago. Although the crowd was large, speeches were made civilly and without fanfare. But as the final speaker concluded near 10:30 at night, somebody threw a pipe bomb at the police. In the ensuing riot between police and the crowd, just over ten people were killed and dozens wounded. Six men, Albert Parsons, August Spies, Adolph Fischer, George Engel, Michael Schwab, Samuel Felden, and Oscar Neebe were arrested for murder. Nobody knew who initiated the violence. But the events witnessed by the likes of Bill Haywood, founder of the Industrial Workers of the World (IWW), and Mother Jones would forever inspire them in their missions on behalf of labor. Mother Jones later said, "those were the days of martyrs and saints." The trial of the six accused aroused and mobilized many throughout the world.

At the trial, August Spies warned:

If you think you can stamp out the labor movement, then hang us! ... Here you will tread upon a spark, but here, and there, and behind you and front of you, and everywhere, flames will blaze up. It is a subterranean fire. You cannot put it out. The ground is on fire upon which you stand.

George Engel, Albert Parsons, Adolph Fischer, and August Spies were convicted. Together, ropes were placed around their necks as they were allowed to utter their last words. Engel shouted, "Hurrah for anarchy!" Adolph Fischer, pleased with the purposefulness of his existence pronounced, "This is the happiest day of my life." Spies uttered, "The time will come when our silence will be more powerful than the voices you strangle today." Parsons, known for extraordinarily prolonged oration, began a long speech that was abbreviated by the drop of the rope.

Many theories exist about who threw the bomb. Some say Pinkerton detectives intended to incite a riot to hurt the labor movement. Others suggest a policeman threw it intending it for the crowd. But the most credible theories suggest that an anarchist or militant did throw the bomb. The effect, however, was that the accused were convicted without a fair trial. And the four men would become martyrs and symbols for socialists and labor movement leaders throughout the world for decades.[8]

In 1893, Chicago hosted a fair called the Columbian Exposition. The same month, Lucy Parsons, wife of the deceased Albert Parsons, raised money for a monument on the martyr's grave. Illinois Governor Atgeld dedicated the monument and announced a pardon for Fielden, Scwab, Neebe, and the four men that were hung. Altgeld wasn't as concerned with the bomber's identity as he was with justice.

Ironically, just as the Columbian Exposition concluded, another momentous labor strike hit Chicago. The Pullman Strike in the summer of 1894 was as bloody as any strike in the nation's history. Eugene Debs organized the Pullman workers who lived in substandard conditions in a city established for the workers who built the Pullman cars for trains. The workers were required to purchase their goods at the Pullman store and live within the company town limits. The workers lived and worked under precarious conditions; Pullman used his management to report any substandard or disgruntled workers so they could be quickly blacklisted, fired, and removed from their homes and the town. Because the strike disrupted the mail, President Grover Cleveland sent in federal troops to break it up amidst protest from the sympathetic Governor Altgeld. Altgeld warned against the use of violence toward the protesters:

While some men may tamely submit to being clubbed and seeing their brothers shot down, there are some who will resent it, and will nurture a spirit of hatred and seek revenge for themselves.[9]

On July 4, two thousand armed U.S. troops arrived in Chicago. They arrested Debs and violently ended the strike. In the aftermath of the Pullman strike, because of the force used by the United States government, the unions were severely weakened. Several more decades would pass before labor would gain significant strength again.

The labor movement in baseball paralleled the movement at the national level. From the 1870s through the turn of the century, management and labor fought over issues including property rights of the owner, player rights to collective bargaining, working conditions, and salary caps. Similar to the chronology of the labor movement in Chicago, the movement in baseball gained momentum in the 1880s and culminated in the early 1890s with the National League monopoly prevailing. Labor would not significantly challenge management for years. In April of 1900, labor leader Samuel Gompers considered unionizing baseball players. Unionization would have required coordination by a committed outsider like Gompers. With players separated by the distance between the towns in which they played, organization and consent were difficult. But Gompers said that the major barrier was the timidity of the players. There just wasn't enough interest or will.

In 1900, Debs ran for President of the United States as the candidate for the Social Democratic Party. With running mate Job Harriman, he won .6% of the popular vote.[A] Over the next year, a man named Leon Czolgosz visited Chicago anarchist Emma Goldman,[B] a political activist inspired by the Haymarket affair. She was a renowned and inspirational lecturer who attracted large crowds. Unbeknownst to Goldman, her lectures inspired Czolgosz. On September 1, 1901, the anarchist Czolgosz assassinated President William McKinley. Soon after he assumed the presidency, former Vice President Theodore Roosevelt boldly lashed out and promised "death, imprisonment, and deportation of all Anarchists."[10] Americans shared Roosevelt's sentiment. Over the next two decades, those who challenged the status quo were often viewed with contempt and compared with the left wing anarchist movement of the day.

Baseball players had yet to mount a significant challenge against the reserve clause and the baseball monopoly. But the labor movement in America outside of baseball was showing signs of resurgence. In recent years, President Theodore Roosevelt introduced an era of New Nationalism, asserting that the

---

[A] He would run for president in 1904, 1908, 1912, and 1920 with considerable success.

[B] Goldman founded the anarchist journal known as Mother Earth. She was an outspoken advocate for birth control, draft evasion, atheism, freedom of speech, socialism, peace, and rights for homosexuals.

President served as the "steward of public welfare." And he stated, "labor is the superior of capital and deserves much the higher consideration... I wish to see labor organizations powerful."[11]

Hal Chase seemed the unlikely poster boy for the labor movement in baseball. He was incapable of organizing anything. But he was irreverent – an Organized Baseball anarchist. He had little respect or regard for the rules and threats of the National Commission. And he was not only willing to ignore them; he was willing to challenge them. And he would challenge them in the heart of the national labor movement, Chicago, against baseball's most powerful owner, Charles Comiskey. He had little choice. The National Commission challenged Hal Chase. Few challenged Hal Chase at anything and won.

And while Hal would naturally avoid conflict, he never backed down from a challenge. Significant progress against the baseball monopoly would not occur for decades. But with Chase and others bold enough to risk their livelihood, seeds for change were planted. And in the battle that would span another fifty years, those who challenged the status quo suffered from the purposefully manipulative muckraking perpetrated by cruelly vengeful opposition.

Chase certainly understood the risks he faced by challenging Comiskey, Johnson, and Organized Baseball. He likely had fallback strategies worked out in his head. First, he knew the significant wealth behind the new Federal League, including that of oil man extraordinaire Harry Sinclair. Perhaps the league would survive and players would realize their true market value. In the waning years of his career, he certainly held out hope that he could cash in before he retired. Second, he could hope for reconciliation between the leagues. In the past, owners had short memories regarding grudges toward star players when building their rosters. And last, Chase likely counted on a fallback in the California League and the always-welcoming arms of Cy Moreing in Stockton.

Concerned about an uncertain future, Chase cut back on his alimony payments to Nellie. When Nellie went to court to force payment, Hal claimed that a reduction was appropriate considering the financial uncertainty of the new league. The court sided with Chase.

On June 25, 1914 the Buffalo Bisons hosted Hal Chase Day in a game against Pittsburgh. The team handed out photos and biographies of the player to fans at the ballpark. Comiskey had ordered that Chase be served an injunction preventing him from playing for the Feds.

When Chase appeared at the ballpark, he was to be served the papers enforcing the injunction. Team officials devised a scheme to sneak Chase into the stadium unnoticed – in drag. Chase would enter the park secretly disguised as a woman. They placed his uniform in a tool shed under the grandstands and inconspicuously escorted Chase into the shed hours before the game. With Chase in hiding, he could not be served papers before the first pitch. Reporters learned that Chase was hiding in the tool shed, and began banging on it to get a statement.

224

Chase remained in the shed in total darkness as the reporters pounded on the walls.[12]   One newspaper reported that the surreal scene illustrated the absurd conditions of the game:

> *... presented one the opportunity to ruminate on the vagaries of the game, which left a stellar performer locked in a closet.[13]*

In the bottom half of the first inning, after the opposing team took the field and the pitcher had warmed up, the umpire shouted "Play Ball." Hal opened his tool shed and walked on to the field toward home plate. The crowd greeted him with a tremendous roar. When he entered the batter's box, his eyes had still not adjusted to daylight; Chase struck out on three pitches.[14]   As Chase returned to the dugout from the field at the end of the second inning, while in the company of the Buffalo team attorney, he was served the papers preventing him from playing in the game.[15]   Chase was escorted off the field.

Hal Chase became one of the first baseball players to challenge the reserve clause in court. He intended to fight the injunction. Judge Herbert P. Bissell, former mayor of Buffalo, presided over the case and unfortunately dismissed the argument that Organized Baseball's structure violated federal anti-trust laws. But he made the following seminal statements regarding baseball players and their servitude:

> *No opportunity is afforded the player to solicit employment upon his own account. No right is afforded to enable him to resist an unjust limitation upon his power to earn. No consideration is afforded either to himself or his family with respect to choosing a home. In short, he is placed where he must at all times while playing in Organized Baseball, consider that his home is only the place in which his services are for the time being controlled...The baseball player is made a chattel.[16]*

Judge Bissell added in defense of Chase that baseball had become a monopoly.

> *A species of quasi-peonage unlawfully controlling and interfering with the personal freedom of the men employed...Organized Baseball is now as complete a monopoly of the baseball business for profit as any monopoly can be made. It is a contravention of the common law in that it invades the right of labor as a property right; in that it invades the right to contract as a property right; and in that it is a combination to restrain and control the exercise of a profession or calling... If a baseball player like the defendant, who has made baseball playing his profession and means of earning a livelihood, desires to be employed at the work for which he is qualified and is entitled to earn his best compensation, he must submit to dominion over his personal freedom and the control of his services by sale, transfer, or exchange, without his consent, or abandon his vocation and seek some other kind of labor. While the services of these baseball players are ostensibly secured by voluntary contracts, a study of the system ... reveals the involuntary character of the servitude*

which is imposed upon players by the strength of the combination controlling the labor of practically all of the players in the country. This is so great as to make it necessary for the player either to take the contract prescribed by the Commission or abandon baseball as a profession and seek some other mode of earning a livelihood... The quasi peonage of baseball players under the operations of this plan and agreement is contrary to the spirit of the Constitution of the United States.[17]

Contractually, Bissell found in favor of Chase due to the lack of mutuality in the contract and the unenforceability of the injunction:

The absolute lack of mutuality, both of obligation and remedy, in this contract, would prevent a court of equity from making it the basis of equitable relief by injunction or otherwise.   The negative covenant, under such circumstances, is without a consideration to support it, and is unenforceable by injunction.

Judge Bissell found in favor of Hal Chase. Whether challenged in a pool hall, card game, baseball field or court of law, Hal Chase often proved victorious. More important, once challenged, Chase never backed down from the fight.

But the fight with Comiskey would ultimately alienate Chase from the American League and begin a protracted battle between Chase and the betrayed Chicago White Sox owner. Their feud was far from settled; the grudge would last for many more years.

Few historians have considered Hal Chase as a courageous labor leader. Like many others who stood for players' rights, his actions were dismissed as convenient and self-interested.   Perhaps only Hal Chase saw himself as a courageous and outspoken emissary for change. The day after the ruling, on July 21, Chase commented on his battle with Comiskey:

I am greatly pleased.   I knew I was right to challenge them and went ahead with the fight.   This is the second big defeat Organized Baseball has suffered...and I know there are many big league players who feel the same as I do, but did not have the courage to fight.   Now that I have won there may be others who will join me in my fight for what is right.[18]

Ninety-five players left major league baseball for the Federal League, but Ban Johnson admittedly held a grudge with two individuals – George Stovall and Hal Chase. Stovall raided the major leagues like nobody had done since Clark Griffith raided the National League for Johnson when they established the American League together. And Hal Chase had betrayed Ban Johnson's trust. Johnson stated, "... there's no blacklist, but Stovall and Chase are not the kind of men the American League wants."

[1]   Hoganites Are To Start Training February 23. Los Angeles Times. Jan 21, 1914. pg. III2

[2]   Feds Open to Packed Park. Los Angeles Times, Apr 14, 1914. pg. III1

[3]   Antlered Army to Lay Siege. Los Angeles Times Apr 24, 1914

[4]   Big League War Is On: Chase Plays with Feds, Los Angeles Times. Jun 22, 1914. pg III1

[5]   Hal Chase Foils Comiskey. Los Angeles Times. Jun 23, 1914. Pg. III1

[6]   Death in the Haymarket. James Green. Pantheon Books

[7]   The Haymarket Tragedy. Paul Avrich. pg. 215

[8]   Death in the Haymarket. James Green. Pantheon Books

[9]   The New Encyclopedia of Social Reform. William Dwight. 1908 p. 167

[10] Erich Rauchway. Murdering McKinley: the Making of Theodore Roosevelt's America (New York: Hill and Wang. 2003

[11] 1912: Wilson, Roosevelt, Taft & Debs – the Election that Changed the Country. James Chace.

[12] Buffalo Express. June 26, 1914

[13] Buffalo Express. June 26, 1914

[14] The Sporting News. September 18, 1941. Lester Grant (Oakland Post Enquirer)

[15] Chase is Ruled Out. Los Angeles Times. Jun 26, 1914. pg. III1

[16] American League Baseball Club of Chicago v. Chase, 149 NYS 6 (1914)

[17] American League Baseball Club of Chicago v. Chase, 149 NYS 6 (1914)

[18] Buffalo Evening News. July 21, 1914

Chapter 19

The Joy Is In The Journey: Hap Hogan Leads the Vernon Tigers

The 1914 Pacific Coast League season was marked by the league's financial plight, the ascension of Harry Wolter as a star for the Los Angeles Angels, and the demise of Frank Arellanes as a Venice Tiger.

In July, the league owners and managers met in San Francisco to address declining revenues. Baseball throughout the state of California was in the doldrums. The Federal League's ability to recruit players from the minor circuit contributed to the difficulties. Cal Ewing's considerable investment in a ballpark in San Francisco that was inhospitable to spectators didn't help matters. And attendance in Venice dropped in spite of a robust squad. Harry Wolverton took majority ownership in Sacramento with the Mission club and struggled at the box office and on the field.[A] During the season, the league terminated Wolverton and the Missions' membership for failure to pay salaries and meet the financial obligations of the league. Wolverton claimed to have lost his personal fortune of nearly $50,000. The attendance slump throughout the league sealed the Missions' fate. Wolverton had hoped for support from the league, but the league was in no position to provide it. At a meeting at the St. Francis Hotel in San Francisco, the owners decided to find a buyer for the Missions.

The league took measures to improve financial conditions. Part of the plan involved creating a more wholesome experience at the ballpark. They attempted to clean up an ever-present intolerable atmosphere in the stands. The papers reported activities at a Venice Tigers game,

> *A low-brow gent belched cusswords... until picked up by the park officer and dropped on the other side of the fence. This same untimely fate awaits others who labor under the delusion that four bits buys them a reserved right to abuse the players.... profane language will not be tolerated.*

The league also agreed to control salaries by imposing a $5,000 monthly salary cap per team. It cut the roster sizes to eighteen players. And it agreed to use only one umpire in each game rather than two. The decision would put three umpires out of work.

Charlie Graham worked into the winter trying to find a buyer for the Sacramento club. He said, "business men want the team and think we can arrange

---

[A] Charlie Graham and Lloyd Jacobs were minority owners.

the matter." At times, it seemed the squad would remain in Sacramento with Graham organizing ownership from members of the city. Ultimately, however, the team found a buyer in Salt Lake City for the 1915 season.

In the same off-season, Henry Berry decided to sell the Los Angeles Angels squad and instead purchase the San Francisco Seals team from the struggling Cal Ewing. Berry arranged the sale of the Angels team to Tom Darmody, who was already a large stockholder in the club. Henry purchased the Seals with his brother Clarence Berry, the Klondike King. Clarence had passed on opportunities to own a club to avoid competing with his brother. But with the purchase of the Seals the "richest man in baseball" joined the former owner of the Los Angeles Angels in an effort to lift the franchise in San Francisco that was beleaguered by the financial burden created by the club's relocation to Ewing Field.

Whenever new ownership was discussed, Hap Hogan's name was raised as manager. And to induce him away from Maier, he was offered ownership interest. Hogan admitted that his loyalty belonged to Maier, but that being a mogul attracted him.

Both Graham and Berry contacted Hogan about joining their squads. Graham wanted Hogan to manage Sacramento if the team remained there. Berry wanted Hogan to manage the Seals. And a potential franchise in Seattle also courted Hogan. But Hap remained in Venice with Maier.

With the change in ownership in Los Angeles, Darmody inherited one of the best outfields in minor league baseball. Harry Wolter, Rube Ellis, and Harl Maggart were considered in a class above all other outfields in the Pacific Coast League and many in the majors. Harry Williams reported,

> *Los Angeles has the greatest outfield in its history - regarded by many competent critics as superior to anything in the history of the minor leagues.... Here is an outfield with a combined hitting power of .315. Put that in your pipe and smoke it! Coupled with this is a total of 102 stolen bases, proving that speed and hitting power are written all over that outer garden.... with 292 runs scored to date, they top all other Coast League outfielders...*[1]

By the time Harry Wolter returned for the winter to coach at Santa Clara, he had amassed far more hits during the past season than anyone in the Coast League for many years. He led the league in hitting with a .330 average. Wolter's manager Pop Dillon posted a record that exceeded Wolter with 275 hits in 188 games more than a decade before.[2] And Dillon did not hesitate to remind Wolter of his superior mark. The two developed a healthy rivalry. In the midst of a torrid streak, Dillon needled Wolter that he lacked power. Dillon bet Wolter a suit that he wouldn't hit a home run the entire season. In a game against cross-town rivals Venice, Wolter hit a ball into the right field bleachers to win the competition.[3]

Conversely, Frank Arellanes started the season well, but ended on a sour note. Playing for the lowly Missions, even though he pitched well, he received no run support. He lost in April after giving up only three hits. In June, the newspapers noted the poor run production when he took the mound. In July, he shut out the Angels 3-0. And in August he lost a close game on errors. But in September, Arellanes got rocked in a game in Portland. He could not blame his teammates for his poor performance. He relinquished seventeen hits, one to every player on the opposing team. Then on October 2, the reason for his poor play came to light. The thirty-two year old Arellanes was arrested at his hotel for committing crimes the night before his abysmal performance in Portland. Frank was one of five players from Portland, San Francisco, and Oakland accused of violating the Mann Act. The papers reported that Arellanes was arrested in connection with white slavery, a term sometimes used to describe prostitution. The charge against Arellanes was a statutory offense because the girl he allegedly met was fourteen years of age. The girl claimed she became acquainted with Arellanes by phone and that he took her to a hotel and to the clubhouse at the baseball park when nobody else was there. Police reported that Arellanes gave liquor to the girl, which was corroborated by a waiter who served them. Arellanes denied the charges. If his performance the next day were used as evidence, the grand jury would certainly have convicted Arellanes.

But Arellanes was soon back playing ball on the Coast. In 1915, as the PCL teams cut their rosters to reduce expenses, fifty players were cut from the league, including Arellanes. Fortunately for Frank, he signed with Denver in the Western League, and later returned to the Pacific Coast League for 1916.

In February, Ed Maier scheduled a week of spring training at his Maier Ranch. The team worked itself into shape before heading to San Diego[A] for more extensive training. During the week at the ranch the players played baseball, but they spent more time living the life as guests of Maier. They hiked the foothills and played tennis, golf, pinochle, checkers and other activities that Hogan hoped would strengthen their wind.[4] Good food, rest, and clean living were certainly part of the agenda as the players refreshed their outlook and stepped away from possible negative influences of friends and the city.

Ed Maier believed he had the best team ever assembled on the Coast. Certainly as each season approached, the owners claimed a championship was imminent. But unlike other years, Maier knew that the 1915 squad could bring him and Hap Hogan their first Pacific Coast League title. Hogan had been close before, placing second in 1911 and 1912. But he had yet to claim the crown.

[A]   When they arrived in San Diego, the team turned around and came home. They complained that San Diego didn't even have a grass diamond. So the squad played the Chisox in Anaheim on their way back.

Hen Berry felt he had the class of the league in San Francisco behind young Harry Heilmann, power hitter Ping Bodie, and new manager Harry Wolverton.[A] But Hogan was highly regarded within the league for being able to tactically scratch out the victories needed to defeat the northern foe. Hogan's admirers touted him for being clever, smart, and tricky. His team could always compete, but critics wondered if his team could ever win the pennant. Many claim he was too nice a person; he was far too easy with his men.

In the opening series in Salt Lake, in front of ten thousand and following a parade organized by the Rotary that was headed by a brass band, Hogan demonstrated his "tactics" against star pitcher Lefty Williams. Although Williams never cracked, the newspaper noted that Hogan chanted at the pitcher throughout the game to distract him. As usual, Hogan was the center of attention.

When the team opened its season in Los Angeles on April 20, Hogan and Maier spared little expense creating a spectacle to usher in the new season. Prior to the game against the Berry brothers' San Francisco Seals, Hap Hogan and Harry Wolverton rode elephants down the streets of Los Angeles in a parade that included a twenty-four piece band, a calliope, clowns, dancing girls, seals, and caged tigers. As was fast becoming the custom around the Venice and Los Angeles teams, celebrities graced the stands. Jim Jeffries was present on the field, and Charlie Chaplin caught the first pitch.

For the next two weeks, Hogan's squad won most of its games while Hap displayed his customary antics in the field. In tight situations, he'd often substitute himself as a batter. The accomplished pinch hitter relished the opportunity to rattle the pitcher to gain an advantage. He'd sometimes walk to the plate while pointing his bat at the pitcher like a sharpshooter holding his musket. Other times he'd dance a jig at home plate. And he talked incessantly to the pitcher and catcher throughout his at bat.

Hogan had yet to implement the great play he had unveiled in January of 1914. By now, certainly every defense in the league had forgotten any mention of it. With the bases loaded and two outs and a full count, Hap schemed that if the runner on third dashed for home as the pitcher began his motion, the pitcher would become rattled and throw ball four, forcing in the winning run. The Pacific Coast League would soon witness Hap's wizardry in action.

In a game on May 7, Hogan was feeling under the weather. Despite being burdened by a bad cough and general weakness, he endured through an extra inning game. Venice was tied in the fourteenth inning with the bases loaded. A strong hitter, Lefty Decanniere, was due to bat. Hogan subbed himself in for

---

[A] Hen Berry would send Wolverton a telegram in August as the season approached its end, "Go as far as you like, regardless of cost, to get players to win pennant," Berry Wants to Get Coast Flag, LA Times, August 25, 1915 p. III4

Decanniere. With each pitch, Hogan stepped out of the box and motioned signals to the base runners. He worked the count to three balls and two strikes. Then he stepped out of the batter's box and motioned for a squeeze play. With the next pitch, the runner from third raced for home plate. Hogan squared to bunt, expecting the pitcher to throw a ball. But the pitch was a strike, and Hogan pulled the bat back and hit a weak grounder. Fortunately, the shortstop moved out of position and the ball rolled through the hole scoring the winning run.

Hogan had implemented the play he had bragged about in his pool hall. And it had worked, although not as planned. But he would never attempt the play again.

One reporter once wrote about Hap,

> *Hap will never quit. When he passes it will be in harness, and his shroud will be a baseball uniform.*

And Hap often joked with Hen Berry about never retiring:

> *I want to wind up my career catching for you. And I'll tell you why: I want to be an angel when I die.*

Somehow, Hap always knew he would play baseball right to the end. When Hap went home after the game, he wouldn't acknowledge for a few days that he was sick. He insisted all he needed was a dip in the ocean, so he drove with friends for a swim in the surf. The swim worsened his condition and forced him to bed. A few days later, his relatives in Santa Clara received a message that read, "Hogan very low." The diagnosis was pneumonia, and doctors expected Hap to endure through the crisis once his fever broke. His temperature had risen to 104, but had since fallen back to 102. Because of Hogan's strength, physicians expected a recovery.[5]

But Hogan's condition worsened. Weakened, Hogan asked how the Tigers had fared in the recent series. When he heard that Venice had won 4-3, the always-optimistic Hogan uttered his last words,

> *I knew it would be that way.*

Thousands attended Hap Hogan's funeral on May 19 organized by the Los Angeles Elks club 99. Hogan had planned his funeral and had asked to be placed in a purple and white casket in the colors of the Elks Club. The attendants came from all social circles - sport celebrities, city officials, baseball players and owners, and other prominent people as well as "newsboys, bootblacks, college men, schoolboys, and persons of every walk of life." Nearly three hundred cars parked near Christ Church in Los Angeles. Frank Chance escorted the remains from the altar, as did Orval Overall, Walt McCredie, Tom Darmody, Cal Ewing, Spider Baum, Eugene Doyle, Jack Jeffries, and Venice Mayor Ed Garety. Pallbearers were ballplayers Johnny Kane, Dick Bayless, Walter Carlisle, Roy Hitt, Doc White, and Lefty Decanniere. The Los Angeles Times reported,

According to many of those who attended the service Hap Hogan's funeral was the greatest demonstration of love and loyalty ever accorded any public character in Los Angeles.

On the day that the Lusitania was sunk killing 1,198 passengers and 128 Americans leading to Woodrow Wilson's decision to enter the United States in to the Great War, Cal Ewing paid a tribute to Hap Hogan, a great baseball man who was one of the few who remained in the Pacific Coast League from its inception throughout his career. Ewing said about Hap,

One of the kindest men I have ever known and as honest as the day is long. He was popular in all cities of the PCL and was popular when his team was down as well as up. He was a favorite of children who came out to see Hap.

At the next games scheduled in the Pacific Coast League, all teams paused and bowed their heads before play for five minutes of silence. Even in a game played in Oakland, not a sound was heard from the grandstands or bleachers. The fans treasured the opportunity to mourn along with those from Los Angeles. Ed Maier decided to pay tribute to Hap by retaining his name on the roster as manager until the end of the season. Hogan had never won a championship. As a strong contender in 1915, if the Tigers were to win the title, Hogan would go down in the record books as having won as manager. The thoughtful consideration revealed Maier's kindness. In the end, however, the San Francisco Seals won the championship.

Former teammate, friend, and sportswriter Winnie Cutter said of Hogan,

There was something about Hogan's personality which was bound to make him liked by all who had ever been closely associated with him.[6] ... Hap treated ballplayers like they had hearts and feelings -- and as a result, they worked hard for him.

Hogan left his wife, Mrs. Laura Bray, widowed and without a source of livelihood. On May 26, she reported to the probate court that her husband's estate consisted of ten shares in the Venice Athletic Club, worth $1,000, and his last check from the Venice Tigers for $300.[7] To provide assistance to Hap's widow, a month after Hogan's death Los Angeles Angels' owner Tom Darmody convinced the Pacific Coast League to donate to her all revenues from games played on one day. In Los Angeles, attendance exceeded 10,000. Hollywood actors played a warm-up game, and Charlie Chaplin sold scorecards in a display of support.

A month later, Maier's Venice Tigers moved back to Vernon. Ed Maier had built a new ballpark at considerable expense in Venice. But like Cal Ewing in San Francisco, he soon realized it was a bust. The stadium had featured a circular fence that was an even 375 feet in all directions from home plate. Made of wire, fans could drive up to the fence and watch from their cars. When Maier decided to return to Vernon, he moved the entire stadium fourteen miles east toward the city's center. Carpenters numbered every piece of lumber, disassembled the grandstands, cut the grass, rolled it into strips, and put everything back together in Vernon.[8]

The Angels' Washington Park also moved in 1915. The city wanted to cut Hill Street through the previous location. So the park was disassembled and moved toward Main Street.[9] At the new location, Wolter continued to patrol the outfield and feast on Coast League pitching. He wanted to return to the majors to show them they had been wrong about him. Miller Huggins of St. Louis showed interest. Huggins felt that the Cards would have won the pennant the prior year with Wolter hitting for him. And with outfielder Lee Magee jumping to the Feds, a spot in the outfield was open. The only reason the major league teams lost interest in Wolter was because they didn't anticipate a full recovery from his broken leg. But the 1914 Pacific Coast League batting crown dispelled any concerns. Huggins sent the Angels an offer for Wolter. The Angels rejected it.[10]

As usual, Wolter didn't report for spring training. He trained with the Santa Clara squad while coaching. But he said he had no interest in the majors or the Federal League even though he had a standing offer from Fielder Jones. Married and living in Redwood City, he preferred playing in California, preferably Northern California. He desired a trade to San Francisco, but was willing to work with the Angels. Harry Williams of the Los Angeles Times sent a wire to Wolter's home asking him about his status with the Angels. He replied,

> As far as I know there is but little difference between myself and the Los Angeles club. I wrote to President Darmody while Tom Stephens was still part owner of the team that I would be glad to see ether of them and talk the matter over... The salary they offered me is the same as last year. In view of the showing that I made, I feel that I am entitled to a raise.[11]

He ignored the ticket the Angels sent him for transportation to Los Angeles. He claimed that if he couldn't come to an agreement, he would just work with his wife in her business. They had two steam laundry businesses, one in Redwood City. And he was up every morning at 6:45 to assist and learn. By the time afternoon rolled around, he coached and worked out at Santa Clara.[12] Wolter claimed that his business made him independent from baseball. But Wolter was a straight shooter. He postured only to improve his salary, which he rightfully deserved after a stellar season. After a trip to Los Angeles and a meeting with Pop Dillon, Wolter indicated he would likely come to an agreement before the end of March. Coincidentally, Santa Clara's season would end approximately the same time.[13] The papers reported that Wolter dispelled rumors that he'd trade baseball for becoming a dryer in a powder plant.

Wolter started the season where he left off the year before by hitting .361 in his first eighty-four at bats. He battled future Hall of Famer Harry Heilmann throughout the season for the batting title. He hit around .360 through most of the season and was fast closing in on Heilmann and league leader Bunny Brief in

September. But on September 2, Wolter badly pulled a muscle that derailed his bid for a second consecutive crown.

> *'I didn't know what had happened when that pain shot through my leg,' declared Wolter. 'It felt like a hard electric shock, with a few extra volts thrown in. And, believe me, third base seemed ten miles from me ...'*[14]

Two weeks later he entered a game against Salt Lake City, but Wolter's leg had not fully recovered. The Los Angeles Times reported:

> *Harry Wolter was back in the game ... his bum leg was far from right and threatened to crumble at any moment. In fact, it did not seem like the same old leg. All the rubber and life seemed to have departed out of it, and it worked like two pieces of scantling held together with a cast-iron hinge.*[15]

Bunny Brief finished the season with a .366 average to with the batting title, followed by Heilmann at .365. However, Wolter's .361 average spanned 145 games whereas the other two played in fewer than 100 games. Wolter didn't win the title, but he did reinforce his reputation as one of the premier hitters in the Pacific Coast League.

During 1915, Doc Strub wed San Franciscan Vera Wood, a devoted Catholic woman, at the St. Francis de Sales Church in San Francisco. The Wood family hosted a wedding and reception that received considerable mention in the society section of the San Francisco newspapers. Several hundred guests attended.

> *Before the altar was an abundance of pink roses, carnations and potted palms. The gown worn by the bride was a handsome combination of satin, brocaded chiffon, silver embroidery and pearls. The tulle veil, which came to the hem of the court train, was secured with a wreath of orange blossoms about the bride's head. The bouquet of lilies of the valley was similar to that which recently won the prize at the exposition as being the most beautiful. It almost covered the front of the gown with its streamers of tulle, with true lovers knots tied with sprays of lilies.*[16]

After a reception at the home of Mrs. Alice Wood, the couple honeymooned in New York City and returned home through the Panama Canal, stopping along the way during a three-month trip. The grand style of the wedding and the elaborate length of the honeymoon indicated opulence. Strub demonstrated success and means not ordinary in the early 1900s.

Likewise, Hal Chase demonstrated success in the new Federal League. After fielding a team called Hal Chase's All-Stars that played against coach

Tramutolo's Santa Clara squad[A] before reporting to Buffalo, Chase hit .291 in his second season for the Bisons, after hitting .347 the previous season. He starred for what was a mediocre team. Perhaps most interesting was Chase's home run total. He hit seventeen home runs. The Federal League was the first league to adopt a more lively baseball to increase run production. In the midst of the deadball era, home runs were uncommon. Balls were relatively soft, and the same dirtied ball was used throughout the game. Not for five more years would major league baseball make changes to rules to encourage more production. But the Feds were more progressive, at least in adopting a new ball.[17] The Fed's "lively ball" exemplified the many changes that occurred in the rules over decades that would make futile statistical comparisons of players from different eras.

The Federal League enjoyed limited success and was kept afloat by the backing of considerably wealthy individuals. Robert Ward, one of the prominent "angels" and founder of the financially successful Ward Baking Company, contributed between $1 million to $1.5 million to be a baseball magnate. He was the President of the Brooklyn team and the President of the Federal League. He also backed the teams in Kansas City, Pittsburgh, and Indianapolis.[18] Another significant backer, wealthy oilman Harry Sinclair, also brought considerable resources to bare to support the league. His considerable power enabled him to wreak havoc with Organized Baseball, if he so chose. However, Sinclair invested most of his energy and finances into building his considerable oil empire.

Sinclair had the uncanny ability to prospect for profitable oil land. He purchased land in Oklahoma that made him a millionaire before he turned thirty. He continued to invest in new land, and as the price of oil fluctuated, Sinclair bought wells when prices were low, and sold oil when prices were high.[19] By 1915, he had begun building the largest independent oil company in America.[B] Like many wealthy men, Sinclair also took an interest in horse racing and baseball. He owned various minor league teams and backed teams in the Federal League.

Organized Baseball didn't sit back and allow for the Federal League to gain strength. It attacked the new league in court arguing a violation of the reserve clauses in contracts. Chicago Judge Kenesaw Landis heard the case. Landis typically carried out the desires of the status quo, whether that involved fighting monopolies under the Roosevelt Administration, upholding an unjust

[A] Hal Chase's All-Stars Tackle the Varsity Team Today, Jan 22, San Francisco Chronicle, pg. 4. Coach Tramatulo would eventually become one of the pallbearers at Hal Chase's funeral.

[B] In the novel Oil, by Upton Sinclair, or the academy award winning movie "There Will Be Blood" made from the novel, the main character Daniel Plainview is likely based on the combined characters of E.L. Doheny and Harry Sinclair. Like Sinclair, Plainview had an ability to find and purchase land bountiful with oil, ahead of the larger oil companies, that made him extremely wealthy.

conviction of boxer Jack Johnson for violation of the Mann Act, or later advancing President Wilson's agenda to root out seditious acts during World War I. Rather than act to decide the case between the baseball leagues, Landis instead chose to broker a settlement. His close friend, Judge George Williams of St. Louis, was the former attorney for the St. Louis Federal team owner Phil Ball and the St. Louis American's owner Robert Lee Hedges. Williams convinced Landis to give him time to broker a settlement. Hedges and Ball met with Ban Johnson and served as mediators with others within their respective leagues.[20] Many scenarios were considered, including a third league. But more important, the discussions demonstrated that both leagues were willing to consider an amicable end to the past hostilities. Some owners in the Federal League likely preferred the end of the fledgling league in exchange for partial ownership in major league franchises.

Then in October of 1915, Federal League President Robert Ward died. Nearly a month later, the Federal League perished. As the writing was on the wall, Harry Sinclair stated that he still had a lot of fight in him. He vowed to establish a team in New York City. But when the leagues merged, Organized Baseball denied Sinclair entry into New York. But they did agree not to blacklist players and to allow owners such as Sinclair to sell their players back into the major leagues.[21]

By February of 1916, the suit of the Federal League against Organized Baseball based on alleged violation of the Federal anti-trust laws was largely moot. The leagues had brokered a settlement.[A] United States Circuit court Kenesaw Landis dismissed the case on a motion made by the Federal League.

One franchise, however, disagreed with the dismissal. The Baltimore team pursued their own case, which would be decided by the Supreme Court seven years later in one of the most noteworthy rulings in baseball history.

Many felt that by delaying, or even avoiding a decision, Landis assured the financial demise of the new league. But rather than view himself as an impediment to the judicial process, Landis defended his actions by claiming he sought what was best for the whole. And while his comments often espoused his intentions to preserve the great virtues of the game, his hollow rhetoric didn't address his responsibility as a Judge to first and foremost pursue justice:

> *I want you gentlemen to leave this court with the understanding that there was not the slightest bit of evidence produced from which the most*

[A] Two Federal League owners were allowed to purchase existing major league teams. Charles Weeghman, who had been President of the Chicago Whales, took controlling interest of the Chicago Cubs of the National League from Charles P. Taft of Cincinnati. Philip Hall and his associates, who were connected with the St. Louis Terriers, gained control of the St. Louis Browns of the American League from Robert Hedges, John E. Bruce, and others.

suspicious person could have obtained anything with which to impute the honesty and integrity of any player of the cleanliness of the game... My decision would not have allowed either of the litigants to leave the court the absolute victor... Therefore I decided that this court had a right to postpone the announcement of such an order, and that is the reason it was postponed.[22]

Even though Landis would develop a reputation as an autocrat, in many cases, he delayed most decisions in order to first assess the direction of political winds. Inevitably, he did rule either justly or unjustly with conviction. But unlike the perpetuated myth, individualism did not fuel his conviction. His conviction came from knowing that his rulings supported the status quo and the powerful. In the Federal League case, his actions clearly benefited major league baseball at the expense of the Feds. For his service to Organized Baseball, he would eventually be rewarded with the commissioner's position.

As the Federal League assets were split up among the remaining owners, Hal Chase became the property of Harry Sinclair. He remained under a guaranteed contract for the next season. Sinclair was obligated to pay Chase whether he played or not. Surely Sinclair would attempt to sell Chase as a matter of administrative cleanup. But Sinclair would find no bids for Chase from the American League. Ban Johnson and Charles Comiskey would not allow Chase back into their league. Comiskey and Johnson were entitled to their grudges. When Chase jumped to the Feds, Johnson viewed Chase's actions as a betrayal. In an interview on August 21, 1918, Ban Johnson later admitted that Chase was overtly blacklisted.

Hal Chase is barred from American League baseball, has been ever since he left Comiskey's club. It was decided then that he was wrong in his treatment of Comiskey, and our league agreed never to reinstate him.[23]

Chase had little concern for either Johnson or Comiskey. They meant as little to him as he did to them. "Screw those bastards," he mumbled to himself under his breath. "I don't need them for nothin'."

---

[1] Angel Outfield is Unsurpassed, Harry A. Williams, Los Angeles Times, Sep 24, 1914. IV3
[2] Several Angels May Play Ball in Cuba, Harry A. William, Oct 23, 1914, pg. III3
[3] Seraphs Swamp tigers Twice and Win Series, Clyde A. Bruckman, LA Times, 8/17/1914, Pg. III1
[4] Hogan to Get Three Players from Rowland, Los Angeles Times, 2/18/1915
[5] Handicap Meet is Canceled, San Francisco Chronicle, May 15, 1915, pg. 7
[6] Hap Hogan's Busher Days, May 23,1915, Los Angeles Times, pg. VII7
[7] Estate of Hap Hogan Is Valued at $1300, San Francisco Chronicle, May 27, 1915, pg. 8
[8] Them Were The Days, Jeane Hoffman, Los Angeles Times, June 16, 1953, Pg. C3
[9] Them Were The Days, Jeane Hoffman, Los Angeles Times, June 16, 1953, Pg. C3
[10] Cards After Harry Wolter, Harry A. Williams, Los Angeles Times, pg 17, Feb 27.1915

238

[11] Wolter Explains Why He Has Not Reported. Harry A. Williams, LA Times, March 15, 1915, Pg. III3

[12] Wolter Hints He Is Willing To Compromise, SF Chronicle, Mar 9, 1915, Pg. 5

[13] Harry Wolter Here And Intends To Be an Angel, LA Times, Mar 16, 1915, pg. III3

[14] Harry Wolter is Laid Out, Sep 3, 1915, Los Angeles Times, pg. III2

[15] Los Angeles Times, Sep 16, 1915, pg. III1

[16] Wedding Bells ring Merrily in Oakland, San Francisco Chronicle, April 18, 1915, pg 16

[17] Who Will Furnish Balls To Fedreals, Los Angeles Times, Jan 14, 1915, pg. III1

[18] Ward Lost Million in Federal League, New York Times, May 6, 1917, pg. 17

[19] Kansas State Historical Society

[20] Judge Landis Behind Peace, Los Angeles Times, Apr 27, 1915, pg III

[21] New York Times, Dec 3, 1915

[22] Judge Landis Handles Federal League Anti-Trust Case, Chicago Daily Tribune, Feb 8, 1916

[23] Cincinnati Times-Star, August 21, 1918

Chapter 20

Major League Baseball: The Mighty Steamroller

When the Federal League folded, Cincinnati sportswriter William Phelon wrote in Baseball Magazine "Organized baseball is a mighty steamroller. It may roll slowly, but it crushes everything that opposes it, sooner or later."[1] Phelon's comments were prompted by the demise of the Feds, but they applied to the effect that the National Commission had on individuals as well. Ban Johnson and the American League had just begun to steamroll Hal Chase.

As a free agent, Chase wanted to play for his old friend Hen Berry and ex-manager Harry Wolverton with the San Francisco Seals in the Pacific Coast League.[2] However, he had a guaranteed contract with Harry Sinclair for $8,000. The PCL had a salary cap that prevented any team from paying more than $4,000 for any player. So Chase proposed to Sinclair that he sign with the Seals for $4,000 and receive only $4,000 from Sinclair. No finagling in the PCL contract could land Chase in the league without Sinclair's agreement to Chase's proposal. The St. Louis Americans showed interest in Chase, but Ban Johnson would not allow Chase to play again in the American League. National League teams, including the Cincinnati Reds and New York Giants, began to court Chase. Ban Johnson was certainly irked when his nemesis John McGraw displayed interest in Chase, the prodigal son.

Technically, if Chase returned to the major leagues, he remained the property of the Chicago White Sox. Whatever National League team he joined would need to pay or trade with the Sox. Rumors circulated that McGraw was willing to trade Fred Merkle to the Sox in exchange for the right to sign Chase. In March, Hal flew to meet with the Giants to discuss a contract.[3] But his first choice was to remain in California.

As a free agent in the winter of 1915-16, Chase had the freedom to play wherever he wanted without facing a ban. Like a pig in slop, Chase relished playing near his hometown. In December he played in a game at Santa Clara College where famous pilot Art Smith was honored. Smith became known for his daredevil flying – loop to loops, nose dives, night sky writing, and dropping bombs that exploded in the air that cascaded lights in the sky.[A] Smith put on a show for 12,000 at Santa Clara before the game. The school sent invitations to

---

[A] Santa Clara College had a strong tradition in aviation. The University had a long relationship with the father of aviation, John J. Montgomery, who was an inventor and professor at Santa Clara. In 1883, he made the first manned, controlled, heavier-than-air flight in the United States. Arguably, Montgomery received the first patent for an airplane, although Montgomery called it an aeroplane.

friends and alumni from from miles around for the event. The professional baseball players in the exhibition game included Duffy Lewis, Harry Hooper, Dutch Leonard, Ping Bodie, Harry Wolter, Joe Gedeon, and Justin Fitzgerald.[4] Harry Wolter had coached Santa Clara the previous season, but was replaced by Thomas Ybarrando[A] as Wolter pursued a head coaching position with Stanford.

The local stars continued to play in exhibition games throughout the winter. In February, Chase joined a team of San Jose All Stars once again in a game against Santa Clara College. With retired pitcher Elmer Stricklett umpiring the game, Chase took the field with friends Frank Arellanes, Harry Wolter, and two participants from the prior year's World Series, Duffy Lewis and Eddie Burns. With the Seals' Harry Wolverton in attendance, the stars won 9-5 amidst reports that Chase would likely play for the Seals the following year. He even began working out with the team in San Jose at Luna Park and was listed in the Seals' pre-season roster.

Where Wolter would play in 1916 was also still uncertain. For months, rumors circulated that he would be the next manager of the Los Angeles Angels. Wolter claimed that he didn't give the rumors any credence, and said he would return the following season to give his best as a player.[5] But Wolter did want the manager position. At first, Nixey Callahan was offered the job. Disappointed, Wolter agreed to return the next season. But in January when the Angels named Frank Chance the manager instead of Wolter or Callahan, Harry considered retiring from the Angels. Wolter probably could have come to terms with another selection, such as Callahan. He had the richest contract in the Pacific Coast League, so he could overcome a bruised ego and return to the fold if the selection had not been Chance. But he had a grudge with Frank Chance ever since he played for him in New York. When Chance was manager of New York, he had released Wolter to the minors after he broke his leg. Chance claimed that he had nothing to do with Wolter's departure; he had been instructed by Frank Farrell to waive Wolter after he broke his leg. Chance explained that he actually tried to help Harry. When Farrell instructed him to release Wolter, Chance immediately called Hen Berry. Within three days, Berry had offered Wolter a contract with the Angels.[6]

At first, Wolter simply refused to report for spring training, which he never did in the past anyway. But Frank Chance was strict about players reporting for training. A paper said the following about Chance:

> *Frank Chance was never a chap who liked to be obeyed half way. As a matter of fact, he is just about as strict a disciplinarian with his ball players as you would care to meet.*[7]

If ever Chance had met his match in terms of hardheaded obstinacy, it was with Wolter. Wolter would not report for spring training. Instead, he agreed

---

[A] Fitzgerald would take over from Ybarrando

to become the head baseball coach at Stanford University. Wolter used one of the only negotiation tools that existed for ballplayers; he demonstrated that he didn't need Organized Baseball. Wolter made the announcement on the phone from his home in Redwood City. He had planned a trip to Los Angeles to discuss business, but he cancelled the trip and decided to correspond with the Angels through the mail. He had done this in the past with Hen Berry by stating "Come to me if you want to talk with me."

Chance expressed his sentiments in the newspapers by having reporters write that the Angels had catered to Wolter in the past. They didn't say, however, whether they would continue to do so in the future, and did admit that Wolter was too valuable to lose. Wolter always favored a trade to the San Francisco Seals. And if the alternative was to lose Wolter without any compensation, a trade to the Seals appeared likely. It seemed that Hal Chase and Harry Wolter would once again be teammates, this time under Hen Berry in San Francisco.

But as the season approached and reality supplanted speculation, Harry Sinclair disposed of Chase to the Cincinnati Reds. The team's first baseman had broken his collarbone and the team was in need of a replacement.[8] The Reds matched Chase's salary from the Federal League, which exceeded anything the Seals were allowed to offer. He received a three-year contract for $25,000. And although Chase claimed that he preferred to play for the Seals and only joined the Reds because he was "forced to play" because he became the Reds' property, Chase would never have played anywhere for less money. He claimed that the Berry brothers and the Seals were working out an arrangement to give him 10% ownership, the maximum $4,000 salary, plus a $4,000 bonus that would be constructed to get around the league's salary cap. But the terms were never worked out.[9] For Chase, the dream of playing in California would remain a dream.

By the end of March, Wolter reported to the Angels training camp in Lake Elsinore. Shortly thereafter, Stanford announced that Jack McCarthy would replace Wolter as their baseball coach. Wolter only coached Stanford for a month. The temporary position served as leverage in negotiations. But Wolter would not have taken the provisional role for selfish reasons; he did consider the head coaching position at Stanford as an attractive option.

When Wolter arrived at spring training, he encountered ex-Santa Clara coach Joe Corbett, who had starred for the Angels on the mound over a decade before. One of the league's best pitchers at one time, Corbett vowed he was strong enough to stage a comeback at thirty-eight, nearly twenty years after winning over twenty games in the major leagues.

At Maier Ranch, the Vernon Tigers began training for their first full season without manager Hap Hogan. Maier kept the atmosphere light by organizing a turkey-eating contest. Each competitor was given a turkey and twelve ears of corn. Trainer Shine Scott came from behind for the win. Shine strategically began the contest by eating the turkey, because as Scott explained, you can buy corn cheap, "but the price of turkey roosts powerfully high." Besides, he said there was nothing in his contract that required him to eat corn. Over the years, Shine Scott had become more than a trainer to the club. He had become a fixture and an institution. His whole life revolved around the Vernon Tigers. Shine was under contract to Maier, but Maier admitted that Scott drew up the contract himself. In contrast to the player contracts that provided that owners give ten days notice before releasing a player, Scott wrote in that he required ten years notice. Maier didn't argue with Scott over the matter.

Maier signed Frank Arellanes in the winter. If the Federal League had survived, Arellanes reported he would have arranged a contract with its Buffalo franchise. Buffalo's Harry Lord, Chase's friend and Arellanes' former Boston teammate, had recommended Frank.

Maier also forged an excellent relationship with Comiskey and the Chicago White Sox organization over the years that proved a source of players. Other PCL owners also remained close to the team that traveled to the Coast each spring. The prior year, the Chisox requested a permanent relationship with the Los Angeles Angels, although that never transpired. Not coincidentally, many players involved in the team's alleged fix of the 1919 World Series played in the Pacific Coast League. Maier's Vernon team featured Swede Risberg, who tore up California pitching. Joe Gedeon and Lefty Williams were close friends who had played together on Salt Lake City. When they were called up to the Sox, manager Blankenship sought to acquire Morris Rath as compensation. Chick Gandil had played for Charlie Graham a few years back. And Buck Weaver starred for the San Francisco Seals at one time.[A]

As soon as the Tigers assembled at Maier Ranch, Arellanes showed good form. In a game between the Yannigans[B] and the regulars, Frank won 10-5. The paper reported that he had his spitter working to perfection. He continued to win, perhaps with spirits lifted by the $500 bonus check that Sacramento sent him for winning twenty-five games the previous season.

As the Pacific Coast League season began, Henry Berry and Johnny Powers made sure that Hap Hogan would be remembered. Nearly a year after his death the league agreed to pay tribute to Hap with a moment of silence at each

---

[A] Lefty Williams, Buck Weaver, Chick Gandil, and Swede Risberg were four of the eight White Sox permanently banned from Organized Baseball. Joe Gedeon was implicated as a possible organizer of one of the fixes. And Morris Rath was the Cincinnati Reds batter who White Sox pitcher Ed Cicotte hit with a pitch to signal to gamblers that the World Series fix was on as planned.

[B] A term used to describe the second string players.

league game. The quiet reflection for Hap was countered by joy in the Graham household. Charlie and his wife were graced with a baby boy, Joseph.[A]

Chase, Wolter, and Arellanes had excellent seasons in 1916. Arellanes won his first three games and was 7-2 by July. Wolter's strong hitting had major league teams warning the Angels that they should either sell Wolter or risk losing him during the upcoming draft. Wolter was ultimately sold to the Chicago Cubs, but remained with the Angels through the season. Joe Tinker of the Cubs demanded that Wolter report right away. But the Angels refused. Owner Johnny Powers told Frank Chance to go work out the differences with his old infield mate, part of the legendary Cub trio of "Tinker to Evers to Chance."[10] Powers' dogged resistance brought the Angels the PCL championship.

Chase won the National League batting title with a .339 average. He also led the league in hits and runs, and as usual, was the best defensive first baseman in the game. But the Reds still finished more than thirty-three games behind the pennant winners. During the season, the Cincinnati Enquirer reported that Chase would become the team's next manager. It announced that the current manager, Buck Herzog, would be traded to the New York Giants and that Chase would replace him.

Instead, Herzog was traded for Christy Mathewson, who became the manager. Even in the interim until Mathewson reported to the team, Chase did not lead the team. Catcher Ivey Wingo was given the role. But Chase claimed no animosity. He responded by closing out an outstanding season and stated, "Matty was an ideal manager and I cannot conceive how any player could have trouble with him."

Chase did not return to California right away as he usually did in the fall. He covered the World Series between the Red Sox and Brooklyn for Tom Swope of the Cincinnati Post, attended to business interests in the East, and played in an All-Star game in Kansas City.[11]

Off-season rumors circulated about Frank Chance leaving the Angels to manage the Cubs. Chance claimed that if he did take a position in the majors, he would recommend Harry Wolter for the manager position with the Angels. With a backhanded compliment, Chance admitted that Wolter was a crabby player, but explained that he too had once been the same way. He petitioned that the managerial responsibilities were just what Wolter needed "to steady him." Wolter may have received a better reference from an enemy. For the 1917 season, Wolter reported to the Chicago Cubs.

Chase returned to Cincinnati to play for manager Christy Mathewson.

[A] Joseph was one of four Graham children.

[1]   Baseball Magazine. March 1916
[2]   Hal Chase Admits He Wouldn't Mind Playing With the Seals. Harry B. Smith. San Francisco Chronicle. Dec 25, 1915, pg. 6
[3]   Fred Merkle and Hal Chase May be Traded. Los Angeles Times. Mar 10, 1916 Pf. III1
[4]   Art Smith Star At Santa Clara Game Today. SF Chronicle. Dec 12, 1915, pg 40
[5]   Hal Chase Admits He Wouldn't Mind Playing With the Seals. Harry B. Smith. SF Chronicle. Dec 25, 1915, pg. 6
[6]   Wolter May Make Trouble. Harry A. Williams. Los Angeles Times. Jan 8, 1916, pg. 16
[7]   Some Salaries to Be Raised: Others Lowered -- Harry Wolverton. Harry B. Smith. SF Chronicle. Jan 16, 1916, pg 47
[8]   Hal Chase to Join "Cinci." Apr 7, 1916. Los Angeles Times, pg III2
[9]   The Sporting News. September 18, 1941. Lester Grant (Oakland Post Enquirer)
[10] Powers Refuses Cubs' Demand For Immediate Delivery of Wolter. LA Times, Aug 29, 1916, pg. III1
[11] Chase Will Not Winter in California. SF Chronicle. Oct 13, 1916, pg. 6

Chapter 21

Baseball Woes Trivial Amidst Global Pandemonium

On April 6, 1917, the United States declared war against Germany and joined the conflict in Europe. The isolationist Woodrow Wilson could no longer remain neutral in the face of perceived and real threats internally and externally. British intelligence presented reports that Germany contacted Mexico regarding an overthrow of the United States by promising the Southwestern United States in exchange for support. At the same time, suspected German conspirators in major cities were arrested to avoid an uprising from within. When Wilson appealed to the American people, he said,

> *It is a fearful thing to lead this great peaceful people into war, into the most terrible and disastrous of all wars, civilization itself seeming to be in the balance.*

After declaring war, the United States drafted four million men, including nearly half of the major league baseball players. Over the next year, the country would send ten thousand soldiers each day to fight in France against the Germans.

By June, President Wilson passed an Espionage Act that threatened to convict anyone who interfered with the operation of the United States armed forces, which included attempts to cause "insubordination, disloyalty, mutiny, refusal of duty, or willful obstruction of the recruiting or enlistment service of the United States." Wilson feared that dissent in a time of war constituted a threat to the war effort. In 1918, Wilson altered the act to also criminalize "sedition," or any opposition to the government.[A] Facing the bona fide threat of a German invasion, and having witnessed the Russian Revolution in 1917 that ended Csar Nicholas II's reign, President Wilson acted swiftly to subvert any dissident internal organization.

It was not a good time to be an "outsider" in America. Anarchists and socialists were rounded up. Anyone perceived as a threat to the United States or its institutions, including Baseball, were lumped together as non-conformist nuisances.

Over the next year, Judge Kenesaw Landis would use the Espionage and Sedition Act, at the direction of the President, to convict large groups of socialists

---

[A] In time, the Act was considered unconstitutional unless actions represented a "clear and present danger," or "imminent lawless action." But as the country entered the Great War, the Act was considered necessary and constitutional.

and draft protesters. Bill Haywood, founder of the labor union IWW, who had been inspired by the Haymarket Tragedy he witnessed in Chicago in 1886, was found guilty along with more than one hundred other socialists and union activists. Haywood and fourteen others were sentenced to twenty years in prison.[A] As was the case with many decisions by Landis, justice took a backseat to political expediency.

During 1917, the war effort consumed baseball. Over the next year, the Secretary of War issued a "work or fight" order that required that all eligible men, including professional baseball players, report for duty. Of the half of the league that didn't report, many of the others worked in industries that supported the war effort.

Gambling in baseball had been a constant for decades. During the first World Series in 1903, Lou Criger claimed he was approached by gamblers to convince Cy Young to throw the Series. In 1904, Barney Dreyfuss bet heavily on his team. In 1905, Rube Waddell sat out the series with a "sore shoulder" that some say earned him $17,000 from gamblers. That same year, John McGraw bet $400 on his Giants to defeat the Athletics. In 1908, the Boston Nationals didn't have its license renewed by the city because of too much gambling at its park. The same year, McGraw's Giants attempted to bribe umpire Bill Klem in the one-game playoff with the Cubs to see who would win the pennant. In 1911, Garry Herrmann, owner of the Cincinnati Reds stated he would no longer deliver telegrams to facilitate gambling. In 1912, the Philadelphia Athletics had twenty-five men arrested because of gambling at its ballpark. The same year, the Philadelphia Phillies President wrote articles for the Chicago Post accusing the Cardinals' manager Roger Bresnahan of having thrown key games to the Giants to help them beat Philly for the National League pennant. He also claimed that the umpires were "controlled" by McGraw. The owner was banished from the league for making his claims public, but Bresnahan was also soon released. Gambling was rampant.

But in 1917, perhaps because of the war, baseball's gambling problems reached new heights. On June 16 in a game between the Chisox and the Bosox, the outcome of a game was changed because of gamblers. Before the third out in the fifth inning at a game in Fenway Park, gamblers instigated hundreds of fans to run onto the field before the game could become "official" and cause steep losses. When the crowd descended upon the field, the umpires were forced to suspend the game and replay it another day.[1]

[A] Eugene Debs, Socialist Party leader who had run for President against Woodrow Wilson in 1912 and had been the organizer of Chicago's Pullman strike in 1894, was convicted and sentenced for ten years for speaking out against the draft. In 1919, Victor Berger, a Socialist elected to the House of Representatives, but denied the office, was sentenced as well.

In early September, as the eventual World Series winner Chicago White Sox were closing in on the pennant, they sent a $1,100 payment to the Detroit Tigers to "lay down" for four games.[2] The money was raised through a collection taken up among all of the Chicago players and sent "as a gift" to Detroit in appreciation for their competitiveness during the season, particularly against the White Sox' foes. This kind of payment was considered customary. Chisox player Swede Risberg admitted in 1927 to the payment. And in defense, Charles Comiskey did not deny the payment. He merely claimed that sending such presents was an old baseball custom and was not meant to bribe any players.

In truth, many bribes occurred at the end of the seasons between teams and players. Some teams bribed other teams to sew up a pennant. And players were given bonuses at year-end if their teams finished second, third, or fourth, so teams bribed other teams to assure their bonus money. Some players who wanted to improve their batting average or extra-base hit totals prior to contract negotiations bribed pitchers to throw them easy pitches to hit. There was hardly a player, owner, or manager who didn't know about some payment for services rendered.

Hal Chase certainly knew of the custom. And many historians would write that Chase had already been involved with fixing games. But only two things were certain – first, counter to many claims, Chase had not yet been accused of any game fixing. The only source for allegations was the media that served as the owners' puppets. With Chase's recurring injuries, certainly owners became frustrated with his inability to always play at full speed, which fueled criticism. Second, Chase was one of the most tenured players in the game and had produced at the highest level over many years. Over the same period of time, thousands of players had attempted to break into the competitive arena. In spite of effort and skill, few succeeded. Yet many claimed that Hal Chase was gifted enough to give less than full effort and still be one of the game's most productive players.

Many seemingly credible modern day writers, including Bill James and Eliot Asinof, who have earned credibility and distinction, have maligned Chase, painting him even up until 1917 as a "troublemaker" and the cause of the evil in baseball. These claims created a convenient villain as well as the conflict and drama that would make their writing more marketable. But their cases inaccurately blend fiction and non-fiction. At times, the writers were blatantly incorrect with their facts. At other times, they editorialized in a manner that painted Chase as "the outsider," the anarchist, and rebel.

When referring to 1917 and 1918, writers often contrasted the chaste Mathewson with the evil Chase; Mathewson became the embodiment of the ideal baseball player in terms of character and ability. Chase became the embodiment of an unruly insubordinate. Yet, in the context of the facts up until this point in time, Chase was not a villain. Chase was no more a troublemaker than any other baseball player. But he did stand up to Ban Johnson and Charles Comiskey, and for that, writers from every era have at times unfairly perpetuated the myth of Chase as a ne'er-do-well.

During the era, the baseball union was too weak to provide players such as Chase support when dealing with Organized Baseball. So Chase fended for himself. The President of the Players' Union, Dave Fultz did threaten owners with strikes if they didn't meet with him to listen to grievances. Players were upset that after the Federal League folded, their salaries were cut back to the levels in place before the competing league formed. In many cases, the owners ignored their contractual responsibilities once they faced a lack of competition. But Fultz' ideas didn't often jibe with the players. For example, Fultz wanted players to sign a no-drinking pledge. He also wanted to expel players who didn't hustle. Players never took him seriously enough to organize a powerful base. Baseball ignored the toothless Fultz. And with a weak union, the owners not only didn't concede to player demands, they often ignored their obligations. As one who dared to challenge the National Commission, Chase was publicly maligned. The truth was much less dramatic than what has often been portrayed.

In 1917, Chase had posted another fair season for manager Christy Mathewson. His batting average slipped considerably from the previous season to .277, but Chase was productive at the plate. In the league, he was first in at bats, second in RBI, fourth in extra base hits, and fifth in total bases. Over the past three seasons, he had been one of the most consistent RBI men in baseball, averaging eighty-six each year. The Reds played better under Mathewson. After initially competing for the league lead, the Reds fell eventually fell well behind the pennant winning New York Giants toward the end and finished fourth.

At season's end, Chase and Christy Mathewson traveled through the country selling bonds together to support the U.S. efforts in the war. Chase also promoted the new book published by Spalding and "written" by Chase entitled How to Play First Base. Spalding published a series of books that offered instructions about playing the various baseball positions. The books also served to advertise the company's

How to Play First Base, by Hal Chase

athletic equipment. As the preeminent first baseman in baseball, Chase was asked to lend his name to the tome.

In February of 1918, Ban Johnson announced at the Winter Meetings that he had enough with the game's escalating gambling problem. He announced,

*If any club owner fails to do his utmost to stamp out gambling, he will
lose his franchise. If any American League player is caught associating
with gamblers at any time, his immediate expulsion will follow. I mean
business and I am preparing to go ahead with a policy that will suppress
an evil that, unless checked, will undermine the national game.[3]*

The San Francisco Chronicle noted that gambling caused a lot of trouble
in Pittsburgh as well as Boston. And in San Francisco, the paper noted that there
were men who bet on the games and on the plays during a game. They reported
that although there had been efforts to suppress them, they often persisted in full
view. The prior year in Oakland, bold gamblers paid off betters right in the
grandstands. The newspaper expected that PCL President Baum would follow in
"Fat Ban's" lead and issue an edict against gambling in the league.

Charlie Graham wasn't much of a gambler. Perhaps best described as
"staid," Graham only played poker for the sake of passing time on long road trips.
Former owner Mike Fischer called Graham the greatest poker player that ever
donned a Coast League uniform. And many ballplayers became very good poker
players on the long train trips. But according to Fischer, Graham never lost.

*He had to owe in the first pot, but after that it was all Graham. Before
they were back, all the money belonged to Graham and most likely the
whole crew would be in debt to him. Graham never took a chance – he
played his cards close up.[4]*

So when the conservative Graham was willing to gamble on a new
franchise in the Pacific Coast League, he successfully courted financial backers,
including friends Doc Strub and George Putnam, a man from a wealthy
Sacramento family, and C.J. Heeseman of Sacramento. At first, he wanted to
replace the Sacramento team that had moved to Salt Lake City. He felt that the
timing was finally right for Sacramento to succeed as a baseball town because of
the profliferation of roads and the increase in auto usage. He claimed that people
could come to Sacramento from miles around to see a game.

Graham contacted McCredie in Portland about purchasing his team and
moving it to Sacramento. But Heeseman and Graham decided that they didn't
want to pay anything for a new team. They planned to petition the league for a
new franchise, pay nothing for the right, and build a team from scratch.[5]

But George Putnam insisted that the best minor league baseball town in
America was San Francisco. So Graham approached the Berry brothers about
selling the S.F. Seals.[6] On February 25, 1918, Charlie Graham, Doc Strub,
George Putnam, and Tom Stephens purchased the San Francisco Seals. Doc Strub
provided much of the financing. While Strub initially stated he would assume a
background role due to his varied business interests, he became the team's
President. Graham assumed the role of General Manager, Putnam was Secretary,
and Stephens became the Treasurer. Graham resigned his role with the
Sacramento club and disposed of his business interests in the capital city.

Excited about the opportunity to build a successful franchise in San Francisco, one of Strub's first announcements was that he wanted a lot of "Harry Hoopers" for the Seals. Strub remembered the first time he saw Harry Hooper play in 1907 when he showed blazing speed down the first baseline after grounding a ball to Strub. To Strub, Hooper left an impression with both his speed and the three World Series championships he had won with Boston since that game in Alameda. To Strub, Hooper symbolized the undiscovered young talent that would develop into superstardom. To that end, Strub and the other new owners would be as successful as any minor league ownership in baseball history producing stars for the major leagues. As the new owners assembled their wish lists, Charlie Graham commented that he needed a player like Hap Hogan who understood how to entertain. He admitted that Hap may not have been the best player, but he filled the stands.[7]

Strub filled the stands by organizing boosters from the local Elks' Club and Olympic Club of which the Doc was a member. Graham spent more time fortifying the team. In need of an outfielder, Graham tried to claim Harry Wolter from the Chicago Cubs. Graham and Cub owner Weeghman negotiated terms that would bring Wolter to the Seals, but Weeghman sold Harry away to Sacramento instead. Even though Graham protested to President Baum, Wolter slipped through Graham's fingers.

As the season started, the league still suffered from financial difficulties. The rosters had been reduced and the one-umpire system was still in effect. Frugality was the rule of the day, and development of young players was the mode for survival. But Charlie Graham commented in the newspapers that he was comfortable with the one-umpire system. In any situation, Charlie Graham would make lemonade out of lemons.

Sometimes Graham was given a plum rather than a lemon, as was the case in 1917 when the team signed pitcher Frank O'Doul. The twenty-one year old southpaw, known by his nickname "Lefty," showed immediate promise and was assigned to veteran Ham Iburg for mentorship. During the 1918 season, O'Doul won twenty-five games against nine losses in a shortened season. The New York Yankees signed him for the 1919 season.[A]

Frank Arellanes would not prepare for the 1918 season. After a decade as one of the top pitchers in California, the new manager of the Vernon Tigers, George Stovall, released the aging pitcher. Arellanes would no longer be invited

---

[A] He was unsuccessful in four seasons in the major leagues as a pitcher due to arm trouble. But he would return to the Seals as a hitter, and would return to the majors and become one of the greatest hitters in the history of the game. His career batting average of .349 ranks fourth all-time. He is the only player since 1900 who ranks among the top twenty in career batting average who isn't in the Hall of Fame other than Shoeless Joe Jackson, who ranked third all-time but was subsequently banned from baseball.

to the bashes at Maier Ranch. For the first time, Arellanes would face life without baseball.

In the winter, eight hundred more Shriners attended a Maier feast featuring barbecued beef, mutton, and bulls' heads served with beans and Spanish fixings. To enliven the festivities, Ju-Jitsu and Japanese sword combats were demonstrated. The always-charitable Maier sent the leftovers to the local orphanages. In 1918, however, Maier turned over the ranch to the military. The Woman's Land Army used the Maier Ranch as its headquarters. The Woman's Land Army organized women, known as "Land Girls," to replace men in agricultural jobs who were called to serve in the war.

The war had a far-reaching impact on all of American life in 1918. Religious leaders used the chaos to push for prohibition in all of Los Angeles County, including Venice and Vernon, where the Tigers played. Much of the argument against the sale of liquor claimed that it contributed to the drunkenness of the military, which was true to an extent. Vernon, and Doyle's Bar, had attracted off-duty military that congregated in the wet town and sometimes contributed to delinquency. In April, all of the bars were closed. Many claimed better "moral and economic conditions" due to the closure. They cited fewer idle men and a noticeable reduction in arrests. But with large cafes, grills, liquor stores, and bars closed, rents dropped and the county suffered from lost tax revenues.[8]

The Los Angeles City Council debated the closure of bars, including Doyle's Bar in Vernon, cited as one of the largest contributors to crime and drunkenness. Advocates of prohibition claimed that it wasn't fair for taxpayers to bear the burden of paying police to control Vernon's problems. Jack Doyle agreed to hire twenty plain-clothes men to patrol his establishment to keep trouble to a minimum. He also agreed to watch for those purchasing liquor on behalf of military men. And he vowed not to allow the military to attend or participate in boxing matches on his premises.[9] Due to the need for the tax revenues, the county couldn't afford not to allow liquor sales.

Pastor Dr. J. Whitcomb Brougher, a prominent fundamentalist Baptist preacher from Glendale, visited Doyle's Bar to witness what many called "The Vernon Hellhole." After meeting with Jack Doyle and spending time at the bar, he commented that Doyle is:

> ... about the cleanest man that I have ever seen in the saloon business... last night they [Vernon bars] were packed to capacity with men, young and old - laboring men, clerks, movie actors, and men who are rich and men who are poor. If a man got a little hilarious and showed signs of intoxication, one of the policemen would hurry him out along the sidewalk, put him the street car and tell him to get on and go... But the saloon keepers of Vernon are no more to blame for this situation than is any man or woman who has voted to license the saloon and let it do

*business ... The saloons at Vernon and Venice, and in every other place
in our country today should be closed and the whole nation made dry
during the time ... of the war.*[10]

Later in 1918, both Dr. Brougher's church halls and Doyle's Bar would
close for another reason – the outbreak of flu pandemic. Bars, churches, dance
halls, and other places where people congregated in Los Angeles were closed.
Jack Doyle had closed his bar at 11 AM on October 19, well before authorities
required him to do so. With his available time, he helped to sell Liberty Bonds.
Boxing bouts were postponed until after the pandemic ended, which ended many
boxers' careers and created a long hiatus for the rest who had become accustomed
to fighting multiple times each month. One bright spot was the sales of lemons.
Lemon sales surged as the Chamber of Commerce reported that sucking on a
lemon proved a defensive measure against the illness.[11]

The Spanish Flu pandemic of 1918-1919 killed more people, up to forty
million worldwide, than World War I. It was the most devastating epidemic in
recorded history; it killed more people in one year than the Bubonic Plague killed
in four years in the 1300s. As the war approached its end, and when nobody could
imagine a bleaker outlook for mankind, the pandemic struck the globe. One in
five people in the world were infected; 2.5% didn't survive. People often died
rapid deaths. After becoming infected in the evening, many died by morning.
The flu began to spread first in the United States in March. By August, a virulent
strain appeared in Europe and Africa.[A]

Baseball players during 1918 not only witnessed the threat of a World
War, but the horror of the flu, which could claim anyone with little notice.
Additionally, the season was shortened due to the War. As of Labor Day on
September 2, the season ended.[12] The Chicago Cubs and the Boston Red Sox
were scheduled in the 1918 World Series after the shortened season, but debate
continued whether the series should be played. The World Series winners each
expected $2,000, and the losers anticipated a bonus of $1,400. With attendance
down and the season shortened, there were fewer funds to pay the players. The
second, third, and fourth place teams didn't get their usual share. And the World
Series cuts were reduced to less than $1,000 for the winners. The players filed a
grievance with the National Commission, but the Commission showed them no
support. The players' union was virtually non-existent. The teams refused to take
the field for game five. The Boston mayor successfully appealed to the players to
complete the Series for the sake of patriotism. The players did complete the
Series, but patriotism wasn't the only motivation.

A year later, on a train to New York shared by the Cubs and the Chisox
at the end of the 1919 season, the Cubs admitted to the league-leading Chisox that

---

[A] The flu was first detected in the United States. But it received much press when it
spread to Spain from France.

they had fixed the previous year's World Series in 1918. They said they had conceded the contest to the Red Sox to make up for the income lost from the reduction in their World Series bonus. Players on the Cubs implicated in game fixes during their careers included Bill Killefer, Fred Merkle, Claude Hendrix, and Grover Cleveland Alexander. The mention of the fix to the White Sox on the train in 1919 was perhaps the seed that piqued the interest of Ed Cicotte, Lefty Williams, and Chick Gandil as they devised a plan to fix the 1919 World Series with the Cincinnati Reds. And why not? Since the Federal League failed, the owners weren't honoring their contracts, the National Commission ignored grievances, and the players' union was ineffective. So the ballplayers took care of business on their own.

Charles Comiskey's right hand man, Harry Grabiner kept a diary found years later in the Chicago White Sox ballpark. In it, Grabiner kept notes about many players involved in fixing games, including Hall of Famers Pete "Grover Cleveland" Alexander and Rabbit Maranville. Grabiner also noted how journeyman pitcher Gene Packard had allegedly played a key role fixing the 1918 World Series.[13] The Cubs were the heavy favorites. But Babe Ruth, Harry Hooper, and the Red Sox prevailed against the suddenly hapless Cubs.

Just as the Cubs and probably many more baseball players sidled up to gamblers at the end of the shortened 1918 season, so did Hal Chase. Before the season ended, Chase allegedly approached relief pitcher and teammate Jimmy Ring as he took the mound in a tie ballgame. According to Ring, Chase said he had bet on the opponent and offered Ring $50 to throw the game. Ring refused, but still gave up the winning run. After the game, Chase allegedly handed Ring his $50 in the lobby of the Majestic Hotel. Ring informed manager Christy Mathewson, who took the matter up with National League President. A few weeks later, Mathewson suspended Chase indefinitely for "indifferent work." Chase had his salary suspended. Chase countersued in order to receive what he was contractually owed. The case went to court. At the same time, National League President Tener resigned and was replaced by John Heydler. Heydler investigated the claims against Chase between August 16 and August 21. Reds Manager Christy Mathewson and President Garry Herrmann charged that Chase violated Section 40 of the League Constitution:

> *Any person who shall be proven guilty of offering, agreeing, conspiring or attempting to causes any game of ball to result otherwise than on its merits under the playing rules, shall be forever disqualified by the President of the league from acting as umpire, manager or player, in any capacity in any game of ball participated in by a league club.[14]*

The league investigated various claims about Chase betting on games and approaching players in a brazen manner predominantly in July. The league obtained affidavits from Jimmy Ring, Mike Regan, Pol Perritt, and John McGraw.

Another incident during the season, an alleged fix coordinated with teammate Lee Magee, was not yet known.

While the case was investigated, Chase spent some time away from baseball with a lover in New York named Billy. Chase was sent a letter from "Billy" during this period. Billy asked that it be destroyed after Chase read it. Unfortunately for Chase, he failed to destroy the letter, which later surfaced as evidence in divorce proceedings with Anna. The Cincinnati Times-Star published the letter in 1921.[15]

Before the investigation into allegations against Chase was fully vetted, Hermann wrote a letter to Heydler regarding the Chase matter. Hermann recommended what would become an ongoing practice in Organized Baseball – he advised not to publicly discuss the findings for fear of a black eye to baseball. Or perhaps by stating that the findings weren't going to be revealed, Hermann intended to imply guilt without having to provide proof:

> *In discussing this matter in a confidential way with Johnson last Sunday night, he was strongly of the opinion that if the testimony warrants expulsion, that the reason for it should not be made public. The evidence is so damaging that he believes - and I agree with him - that it would be a severe black eye for the game if the details became fully known.[16]*

Christy Mathewson was not present for the inquiry in January. Serving in the military, Matty forwarded his testimony in writing. He wrote that he had no proof of any wrongdoing, but suspected from his poor judgment in the field that Chase was purposely making bad plays. He cited hesitation fielding bunts, throwing late to bases, missing balls thrown wide to the bag, fielding grounders with one hand, playing too close to second base, overplaying bunts, and not covering first base. On many calls for bunts or hit and run plays, Mathewson noted that Chase was so unreliable that he discontinued calling for the plays.

Mathewson's testimony on the surface may seem anecdotal. But the testimony was incriminating for various reasons. First, Christy Mathewson's judgment and character were beyond reproach. Second, Chase's reputation as a smart player, backed by Charlie Graham's comments that Chase had the greatest instincts of any fielder, supported Matty's claim. Furthermore, Chase was considered by many to be the greatest hit and run batsman in baseball history. It would then appear suspicious that Matty couldn't rely on him in that role. However, Heydler noted that in one game cited by Mathewson, Chase won the game with a three-run home run.[A] While Matty's testimony highlighted suspicious play, there was no proof of impropriety.

[A] Chase hit .301 for the season, although he was not among the offensive leaders in any categories.

Alleged Incidences of Chase Fixing Games

AFFIDAVIT	EVENTS	OUTCOME
Pol Perritt, New York Giants Player	Chase approached him at the Polo Grounds in New York. He said Chase gave a vague statement that if he would let him know which game he was to pitch, Chase would make sure "he would have nothing to worry about."	Perritt was disgusted. But Chase asking Perritt to play poorly against the Reds was not considered significant issue.
John McGraw	Pol Perritt told McGraw that he had been approached by Chase at Polo Grounds.	McGraw only knew about a vague comment second hand. McGraw, knowing that the Reds would release Chase, hung around the case out of efforts to sign Hal for the Giants
Jimmy Ring	Cincinnati Reds teammate asked by Hal Chase to lose a tie game.	Testimony was weak in front of Heydler.
Mike Regan	Chase approached in Boston and asked if he would like to make $200 when they arrived in New York. Regan showed some interest, so Chase said he would fill him in New York.	No conclusive evidence against Chase.
Greasy Neale	Admitted to working with Chase betting for the Reds. Chase told him he had made $500 in a series against the Phillies. Neale wanted in.	Allegations did not involve Chase betting against the Reds.
Lee Magee	Chase and Magee allegedly bet on games at the end of 1918. Magee claimed that Chase bet against the Reds, but Magee's testimony was suspect. But the event, uncovered in the future, was further implication of Chase in betting on games.	Details not yet known

Only Ring's testimony could become incriminating because it involved bets against his team. Betting for one's own team was a common practice. It did not even represent a violation of the National Agreement. Additionally, the evidence presented against Chase was inconclusive. For example, McGraw testified that he knew Chase conversed with players, but had no evidence of what was said.

When Heydler questioned Ring, the pitcher was vague and unsure. Heydler persisted in his questioning in an attempt to establish a coherent case, but he could not get the answers that would prove Chase's guilt. On the other hand, Chase appeared assured and convincing. He not only was eloquent in his own defense, but he brought with him I.O. De Passe, L.E. Rich, and New York newspaper man Sid Mercer to testify as character witnesses. Three lawyers, including his wife's brother Rudolph, represented Chase legally.

Heydler exonerated Chase and concluded that no game was decided by anything other than its merits.

> *There was no evidence whatever produced at the trial to show that Chase had made a bet, and the only direct evidence as to his crookedness was made by Player Ring. On the stand, however, Ring was a poor witness and made statements differing from what he had stated in his affidavit, so much so, in fact, that I brought him back here Monday for further testimony. To have found Chase guilty on this man's unsupported testimony would have been impossible.*[17]

From that point forward, Heydler prohibited players from betting on any baseball game, whether for or against his team.

In the end, it appeared that Chase did bet on baseball, but it was the custom at the time. There was no proof he actually bet against his team. And John McGraw was unconcerned about the claims against Chase. He awaited Heydler's decision intently so that he could sign Chase as soon as the Reds let him go. Chase was not welcome back in Cincy. He continued to pursue back wages totaling $1,600 for the end of the season. Ultimately, however, he agreed to drop the suit as long at the Reds agreed to trade him to McGraw. McGraw agreed to make up the difference in his contract with New York. On Feburary 13, Hal Chase signed to play for the Giants in 1919.

The year 1918 had been one of the most tumultuous in baseball and world history. The Russian Revolution, World War I, and the Spanish Flu Pandemic put into perspective the insignificance of an uncovered base or missed hit and run signal. The troubles of any and every man were more significant. That is perhaps how Christy Mathewson could accept a coaching role in 1919 in New York alongside John McGraw and Hal Chase. The challenges of each new day were too significant to dwell on the pettiness of the past. For many, however, there would be no future. The war had taken its toll on the world. And those spared faced a more formidable challenge from the flu bug. The tragedies of both the war and the flu would afflict those in baseball and California. While serving time in 1918, Christy Mathewson was accidentally exposed to poisonous mustard gas during a training exercise.[A] The poison caused tuberculosis that would lead to his untimely demise only seven years later. And in December 1918, pitcher Frank Arellanes, who had been released by the Vernon Tigers in 1917, became one of

---

[A] Part of the reason Matty couldn't testify in person in the Chase incidence was because he was recovering from the exposure to the gas. The war had ended on Novermber 11, 1918, but in January 1919 when Chase's case was heard, Matty was still in the hospital. Ty Cobb and Branch Rickey also served in the unit, called the Gas and Flame Division.

the many who contracted the Spanish Flu. At the age of thirty-eight in San Jose, Arellanes died from the disease on December 13.

[1]   The Dark Side of the Diamond, Gambling, Violence, Drugs, and Alcoholism in the National Pastime, Roger I. Abrams.
[2]   Calls Players in New Scandal, Los Angeles Times, Jan 3, 1927, pg. 9
[3]   Port Talk, Ed R. Hughes, San Francisco Chronicle, Feb 26, 1918, Pg. 10
[4]   Hot Stove League Waxes Exceeding Warm, Harry B. Smith, SF Chronicle, Feb 4, 1917, pg. 40
[5]   Sacramento to Get A Berth In Coast League, SF Chronicle, Dec 10, 1917, pg 6
[6]   Sacramentans Dicker to Buy the S.F. Seals, SF Chronicle, Feb 24, 1918, Pg. N7
[7]   Port Talk, Ed R. Hughes, SF Chronicle, Feb 26, 1918, Pg. 10
[8]   Benefits of No-Saloons Outweigh Ill Effects, LA Times, Apr 21, 1918, pg. II1
[9]   Army Not Likely to Close Vernon Bars, Los Angeles Times, May 5, 1918
[10] Pastor Raids Vernon Bars, Los Angeles Times, May 6, 1918, Pg. II3
[11] Flu Closes Vernon Bars, Los Angeles Times, Oct 20, 1918, pg I8
[12] The Pacific Coast League also abbreviated the season in July.
[13] Cubs-Red Sox Series framed by WWI, strike threat, By Timothy M. Gay, Special for USA TODAY, June 9, 2005
[14] Heydler Reserves Decision in Case, New York Times, January 31, 1919
[15] Cincinnati Times-Star, January 26, 1921
[16] Letter from Herrmann to Heydler in Chase File, National Baseball Hall of Fame and Museum, Cooperstown
[17] Heydler letter to Herrmann, Chase File, National Baseball Hall of Fame and Museum, Cooperstown

Chapter 22

Gambling Is Growth Industry During An Apocalypse

Chase became involved with gambling in baseball in 1918. If he had gambled prior to that, it certainly wasn't as overt as during the past year in Cincinnati. And moving back to the city of New York put Chase in closer contact with corrupt elements. The Giants had recently been sold to Charles Stoneham and had maintained its relationship with Tammany Hall politics since Freedman, through the ownership of Brush, and into the Stoneham regime.

Stoneham opened his own stock brokerage firm in 1913 at 41 Broadway in Manhattan called Charles A. Stoneham & Co. A fervent gambler, Stoneham owned numerous gambling operations, including a racetrack, a casino in Havana, Cuba, and billiard parlors, including one co-owned with Giants manager John McGraw. At the time, there were no restrictions preventing owners from involvement in gambling ventures. Stoneham participated in Tammany Hall politics and was close to Governor Al Smith. Stoneham also sometimes associated with leaders of organized crime, including notorious crime boss, Arnold Rothstein. Rothstein had assisted in brokering the deal between former owner John T. Brush and his successor Stoneham. A regular at the Giants' baseball games, Rothstein enjoyed one of the best seats in the stadium. He was also a business partner with Stoneham in a Havana racetrack and in a rum import business during prohibition.[1]

Stoneham's brokerage business would fail in 1921. Investors with accounts in the millions were sent thank you letters and told that their investments would be transferred to the firms E.M. Fuller & Co., E.H. Clarke and Co., and E.D. Dier & Co. The Dier & Co. collapsed in what was the first of a series of failures involving the firms to which the Stoneham & Co. assets were transferred. During the investigation of the Fuller case, Stoneham became a central figure and was summoned to Federal court to testify. On Aug 31, 1923 he was indicted by a Federal grand jury for perjury. In September 1923, he was charged and later acquitted of using the mail to defraud during the transfer to the Dier firm.[2]

To Chase, who grew up playing baseball in New York for owners Farrell and Devery, the experience under Stoneham was familiar. He certainly knew those involved in fixing games.

Chase's involvement with gambling, as well as alleged infidelity, impacted his marriage. In March, Anna filed for divorce after six years of marriage. She claimed that Chase stopped financially supporting her, was unfaithful, spent money on gambling, and exhibited wasteful consumption. She claimed the problems worsened over the past year, and that she remained with him because he promised to change. Just two months before, Anna's brother offered legal support Hal's case against the Cincinnati Reds. But by March, she had had enough.[3]

There was little question that Chase gambled on games. Gambling by players was customary until outlawed at the beginning of 1919. Not only did Hal's wife and teammates claim that Chase gambled, later in life Chase admitted that he enjoyed placing inconsequential wagers on games.

What many claim, however, is that Hal Chase was unique because he gambled against his own team. If Chase had thrown games, he was certainly not alone. And the claim against Chase has yet to be proven. But an incident with Lee Magee, a teammate with Cincinnati in 1918, added to the body of accusations dealing with Chase "laying down." Perhaps Chase's involvement with Magee would never have been exposed if Magee had kept quiet. During the prior season, Chase and Magee allegedly approached a gambler in Boston and agreed to each give him $500 in exchange for one-third of the gambling winnings when the Reds lost a game to the Braves. But the Reds won.

Magee had done his best to lose the game, although he later testified that he thought he was betting for his team. But Magee's play was suspicious. He kicked balls in the field, ran the bases poorly, and threw the ball away allowing the tying run to score and send the game into extra innings. Ironically, Magee scored the winning run. He came up with two out and nobody on base. He hit a weak ground ball that he expected to result in an out. But the ball hit a pebble and caromed into the outfield. Mathewson then gave him the signal to steal second. Although Magee broke late, the catcher threw the ball into the outfield. The next batter, Edd Roush, hit a ball to the outfield wall. It was reported that Magee was so slow running the bases that Roush was heard screaming, "Run, you dirty son of a bitch!"

Despite Magee's efforts, the Reds won. Not wanting to part with his $500, Magee stopped payment on his check to Jim Costello, operator of a pool hall in the Oxford Hotel in Boston. Because Magee stopped payment on the check, when Magee next returned to Boston in June 1919, Costello served him with papers demanding the money. Because Magee refused to pay his debt to a gambler, the Magee and Chase case would eventually have its day in court and in the press. The exposure was something that the owners and league presidents detested, as it undermined their life-long efforts to promote the game and keep skeletons in the closet. The following year, Heydler would re-open the investigation against Chase in light of new evidence from Magee.

At the end of the 1919 season, as was the case at the end of each major league season, the various teams conspired to bribe players to win games, toss games, and bolster statistics. In one instance, on September 10 Heinie Zimmerman allegedly approached his fellow Giants' teammates Fred Toney, Benny Kauff, and Rube Benton about throwing games to Chicago. The Giants finished nine games behind the pennant winners Cincinnati Reds. The Chicago

Cubs were a distant third, twenty-one games back at the end of the season. The outcome of the games had virtually no bearing on the outcome of the standings. Thus the normally competitive players justified making additional cash by throwing games. The Giants won the game, with Toney and Kauff playing well in the victory. After the game, the two claimed to have reported Zimmerman to McGraw. The truth may not be known, but in the many stories that relate the various conspiracies to fix games, a pattern emerges; both the accuser and the accused were often involved. Those who claimed to report one offender often did so to deflect suspicion. For example, Fred Toney, only two weeks later, was reported to have associated with individuals discussing the fix of the upcoming World Series. And McGraw was never distant from allegations about wrongdoing. The Giants symbolized "dirty baseball," and for nearly two decades McGraw had been its mentor. Zimmerman understandably denied involvement and added that everyone was connected with criminals, including McGraw.[4]

After that game, Rube Benton said he took a cab with Buck Herzog and Hal Chase to a Chicago restaurant. He said that Herzog asked him if he wanted to make some money by dropping the next day's game to Chicago. He said that Chase remained quiet throughout the conversation, but his involvement was implied. Benton said that he didn't accept the offer, and he went on to win the game.[A]

Cheating was perpetrated throughout baseball by both the mediocre and the superstar. Zimmerman, Toney, Benton, and Kauff were stars on the Giants. Their names, however, would be forgotten by many as the decades passed. But legendary players and future Hall of Famers also tossed games. On September 15, the Cleveland Indians allegedly laid down in a game with Detroit. Smoky Joe Wood, former superstar pitcher for the Boston Red Sox, and former teammate and player/manager Tris Speaker made arrangements with Detroit's Ty Cobb and Dutch Leonard to bet on a Cleveland loss to Detroit. Cleveland finished only three and a half games behind the White Sox. Detroit was in close contention with the Yankees for third place. The details of the fix would not surface for many more years. The following letter from Joe Wood to Dutch Leonard eventually served as evidence that gambling occurred.

Cleveland, O., Friday

Enclosed find certified check for sixteen hundred and thirty dollars ($1,630).

Dear Friend "Dutch":

The only bet West could get up was $600 against $420 (10 to 7). Cobb did not get up a cent. He told us that and I believed him. Could have put

---

[A] Testimony was part of the Grand Jury Investigation in Chicago related to the Black Sox scandal in an effort to implicate Chase in baseball gambling rings.

some at 5 to 2 on Detroit, but did not, as that would make us put up $1,000 to win $400.

We won the $420. I gave West $30, leaving $390, or $130 for each of us. Would not have cashed your check at all, but West thought he could get it up to 10-7, and I was going to put it all up at those odds. We would have won $1,750 for the $2,500 if we could have placed it.

If we ever get another chance like this we will know enough to try to get down early.

Let me hear from you, "Dutch."

With all good wishes to yourself and Mrs. Leonard, I am, always,

Joe Wood [5]

Ty Cobb also sent Leonard a letter about gambling at the end of the 1919 season.

August, GA, Oct 23, 1919

Dear Dutch: Well, old boy, guess you are out in old California by this time and enjoying life.

I arrived home and found Mrs. Cobb only fair, but the baby girl was fine, and at this time Mrs. Cobb is very well, but I have been very busy getting acquainted with my family and have not tried to do any correspondence, hence my delay.

Wood and myself are considerably disappointed in our business proposition, as we had $2,000 to put into it and the other side quoted us $1,400 and when we finally secured that much it was about two o'clock and they refused to deal with us, as they had men in Chicago to take the matter up with and they had no time, so we completely fell down and of course we felt badly about it.

Everything was open to Wood and he can tell you about it when we get together. it was quite a responsibility and I don't care for it again, I can assure you.

With kindest regards to Mrs. Leonard, I remain, sincerely,

Ty Cobb [6]

Both Cobb (Detroit) and Wood (Cleveland) referred to betting on the game of baseball, an act that had been outlawed by the National Commission. And the bet was on Detroit, which meant that those with Cleveland bet against their team. Cobb admitted later that betting really wasn't his thing, and that he was uncomfortable doing it. As much as it was "trendy," the amount of money wasn't significant for Cobb even if the ethical implications failed to deter him. The considerable money that changed hands between Wood and Leonard indicated culpability. And the letter from Wood was quite specific.

The letters surfaced years later when Leonard went public due to a gripe with Cobb. At first, he attempted to sell the documents to the highest bidder. He would never testify, however, because he didn't want to face Cobb. He said he feared being physically attacked by "that wild man" and was concerned that Cobb might even try to shoot him. No matter what would later be decided by Organized Baseball, it seemed clear that if Chase was involved "throwing games," he was not alone. Yet he would soon become the lone symbol of a baseball traitor.

The day after Cleveland and Detroit played their game in question, White Sox players Chick Gandil and Ed Cicotte met in New York at the Ansonia Hotel on September 16 with gambler and former ballplayer Bill Burns and ex-boxer Billy Maharg to concoct a plan to fix the upcoming 1919 World Series. Having heard the Cubs' players relate on the train to New York that they had profitably fixed the prior year's Series, Gandil and Cicotte made inquiries to find those who could broker a deal that would earn them $100,000 in exchange for their services. The meeting represented the beginning of the "Black Sox Scandal" that would lead to the expulsion from baseball of eight Chicago White Sox players for intentionally losing the series to the Cincinnati Reds. In one of the meetings, Gandil expressed to organizer Sport Sullivan that the idea of taking on seven or eight players in a plot to fix a World Series scared him. To that, Sullivan replied, "Don't be silly. It's been pulled before and it can be again."[A]

The season was still a few weeks from its regular conclusion. Hal Chase completed the year in good status with the Giants. In fact, during the last few weeks of the season, Christy Mathewson managed Chase. McGraw had been grooming Matty to take over for him when he retired. Little did McGraw know that Matty had only a few more years to live. Nonetheless, during the last two weeks of the 1919 season, McGraw put Matty in charge when he traveled with Charles Stoneham on business to scout oil properties in Texas and to visit gambling casinos and racetracks in Cuba.

Chick Gandil joined Cicotte for a second meeting with Bill Burns at the Ansonia Hotel on September 22. This time, Burns had others with him, including Hal Chase,[B] former boxer Abe Attell, and David Zelser (using the name Bennett). Chase later said that Burns had asked to meet him. They threw back some drinks.

[A] "Blackest Secret", Mel Durslag interview of Chick Gandil, Sports Illustrated, September 17, 1956. In the interview, Gandil admitted being ringleader and said "I feel we got what we had coming."

[B] There has been speculation that Chase's teammate at Santa Clara College, pitcher Bobby O'Keefe, played with Burns in Cincinnati and introduced him to Chase. But it really doesn't matter how Burns and Chase met. And the introduction doesn't implicate O'Keefe. What seems clear is that when the Chisox sought financing for their plan, they were able to quickly assemble a group. That may not mean that the group was the hub for gambling. Rather, gambling was so prevalent that assembling interested parties was not difficult.

Then Burns asked, "Hal, what would you think if I told you that the World Series between the White Sox and Cincinnati could be swung to the short-ender?" Chase replied, "... Someone would make a lot of money out of it."[7] Chase later commented that from his conversations with Burns, who said he approached Arnold Rothstein for backing, he felt confident the Series would be fixed and that he did bet on it. Perhaps there was more to Chase's motivation. He likely enjoyed playing a small role in sabotaging his enemies Charles Comiskey and Ban Johnson. Perhaps he reflected very briefly and thought, "Screw them!" They would have done the same to Chase.

The truth about the fix may never be known, but it can be inferred. Burns contacted individuals who could raise the $100,000 to finance the fix. To that end, Chase became involved. Knowing Chase, if he could have been involved he would have been involved. He would have relished the role of outsmarting the system and using his wits and celebrity to broker events more than he would appreciate the financial opportunity. He and the others were very likely the front men for Rothstein or other potential investors, including Sport Sullivan. Attell was known as a Rothstein associate. But Chase and Attell did not "organize" the fix. Chase had never been capable of organizing anything in his life. But he and the others could broker an arrangement between the players and the individuals who could provide the financing. Evidence suggests that the White Sox players sought the gamblers, rather than the other way around, and that Chase and others helped with the introductions. Chase later admitted that having known about the fix, he should have reported Bill Burns to John Heydler, President of the National League. But Chase said he had "never had any use for a stool pigeon or a squealer."[8]

On September 27, Benton later testified that he was in his room when roommate Jean Dubuc, another New York Giant, received a telegram from Burns that the fix was on. Two days later, in a final meeting at the Ansonia Hotel prior to the start of the World Series, Burns allegedly met with Chase, Toney, Dubuq, and Zelser (known as Bennett). Zelser appeared to be the official front man for the financier.

Following the meeting, Chase didn't even attend the World Series. He went on a fourteen-game barnstorming tour with other Giants and umpire Bill Klem in upstate New York, New England, and Quebec as he had done in previous years. It appeared that any role he played in the fix, which was likely no more than an intermediary, was completed.

Rumors abounded that Chase made $40,000 betting on the Reds. But his limited financial means following the 1919 season didn't support such a claim. Chase was not one who needed financial motivation to be involved. He liked challenges and would have participated in the fix regardless of money. And following the Series, he appeared to be financially unstable. In contrast, Chick

Gandil purchased a new home near Los Angeles, a new car, jewelry, and had a flush bank account when detectives investigated his financial records in 1920.

No matter, Chase admitted to gambling on the series. And Gandil and Ed Cicotte admitted that the Series was fixed. But Hal Chase or the Chicago White Sox players didn't spoil baseball by fixing the 1919 World Series. From the onset of baseball in America, gambling permeated the game. Nobody needed to attract the gamblers to the game. Baseball had been spoiled long before 1919.

While the baseball season came to a close and players attempted to line their pockets from bets and bribes, the havoc that unfolded in the World Series paled in comparison to the national spectacle in Boston in September. Dissatisfied with stagnant wages and poor working conditions, the Boston Police attempted to unionize. When Police Commissioner Edwin Curtis would not recognize the union, the police force threatened to strike. On September 9, over a thousand Boston policemen went on strike at 5:45 pm. Curtis and Governor Calvin Coolidge attempted to replace the striking policemen, but many replacements didn't arrive until the following morning. Riots and public chaos consumed the city that night. Looters and armed gangs paraded through the streets unopposed. Widespread civil unrest ensued. Perhaps the national press exaggerated the accounts, but the events did become prominent nationally. In the aftermath, Governor Calvin Coolidge fired many of the striking policemen and replaced them from a pool of unemployed World War I veterans. His firm response to the striking police made him popular and propelled him onto the national stage, leading to his nomination for vice-president with candidate Warren Harding in 1920. Coolidge's ascension in national politics revealed a national sentiment that favored the tough handling of labor unions and those who challenged the status quo.

Following World War I, current President Wilson continued to aggressively squash free speech and opposition to the status quo. After convicting Bill Haywood, Eugene Debs, and other socialist and labor union leaders, Wilson had socialist political leader Victor Berger sentenced to prison for his opposition to war and the draft. The trial in February had been presided over by Judge Kenesaw Landis.[A] National hostility grew toward "outsiders," like the German Berger, or the striking policemen in Boston who symbolized a threat to peace, freedom, and the American way of life. Both the powerful and the press fanned the flames of emotions that created a mob mentality that opposed anyone who appeared as a "troublemaker." And the mob would staunchly demand that an example be made of those troublemakers, as would be the case when the perpetrators of the 1919 Black Sox Scandal came to light.

[A] The conviction was appealed, and ultimately overturned on January 31, 1921 by the Supreme Court, finding that Judge Landis improperly presided over the case after the filing of an affidavit of prejudice. Berger et al. v. United States, 41 S.Ct. 230, 235 U.S. 22 (1921).

In 1919, the Pacific Coast League continued to struggle through a difficult financial period. New San Francisco Seals owners Strub, Graham, and Putnam created a new strategy to survive. Whereas Graham began his career as an "outlaw" to Organized Baseball, he had since abided by the National Commission and developed a formula for financial survival. Rather than rely solely upon income from ticket sales, Graham acted as a scout, sending many players to the major leagues in exchange for a fee. Sometimes, he recommended players on other teams, such as Harry Wolter and Frank Arellanes. Other times, he sold his players, including Harry Hooper and Chick Gandil. Graham explained to Strub and Putnam that to survive, they needed to develop young talent for the major leagues.

So the owners hired veteran Spider Baum in February 1919 to develop their young pitchers.[A] Another aspect of their strategy involved developing amateur leagues that would prepare young players. Graham and Strub remembered the Examiner Game tournaments in the late 1890s that had developed so much young talent in the Bay Area and throughout California. Thus, at the end of the 1919 season, Doc Strub founded one of the largest winter leagues in the history of baseball. It contained more than thirty amateur teams to whom the San Francisco Seals offered a $1,000 purse for the winning squad.[9]

The Vernon Tigers survived by producing a winning team and with showmanship at its games. The Tigers would win the pennant in 1919. At the beginning of the year, Ed Maier sold a portion of his squad to Roscoe "Fatty" Arbuckle, one of the most successful and wealthy silent movie stars of the era. Arbuckle purchased Tom Darmody's shares and became President of the team. Arbuckle and other stars, including Charlie Chaplin, had adopted the Vernon squad in recent years. At opening day on May 25, a large Hollywood contingent appeared to watch the sold-out game from the grandstands. Tom Mix was there in one box seat. And the New York Telegraph reported that Fatty Arbuckle, Al St. John, and Buster Keaton put on a sideshow. "Dressed in the garb of the Vernons they staged a game all their own, using a plaster of Paris bat and ball. The result when ball and bat met may be imagined." Throughout the season, Arbuckle and his comedy staff traveled with the team and performed burlesque stunts at the ballparks of the Pacific Coast League. The fans loved the famous actor. The papers reported that his shows were "a riot." The entertainment industry newspaper Variety reported that Arbuckle spent all of his time promoting his team and not his movies.

During the season, Vernon would become involved in a transaction that drove a wedge between two former friends, Ban Johnson and Charles Comiskey. Comiskey and Johnson had been drinking, hunting, and card-playing buddies for

---

[A] Baum would pitch for Salt Lake City in 1920, then later return to the Seals as pitching coach.

years.   Although Comiskey enjoyed joking about Johnson's girth, the two remained friends ever since they formed the American League together. In 1918, Vernon owned pitcher Jack Quinn. The White Sox roster, depleted due to World War I, acquired Quinn from Vernon toward the end of the season.   Quinn performed well.   Many teams then sought Quinn, including the Yankees. Technically, Quinn was still owned by Vernon. So the Yankees purchased Quinn directly from the Vernon club. Comiskey became furious and protested the case. But his good friend Ban Johnson awarded Quinn to New York. From that point on, Comiskey and Johnson became enemies.

The two would no longer share a drink at a bar. Not only did their mutual disgust stand between them, but laws prohibiting consumption of alcohol passed. On June 30, the world's largest bar, Doyle's Bar in Vernon closed due to prohibition. It certainly went out with a bang, however. The night before the national law went into effect, more than sixty bartenders doled out drinks to an estimated one thousand customers in what was the ultimate "last call."[10]   The town was never the same.

> *At night, Vernon's silent streets that were once alive with thousands of boxing followers and before that with the night life crowd who patronized Baron Long's Vernon Country Club; the sporting fraternity that followed the silent movie stars, the dance girls, harlots and gamblers; this strange little community can only look back with fond remembrance and see it as it once was.*[11]

Harry Wolter considered a "last call" on his career.   Playing for Sacramento, Wolter announced that he would no longer play after the 1919 season. He said he had a position waiting for him in the sales department at the Standard Oil Company.[12]   Wolter played for the Standard Oil Company winter league team in the off-season, and perhaps through that association a job offer was implied. He said he had not wanted to play the current season, but was convinced by Sacramento owners. Following the 1919 season, Lew Moreing and Charles Moreing, brothers to legendary Stockton Millers' "outlaw" owner Cy Moreing, purchased the Sacramento PCL team. However, they sold Wolter to Seattle. Adding insult to injury, the Standard Oil Team also sold Wolter to another winter league team. Not only did the trade jeopardize his chances of getting a job with Standard Oil, the sale was particularly damaging to Wolter's ego; he was sold for a half dozen baseballs.[13]

[1] City Games, The Evolution of American Urban Society and the Rise of Sports, Steven A. Riess, p. 198
[2] New York Times, January 7, 1936
[3] Hal Chase's Wife Suing for Divorce, Los Angeles Times, Nov 23, 1920, pg. II11
[4] Conspired In A Hotel, Los Angeles Times, Sep 30, 1920, Pg. I1
[5] Cobb, A Biography, Al Stump
[6] Cobb, A Biography, Al Stump

[7]   The Sporting News, September 18, 1941, Lester Grant (Oakland Post Enquirer)
[8]   The Sporting News, September 18, 1941, Lester Grant (Oakland Post Enquirer)
[9]   Baseball Notes, Los Angeles Times, Sep 19, 1919, pg. III2
[10] A Teetotaler's Bar and Boxing Mecca, Cecilia Rasmussen. Los Angeles Times. Los Angeles, Calif.:Jun 22, 1997. p. B, 3:3
[11] Leonis of Vernon, . Kilty, James, New York: Carlton Press 1963
[12] Harry Wolter to Quit Ball, LA Times, Jul 14, 1919, Pg I5
[13] Harry Wolter and Eldred Sold for Dozen Baseballs, San Francisco Chronicle, Feb 9, 1920, pg 8.

Early California Baseball Men

Photos Courtesy of Fred Lange

J. Cal Ewing, Father of the Pacific Coast League

George Van Haltren, one of the best former major league players not in the Hall of Fame.

Frank "Cap" or "Pop" Dillon. (Los Angeles Public Library)

Charlie Graham at Santa Clara College and as President of the San Francisco Seals in 1947. (Top left photo courtesy of Santa Clara University Special Collections)

William Lange, one of the greatest players in major league history, retired at 28 in 1899.

Kid Mohler, the PCL's star left-handed second baseman, as coach for Navy

Santa Clara Baseball Men

Top: Hap Hogan (bottom left) with Harry Wolter (top right) in Santa Clara College team photo (Santa Clara University Special Collections)

Harry Wolter at Stanford and with New York Yankees

Elmer Stricklett   Hal Chase   Doc Strub

Hap Hogan

National Baseball Figures

Left: Frank Chance arrives in New York to manage the Yankees. Right: Chance dons a more familiar suit, a soiled uniform.

Frank Farrell, Bill Devery, and American League President Ban Johnson

John McGraw (left) shakes hands with Frank Chance (right) in the stands when the 1913 World Tour played in Los Angeles the day Reb Russell defeated Christy Mathewson. The photo reunited two New York managers who heartily greeted each other in spite of their rivalry. The meeting of the two highest paid men in baseball was noted by the caption as further proof that Los Angeles was "the winter baseball metropolis of the world."

Turkey Mike Donlin and Mabel Hite

Edward R. (Eddie) Maier, owner of the Vernon and Venice Tigers and Maier Brewery

Vernon Tigers

Exterior and interior of Jack Doyle's Bar and boxing arena in Vernon. Jack Doyle inset. Electric trolley car transports passengers to Vernon. Sign on trolley advertises the baseball games. Vernon program from 1911 advertises Doyle's Thirst Emporium on its cover.

Silent movie star, comedian, and owner of the Vernon Tigers, Fatty Arbuckle (shown in his baseball uniform) symbolized the influence of stars from the entertainment industry in sports, particularly in Los Angeles, in the early 1900s.

Maier Select Beer Matchbook

Maier Brewery's top seller, Brew "102"

Vintage California Baseball Stadiums

Recreation Park in San Francisco (predecessor to Seals Stadium)

Ewing Field in San Francisco used as ground for rodeo and circus.

Wrigley Field, Los Angeles, CA.

Seals Stadium, San Francisco

Willie Mays in front of Seals Stadium before the San Francisco Giants debut in 1958. This photo framed prominently over the bar at Lefty O'Doul's Restaurant in San Francisco. The Giants played at Seals Stadium until it was demolished in 1960

Miscellanea

Above, Walter Johnson with Calvin Coolidge. Below, the 1911 Lincoln Giants. Walter Johnson and the Lincoln Giants played in the California Winter League, the first integrated professional baseball league in the United States.

San Francisco Seals Program containing photos of Charles H. Graham, Lefty O'Doul, Paul Fagan, and President Graham's son, Charles J. Graham, General Manager.

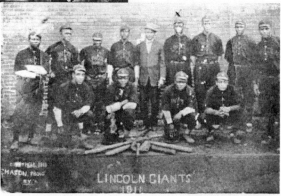

1945 SF Seals Program

Left: Spider Baum as a coach with the SF Seals. Ironically the photo shows Baum's arm getting looked over by the team trainer Baum's callous response to Paul Waner's sore arm shortly thereafter would end Waner's career as a pitcher. Middle: Jimmy O'Connell baseball card. Right: Willie Kamm.

Original class of 1944 inducted into the Pacific Coast League Hall of Fame on display in Lefty O'Doul's Restaurant in San Francisco. Included are Arnold Statz, Frank "Pop" Dillon, Earl Sheehy, Hap Hogan, Raymond French, H. William Lane, Frank Shellenback, Charles H. Graham, Walter McCredie, Herman Pillette, Harry A. Williams, Oscar Vitt, John Bassler, J. Cal Ewing, Jack Leivelt, Otis Crandall, Charles Baum, and Frank O'Doul.

Letter to Shoeless Joe Jackson from fan in 1951 when Jackson operated Joe's Liquor Store in Greenville, South Carolina.

Hello Joe,

I read an article in the sports page about you wanting to here from some one in Iowa so I thought I would write you as I was really a baseball fan of yours. Well Joe lots of things happen and I think they could have been ironed out too. Well Joe I can go quite a few years back as a Black Sox and White sox fan. And why I picked you as my favorite fan I don't know. But I guess if you like a Guy you just do those things.

Those were the good old days.

Joe if we could just get you and all the rest of the boys that played with you for an exabition game wouldn't that be some thing. I'd say the biggest crowd in history would turn out. If that ever happened Joe get me some tickets. Well Joe lets hope the white sox get on top. Well Joe I've never seen you and as a ball player you were a great guy and my favorite.

Well Joe you're a long ways from Waterloo and if I can ever afford a car Im going to try to see you down in Carolina. Thats one place I always wanted to see. Well Joe before I sign off Im sending you the story out of the paper to you. Im sending the pictures of my self and my wife and Daughter. Send them back Joe will you. And if you got a snap shot of your self Id like to get one to remember you by. Well Joe my name is Joe too. I am 50 yrs old and if you want to Id like to know how old you are.

Well Joe its time to sign off.

Yours truly and the Best of Luck to you.

Chapter 23

Hal Chase Becomes Convenient Scapegoat

As a rancher and hotel and tavern operator in Santa Cruz, Elmer Stricklett left baseball before spitballs and betting on a baseball game were considered cheating. By 1920, cheating in baseball had become an epidemic. The American people had developed a fear of the outsider who threatened their cherished institutions. The Espionage and Sedition Act arrests of "outsiders" marked a new low point in America's "red scare," which had been growing for decades. In baseball, the outsiders were the mobsters, whom many feared would successfully upend a game that stood for traditional American ideals.[1]

The infiltration of organized crime in baseball even created a climate of real fear, fear for one's life. During disagreements and legal challenges during the gambling era and the "Black Sox Scandal," individuals made reference to concerns about getting shot. Dutch Leonard would later state he feared that Ty Cobb might shoot him if confronted. And during the 1919 World Series, as sportswriter Hugh Fullerton wrote that the White Sox weren't giving a full effort, he claimed that he was followed and shot at. The problem had become serious, and baseball needed to rid itself from the mob bosses' influences.

The investigation into the World Series fix didn't occur in 1919. If the owners had their druthers, the incident would never be vetted in court. Baseball liked to keep their dirty laundry in their respective closets. Only when incidences reached the courts did facts become exposed to the general public.

Following the 1919 season, Chase remained in good stead with the New York Giants. He remained on the reserve list for the 1920 season.

Chisox third baseman Buck Weaver, who would later be banned from baseball,[A] traveled to California to play in the Winter League less than a month after the Series. He fielded a team called Weaver's All Stars, which featured stars Babe Ruth and Bob Meusel.[2]

Doc Strub also traveled to Los Angeles in the winter. He and new Pacific Coast League President William H. McCarthy traveled to Fresno, Los Angeles, and San Diego to discuss moving the Portland and Seattle teams into California markets. Not only would travel time and expenses be reduced, the move would avoid some of the wrangling that had occurred in previous months. As guests, Strub and McCarthy spent an afternoon at the San Gabriel Country Club playing golf and discussing the issue. While in Los Angeles, Strub was

---

[A] Weaver arguably knew about the fix, but didn't participate in it. But he was banned nonetheless.

approached by a pitcher for the Los Angeles Angels who said he was willing to play where he could get the most money. Strub tutored the pitcher on the proper attitude.

> *You've got the wrong idea. What you want is the opportunity. Then if you make good you can demand and get the big money.*[3]

Strub told the pitcher that he had no intention to outbid Los Angeles. The reserve clause prevented it. Rather than bid for other teams' players, the Seals and other teams needed to find and develop their own talent.

They could, however, sign ex-major league players with some gas still in the tank. In February, former White Sox pitching star Jim Scott was en route to Los Angeles to visit his sick mother. Charlie Graham had been trying to sign him for some time, but Scott indicated he wanted to play in Seattle.[4] But Graham effectively persuaded Scott to join the Seals. Scott would contribute to one of the league's best pitching staffs.

The Giants roster included Hal Chase for 1920. But in January, Lee Magee implicated Chase in a fix from the 1918 season that would make John McGraw change his mind about bringing Hal back. Magee confessed to Cubs owner William Veeck that he had been involved with Chase in wagering on the Boston Braves game with Cincinnati. But he insisted that his bet to the gambler had been on the Reds, not against them. When Veeck responded by cutting him from the Cubs, Magee went to court to get the salary owed him under his contract. If matters didn't go to court, perhaps the Chase involvement would not have come to light. But with matters becoming public, the National Commission began damage control.

The Cubs requested a dismissal of the Magee case by stating,

> *Previous to the making of the contract, the plaintiff was guilty of betting against the team of which he was a member, and sought to win bets by intentional bad playing to defeat said team.*

Organized baseball chewed up and spit out Magee during testimony, and Magee lost his appeal for lost wages. Magee's case was particularly weak because he used the same lawyer who defended both him and Chase in 1918. The lawyer was unable to change his argument relative to the previous testimony and the affidavits submitted. The affidavits could not be false before when defending Chase and now be true when attempting to place blame on Chase.

> *You were the attorney of record for Player Hal Chase when charges were brought against him in 1918; as part of the proceedings there was furnished to you a complete copy of the specifications and affidavits of Messrs. Mathewson, Neale, Ring, Perritt, McGraw, and Regan filed against your client. As you well know, Player Chase, in his sworn answer, presumably prepared by you - and in his testimony given under oath and while attended by local counsel representing you -- denied each*

and every charge made in the affidavits.... You now bring up these affidavits, as alleged charges of the persons who made them and is apparently against your former client, Chase, for if you claim the affidavits are true now, they were untrue in 1919, when the case was tried, and the defense made and testimony given by Chase under your direction in denial thereof could not be the truth if the charges and affidavits are true.

I publicly warned the players in the National League that betting either to win or lose would not be tolerated, and I know of no case where that warning has been disregarded. If you or your client know of any player who has in the season of 1919 made a bet or been interested in one on any game in which his club participated, you are requested in confidence, if you desire, or with full publicity, to name him and direct me to the evidence or furnish it and there will be no delay in acting in the matter.

Likewise, if you can direct me to any player who was guilty of any act of betting or gambling in any previous season, the same result will follow.

At first Heydler probed Magee and his lawyer to come forward with evidence against any player. And Heydler was particularly interested in opening up the investigation once again regarding Hal Chase. In 1918, Christy Mathewson had claimed that Chase intentionally lost games. When Chase was exonerated due to lack of evidence, the Magee incident was not yet known. So Heydler showed a willingness to bargain with Magee to get to Chase in light of the new information. In the end, Organized Baseball decided that both Magee and Chase were blameworthy.

John McGraw was either instructed, or felt the need, to distance the Giants from Hal Chase. McGraw didn't cut Chase. As was the custom when an owner no longer wanted a player, they offered a contract with a significantly reduced salary. McGraw knew Chase would reject it. McGraw did the same thing that year with Heinie Zimmerman who he didn't want back for similar reasons. Chase later stated that McGraw offered him a raise, but going through a divorce, Chase wanted to return to the Bay Area and play in the West. Chase said he "had connections in the West." Indeed, Chase had many connections in the West. He knew Strub and Graham with the Seals. And he remained close with Cy Moreing in Stockton, who still wanted Chase to play for him. And Moreing's brothers in Sacramento could certainly use the services of Prince Hal.

But Hal Chase's stock was sinking. "Organized Baseball" earned its moniker because the owners communicated. And word of Chase's involvement in throwing games circulated throughout. No judge or jury was required to shape the opinions within the consortium. And part of the "damage control" implemented by Organized Baseball was to blame everything on Chase. Chase was fast becoming a scapegoat and the symbol for corruption in baseball.

National League President John Heydler vowed that Chase would never play in the National League again. Years before when Chase jumped to the Federal League, American League President Ban Johnson had vowed that Chase would never again play in the American League. Unless the Feds came back, Chase's career options were becoming limited.

Chase returned to California in February and moved to Los Angeles. In April, he announced he would not return to the Giants. He agreed to travel on weekends to play for the San Jose club in the Mission League.

The May issue of Baseball Magazine announced Hal Chase's "Retirement." The quotes around the word "retirement" implied that the Giants released him because of impropriety. The headline implied more than the decline of Chase's skills. The quotes represented a "wink wink" that Chase was asked to retire for unspecified reasons. The quotes symbolized the beginning of Chase being chastised in the media, one implication piled upon another, until his iconic status as villain formed.

Perhaps as villain, or even suspected villain, Organized Baseball had already privately tried and convicted him. Thus, perhaps Chase had no home in the Pacific Coast League. But Robert Larocca, owner of the San Jose Missions, was hopeful that Chase had some ginger left in his step. There was a chance that Larocca would be granted admission to the Pacific Coast League. But first he would have to demonstrate an ability to fill the stands, even if the team only played on Sundays. Showcasing Chase was Larocca's plan. LaRocca gave Chase part ownership as incentive.

Certainly the strict Charlie Graham would have zero tolerance for Chase and any alleged cheating if the claims were true. On May 3, 1920, Graham declared war on gambling in the Pacific Coast League. He suspended star players Tom Seaton and Casey Smith. He said,

> *Tom Seaton and Casey Smith have been unconditionally released by the San Francisco Baseball Club. I believe that baseball must be kept above suspicion. From time to time, rumors of the most serious nature have reached me regarding both players, their practices and their associates. At first I refused to listen to these rumors, but their persistency and their growth have persuaded me that, whether true or untrue, for the best interests of baseball, Seaton and Smith should be released.*

> *Unfortunately their loss to the club is most serious. They are both classed as among the best, if not the best, pitchers in the league. At this time, when we are making a winning fight for the pennant, it is to be regretted that this sacrifice must be made. But, much as I covet the pennant and anxious as I am to remain in first place, i would rather sacrifice the club in every way than to continue with players who, by their actions and associates, either on or off the field, leave themselves,*

their club, and the game open to suspicion of any kind.[5]

A few days later, Pacific Coast League President W.H. McCarthy banned three men associated with gambling from league games. Roy Hurlbert, part owner of the Colonial Social Club at 207 Powell Street, Charles "Kid" Schwartz, part owner of the Waffle Inn at 126 Ellis Street, and jewelry salesman Martin Breslauer were barred. Upset by the ban, Hurlbert approached President McCarthy on the street near Union Square in San Francisco. Catching McCarthy by surprise with his hands still in his pockets, Hurlbert struck him in the face, and kicked him while he was on the ground until police came to the aid of the President. McCarthy washed the blood from his face and clothing inside the St. Francis Hotel.[6]

President McCarthy would also ban mobster Nate Raymond. Nate Raymond was the Arnold Rothstein[A] of the West. Ironically, years later, Rothstein was shot to death for not paying his debt after losing hundreds of thousands of dollars to Raymond in a poker match. Charlie Graham, Doc Strub, and President McCarthy were adamant about eliminating the dangerous and shady element from the league. The danger hit close to home in August of 1920.

Doc Strub was driving out of the business district in San Francisco on Market Street to his home on Portola Drive in Twin Peaks. Two men drove alongside Strub. A high-speed chase ensued. Strub stepped on the gas and raced to his home where he hid in his garage. The other car followed but did not attempt to enter the residence. The police were called, but nobody was apprehended. The pursuit could have been an attempted robbery. Or it could have been an act of intimidation as Strub and the Seals attempted to clean up San Francisco baseball.[7]

Undeterred by the attack on him or the threat from organized crime, McCarthy publicly stated that he'd rather "close every ballpark than permit gambling." He hired plainclothes detectives to arrest gamblers in the stands at the league's parks. He also hired private investigators and "spies" to report back to him about suspicious activity.

McCarthy had considerable influence in San Francisco. He had Hurlbert arrested and tried. While Hurlbert stood trial, police blockaded his Colonial Club. And detectives roamed Recreation Park to see that no betting on baseball occurred.[8]

Strub and Graham likewise investigated all suspected activity and didn't provide the opportunity of a trial in order to dole out justice. As much as gambling impacted baseball, they were going to enforce the law. Police Chief White argued that the Seals must show their evidence:

[A] Rothstein, an East Coast crime boss, allegedly played a role in fixing the 1919 World Series.

The officials of the San Francisco baseball club have taken into their own hands certain of the provinces of the Police Department, and have taken executive action that presages knowledge of violation of the laws.

The police department wanted to participate in the investigations. Detective Frank McConnell of the gambling detail was assigned to Recreation Park. While Strub, Graham, and Putnam welcomed the attention, they had reason to be skeptical, as gambling had occurred at Recreation Park for two decades without significant curtailment by police. From this point forward, however, the police agreed to investigate all charges and work together with baseball.[9]

When Seaton and Smith were dismissed from the Seals, the manager of the Little Rock Travelers, Kid Elberfeld, contacted them to play for him. But the President of the Southern Association barred the players from the league. When a player in any league in Organized Baseball was charged with throwing games, they were forced into the independent leagues, many of which were in Arizona.

The Pacific Coast League owners and managers banded together against gambling. In addition to Strub, Graham, and Putnam in San Francisco, there was John Powers and J.H. Patrick in Los Angeles, J. Cal Ewing and Del Howard in Oakland, Willliam Lane in Salt Lake City, Bill Klepper, Charles Lockhart, and Wade Killefer in Seattle, Ed Maier in Vernon, Thomas Turner in Portland, and Lew Moreing in Sacramento.[10]

The owners in major league baseball were much less interested in uncovering the unsavory details of gambling and corruption. For one thing, they understood it was widespread. Second, many star players could be implicated which would deplete their franchises. Third, the publicity would damage the reputation of the game. And finally, the investigation could lead to their respective doors. Baseball preferred to handle issues on their own and keep the dirty details hidden from the public. But baseball did have one crusader in Ban Johnson.

Ban Johnson, who perhaps more than any administrator worked to create "clean baseball" for two decades, had seen enough. His sole responsibility as American League President was to create and sustain the virtues that made America's game popular. When he formed the American League, he attempted to eradicate gambling from the parks. When the league merged with the National League, he compromised out of necessity, as gambling had become inseparable from the sport. He had compromised when he allowed the likes of Devery and Farrell to own the league's most important franchise in New York. Like his former National League counterpart, the deceased Harry Pulliam, he became tired of simply carrying out the desires of the owners at the expense of the game's integrity. He was through with compromise. Ban Johnson would turn on the owners and attempt to expose the 1919 World Series fix by ensuring that the incidences would be investigated in the courts and not resolved by the owners. Like the owners in the Pacific Coast League, Johnson personally investigated claims of impropriety. And he provided the authorities with the details that would lead them like a trail of crumbs. Because Johnson chose to expose baseball in order to clean it up, he alienated himself from the other owners, including his old friend Charles Comiskey. During the summer of 1920, Johnson began his personal investigation and combined what he would learn with what he already knew after years of fighting the contagion.

During the summer of 1920, as part of the war on gambling, baseball began leaking information regarding various scandals to the public. The Pacific Coast League would accuse Hal Chase of attempting to fix games in its league. Separately, the 1920 pennant won by the Vernon Tigers was allegedly fixed, leading to player bans. And a grand jury in Chicago would soon reveal that the 1919 World Series had been fixed.

The Chase affair began at the end of July at the Lankershim Hotel in Los Angeles. The Lankershim was located downtown at the corner of Broadway and Seventh. For decades, it was the hotel of choice for baseball people when in town. Now living in Los Angeles, Chase met with pitcher Spider Baum of the Salt Lake City club at the bar to discuss baseball in the Pacific Coast League. Baum was particularly sensitive to the advances of anyone related to gambling. Loyal to the league, Baum had played in the California League or Pacific Coast League for over two decades. Additionally, team owner William Lane had asked Baum to perform the role of a spy and report back any questionable behavior. Chase later explained that their conversation was casual. Chase had known Baum for years. Baum's first game with the Los Angeles Angels was also Chase's debut as a professional. Chase claimed to ask if Baum had any insights for him that would help him with some bets. Baum admitted that he didn't have anything special to offer, but did recommend betting on teammate Walt Leverenz because he rarely lost. Chase felt that their meeting was friendly and benign, but Baum immediately reported Chase to league President McCarthy claiming that Chase offered him $300 if he would throw games. Baum explained that Chase said he had friends willing to bet large sums of money on games "provided that they had an edge."

A week later, on August 3, 1920, McCarthy banned Hal Chase from all Pacific Coast League parks. McCarthy made the following statement:

> I have this day notified all clubs of the Pacific Coast League that admission to our parks shall hereafter be refused Hal Chase. If reports are true, Chase has done more discredit to baseball than any single individual. It was hoped that his activities would be ended with his elimination from the major leagues and would not extend further.... Last week, at Los Angeles, however, Chase, so it has been reported to me, approached pitcher Charles A. Baum of the Salt Lake club with a proposition to make some easy money. I have this in a signed statement from Baum. Chase went on to explain that he had some friends who

were willing to bet large sums of money on ball games, provided they had "the edge."

Chase will not hereafter be permitted in any park in our league. It is unfortunate that no further punishment can be imposed. Certainly there is no punishment too severe, but perhaps the contempt of men and women who love baseball who believe in clean sport will prove sufficient penalty... The task of keeping baseball clean is not the easy one I had hoped. Today's developments prove it. but I am determined, and my directors are determined that no matter what the sacrifice, baseball on the Pacific Coast is going to be clean and above suspicion.[11]

The key to McCarthy's comment was "if reports are true." The reports he referred to were the rumors circulating throughout Organized Baseball about Chase. His cases with Mathewson and Magee were public, but would not by themselves represent actions causing "more discredit to baseball than any single individual." Although hyperbole was common, McCarthy likely referred to knowledge of Chase's involvement in the 1919 World Series fix, which had not yet become public. Ban Johnson's private investigation indicated involvement by Chase. Even before the investigation, Chase was persona non grata to Johnson – not for gambling, but because Chase jumped to the Federal League. Baseball had become its own judge and jury, and had begun defaming Hal Chase. Certainly as McCarthy took a hard line against gambling, he wasn't as concerned about feelings or reputations; he could ban today and ask questions later.

The same day, Mission League President Jim Nealon banned Chase from the Mission League. The two bans were greater tragedies than any ban from John Heydler or Ban Johnson. Chase always had a dream to play in California. He never held the major leagues or the National Commission in high regard; he used Organized Baseball as much as Organized Baseball used Hal Chase. But for Chase, California baseball was home. The businessman Hal Chase would say he had "connections" in California. But the little boy inside Hal Chase would declare he had friends in California. Chase had played against President Jim Nealon for years in the California League. Chase had played for and with Doc Strub and Charlie Graham since he was a teenager. Even at home, baseball's doors were closing rapidly for Hal Chase. Nealon admitted that he didn't have any evidence. In addition to Baum's report, Ban Johnson likely influenced McCarthy. And McCarthy influenced Nealon.

The action of the Coast League directors barring Chase from all Coast League games is sufficient proof to me that Chase is not a fit player for the Mission League. He must sever all connections with San Jose.... interest he has in the San Jose ball club must be forfeited.[12]

Mission's owner Robert Larocca protested that Chase never had a hearing. He didn't plan to abide by Nealon's ruling. The indignant Larocca told Chase to report to the Sunday game against Hollister. It would be Hal Chase's last game in front of his home crowd. But it would be memorable.

On August 8, a crowd of 1,400 attended the game in San Jose. Nealon instructed the umpire to forfeit the game if Hal Chase attempted to play. At the start, Chase didn't play. But upon seeing him appear in uniform "the crowd cheered madly." Hollister extended a lead in the first two innings. In the third, the San Jose manager put Chase in to pitch. As Hal walked to the mound, the fans stood and roared with applause. Chase raised his hands to the cheers and basked in one final game of town ball for his local team. The umpire declared the game a forfeit. But the outcome of the game was secondary. The paper reported,

> Chase was a hero in the eyes of the crowd of 1,400 fans and was cheered
> to the echo when he first walked on the field.[13]

Aside from the game's rules, commissions, and administration, when Chase approached the mound, the player and fans enjoyed the purest of moments in baseball – the fan's undeniable appreciation for their hero, and the hero's appreciation for the fan. In the court of public opinion, Hal Chase was still a hero. For a man who was fast becoming the symbol of impurity in sports, Chase simply dreamed of a time when he could play and fans could watch. The fans didn't mind that the game was played as an exhibition. Hollister won 14-9.[14]

Three days later, the Mission League Directors met to discuss the Chase issue. Larocca explained that judgment could not be passed unless Chase had a hearing. But the directors decided to uphold the ban on Hal Chase. Chase was not present at the meeting, but his lawyer James P. Sex, a graduate of Santa Clara College, attended. After the meeting, Sex advised the media that Chase would sue President William McCarthy for defamation of character. Certainly he had a case, but sentiment would be hard to overcome. When President McCarthy heard about the threat, he declared, "So Hal Chase is suing me for defamation of character … I never knew he possessed such a thing."

The sentiment against Chase swelled at a national level in an era when justice took a backseat to order. Editorials written during the month that Chase was banned revealed the national sentiment. In recent weeks, labor leader Samuel Gompers had declared opposition in the upcoming elections to Harding and Coolidge because of Governor Coolidge's position in the Boston Police Strike. In various papers across the country, citizens wrote to the editors expressing their views toward Gompers and the labor movement in general.

New York Times: *As Gov. Coolidge puts it, where there is no profit there is no employment, and the suspension of one man's dividends is the suspension of another man's wages…. If the workers wish to better their position they must help to better the position of their employers.*

Portland Oregonian: *Democratic rule and prosperity do not travel together, for prosperity brings success, which Democrats treat as a crime. The law regards every man as innocent until he is proved guilty, but Democrats regard a successful businessman as guilty until he proves his innocence... In this manner Wilson democracy produced a state of mind unfavorable to business enterprise and expansion.*

Denver News: *Communism in itself is not criminal. It was introduced into American governmental affairs at a very early day, long before the Declaration of Independence and what followed the latter.... voluntary communism is one thing, forced communism is another thing. Compulsory communism is being practiced in Russia by the Lenin-Trotzky dictatorship.*

Worcester Telegram: *Mr. Gompers seems to indicate a mild approval for Mr. Cox and distaste toward Mr. Coolidge, because of his 'attitude toward labor.'*

Kansas City Star: *Those who imagine the execution of a shady trick now and then in business or play pays velvet dividends should consider the case of Hal Chase, a few years ago rated among the best first basemen. Chase jeopardized his professional honor for a little cash in hand and now is not only barred from all of the big leagues in the country, but has just received notice that he many no longer play in an insignificant Sunday league on the Pacific Coast.*

Similar to Eugene Debs, Victor Berger, and the Boston Police, Hal Chases's name was fast becoming synonymous with anarchist, ingrate, and outsider, much like the socialists pursued by the Wilson administration in recent years. Chase was defamed on a national level, even though he never was found guilty of wrongdoing in any court of law.

What influenced McCarthy in his decision against Chase would soon become public, as Ban Johnson would unravel the results of his investigation that implicated Chase and others. Ban Johnson continued his investigation into the 1919 World Series. At the end of August, Cubs President William Veeck received the following in a telegram:

Thousands of dollars are being bet on the Phillies to win today. Rumors that your game is fixed. Investigate.[15]

A grand jury was formed on September 7 to probe the event. With a case open in front of a grand jury, Ban Johnson seized the opportunity to turn the investigation about the Cubs and Phillies into an investigation about the prior year's World Series. He approached presiding Judge Charles McDonald and told him he had more to probe than the one game. McDonald agreed to listen to whatever testimony that Johnson had. The first witness provided to the Judge was Rube Benton, who recounted his cab ride with Herzog and Chase. With a file forming on Chase, Johnson then directed the Judge to the Chicago White Sox players.

To present or follow the ensuing tangled web is perhaps impossible and ultimately fruitless. The Series was fixed. And the investigation revealed that the World Series fix wasn't an isolated incident, but part of widespread gambling done by many players and teams.

At the end of September, the confessions of Chisox players Lefty Williams and Oscar Felsch were made public. Sport Sullivan and Nat Evans, using an alias "Brown," were the identified gamblers. Their confessions jibed with those from the previous day provided by Eddie Cicotte and Joe Jackson. The confessions confirmed that the World Series was fixed. Williams said he and Gandil, Weaver, Cicotte, and Felsch met with Brown and Sullivan at the Warner Hotel. They were supposed to throw the Series for $5,000 each. Gandil negotiated the figure higher. They were given a portion of the payment up front. During the series, Gandil reported that the deal was off. Then Abe Attell and Bill Burns agreed to participate so that each player would make $20,000. They all claimed that they never saw the final payment. They said that Gandil, Weaver, Williams, Cicotte, and Felsch met in Gandil's room in Cincinnati. Gandil said they were to receive a portion of the total $100,000 after each game. Lefty Williams claimed he received $10,000 and gave half of that to Joe Jackson. Pitcher Ed Cicotte admitted he lobbed the ball to the Cincinnati players during the Series so that "they could read the trademark on it." He said that Risberg and Fred McMullen were after him for a week to join them and go crooked.[16]

Joe Jackson called Judge McDonald and pleaded that he was an honest man. But McDonald, having heard the various testimonies, knew differently and replied, "I know you are not." The Judge cut the conversation short and hung up the phone on the star. Fearing that the others had turned him in, Jackson agreed to talk. He told the Judge he received $5,000 from Lefty, but was promised $20,000. He said that even though the team tried its best to lose game three, pitcher Dickie Kerr, who wasn't involved with the fix, pitched the team to victory. The win spooked the gamblers and caused the fix to be pulled.[17]

Many were called to testify, including Chisox manager "Kid" Gleason, Hugh Jennings, John McGraw, Comiskey confidant "Tip" O'Neill, Jean Dubuc, Benny Kauff, Arnold Rothstein, Joe Gedeon, and others. Sportswriter Hugh Fullerton shed light on what would become a point of contention between Ban Johnson and Charles Comiskey – going public with the investigation. Johnson believed that players exploited the knowledge that owners would never go public with news of a fix. The owners' continued reluctance to curb the aberrant players led to increasingly more brazen actions. Johnson believed that only by calling their bluff and exposing them to the public would baseball clean up. Fullerton wrote:

The Chase case gave many players the idea that they could play dishonestly and not be discovered, or if discovered or suspected, would be cleared. They believed the club owners feared publicity so much that they would be safe. The club owners have always adhered to the policy of secrecy and have whitewashed every scandal and charge of crooked work on the grounds that it was 'for the good of the game.' Their policy encouraged the crooked ball players and tempted the weak ones who until then had remained honest.[18]

That players would use as leverage the owners' reluctance to make matters public was commonly known and practiced. Chase used a similar threat with Farrell years before when he warned against defaming him because he could do the same to baseball. In the future, when Ty Cobb would battle baseball in a similar charge regarding fixing games, Cobb used this leverage by threatening to expose items, including teams' doctoring turnstile counts to evade taxes. For Chase in 1920, however, baseball would preempt him with its defamation of Chase, which as PCL President McCarthy stated, made Chase's case against anyone appear weak.

At the end of October, a war between Ban Johnson and Charles Comiskey commenced as Johnson continued to investigate with the intent to make matters public. Johnson failed to attend winter meetings to discuss the state of affairs just days before the Chisox players and others were to be indicted; instead of attending the important meetings, Johnson chose to interview St. Louis owner Phil Ball and player Joe Gedeon about the World Series. In response, Comiskey announced,

In view of Johnson's absence from the ball meeting and because of some of his statements I serve notice that I will close my ballpark and go out of business if Ban Johnson remains president of the American League.[19]

On October 23, 1920, thirteen persons were indicted for "throwing games" in the 1919 World Series. They included Hal Chase, Abe Attell, Bill Burns, Sport Sullivan, "Brown", Joe Jackson, Oscar Felsch, Eddie Cicotte, Lefty Williams, Swede Risberg, Chick Gandil, Fred McMullen, and Buck Weaver. All charges involved conspiracy to commit illegal acts and were punishable by imprisonment.[20] The testimony claimed that Chase approached Attell and asked him to raise $100,000 to compensate the Chicago team. Attell approached various gamblers with the proposition.

On October 25, gambler Arnold Rothstein testified. Rothstein said that he was approached, most likely by Chase and Attell, but refused to take part in the deal. But money sent during the series came from initials "A.R."[21] Rothstein was found guiltless. The Chicago White Sox Attorney made a statement that Rothstein not only didn't finance it, he did everything in his power to prevent it.[22] Rothstein was certainly handled with kid gloves. It seemed that Comiskey wanted to keep Rothstein out of the case. Fearing that he would take the fall for Rothstein, Attell came forward and said Rothstein was involved all along. He stated that he had been just a small-time hustler.

> *At the time of the World Series I was broke. Five days before I sold my wife's platinum and gold wedding ring for $125 to a man in Chicago. When I went to New York to borrow money, I was given the information about the Series by Hal Chase and Bill Burns... Chicago has exonerated Rothstein in regard to the baseball scandal. In the grand jury room they indicted Hal Chase, who is broke and has not got a dollar. They indicted me, and I'm in the same position. They indicted Bill Burns who had a little money, but who had not a big enough stake to put up.[23]*

A competitor to Rothstein on the West Coast was behind fixing games in the Pacific Coast League. Even though President McCarthy worked hard to eradicate gamblers from the league, the outcome of the 1920 season came under suspicion. Fatty Arbuckle's Vernon team edged the Los Angeles Angels for its second consecutive PCL pennant in a dramatic closing-day doubleheader between the teams in front of 25,000 fans at Washington Park. Vernon finished ahead of the Angels by one and a half games. During the last two weeks of the season, rumors proliferated that opposing players had been bribed to guarantee Vernon the flag. Perhaps Hal Chase was one of the participants in the bribes. But when the league completed its investigation, Salt Lake player Harl Maggart and Babe Borton of Vernon were also charged based on separate incidences.

President McCarthy and Doc Strub traveled to Oakland where Maggart was playing at the end of the seasons in an attempt to gather additional information. But Maggart only admitted that he received $300 from Borton, but it was for other gambling debts. Criminal charges were brought against Borton in Los Angeles in October 1920, but Borton counterattacked arguing that he wasn't to blame and that the Vernon squad had won the title by bribing opponents. The players were cleared of charges based on a technicality. But President McCarthy expelled them from the league.

[1] City Games, The Evolution of American Urban Society and the Rise of Sports, Steven A. Riess, p. 300
[2] The California Winter League, William F. McNeil.
[3] Baseball Notes, Los Angeles Times, Jan 28, 1920, pg. 17
[4] Jim Scott Here, But Does Not Talk Baseball, San Francisco Chronicle, Feb 6, 1920, pg. 10
[5] Graham Makes No charges, But Says Baseball Must Be Kept Above Suspicion, San Francisco Chronicle, May 8, 1920, pf 14
[6] Three S.F. Men Barred From Baseball, SF Chronicle, May 10, 1920, pg. 1
[7] Doc Strub Steps on Gas, Eludes Holdup Men, SF Chronicle, Aug 28, 1920, pg 14
[8] Gambler Held For Attacking Baseball, SF Chronicle, May 12, 1920, pg. 10
[9] White Calls Baseball Heads In Gambling Quiz, SF Chronicle, May 14, 1920, pg. 1
[10] Baseball Records, Pacific Coast League, From 1903 to 1940 Inclusive, Published in Conjunction with Helms Athletic Foundation, pg. 13

[11] San Francisco Chronicle. August 4. 1920

[12] San Francisco Chronicle. August 4. 1920

[13] Chase Pitches; Game Forfeited to Hollister. San Francisco Chronicle. Aug 9. 1920. pg 10

[14] Chase Cause of Forfeited Game. Los Angeles Times. Aug 9. 1920. Pg. 17

[15] Eight Men Out. Eliot Asinof

[16] Conspired In A Hotel. Los Angeles Times. Sep 30. 1920. Pg. 11

[17] Conspired In A Hotel. Los Angeles Times. Sep 30. 1920. Pg. 11

[18] Hugh Fullerton. New Republic

[19] "Ring" In Another Plot. Oct 20. 1920. AP Wire. LA Times. Pg. 1111

[20] Jury Indicts Thirteen Men. Los Angeles Times. Oct 23. 1920. Pg. 118

[21] Testimony May Be Sensational. LA Times. Oct 26. 1920. Pg. 1111

[22] Attell May Be Brought Back. Oct 27. 1920. pg. 1113

[23] San Francisco Chronicle. October 28. 1920

Chapter 24

San Francisco Seals Success Truly Scandalous

Facing the loss of eight of his players, including his stars, White Sox owner Charles Comiskey was displeased with the outcome of the grand jury investigation in Chicago. And he held Ban Johnson responsible. He and Johnson had a history of feuding, but they always seemed to "bury the hatchet." In fact, a newspaper article from 1906 entitled "Bury the Hatchet" discussed how they both agreed to shake hands during one of their biggest feuds when Johnson wouldn't allow Comiskey to sign Nixey Callahan because of Callahan's prior involvement with the successful independent league team, the Logan Squares. They wrangled on and off over the years, including the rift over Vernon pitcher Jack Quinn, who Johnson awarded to the Yankees even though he had played the prior year for the Chisox.

By the end of 1920, Johnson felt his power waning as talk of naming a single baseball commissioner circulated. He had approached Judge McDonald about investigating gambling in baseball in an attempted power grab. Comiskey counteracted Johnson's attempts at justice and exposure by covering up as much as was possible. On the surface, Comiskey disingenuously pursued justice. He engaged a campaign to discredit Johnson, claiming that he had approached Johnson before the World Series about the fix and Johnson did nothing. He also offered a reward to anyone who had information regarding gambling. Most saw right through him. Some joked that Comiskey just wanted the evidence so he could bury it before anyone would see it. The proud Johnson was going to do his best to reveal the events of the Series, even if at the expense of Comiskey and other owners.

Hal Chase had few places to turn at the end of 1920. He completed the divorce to his wife Anna, who added to the public stoning of Prince Hal by claiming "extreme cruelty and gross neglect of duty." She said he was guilty of "gambling, dissipation, and immoral conduct, wasting his money on other women, losing large sums in gambling, and refusing at all times to contribute to the support and maintenance of his wife." She claimed to be humiliated by the press coverage and claimed Hal didn't support her financially.[1] Anna said she never heard about any accusations of gambling until Christy Mathewson suspended him in 1918. She said he told her, "They got the goods on me." She said she was of the opinion that while with the Giants in 1919, "she was sure he was throwing games there, too." As for the involvement in the 1919 World Series, his wife, who was filing for divorce, said Chase told her, "I knew of it and I did what I could to help it along."[2]

One person who came to the support of Hal was Cy Moreing, the ultimate outlaw and baseball purist. Moreing offered Hal a job in the Sperry Flour Company at $300 per month, which would have been sufficient to support him handsomely. It would also have assisted Hal in the difficult transition from baseball. Chase later admitted that he blew the opportunity to get through the rough times and learn a trade.[3] His life was in an apparent downward spiral. Perhaps the honest, caring, reliable Hal Chase that was buried deep within the now burdened man knew better than to join up with Moreing, fearing that he might disappoint him. Perhaps Hal knew he wasn't worthy of Moreing's charity and was too proud to accept it. In hindsight, Chase's decision to turn down Moreing marked a turning point in his life that would lead to destitution.

Charles Comiskey and the owners of major league baseball made an offer to Judge Landis in November of 1920 that he didn't refuse. Needing one baseball commissioner who would act in concert with the wishes of the owners, Landis was called upon as part of the damage control required in the wake of the Black Sox Scandal. Landis had always loyally and firmly supported the interests of those who appointed him. Although he would appear autocratic, he would act unequivocally to carry out the demands of his employers, the baseball owners. With his appointment, the power of the League Presidents diminished, which further fueled Ban Johnson in a futile quest for power while serving in a pathetic lame duck capacity in the coming years.

Comiskey, Rothstein, baseball owners, or some supreme power took the matters of the 1919 World Series into their own hands. In the end, the players were still banned from the game. So what would transpire in the court was likely the attempt to hide incriminating evidence.

When the players were called to testify in court and present the testimonies offered during the grand jury that had already been made public, they were told to deny that they had confessed. One by one, the players denied any previous confession. The judge warned the players that their denial would represent perjury because of their previous testimonies, which had already been printed in the papers. Yet all the players denied the charges.[4]

Perhaps not unsurprising, in March Judge Dever was told that the grand jury testimony had been stolen and that a "conspiracy had hampered the State." When the judge was told, he could not prevent laughing out loud at the strange and not so unpredictable twist of fate. Even though the previous testimony had been made public in the papers and everyone knew that the fix did occur, the court could not find the original evidence. The Rothstein file was also stolen. The Judge and State Attorneys agreed to close the case. The accused were banned from speaking about it.[5] Judge Landis soon banned all eight players permanently from Organized Baseball.

In a few more months, all players were acquitted. So in 1924, Joe Jackson's innocence entitled him to sue Comiskey for back wages of nearly seventeen thousand dollars for 1921 and 1922 that were contractually owed. Jackson's lawyer counted on the strong testimony on Jackson's behalf by Oscar Felsch and Swede Risberg. What they didn't expect was the curious reappearance of Jackson's 1920 grand jury testimony that had been lost during the Black Sox trial. Jackson was charged with perjury. Comiskey and Jackson agreed to a reduced settlement out of court, and the perjury charge was dropped.[6]

Hal Chase, however, was still subject to conspiracy charges. On April 25, 1921 Hal was arrested in San Jose. Chase had his lawyer James Sex file with the local Superior Court a writ of habeus corpus; he claimed that the indictment was faulty and that he was being held illegally. He was later released on bail of $3,000.[7] Chase claimed that Ban Johnson and Charles Comiskey were railroading him because he had defected to the Federal League. Chase was never pursued. Perhaps Organized Baseball decided it was best if Chase didn't testify to avoid opening up Pandora 's Box.[A]

Cubs manager William Veeck was quoted about gambling in baseball and Landis. He said,

> *Landis' great wisdom was in understanding that any attempt to investigate all of the gambling and fixing of the past would not only be impossible from a purely administrative point of view, but would open up a can of worms that would be eating away at baseball for the next decade.*[8]

Landis never formally banned Hal Chase from Organized Baseball. But if there ever was an informal blacklist, Hal Chase was certainly on it. Chase, Seaton, Smith, Gandil, Cicotte, Williams, Weaver, Jackson, Felsch, and Mullens would not be welcomed on any team in Organized Baseball. Only independent leagues and teams would play them. Hal Chase's new team was the Del Monte Canning Company team in San Jose, which he played for in August and September.

In hindsight, President McCarthy of the Pacific Coast League came under scrutiny for how he investigated the gambling in the league the previous year. Just as dissension surfaced in the major leagues over how to handle the problems, the PCL teams divided for and against McCarthy. Those who supported him were the teams in Northern California – Sacramento's Lew Moreing, Oakland's Cal Ewing, and San Francisco's Strub, Putnam, and Graham. The others wanted to see McCarthy removed. California's Governor William Stephens stepped in and asked him to remain in office until he completed cleaning up baseball. McCarthy said he couldn't ignore the call to serve after being contacted by fans, players, sportswriters, and people from all walks of life

---

[A] Hal Chase only appeared in court for gambling in the Magee case, for which he was acquitted.

requesting that he return in light of the gambling issues in the league. "If there ever was a doubt in my mind as to the hold baseball has on the people, this experience has certainly removed it," he explained.

Scandals were a regular occurrence in the 1920s. Perhaps the most lurid in the annals of the Pacific Coast League was the Fatty Arbuckle scandal at the Saint Francis Hotel in September 1921. Arbuckle held a party in his 12th floor suite that lasted for days. One of the guests was Virginia Rappé, a young actress. During the party, Arbuckle allegedly found Rappé passed out on the bathroom floor. He reportedly picked her up and placed her on the bed, then left to get help. When he returned with a few others, they found her screaming in pain. Four days later, Rappé died. Later one of the partygoers told the police that Arbuckle had raped Rappé with a foreign object that caused her death. Roscoe was arrested for murder. He was acquitted of the charges. But Arbuckle's days as owner of the Vernon Tigers were over, as Ed Maier resumed control of the franchise.

One of the largest scandals of the decade surfaced in 1922. President Harding headed the most crooked cabinet in United States history. A friend of the President, Ty Cobb was invited to the inauguration and became a regular at White House poker games when in town to play the Washington squad. Cobb explained that there was a lot of money bet on the games. He saw as much as ten thousand dollars on the table in one stud game. He said that Harding surrounded himself with crooks that drank hard and became careless. He claimed to sit back, drink lightly, and clean up about twelve times each year.[9]

But Harding's administration was more than just sloppy. In April of 1922, the Wall Street Journal uncovered what would be known as the Teapot Dome Scandal. Secretary of the Interior Albert Fall leased oil fields at Teapot Dome in Wyoming to independent oilman and former Fed League owner Harry Sinclair without making the bidding competitive. In essence, Fell received kickbacks in exchange for Sinclair's rights to drill on the government property for a rate that was below the market. Fell leased other property to Los Angeles oilman Edward Doheny under the same circumstances. Since Harry Sinclair had sold Hal Chase to the Cincinnati Reds, he had developed Sinclair Oil into the largest independent oil company in the United States. The Teapot Dome Scandal represented corruption at the highest levels of government and business in America. Fell was convicted. Sinclair was acquitted of conspiracy, but was charged with contempt for lack of cooperation and convicted of jury tampering. Harding's cronies and appointees robbed the government in many instances while he was in power; the Teapot Dome Scandal represented the most egregious example. Harding may not have known about the many crimes, but he was unable to stop them.[A] Harding's friends, who lost to Cobb in poker what they had stolen

---

[A] Harding's administration would pardon many convicted under the Sedition Act, including Eugene Debs.

from the American people, became a thorn in the President's side. Harding said, "I have no trouble with my enemies, but my damn friends, they're the ones that keep we walking the floor nights!"[10]

Baseball wasn't all about scandals, however. For every unsavory event, there were many more acts of goodness and community. One example was an exhibition game played at New York for the benefit of Christy Mathewson on September 30, 1921 between the New York Giants and a group of Old Timers. The game raised a large sum of money to assist Mathewson, who was recovering from tuberculosis. Twenty thousand people attended. Baseballs autographed by President Harding, Vice President Coolidge, Babe Ruth, Mathewson, George "Highpockets" Kelly, and Honus Wagner were sold.[11] Over the past year, Matty had been bedridden and near death at times from the tuberculosis that developed following the damage to his lungs in WWI. One lung collapsed completely in December of 1920, and while his condition was serious, the doctors at the hospice in Saranac, New York were hopeful for an eventual recovery.[12]

There were no scandals in San Francisco under Strub, Graham, and Putnam either. The Seals' owners were about to embark on the most successful run of any minor league franchise. Even though the Seals finished just three games behind the Los Angeles Angels in third place, they were having fun. Los Angeles Times sportswriter Harry A. Williams reported that when asked, Doc Strub replied, "Don't we have fun?" Williams said that since Doc was paying for everything, he ought to know.[13] The truth was Doc Strub would always say "We're having fun." Not that he was a jokester. He was a businessman. But he knew that his business was creating fun for others. If you ever asked the Doc to sum up his goal as a businessman in three words, he would concede, "to have fun."

But life wasn't all fun. The exhilaration of success was often accompanied by the tedium of politics and the darkness of tragedy. For Strub and Graham, their political battle during 1921/1922 was convincing Organized Baseball that the Pacific Coast League should not have to submit to the draft. Strub said he would even oppose Judge Landis. He declared that the Pacific Coast League was on par with the major leagues in terms of quality and shouldn't have to relinquish its best players each year in the draft.[14] In January 1919, the Pacific Coast League had served noticed upon the major leagues that it no longer wanted to be subjected to the draft. The major leagues agreed. But the issue was contested each year until it was ultimately overturned.[15]

Graham spoke out against the draft arguing that his responsibilities were to his patrons ahead of the interests of Organized Baseball.

> *To our people the American and National League races are secondary. Their main concern is what kind of a team San Francisco will have. That interest is our sole asset. No one can deny that the interests of our patrons are paramount, yet this duty of minor league owners to their*

patrons is one factor in the draft question entirely overlooked by its advocates.

Graham said that if the draft were in place this year, he would have had to sell five or six players, which would have ruined the club. He would have had to let go of the players at a fraction of their value. "What right have the major leagues to ask us to let them draft our players at an arbitrary price for less than they are worth?"

This issue had plagued the league ever since its inception when Jim Morley lost players the first year that the PCL joined Organized Baseball. And nearly two decades later, the same issues persisted.

The Seals knew what they needed to do to preserve the value of their franchise players. Just as Morley had done, they needed to sell them to the major leagues during the season to the highest bidder before any of them were drafted. In 1921, they sold one of their stars, Jimmy O'Connell to John McGraw's Giants.

George Putnam discovered O'Connell, who starred at centerfield for Santa Clara College at eighteen years of age in 1919. Impressed with Jimmy's hitting, Graham convinced O'Connell to turn professional. While O'Connell showed potential as a hitter, he proved to be a liability in the field. Graham struggled over where to play him, hiding him in the outfield or at first base. In 1921, playing first base, he led the team in hitting with a .337 average and stole 23 bases, but led the league in errors by a first baseman. John McGraw overlooked the poor fielding and wanted O'Connell's bat on the Giants. He paid $75,000 in November 1921 for O'Connell, a record price for any minor league player up to that point. The genius of Graham, Putnam, and Strub was in how they negotiated the sale of players to the majors. O'Connell was considered a "can't miss" major league star, but Graham convinced McGraw that he could use another year of seasoning in the minors. McGraw agreed. O'Connell played the 1922 season for the Seals and hit .335 with 39 stolen bases. And he proved popular with the fans as the newspapers touted the Seals' star as the future New York Giant first baseman.

In March, the owners celebrated the new season and O'Connell's future at a luncheon hosted by the President of Santa Clara University. O'Connell, Graham, Strub, and Putnam gathered at San Francisco's trendy Marquard's Café[16] where O'Connell received comparisons to baseball's best young players, including Babe Ruth. Ruth was familiar to Californians, having barnstormed in the winters. Because of his recent barnstorming, Commissioner Landis had penalized Ruth; Landis wouldn't let Ruth play until May 20 rather than on the approaching opening day on April 12.[17] But those who witnessed Ruth's keen eye and unprecedented power at the plate knew that no Pacific Coast Leaguer, including O'Connell, compared to him even before he set records in New York. Some commented that he would hit 100 home runs if he played in the Pacific Coast League, particularly in the thin air of Salt Lake City. O'Connell would still need to prove himself at the major league level.

On the heals of the O'Connell deal, Graham negotiated with the Chicago White Sox to sell another star, Willie Kamm, who the Sox needed to replace the banned Buck Weaver at third base. Doc Strub had discovered Kamm as a nineteen-year-old amateur at Recreation Park. As manager of the Seals over the past four seasons, Graham developed young players like O'Connell and Kamm. For two years, Willie had hit under .250 and led the league in errors. But in 1921, he grew stronger, led the league in fielding, and hit a respectable .288. In 1922, O'Connell and Kamm led the Seals to the pennant.[A] Kamm hit .344, second highest in the league. As the 1922 season began, the Chicago White Sox approached Graham about making a deal. But in May, Charlie Graham took a sudden leave of absence. George Putnam took over the negotiations with Chicago. The team also hired ex-Pittsburgh player Dots Miller as the new manager to replace Graham. Putnam negotiated an historic deal, selling Kamm for $100,000 and three players. Strub, Graham, and Putnam framed the check, which represented the richest deal in the history of minor league baseball, and hung it permanently in the team's business office. Kamm played through the 1922 season with the Seals.

As the fortunes of the Seals changed for the better, the Graham family experienced tragedy. Graham's leave of absence from the franchise was predicated on a calamity May 7, three weeks before Putnam negotiated the Willie Kamm deal in Graham's absence.[18] Charlie's six-year old son Joseph was with his grandmother at the Santa Clara campus, which for many years was intersected by the city's most important thoroughfare, "The Alameda." Hap Hogan's brother Harold Bray was driving down the Alameda when the young Graham ran across the street to his grandmother without observing the approaching car. Hours later, toddler Joseph Graham died of injuries from the auto accident at a local hospital.[19]

---

[1]   Anna M. Chase vs. Harold H. Chase, State of Ohio, Court of Common Please, Hamilton County, Division of Domestic Relations
[2]   Cincinnati Commercial Tribune, January 27, 1921
[3]   The Sporting News, September 18, 1941, Lester Grant (Oakland Post Enquirer)
[4]   Confessions of Players Denied, Feb 13, 1921, Los Angeles Times, pg. 18
[5]   Scandal Cases in A Collapse, Los Angeles Times, Mar 18,1921, Pg. III2
[6]   Eight Men Out, Asinof, , pp. 289-292
[7]   Hal Chase Is In Toils, Los Angeles Times, Apr 26, 1921, Pg. III2

[A]   Jim "Death Valley" Scott won twenty-five games and had an ERA of 2.22. Scott had pitched nine seasons for the Chisox amassing a 2.30 ERA over that time. His best season was 1915 when he was 24-11. Scott served in the World War I until 1919, then signed with the Seals in 1920. Ollie Mitchell was 24-7, Bob Geary was 20-9, and Doug McWeeny, who was received in the sale of Kamm, was 15-7. The offense was supported by Bert Ellison who led the league with 141 RBI, Hal Rhyne, Joe Kelly, Gene Valla, Sam Agnew, and Pete Kilduff.

[8] The Hustlers Handbook, Bill Veeck
[9] Cobb, A Biography, Al Stump
[10] American Decades, The Gale Group, 2001
[11] History of Baseball in California and Pacific Coast Leagues 1847-1938, Lange
[12] 'Mathewson Doing Well', Says Doctor, Dece 22, 1920, New York Times
[13] Sports Motoring Filmland Drama, Harry A. Williams, Los Angeles Times, 9/8/1921, pg. III1
[14] Coast Circuit May Apply for Major League Status, Dec 18, 1921, pg. 102, New York Times
[15] Baseball Records, Pacific Coast League, From 1903 to 1940 Inclusive, Published in Conjunction with Helms Athletic Foundation, pg. 17
[16] O'Connell Guest, Santa Clara Lunch, SF Chronicle, Mar 30, 1922, Pg. I5
[17] Fans Want Babe Ruth Reinstated, New York, March 29, 1922
[18] $510 in Phone Tolls Cost Kamm Deal, SF Chronicle, May 30, 1922, pg. 8
[19] Son of Baseball Magnate is Dead, Los Angeles Times, May 8, 1922, pg. III2

Chapter 25

Jimmy O'Connell Too Honest For His Own Good

In April and May of 1922, the Supreme Court of the United States considered the lawfulness of the reserve clause in major league baseball. When the Federal League disbanded, the Baltimore franchise opted to challenge the baseball monopoly in court. In lower courts, they had won a significant settlement. But on appeal, the case went to the Supreme Court. The case of Federal Baseball Club of Baltimore, Inc. vs. National League of Professional Baseball Clubs was decided in May. Supreme Court Justice Oliver Wendell Holmes upheld the position of the Court of Appeals preserving the reserve clause.

> *The fact that the [owners] produce baseball games as a source of profit, large or small, cannot change the character of the games. They are still sport, not trade.*

Holmes concluded that baseball exhibitions, although a business, did not constitute interstate commerce as intended in the antitrust laws. Traveling across state lines constituted "a mere incident" rather than the result of commerce. He ruled that baseball was an exhibition, as the activity is not related to production, but to the personal effort and exhibition of individuals.

Baseball thus became immune to antitrust laws that restricted businesses from behaving in an unfair or monopolistic manner. The progress of past players including Hal Chase, unions, and competing leagues were dealt a significant setback. The National and American Leagues would never face any competition from other leagues. And more than a half-century would pass before players would challenge the reserve clause in court and win. Hal Chase was one of the few players in the game's first century to successfully challenge the clause in court.

Chase had won a battle against the reserve clause; but if Chase's goal was to play Organized Baseball, perhaps he lost the war. Disbarred from the game, he played sparingly in the southern portion of San Jose with local children in vacant lots. He lived on a ranch of a friend, Harold Rogers. Toward the end of 1922, he worked in his father's lumberyard, and moved into his parents' home at the end of the year to assist them and himself. His mother was in her seventies and his father was becoming frail with heart issues. All the while, he had not let go of the desire to play professional baseball once again. Still not yet forty, Chase maintained the vigor to continue playing.

Just starting their major league careers, Kamm and O'Connell completed the 1922 season with the Seals before shipping off to their teams. The future was bright for the two young stars. On October 2, Jimmy O'Connell married Esther

Doran in Southern California. Two weeks later, the Seals celebrated Willie Kamm Day at the Valencia Street Recreation Park at which Kamm was presented over $1,000 to purchase a diamond ring.

Starting a career in college baseball was Harry Wolter, who retired from playing and took the head baseball coaching position at Stanford University in December of 1922. He once held the same position for less than a month while he negotiated to play for the Los Angeles Angels in 1916. But this time, he would remain, as was customary for the steady and stable Wolter. Now working within a few miles of his home in Redwood City, Wolter remained the head coach on "the farm" for twenty-seven uninterrupted years.

The Seals continued to develop young talent in the tradition of Ping Bodie, Harry Heilman, Lefty O'Doul, Jimmie O'Connell, and Willie Kamm who they blended with ex-major leaguers and experienced veterans including Bert Ellison, Jim Scott, and Spider Baum. One of the new young talents was named Paul Waner. Waner battled for a spot as a pitcher in the winter while on the Seals reserve Yannigans team. Pitching coach Spider Baum looked on as Waner pitched inter-squad games to prove his worth. In one game, Waner's arm stiffened. He called timeout and told Baum that his arm was getting sore. The veteran who pitched for two decades in the minors showed little compassion. He callously told the rookie, "Make it or break it."

Waner continued to throw until he badly injured his arm. The next day, he couldn't throw a ball and feared that his career was over. He managed to hang around the club at practices and offered to shag balls for hitters during batting practice. On most days, crony big leaguers Jimmy O'Connell, Willie Kamm, and Lew Fonseca, a former St. Mary's and Seals star who had hit .361 for the Cincinnati Reds in 1922, stayed after practice to hit balls. In the jargon of the day, the three players were "thick," meaning they were close. Waner quietly fielded for them and threw the balls back to the infield underhanded. He shagged for them for more than a week, never once taking a turn at the plate. As long as he wasn't told to go home, Waner was happy to shag for the stars.

Then one day they asked if he would like a turn at bat. The 135-pound Waner proceeded to hit a few balls over the right field fence 370 feet from home plate. A carpenter who was repairing a roof beyond the fence stopped to take notice when one ball landed close to him. Then Waner hit another onto the roof. Waner kept sending line drives into the vicinity of the carpenter.

After the practice, the big leaguers gave the silent treatment to the rookie. But word traveled to manager Dots Miller. At dinner, Miller approached Waner and told him to play with the Regulars. He started the 1923 season at first base. Then Miller tried him in the outfield for a game in Salt Lake City on a hot day. The Salt Lake manager was Duffy Lewis, former St. Mary's and Boston left fielder. In addition to being part of the greatest defensive outfield in baseball history[A] and manager, Lewis was the league's leading hitter having hit .401 for Salt Lake in 1921.[B] Lewis knew that Waner's arm was lame, so he encouraged his players to take the extra base when possible. He told them that when Waner had the ball, "duck your head and start running." But that day in the desert heat, Paul Waner's arm felt strong for the first time in months. He practiced with no pain during warm-ups. In the second inning, a player hit a ball deep into the gap in the outfield. Waner threw out the runner at second by fifteen feet. Another runner tried to score from second base on a single. Paul threw the ball all the way from right field on a fly to home plate to nail the runner. After throwing out four men, nobody ran on him any more.[1] Paul Waner hit .370 for the next two seasons. Graham shopped Waner to Dots Miller's former team, the Pittsburgh Pirates. The Pittsburgh scout and Oakland Oaks' coach, Joe Devine, said that because Paul was so small, he'd have to hit .400 to make it to the big leagues. The next season Waner hit .401. In 1925, Charlie Graham sold Waner to Pittsburgh with shortstop Hal Rhyne for $100,000.

Once in Pittsburgh, Paul Waner told the President of the Pirates that he had a younger brother who was even better than he was. So the Pirates signed Paul's brother Lloyd. While in the minors, Lloyd hit .350 and was named the league most valuable player. But the big club was wary of Lloyd because the younger Waner was just 130 pounds and only twenty years old. But the team called him up and put the Waners together in the outfield. The brothers combined for 460 hits that year, leading the Pirates to the pennant. Along with Pie Traynor at third base who batted .340, Lloyd hit .355 and Paul hit .380.[C]

Hal Chase likely felt he had as much pop still left in his bat as the Waner brothers. In 1923, he moved to Nogales, Mexico where he managed the Nogales Internationals near the border with Arizona in the Southwestern United States.[2] The location was convenient because of baseball's popularity in Mexico, and because liquor could be obtained in Mexico while the United States was regulated by prohibition. The element of available liquor was not just an attraction to Chase, but important to the success of the local baseball. The league was popular and often rowdy. Just as the border with Mexico liberated the alcoholic lawfully seeking a drink, the border also offered the banned ballplayer the opportunity to play and manage without interference from the authorities in Organized Baseball.

[A] Lewis played with Hall of Famers Harry Hooper and Tris Speaker. Lewis had become so adept at fielding balls off the green wall at Fenway Park, that left field was nicknamed "Duffy's Corner."

[B] The ball traveled well in Salt Lake City, which may have contributed to the batting averages and home run production for the team. Salt Lake also featured hitter Paul Strand led the league in batting and home runs in 1922 with a .363 average and twenty-eight dongs. He followed up in 1923 with an even more impressive .394 and 43 home runs. Connie Mack paid $100,000 for Strand.

[C] Paul and Lloyd Waner are in the Baseball Hall of Fame.

Chase toured Mexico with his team on a trip that took them all the way to Mexico City. Chase discussed with locals about a league for Mexico. But until 1925, there wasn't enough interest or players to create a league outside of Mexico City. Players from Cuba were brought in to fill out the rosters because of the lack of local talent. Perhaps Chase was ahead of his time proposing such a more widespread Mexican League. A year later, he would return to discuss a role in the league that started to take shape. But in 1924, he remained a free agent in an independent league in Arizona, called the Copper League.

Chase had left major league baseball, but he wasn't forgotten. He had established a legacy as one of the sport's gamblers. His legacy also continued to grow as a great first baseman. For years, star players, managers, and journalists would refer to Chase whenever describing the prototypical defensive first baseman. The references continued for more than fifty more years, well past the point where readers would know Hal Chase first hand, or even know his name. But sentimental old-timers as well as old school traditionalists would allude to Chase's excellence for decades. In 1923, writer Ed O'Malley referred to Hal Chase as "the king of all first sackers."[3]

Still considered baseball royalty because of his deftness with the glove, Prince Hal accepted a "job offer" with the Saginaw Manistee Lumber Company in Williams, Arizona. Chase was considered a deadhead baseball bum, which meant he became a journeyman ringer, a hitter for hire. He was also considered a great manager. The papers noted how he whipped a group of novices into a competitive team. By June, however, Chase had jumped to a competitor team in nearby Jerome, where he led the Miners at first base and as manager.

While Chase was handling a group of lumbermen and miners, Harry Wolter was overseeing some of America's best and brightest at Stanford. Wolter faced a familiar and friendly opponent when he played against University of Southern California at the Los Angeles Coliseum. Former Cleveland great, gentleman, and future Hall of Famer Sam Crawford coached the Trojan team after finishing his career with the Los Angeles Angels of the Pacific Coast League from 1919 to 1921, where he led his team to finishes of second, fourth, and first places.[A]

Meanwhile, Willie Kamm played well for the Chisox, particularly on defense. But Jimmy O'Connell didn't play much under McGraw, which was typical for a rookie under McGraw, who often benched the younger players. At the end of 1923, the two received word that their former Seals manager, Dots

---

[A] He hit .359 in 1919. My favorite story about the humble Crawford is that when he retired in Palmdale, California, he received word that a message awaited him at the post office in 1957. The seventy-seven year old learned that he had been inducted into the Hall of Fame. When people in town heard, they were surprised because he had never mentioned that he played baseball. Crawford retired in anonymity.

Miller, succumbed to tuberculosis at the age of thirty-six. Miller had been replaced as manager with Bert Ellison due to illness and spent his last months under care at a facility at Saranac, New York with Christy Mathewson, also under care at the same facility. When Miller passed away in upstate New York in September, O'Connell and New York managers Miller Huggins and John McGraw attended his funeral.

The following season, O'Connell hit .317 for McGraw, but played in only fifty-two games. Because O'Connell was touted as the next great star when signed, in a backup role the newspapers called him the "$75,000 bust." By the end of the 1924 season, his major league career would end.

At the end of the 1924 season, the New York Giants were close to securing another pennant. Facing the lowly Philadelphia A's, somebody on the Giants considered approaching the Philadelphia A's players to ask them to "lay down." Certainly such a proposition was welcomed by McGraw, if not orchestrated by the manager who coined the phrase, "it ain't cheating if you don't get caught."

McGraw played a lead role in defining a culture in the deadball era that would filter down to future generations of players and managers. Fans attracted to the purity of the game also paradoxically cheered those who won at any cost. The dirty player who threw the spitball, stole signs, brushed back hitters, or slid hard with sharpened spikes was quietly admired. Historian Harold Seymour said,

> For good or bad, a consuming urge to win and a willingness to cut a few corners, if necessary to do so, have been a part of the American character since frontier days. These traits, which have contributed toward making the United States the kind of nation it is, were amply reflected by professional ball. [4]

Throughout his baseball career, McGraw usually found a way to win. In 1924, he certainly possessed great players such as Bill Terry, Frankie Frisch, Ross Youngs, George Kelly, and a young Hack Wilson. But talent alone didn't win the games. McGraw was known as a great field manager who motivated players and made good decisions. He was a great tactician. Even though he was uneducated, he ironically was credited for bringing a "scientific" approach to the game by manufacturing runs through bunts, steals, and hit and runs. The talent and coaching had produced a league leading .300 team batting average and a slugging percentage of .432. But in 1924, that wasn't enough for McGraw. He wanted more than talent and good coaching – he wanted an edge.

With a few games left to play in the season and leading the Brooklyn Robins by only one game, McGraw was looking for a win over the lowly Philadelphia A's. McGraw was never charged with wrongdoing. But it was likely he was involved with cheating during the series with the A's. In the end, Jimmy O'Connell was assigned as the messenger, and ultimately the scapegoat. Coach Cozy Dolan asked O'Connell to approach shortstop Heine Sand, a former

Pacific Coast Leaguer, who led the Phillies in putouts and would be in a position to throw games. As a good soldier, O'Connell did as he was told. He offered Sand $500 for "taking it easy" during the game. Sand refused and subsequently reported O'Connell to Commissioner Landis.

Landis investigated the charges. Approaching the opponent and asking them to "take it easy" at the end of the season was about as traditional as turkey at Thanksgiving. But with the heightened sensitivity toward the subject, Landis felt compelled, if not enthusiastic, to research the charges. If he had the opportunity, he would have swept the events under the carpet. But because O'Connell didn't deny the charges, Landis was forced to act.

Coach Dolan denied involvement. The honest and naïve O'Connell, who could not tell a lie, admitted to offering the bribe but claimed that he was following orders. "How would I benefit from paying $500 for a Giants victory?" he told Landis. "Am I the scapegoat?" O'Connell also stated that players Ross Youngs, Frankie Frisch, and George "Highpockets" Kelly were involved.

Pittsburgh owner Barney Dreyfuss, who finished behind McGraw's Giants, pointed out to Landis that neither O'Connell nor Dolan had the means to put up $500 for a fix. He suggested that the source of the arrangement was the Giants' management. Others speculated that organized crime bankrolled it, as they had done in the past. Landis banned both O'Connell and Dolan from baseball. Youngs, Frisch, and Kelly all denied involvement and were acquitted. Landis later said that he would have excused O'Connell if Jimmy hadn't admitted to what had occurred.

Dolan didn't take the ruling lightly. He sued Landis for defamation of character. Ultimately Dolan dropped his suit and agreed to a settlement.

American League president Ban Johnson, disgusted with McGraw, the Giants, and the continuing influence of bribes in baseball, suggested that the World Series be cancelled as a result of the betting scandal. The owners disagreed, but Johnson personally boycotted the games on principle, feeling that corruption still tainted the game. He continued his private investigations and leaked findings from past investigations that had yet to become public. In October, he announced that he knew of the attempted fix of the very first World Series in 1903. Johnson wanted to foster public outrage that would force Landis from his stance of compromise.

Banned from baseball at the age of twenty-three, Jimmy O'Connell and his wife packed their bags for Arizona. The "Copper Leagues" represented one of the only options for a player banned from the game. While O'Connell would play against other banned players as well as Negro players who weren't allowed to play in the major leagues, no other banned players were as young or capable as O'Connell. He would still have a future as a star and a hero in Arizona.

The end of the 1924 season would see the rise and fall of two of

California's greatest baseball players, Walter Johnson and Frank Chance. Perhaps due to the bad karma created by John McGraw and his Giants over the Jimmy O'Connell affair, Olinda's Johnson defeated the Giants by leading the Washington Senators to its first World Series championship. And on September 24, 1924, Fresno's Frank Chance, the Peerless Leader, died from complications related to the health conditions that had plagued him for the past decade.

---

[1] The Glory of Their Times: The Story of Baseball Told by the Men Who Played It, Lawrence S. Ritter.

[2] The Sporting News, September 18, 1941. Lester Grant (Oakland Post Enquirer)

[3] Locals Smother Bees, Ed O'Malley, Los Angeles Times, Oct 3, 1923, pg. III2

[4] Baseball, The Golden Age Harold Seymour

Chapter 26

Baseball Gambling Not An Isolated Affair

A World Series hero, Walter Johnson returned to California during the winter of 1924/25 for two reasons. First, he wanted to purchase one of the Pacific Coast League teams. He also agreed to play in three exhibition games. The first game was in Los Angeles on October 26 between Johnson's White King Soap Company and the Vernon Tigers at Washington Park in front of twenty thousand fans. Johnson's team consisted primarily of Los Angeles Angels players. One of Los Angeles' most wealthy individuals, oil magnate Edward Doheny, caught the ceremonial first pitch thrown by Johnson. Doheny was due to stand trial for his involvement in the Teapot Dome Scandal, but maneuvered a postponement so that he could attend the game. While in Los Angeles, Johnson met with Ed Maier about purchasing the Vernon team, which Maier would sell after the 1925 season to San Francisco banker Herbert Fleishhacker. Chicago Cubs owner William Wrigley, who had purchased the Los Angeles Angels in 1921, didn't want the Vernon team to remain in Los Angeles.

From the days of Hen Berry and Hap Hogan, the Vernon Tigers and Los Angeles Angels teams had graciously shared the Los Angeles market, often playing in the same Washington Park grounds. But because the city of Los Angeles wouldn't make improvements that Wrigley wanted at Washington Park, he built a new stadium at 42nd Place and Avalon Boulevard, in what is now known as South Central Los Angeles. The new Wrigley Field was modeled after the original field in Chicago built eleven years earlier. In a feud with Ed Maier, Wrigley had no intention to share the field with the Vernon franchise. He was willing to share, however, with the Salt Lake City club as he proposed that owner William Lane transfer his team to Los Angeles, which Lane would do in 1926 when the Vernon team moved to San Francisco. Perhaps the feud between Wrigley and Maier discouraged Johnson in his pursuit of the Vernon team. Or perhaps the team just wasn't good enough to interest him. Nonetheless, Johnson continued to shop among the owners of the league.

Johnson then met in the Bay Area with J. Cal Ewing, owner of the Oakland Oaks. He played in an exhibition game between the Pittsburgh Pirates' West Coast scout and Oakland Oaks' coach Joe Devine's "Major League All Stars" and pitcher Walter Mails' "Coast League All Stars." Pitching for Devine's team, Johnson shut out the minor leaguers. He returned to Southern California where he served as Grand Marshal in a Halloween parade. Another attraction in the parade was Babe Ruth who was barnstorming on the West Coast. Commissioner Landis had set a deadline for all exhibition games to be played by November 1. Both Johnson and Ruth had been reprimanded in past seasons for playing in exhibition games in California in the winter. To avoid controversy, the locals arranged a game with both players before the deadline.

The next day in Brea, California, Walter Johnson pitched for the Anaheim Elks against Babe Ruth, who took the mound for the Ruth All Stars. Also featured in the game were Ernie Johnson, Bob Meusel, Rube Ellis, and Sam Crawford. It was featured as the "Only Game in Southern California Where Johnson and Ruth Oppose Each Other." With a tired arm, Johnson gave up four home runs, two to Ruth, who hit one over five hundred feet. Ruth gave up only one run while on the mound.

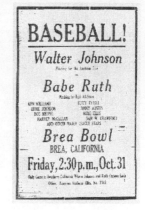

Johnson never did come to terms on a purchase of a PCL club. At one point, a deal was announced. But it fell through and Johnson lost interest. The Pacific Coast League lost an opportunity to bring a star to the circuit that would have certainly attracted fans in all cities. Some owners considered pooling money together to assist Johnson's purchase. But Ewing set a price that was unreasonably high for his mediocre Oaks team, and the entire league suffered by losing out on Johnson's stardom as a result.[1]

Flyer for exhibition game between Walter Johnson and Babe Ruth

The 1925 season would be the last for the Vernon Tigers, which finished the season deep in the cellar. Once again, the San Francisco Seals proved the class of the league, distancing themselves from runner up Salt Lake City. The Seals featured Gene Valla, Paul Waner, Bert Ellison, Hal Rhyne, Smead Jolley, Lloyd Waner, and Gus Suhr. Salt Lake City featured Tony Lazzeri, who set a professional baseball record with sixty home runs (over 200 games), Ossie Vitt, and Lefty O'Doul. Other notables in the league included Seattle's Frank Brazill, Portland's Duffy Lewis, and Oakland's Buzz Arlett.

1925 PCL Stars

PLAYER	ACCOMPLISHMENTS
Paul Waner	Hall of Fame
Lloyd Waner	Hall of Fame
Tony Lazzeri	Hall of Fame
Lefty O'Doul	Fourth highest all time major league batting average.
Duffy Lewis	Started in left field for the Boston Red Sox for three World Series titles in 1912, 1915, and 1916. Eleven major league seasons followed by years as PCL's top hitter.
Gene Valla	From 1922 to 1925 with the Seals he hit .333, .334, .367, and .333.
Bert Ellison	From 1921 to 1925 with the Seals he hit .311, .306, .358, .381 (his 307 hits led the league), and .325.
Hal Rhyne	After 1925, was sold to Pittsburgh with Paul Waner for $100,000
Smead Jolley	Career .305 hitter in four major league seasons. Led PCL in hitting in 1927, 1928, and 1938. RBIs in 1927 and 1928, and won triple crown in PCL in 1928. Also won batting titles in other minor leagues in 1936, 1938, 1940, and 1941. Sold by Seals to Comiskey's Chisox in 1929.
Gus Suhr	Eleven-year major leaguer with Pittsburgh, hit .275 in his career and voted to National League All Star team in 1936.
Ossie Vitt[A]	San Francisco native, played ten seasons in the majors, mostly in Detroit with Cobb and Crawford as a "no hit, good field" third baseman.
Buzz Arlett[B]	Hit .313 for Philadelphia Phillies in 1931 as a 32-year old rookie. He posted the best season ever by a player who played only one season (due to injury, sub-par fielding, and desire for speed in outfield he was replaced). He began in 1919 with Oakland Oaks as pitcher, won twenty-nine games in 1921. In 1926, he moved to the outfield and hit .382. In 2,390 minor league games, he hit 432 home runs with a .341 average. He is the all-time home run leader in Pacific Coast League history.
Frank Brazill	Played two years in the majors. Hit .395 for Seattle in 1925.

For many years through the 1925 season, the cities of San Francisco, Los Angeles, Portland, Oakland, Sacramento, Vernon, Salt Lake City, and Seattle fielded teams in the Pacific Coast League. After the season, the alignment

---

[A] Ty Cobb referred to how he hit Walter Johnson well once he learned that Johnson feared hitting and hurting batters. So Cobb would crowd the plate until he worked the count in his favor when facing Johnson. Johnson hit Oscar Vitt in a game August 10, 1915 and knocked him out for five minutes. The rattled Johnson then uncharacteristically gave up four runs. Cobb apparently observed Johnson's fear of hitting a player during that game, and went on to hit .435 against Johnson the rest of his career. – source: The Ballplayers - Ossie Vitt, baseballlibrary.com

[B] Due to damage to his arm after throwing so many innings early in his career, Arlett had difficulty hitting right handed. So he learned how to hit left-handed. One fan, at the age of eight, saw Arlett play and recalled how he could hit the hell out of the ball from both sides of the plate; not many did that at the time. Arlett became the first switch-hitting power hitter in baseball.

changed slightly. Ed Maier sold the Vernon Tigers to Herbert Fleishhacker who moved the team to San Francisco and named it the Missions, or the Mission Reds. A successful banker, Fleishhacker also became involved in urban sports and the local parks and recreation in the San Francisco area. The previous year, he had built the largest swimming pool in the world in San Francisco called the Fleishhacker Pool. For the 1926 season, William Lane relocated the Salt Lake City team in Los Angeles under the moniker the Hollywood Stars.[A]

In 1925, Hal Chase and other banned players congregated in the Southwest's Frontier League.[2] Four teams comprised the league, including Douglas (Arizona), Fort Bayard (New Mexico), El Paso (Texas), and Juarez (Mexico). The towns' locals pooled $5 to $10 each to form the teams and charged $.50 per ticket to games played in three-game weekend series. The paltry salaries were enough to attract former star players with no other place to play. Fort Bayard and Juarez fielded the league's premier teams. Jimmy O'Connell played for Fort Bayard, situated in the Southwestern corner of New Mexico Northeast of Douglas. Superstar pitcher Tom Seaton, previously banned by Charlie Graham and Seals, led the Juarez team. He became the team's manager while holding a position with the Southern Pacific Railroad in Tucson. Initially, Chase served as player and manager for Douglas, situated in the Southeast corner of Arizona, not far from the town of Tombstone made famous by Wyatt Earp[B] and the Showdown at OK Corral. Chase also owned the Crystal Palace Café in Agua Prieta in Mexico, just across the border from Douglas.

Before the season began, Mexico started a Mexican Baseball League. Chase claimed to be in discussion with the organizers about becoming its commissioner once stadiums were built throughout the country. Baseball was popular and prominent in Sonora, near where Chase played and from where the current Mexican President Plutarco Elias Calles hailed. On March 10, 1925, the Los Angeles Times declared Hal Chase the "Mexican Czar." The paper reported that he had been offered a position by the government of Mexico to organize a baseball league that would ultimately lead to an international series with the United States clubs.[3]

Facing an obvious public relations challenge as he presented his credentials to the Mexican authorities, Chase offered interviews to the media in an attempt to clear his name and secure the position. In one interview, he said he was not a Benedict Arnold, as many had painted him. Rather, he likened himself to Alfred Dreyfus, a name more familiar in the early twentieth century than today.[4]

[A] To confuse matters, the Mission Reds (formerly the Vernon team) would later return to Los Angeles and be called the Hollywood Stars. The former Hollywood Stars, which had come from Salt Lake City, moved to San Diego and became the Padres.

[B] By that time, Wyatt Earp was still alive, but had moved to California. He first moved near San Francisco. Then toward the end of his life, moved to Hollywood. He died in 1929 and was buried in San Francisco.

Dreyfus was a Jewish French artillery officer wrongly accused of espionage in 1894 who was sentenced to life in exile. The true culprit was later identified and Dreyfus was exonerated. Chase was hopeful that the Mexican government would not only hire him, but also provide vindication for the past claims against him.

Perhaps Chase made public his hope of becoming an important baseball figure in Mexico to demonstrate to his ailing mother that he would make good. In San Jose, while Chase discussed becoming a Mexican Czar at his small bar in Agua Caliente, his mother Mary suffered from cancer at the age of eighty-one. In April, she succumbed to the illness, perhaps believing that her son had been exonerated and elevated to a deserved role as a baseball executive. However, when the Mexican government conferred with major league baseball regarding the forty-two year old Chase, the damaging reference from Ban Johnson sealed Prince Hal's fate as merely a barkeep in the desert.

Chase's Douglas team had little pitching and quickly fell far behind Juarez and Fort Bayard. Although he hit .375 through the first half of the season, his team had won only four games against sixteen losses. Conversely, Fort Bayard posted a record of 18-4. Chase left to California to find some recruits for the second half of the season. He returned with banned Black Sox players Chick Gandil and Buck Weaver. For the remainder of the season, the infield for Douglas was as good as most major league teams. Douglas tied Juarez for the second half championship.[5] Batboy Harold Warnock remembered that season and how Hal Chase had given him a first baseman's glove.[6] While Chase proved inconsistent and unreliable as a parent, accounts throughout his life highlight his good heart with children. On more than one occasion, a young boy reflected on how the baseball hero, with few possessions of his own, handed him a baseball glove along with encouragement.

Another good-hearted man, who many inaccurately portrayed as the alter ego to Hal Chase, died in October of 1925. Christy Mathewson finally lost his long battle against tuberculosis at Saranac Lake, New York on the 7th.

For the 1926 season, Jimmy O'Connell forced Chick Gandil, who had moved to the El Paso team, out of the league. Few liked Gandil, who some referred to as "crooked, ungrateful, and rude." In one altercation with O'Connell, Jimmy chased the older Gandil with a baseball bat and threatened that if Gandil didn't leave the league, he would. Gandil was soon given his release. Unlike Gandil, O'Connell was very popular, particularly in Fort Bayard. A doctor at the local hospital that treated patients for tuberculosis founded the Fort Bayard team. The team's games were piped into the hospital for the patients to hear. And the young ex-Giant and team star regularly visited the patients and became their charismatic hero.

To replace Gandil from the previous season, Buck Weaver recruited another Black Sox player, Lefty Williams, to shore up the weak pitching staff for Douglas. Third baseman Cowboy Ruiz, who had played for Chase with the

Nogales Internationals and agreed to defect from Juarez to join Chase the previous season, recalled a game in 1926 between the Douglas and Fort Bayard, who recruited the best pitcher in the Negro Leagues, Kansas City's Bullet Joe Rogan to pitch against Douglas. Rogan shut out Douglas through eight innings. With two outs and nobody on, Buck Weaver came to bat. Ruiz recalled hearing Weaver say to Chase that he was going to lay one down. Weaver laid down a drag bunt and beat the throw to first. Up walked Prince Hal, who represented the winning run. The crowd became loud. Ruiz was thinking that if Chase wasn't so old, he might have had a chance against Rogan. Lefty Williams shouted to Chase to "Get his ass!" Rogan hung a curve ball and Chase hit it well over the left field fence. The crowd ran onto the field, Weaver jumped up and down on his way to the plate, and Hal Chase circled the bases in a slow trot, basking in glory for the last time. As he jogged slowly, relishing every clap and hoot, Hal raised his hand slowly and waved to the fans.[7]

In August of 1926, after another victory over Fort Bayard, Chase and players were returning down Highway 90 back to Douglass. As they passed through Silver City, the car skidded off the road. Chase flew through the windshield and severed his Achilles tendon and shattered a kneecap. If his career wasn't completely over, the years his body would respond were certainly passed.

It was time for Hal Chase to pass the torch to his son, Hal Chase Jr., who was fast becoming a baseball player of reckon in the Catholic Athletic League in the Bay Area. The Sacred Heart High School student played first base, threw with his left, and batted with his right just like his father. Ironically, former Pacific Coast League President McCarthy, who had banned Hal Chase from all Pacific Coast League parks and now served as the President of the Mission Reds, pursued Chase's son for his franchise. Hal's close friend, William Benson, who had introduced Chase to Jim Morley of the Angeles, served as Hal's best man in his first wedding, and scouted for Chase with the Yankees, negotiated terms with the Missions for Hal, Jr. The youngster decided to travel with the team in the summers when school was out.[8]

1926 was a big year for Harry Wolter down on the farm after winning his first league championship in 1925. When Wolter faced off against Sam Crawford at USC in March, he brought with him the greatest athlete in the history of West Coast collegiate athletics. Ernie Nevers was an all-American fullback for the Stanford football team. Wolter, who would complain for years that he couldn't get anyone on campus to talk about anything other than football, was willing to ride on the coattails of the gridiron program in the case of Nevers. The multi-sport superstar was a great hitter and pitcher. After graduation, the former Stanford star agreed to play both professional football and baseball. As a football prospect, he was heralded as better than Red Grange. On the baseball diamond, the papers referred to him as "Another Matty." In 1925, he earned recognition for single-handedly defeating Cal in a three-game series. He pitched and won the final two games. He hit a home run in one game, and a triple and home run in another. In the final game, losing by three in the bottom of the ninth with the bases loaded and two outs, he hit a grand slam to win.

Graham, Strub, and Putnam continued to develop their own stars, even though they continued to sell their best prospects to the major leagues each year. In 1926 they introduced Earl Averill and Dolph Camilli. A 6-time major league All Star, Averill would later be inducted into the Hall of Fame. Camilli was the National League MVP in 1941 and was inducted into the Dodgers' Hall of Fame. The same season, the Oakland Oaks debuted catcher and future Hall of Famer Ernie Lombardi.

At the end of the 1926 season, Hal Chase returned to San Jose to recuperate from his car crash. The Douglas team folded once they lost their star player, who appeared to be done playing ball. But when he recovered, Chase wanted to return to Arizona. And he convinced his first wife Nellie to let him take Hal Jr. with him. After divorcing Chase, Nellie had moved to San Francisco and raised Hal Jr. as a single mother for many years until she eventually remarried. She remained close to Hal's family, particularly his parents, who helped her raise Hal, Jr. Perhaps if Hal's mother were still alive, she'd once again convince Hal that Hal Jr. was better off with his mother. But as a young adult, Nellie afforded Hal time with his son. According to Hal Jr., who remained with his father for approximately eight months, his father left him alone quite a bit while he traveled, had girlfriends, and was absent-minded. Hal likely had good intentions. After losing his mother, and shaken by the crash, he perhaps wanted to make a positive difference in his son's life. But good intentions didn't prepare him for the responsibility of parenthood. During 1927, Hal Sr. was scrambling. He sold the Crystal Palace and bartended in another saloon in Agua Prieta. He also worked selling cars for the saloon owner. It appeared that he was hustling as best he could to keep his head above water in a region where people went to be lost rather than to find better prospects.

Perhaps Hal Chase took interest in the developments of two scandals that hit major league baseball simultaneously just prior to January 1927 - the "Ty Cobb and Tris Speaker Affair" and the Swede Risberg testimony.

In June the previous year, Ban Johnson had begun privately investigating claims that Cobb and Speaker had gambled. On November 3, 1926 Ty Cobb resigned as manager of the Detroit Tigers and announced his retirement. On November 29, Tris Speaker resigned as Indians' manager. Dutch Leonard had recently circulated information about a fix nearly a decade earlier involving the two stars, and he possessed letters to prove it.[A] Following an investigation, Ban Johnson and Landis agreed to let the two stars retire quietly.

[A] Leonard played baseball for the Saint Mary's College of California "Gaels" in Moraga, California from 1910-1911... Leonard broke in with the Boston Red Sox in 1913. In his second year in the major leagues, 1914, Leonard led the American League with a

On December 22, 1926, however, Commissioner Landis opened up Pandora's Box by publicly stating that Cobb and Speaker retired due to gambling. Cobb was irate. Unlike baseball players in the past, Cobb had the means to hire the best lawyers and tear into major league baseball for the faux pas of making public their arrangement.

At the same time, former Chicago White Sox player Swede Risberg, disgusted over claims against Speaker and Cobb, came forward with knowledge of other fixes. He said, "They pushed Ty Cobb and Tris Speaker out on a piker bet. I think it's only fair that the 'white lilies' get the same treatment." The "white lilies" were the many other players involved with throwing games who dodged any accusations. The banned Black Sox player told the Chicago Tribune that he could implicate twenty big leaguers for crookedness. Within days, Landis called Risberg to his office for a hearing. Referring to a September 1917 series against the Detroit Tigers, Swede claimed that Tigers "sloughed off" to the White Sox. Risberg said that he and Chick Gandil had collected $45 each from the White Sox teammates to pay the Tigers to lose. He also claimed that the White Sox "sloughed off" two games for the Tigers in 1919. From El Paso, Texas where Gandil managed the Chino Copper Company, he stated that the entire Chicago White Sox team was involved in "buying" Detroit in 1917.[9]

When fellow Black Sock Oscar Felsch heard of Risberg's claims, he said, "Is that all Swede said?" Landis investigated. Ray Schalk, Eddie Collins, and others admitted to contributing to the pool, which was to be used "as a present for the Tigers to congratulate them for a three-game series they took from Chisox' rival Boston that year."[10]

The practice referred to by the Chisox players was known as "Friendship Games" or "Friendship Alliances." One team paid another team to make a greater effort to defeat an opponent, perhaps leading to a higher finish and a greater cut of a World Series share. Comiskey agreed that such an arrangement was possible, as it had been a baseball custom for many years. The explanation wasn't entirely plausible. But it was an explanation, which is all Landis needed to dismiss the claims and absolve all players.

Landis called the team pools "reprehensible but not criminal." Amidst so much mounting evidence of game fixes, Landis moderated his previously firm stance against gambling and, like his predecessors, found himself compromising out of necessity and damage control. Dismissing one of the two scandals he faced, Landis commented,

---

remarkable 0.96 ERA -- still the record for single-season ERA. Leonard also pitched well in Boston's 1915 and 1916 World Series victories. He won Game 3 of the 1915 World Series, outduelling the Phillies' Grover Cleveland Alexander 2-1. He also won Game 4 of the 1916 World Series against the Brooklyn Robins.

Team pools or incentive money offered others is an act of high impropriety, reprehensible and censurable, but it is not criminal.

The Cobb incident would be settled almost as easily. Cobb hired Charles Evans Hughes, Sr. as his lawyer. The former Republican candidate for President in 1916, Governor of New York, United States Secretary of State, and Associate Justice to the Supreme Court of the United States,[11] Hughes would bring to bear political influence and power that Organized Baseball had never faced. Like Hal Chase had done years before, Ty Cobb claimed to have dirt on baseball that he was willing to expose to protect his reputation. One of Cobb's claims, referred to in his biography, was that baseball owners tinkered with the turnstiles to understate revenues and avoid taxation.[A]

Landis and the owners wanted no part of Cobb and his legal team. Landis conducted an inquiry in early January and called forty witnesses. Cobb claimed that many players confessed to fixing games. The New York Giants and John McGraw fixed many, according to Cobb's biography.[12]

In a last attempted power grab, Ban Johnson declared anonymously on January 12, 1927 about Cobb and Speaker,

Neither will ever be permitted to play in the ranks of organized baseball again.... They were given positions of trust and they failed to keep that trust. No matter what Landis rules, the American League won't have them.

Papers reported that the American League began its investigation two years prior and had yet to publish the results. It would only make the details public if the case went to court.[13] The American League and Ban Johnson were out of step with the owners and Commissioner Landis, who had no intention of vetting the matter in court. The last thing they wanted was the exposure of Johnson's file and the issues Cobb would uncover in retaliation.

Ironically, at the same time that Ban Johnson warned that Cobb and Speaker would never play again in the league, Comiskey approached Speaker about playing for Chicago. Comiskey knew that Ban Johnson's recent statement represented his final act as a baseball administrator. In reaction to Johnson's comments, Landis called a meeting for the 24th of January at the Congress Hotel in Chicago with the American League owners. He demanded that the owners provide him with all relevant facts.[14] He also scheduled meetings with Speaker, Cobb, and their lawyers. At the meeting, Landis and the American League

---

[A] This writer met an engineer in his nineties who worked for the New York Giants in the 1940s on their turnstile technology. He was also a driver for Stoneham and Durocher, who at the time came under criticism for involvement with organized crime. Who knew that technology that appeared not to have changed in years demanded such attention from "engineers"?

owners stripped Ban Johnson of his power. In name only, he would still be President and draw a $40,000 annual salary, but his retirement was announced due to health.[15]

Landis exonerated Cobb and Speaker. The very same day, various American League teams began bidding for Speaker and Cobb. Philadelphia's Connie Mack, ironically a symbol of clean baseball, signed Cobb on February 8. On January 31, Washington signed Speaker for $35,000. Landis justified his having publicized the charges involving Cobb and Speaker because he claimed it was always best to let the fans know the truth rather than form opinion from gossip or heresay.[16]

Whether true or not, most fans believed that Cobb and Speaker were innocent. And most felt that even if they weren't, hurling mud at such a late date didn't accomplish anything. Landis was quite astute at reading papers to learn public opinion before coming to a conclusion. One reporter wrote,

... the only time Landis acts with speed is when he poses for a photograph.[17]

The Speaker and Cobb incident, as well as the Risberg case, highlighted that in all of the gambling of the deadball era, Chase was a minor figure – not a symbol of impropriety. He was part desperado, part smart aleck, part errand boy, part opportunist, and part small-time hustler. But the deeper problem had persisted for years, and would continue into the future.

And the scandals of the 1920s were not limited to California or baseball. In February 1927, the Supreme Court ruled on the symbol of corruption during the decade, the Teapot Dome Scandal, which shed light on practices in government that had persisted for decades.[A]

---

[1]   "The California Comet" Walter Johnson in the Golden State, Hank Thomas and Chuck Carey.
[2]   The Sporting News, September 18, 1941, Lester Grant (Oakland Post Enquirer)
[3]   Hal Chase is Mexican Czar, LA Times, Mar 10, 1925. Pg B1
[4]   Douglas Daily Dispatch, March 10, 1925
[5]   Outlaw Baseball Players in the Copper League: 1925-1927- M.A. Thesis Western New Mexico University, 1989, Lynn Bevill
[6]   Letter from Warnock to historian Lynn Bevill
[7]   The Black Prince of Baseball: Hal Chase and the Mythology of the Game, Don Dewey and Nick Acocella
[8]   Hal, Jr. to Follow in Dad's Steps, LA Times, Jul 21, 1926, pg. B1

[A]   An example of conditions persisting in the past and into the future was the Bureau of Investigation's (now FBI) exposure of the Teapot Dome Scandal through the use of break-ins and wiretaps. When the actions were revealed, the agency was shaken up and a new Director, J. Edgar Hoover, was appointed. He would act in a similar manner for another fifty years. Another example is the following quote from Richard Nixon as a boy about the Teapot Dome Scandal: "When I grow up, I want to be an honest lawyer so things like that can't happen."

[9] Calls Players in New Scandal. LA Times. Jan 3. 1927. pg. 9

[10] Calls Players in New Scandal. LA Times. Jan 3. 1927. pg. 9

[11] He later became Chief Justice of the United States.

[12] Cobb, A Biography. Al Stump

[13] Cobb and Speaker Barred Forever. Jan 13. 1927. pg. B1

[14] Cobb and Speaker Silent Toward Charges. Wesbrook Pegler. Los Angeles Times. Jan 14. 1927. pg. B4

[15] Three American League Clubs Bidding For Tris. LA Times. Jan 25. 1927. pg. B1

[16] Landis Exonerates Cobb and Speaker. Jan 28. 1927. pg. B1. Los Angeles Times

[17] Observations. Bill Henry. LA Times. Jan 29. 1927 pg. I2

Chapter 27

San Francisco's Valencia Vanderbilts

The scandals of the 1920s didn't prevent the decade from being labeled the golden age of sports. Well before television, and before radio became a widespread phenomena, newspapers and newsreels created icons from sports heroes, including Babe Ruth, Red Grange, Jack Dempsey, Bill Tilden and Bobby Jones. The colorful, humorous, and dramatic accounts delivered daily by notable writers Ring Lardner, Hugh Fullerton, Grantland Rice, Damon Runyon, Fred Lieb, Sid Mercer, Irving Sanborn, Harry Williams, Charles Dryden, and Heywood Broun sparked a love affair between America and its champions. The writers were both critics and co-conspirators in promoting sports. Promotion had always been a critical component for baseball. And since the San Francisco newspapers fielded baseball teams in the 1890s to sell papers during a depression, newspapers understood the intimacy of the daily relationship between the fan and sports. Baseball sold papers, and papers sold baseball.

When former Vernon owner Ed Maier opened up his ranch to the Elks and other Los Angeles locals, his publicist Gene Doyle was sure to invite the sportswriters. Perhaps more than any other person in Southern California, Gene Doyle understood how to promote baseball. Ed Maier hired him to promote the Tigers. Involved in sports promotion throughout the West, Doyle was responsible for bringing Babe Ruth to California for annual barnstorming tours.

Los Angeles Times sports editor Harry Williams covered the Pacific Coast league for years, often going no further than a pool hall to find a story from Hap Hogan or Hen Berry, who became his two closest friends. The close relationship between journalist and baseball magnate was common in many cities during the era. And Williams' involvement as a journalist covering baseball eventually led to his being named president of the Pacific Coast League in 1924, a post he filled until 1932.

Baseball popularity soared during the decade. Additional seating capacity was added to many ballparks, particularly in the outfield. Baseball moved out of the "deadball era" into an era of more power hitting and higher batting averages. In 1920, a pitch thrown at his head by Carl Mays killed a Detroit player named Roy Chapman. The changes the league made to prevent injury to batters contributed to more run production. First, the league banned the soiling of balls by pitchers, effectively eliminating the spitball, although pitchers who made a living by throwing it were allowed to continue until the end of their careers. Additionally, balls were replaced during the game as necessary. In the past, a single ball could be used throughout the game even if it was scuffed or discolored. In addition to safety issues, however, the leagues adopted a livelier baseball that would carry further when hit. But perhaps the biggest change to the game resulted from players changing their approach to hitting after witnessing the success of Babe Ruth's power. Ruth hit so many home runs in the 1920s that batters stopped choking up on the bat, taking partial swings, and attempting to direct balls through the infield. Wee Willie Keeler's comment from the turn of the century, "hit 'em where they ain't," symbolized the dead ball culture known for a lack of power hitting. But when Ruth proved that a full, powerful swing could result in a high batting average and home runs that fans loved, other players emulated his style.

The 1920s produced great stars in the Pacific Coast League. Perhaps the greatest star the league would ever know was Frank Lefty O'Doul. In 1927, O'Doul played for the Hollywood Stars and earned the Most Valuable Player award by hitting .378 with 33 home runs. Although fast establishing himself as the leading hitter in the West, O'Doul was not a youngster. At thirty years of age, he had already completed a career in the minor and major leagues as a pitcher. Similar to Buzz Arlett, and in the tradition of the many hitting pitchers that the West produced over the past fifty years, O'Doul reinvented himself into a hitter who would once again attract the attention of major league teams. The New York Giants signed him for the 1928 season as a power-hitting outfielder. He hit .319 as a platoon player. In Philadelphia in 1929 he led the league in hitting at .398 and was second to Rogers Hornsby in the MVP voting behind 254 hits, 122 RBI, 154 runs, and 32 home runs. In 1932, he once again led the league in hitting at .368 for the Brooklyn Dodgers. Although O'Doul played in eleven seasons, five of those seasons from 1919 to 1924 were as a marginal pitcher. The six years he played as a hitter rank him among the best to have ever played the game. But since he didn't break into the majors as a hitter until he was thirty-one, his short but supreme hitting career has yet to earn him a position in Baseball's Hall of Fame.

Although O'Doul played for the Hollywood Stars in 1927, he was always popular in San Francisco. When his team played in the City on September 11, the Seals organized Lefty O'Doul Day at the ballpark. Frank gave bats and balls away to children, who were admitted to the game free of charge.

The old-timer O'Doul represented baseball's fourth generation of players who found success in the major leagues, then returned to California to develop the subsequent generations. The first generation started playing the game in the 1850s, and then produced the players for the majors in the 1880s, including Bill Lange, Fred Lange, George Van Haltren, Ham Iburg, and Spike Hennessey. They in turn developed the next generation of players that included Frank Chance, Charley Graham, Hap Hogan, Hal Chase, Spider Baum, and Walter Johnson. And they would inspire and develop the next generation, headed by O'Doul, who would develop players into the 1950s in the United States and Japan.

Starting in 1927, the old-timers were honored at games held between the San Francisco Seals and Oakland Oaks. On July 30, 1927, before the regularly scheduled game, two teams of old-timers played a three-inning exhibition game. George Van Haltren pitched to Fred Lange, who demonstrated how he had caught Van Haltren without a glove for the Greenhood and Morans in 1885. In Lange's only at bat, he hit a ball over the shortstop's head for a single. Lange shared stories with Doc Moskiman, who manned first base while Fred was picked off. Players in the game included Jimmy Shinn, Brick Devereaux, Jimmy Byrnes, J. Cal Ewing, Charlie Graham, and Bill Lange. League President Harry Williams arrived from Los Angeles to witness the event.

Hal Chase did not attend. He was playing his first game for El Paso in Texas.[1] Even if he had been in the area, perhaps too little time had passed for him to show his face around a Pacific Coast League baseball field. While the other veterans met over food and drink, sang songs, and reminisced about a play, a game, or a fight, Chase likely did the same in a small bar in West Texas. Hal Chase was keenly aware of his legacy as a ballplayer, which grew over time as players and writers recounted his ability.

The Los Angeles Times reported:

Chase is generally credited with revolutionizing the playing of first base. He introduced the system of playing the position deep – far back of the bag where the infield dirt meets the outfield grass. Stories are legendary of Hal's phenomenal style of play, his speed, and uncanny judgment.[2]

Ty Cobb said, "there has been only one first baseman, and that is Hal Chase."[3]

Baseball legend Hugh Jennings said that Chase was the greatest base runner and the best man he had ever seen stealing third. And of the three men who figured most prominent in the development of defensive play at first base, Charles Comiskey, Fred Tenney, and Hal Chase, Hal had been the best.

He was the most supple...most refined... most accurate thrower ... quicker than anyone ... could throw and get back to the bag quicker than anyone ... extremely intelligent. Offensively and defensively there has never been another first baseman of the caliber of Chase... he was as good on the hit and run as anyone... and was one of the best on the squeeze.

He made more difficult plays than anyone else. He instructed players to throw to the bag and expect that he would arrive after it was thrown, which allowed him to play deep. He often picked balls out of the dirt when players couldn't throw accurately without a target.

Eddie Collins said that Chase set a new style for playing the bag. In fielding bunts, he had no equal, and practically no equal at receiving throws. He was probably the best hit and run man in the American League. "You couldn't throw any ball by him if he wanted to hit it."[4] George Moriarity said that Wee Willie Keeler and Hal Chase came closest to perfection in slapping the ball

318

through the position left unguarded in the original "hit and run" attack. Walter Johnson agreed. He said that Hal Chase was one of the smartest batters he ever faced, although he admitted he wasn't a "great hitter." He said that Hal placed the ball well, particularly on a hit and run.

The Los Angeles Times compared Chase to the Yankee first base star Lou Gehrig in July 1927. Gehrig was perhaps the second coming of Christy Mathewson in terms of character, a hero loved by all. But as a first baseman, the Times wrote:

> *He would rather play ball than eat, although he has a tremendous appetite, and he thinks he's lucky to be permitted to play every day. He isn't Hal Chase exactly, for there never will be another Hal Chase. But there is this difference. Chase demanded pay for everything he did, while it is said Gehrig would pay to play first base.*[5]

The writer unfairly contrasted the unselfishness of Gehrig to Chase. He was appropriately compelled to note the undeniable humility and good character of Gehrig. For the writer and many writers of the era, Chase provided a contrasting symbol. The truth, however, was that all Chase ever did throughout his life, and was still doing in the deserts of the Southwest, was play baseball. What the writer could not deny, however, was that the young Gehrig didn't compare to Hal Chase as a first baseman. Grantland Rice would later say tactfully that Gehrig "… may not be as fancy around first as Hal Chase…"

The El Paso team released Hal Chase just over a month following his first game, soon after the allure of the ex-major league star on the roster lost its luster.

Just as the windows of opportunity for Chase to play baseball closed, the doors opened for baseball on an international stage. The game's popularity had spread throughout the world prior to World War I, and in the relative peace of the 1920s, American players once again toured foreign countries promoting the game. Harry Wolter led his Stanford nine in a series of exhibitions throughout the summer of 1928 against teams from the Pacific Islands. He and Mrs. Wolter chaperoned the team as it toured Honolulu, New Zealand, Samoan Islands and Australia. The team drew crowds exceeding 12,000 at every contest. In Sydney, 30,000 attended their game. Wolter's squad won nearly every competition during the tour.

During the 1920s, West Coast baseball thrust itself into prominence. The Pacific Coast League and Charlie Graham's Seals continued to improve to a level perhaps surpassing the major leagues. If the Pacific Coast League didn't relinquish its best players to enrich the major circuit, it would have certainly competed on a level surpassing "Eastern Baseball."

In 1928, the Cleveland Indians offered $100,000 for the entire San Francisco Seals outfield, which included Earl Averill, Smead Jolley, and Roy

Johnson. The outfield was probably the best outfield ever assembled in minor league baseball. When Charlie Graham rejected the Cleveland offer, the Indians proposed that the Seals accept a trade for the entire Cleveland starting outfield and cash. Graham rejected the offer. At the end of the season, Graham sold the three players for a total of $135,000 - Averill for $50,000, Johnson for $50,000[A], and Jolley for $35,000. Graham, Strub, and Putnam had so much success developing players at Recreation Park on Valencia and 15th that they became known as the Valencia Vanderbilts. The minor league San Francisco Seals were considered the second most valuable franchise in sports, second only to the New York Yankees.

The Seals continued to produce future Hall of Famers. In 1928, Seals' manager Nick Williams signed a 6' 2" 150 pound pitcher from the East Bay by the name of Vernon Lefty Gomez. The team didn't need him immediately, as the Seals won another title in 1928. Instead they assigned Gomez to the Salt Lake squad in the Utah-Idaho league. They called him up for the 1929 season, in which he won eighteen games for San Francisco. Charlie Graham and Doc Strub then sold him to the Yankees for $35,000 where he became one of the team's greatest pitchers and Hall of Fame player.

[A] After hitting .375 in 1928 for the Seals, Johnson led the American League in at bats and doubles for the Red Sox in 1929, collecting 201 hits and 128 runs his rookie season. He became a lifetime .296 hitter in the majors. The Seals also featured youngsters Frank Crosetti, Gus Suhr, and Hal Rhyne to go with veterans Duster Mails, Dutch Ruether, and Babe Pinelli.

San Francisco Seals Factory of the 1920s

PLAYER	SOLD TO	FIRST SEASON IN MAJORS	AMT	ACCOMPLISHMENTS
Jimmy O'Connell	New York Giants	1923	$75.000	Short career. Banned from baseball.
Willie Kamm	Chicago White Sox	1923	$100.000	Defensive specialist at third base for Chisox. Voted best third baseman in PCL history.
Lew Fonseca	Cincinnati	1921	Unk	Lifetime .316 hitter, won AL batting title in 1929 at .369
Paul Waner	Pittsburgh Pirates	1926	$65.000	Hall of Fame
Lloyd Waner	Pittsburgh Pirates	1927	Not under contract with Seals	Hall of Fame
Earl Averill	Cleveland Indians	1929	$50.000	Hall of Fame
Lefty Gomez	New York Yankees	1930	$35.000	Hall of Fame
Roy Johnson	Detroit Tigers	1929	$50.000	Rookie season collected 201 hits and 128 runs. Became lifetime .296 hitter in majors.
Hal Rhyne	Pittsburgh Pirates	1926	$35.000	After 1925, was sold to Pittsburgh with Paul Waner for $100.000
Smead Jolley	Chicago White Sox	1930	$35.000	Career .305 hitter in four major league seasons. Led PCL in hitting in '27, '28, and '38. RBIs in '27 and '28, and won triple crown in PCL in '28. Won batting titles in other minor leagues in '36, '38, '40, and '41. Sold by Seals to Chisox in '29.
Gus Suhr	Pittsburgh Pirates	1930	Unk	Eleven-year major leaguer with Pittsburgh, hit .275 in his career and voted to National League All Star team in 1936.
Frank Crosetti	New York Yankees	1932	$65.000	Shortstop for 17 seasons with Yankees. Two all star appearances. Won 8 World Series titles. Became coach for Yankees and other teams. Appeared in 17 World Series as player or coach.
Dolph Camilli	Chicago Cubs	1933	Unk	NL MVP 1941. Dodgers Hall of Fame

Doc Strub and the San Francisco Seals were flying high after 1928. Strub and Graham dreamed of a new ballpark, and spared no expense in designing a replacement for old Recreation Park. In addition to his success with the Seals, Doc Strub experienced financial success outside baseball during the 1920s. Like many during the era, he increased his fortune by using leverage. He grew his wealth by borrowing on margin and investing in the escalating stock market. The San Francisco Chronicle reported that the multi-million Strub estate was invested in the "margin market." He also invested heavily in real estate, and borrowed money to build the new ballpark, Seals Stadium. An astute businessman, Strub took no shortcuts in meticulously pursuing an uncompromising standard for quality in every aspect of his businesses. Strub planned to spend whatever was required to make Seals Stadium one of the most modern stadiums in the country.[6] The park would not be completed for many more years, however, as the financial conditions in the United States deteriorated in 1929.

Between July 1929 and July 1932, the stock market lost most of its value. Many like Doc Strub, who had been wealthy on paper prior to the crash, were broke. One reporter noted that on October 29, 1929, also known as Black Tuesday, Strub was enjoying his customary shave at the St. Francis Hotel barbershop when he was handed the phone. His broker told him he had been wiped out.[7] The available credit that existed prior to 1929 dried up, as banks became conservative and unwilling to lend. And since Strub had invested in the market with borrowed money, when the market dropped, he owed money to banks. Some reports indicated that he owed $1,250,000 to one bank after the stock market crash. But Strub would not accept defeat. Ty Cobb, who lived in nearby Atherton and wanted to own the Seals, had invested wisely in the market and had avoided financial ruin. With the Seals organization facing difficulties, Cobb made an offer to Strub to purchase the club. Strub refused.[A]

Sacramento's Lew Moreing had begun to struggle even before the depression hit. After a strong 1928 season when the team finished tied for first with the Seals, the squad played poorly the next season. Then Lew's partner and brother, Charles, died at 52. Attendance continued to fall and Lew put the team up for sale. In July, he attracted interest from investor Charles Lockhart. But the stock market crash dashed hopes for a sale. The financial meltdown impacted every team in the Pacific Coast League. On November 3, 1929, the league's magnates, including Charlie Graham, George "Alfy" Putnam, Lew Moreing, Spider Baum, Cal Ewing, Harry Williams, and Bill Lane met at the St. Catherine Hotel on Catalina Island, twenty-six miles off the coast of Los Angeles to discuss strategy to keep the league alive.

The executives traveled from the mainland aboard the 310-foot luxury steamship SS Catalina to the island that William Wrigley had purchased and

---

[A] Cobb wanted to own a major league team. In an interview in 1950, Cobb later stated that the owners in major league baseball were crooks who kept him from owning a team. He said, "There were crooked lawyers and Tammany Hall ginks and bootleg whiskey smugglers who held important jobs in the game…" Cobb, A Biography, Al Stump.

turned into a popular tourist destination. Wrigley also built a baseball training facility on the island where the Chicago Cubs conducted spring training.[A]

The island gathering occurred eight months after the league administrators learned of the death of Hen Berry, the great former owner of the Los Angeles Angels. Attending to his oil facility in Surprise, California near his home north of Maricopa in Kern County at the Southwestern edge of the San Joaquin Valley, Berry's automobile plunged off a highway and down a ravine due to a steering malfunction. He was 59 when he died.[8] His best friend, sportswriter and league President Harry Williams, credited Berry with saving the Coast League when it was in bad shape after the San Francisco fire of 1906. Henry had taken over the Los Angeles club with the gold he made in Alaska.

There was never a more picturesque character in the Coast League than Henry, and I do not except my other dear friend, the late Hap Hogan.[9]

The owners could use more Hen Berry's now with the depression threatening the league's viability. The owners discussed creative ways to deal with the financial challenges. Its leaders would never give up. Perhaps more than anyone, Lew Moreing demonstrated the perseverance to keep competitive baseball on the Coast.

With his back to the wall, Lew did not give up on his franchise. He had invested most of his net worth in the organization. If it failed, he failed. So he developed a plan. He knew too well that the heat in Sacramento made day games less appealing for fans. So he vowed to install lights and play night games after temperatures cooled. In the middle of the depression, Moreing invested $10,000 in lighting. The first night baseball game in the Pacific Coast League was played at Moreing field on June 10, 1930 before a sell-out crowd. The same month, the San Francisco Seals received $75,000 for Frank Crosetti from the New York Yankees. With ingenuity and hard work, the organizations treaded water through difficult times until conditions improved.

There would be no guarantees, however. During stressful periods, the small markets like Sacramento suffered the most. Moreing valiantly installed lights to increase the value of his franchise. But like many others during the depression, Moreing experienced a string of business failures and continued to struggle through the 1934 season.

The San Francisco Seals were more fortunate. On March 13, 1931, they opened Seals Stadium at a cost of more than $1 million. The stadium seated 25,000 and was equipped with the most powerful lighting system in the United States. Strub, Graham, and Putnam also spent $6,000 on an announcement system that replaced the megaphone to introduce batters. The stadium also featured a

---

[A] Nineteen future Hall of Famers trained on the island before the Cubs moved their spring training facility to Mesa, Arizona.

private viewing area that Graham used exclusively to showcase players for major league managers and scouts. When he hosted the Giants' John McGraw in the "tower," the impressed manager told Graham "…You'll have major league baseball here someday, Charlie."[A]

Strub and Graham partially based their franchise success on a brand of "clean baseball" and personal development. Unlike major league owners and administrators, they never compromised their principles. When they purchased the team from Hen and C.J. Berry, they brusquely confronted the league's gambling problem. And they required exemplary conduct from their players and coaches since personal development was a hallmark of their franchise. In a display of their dedication to uncompromising ideals, they fired veteran coach and scout Nick Williams at the end of the 1931 season. Williams had discovered and developed superstars including Paul Waner, Earl Averill, Lefty Gomez, Gus Suhr, Frank Crosetti, and Smead Jolley. But when his conduct didn't measure up to the required standards of the organization, Williams was asked to resign. The public would never have learned about the organization's discreet and tasteful handling of Williams' situation. But Williams inexplicably publicized that he was fired due to personal habits. Even when the manager demonstrated success, having won two pennants and discovering many star players, Graham, Strub, and Putnam required a high standard from their employees.

The organization's character contributed to the trust it engendered from major league teams, which helped it to survive the difficult financial conditions of the Great Depression.

---

[1] Account from manuscript by S.L.A. Marshall called Bringing Up the Rear: A Memoir. Marshall Collection at the University of Texas, El Paso
[2] Hal, Jr to Follow in Dad's Steps, Los Angeles Times, Jul 21, 1926, pg. B1
[3] Hal, Jr to Follow in Dad's Steps, Los Angeles Times, Jul 21, 1926, pg. B1
[4] Twenty One Years of Base Ball, Eddie Collins, Jan 25, 1927, Los Angeles Times, Pg. B2
[5] Gehrig Wallops Way To Become Bambino's Chief Rival as Home-Run King, LA Times, Jul 23, 1927, pg. A4
[6] The Giants Encyclopedia, Tom Schott and Nick Peters
[7] Art Rosenbaum. San Francisco Chronicle. San Francisco, Calif.: Mar 8, 1985. pg. 80
[8] "Hen" Berry Is Killed As Car Leaps Down Ravine, Mar 14, 1929, LA Times, pg. B1
[9] Williams Tells of "Hen" Berry, Harry A. Williams, Mar 17, 1920, Pg. A5.

[A] Indeed, major league baseball came to Seals Stadium in 1958 when Willie Mays moved from New York. McGraw and Graham would not be involved.

Chapter 28

DiMaggio the Ultimate Thoroughbred

H al Chase was selling Marmon "8" automobiles in Douglas, Arizona in 1928[1] when sister Jessie convinced him to join her and her family on her ranch in Lindsay, California. Years before Hal had purchased the land in the Southeastern San Joaquin Valley near the southern edge of the California gold country in the Sierra Nevada foothills. Jessie loved Hal. From his first game with the Los Angeles Angels, she had proudly saved every newspaper clipping about her talented brother. Prospects in Douglas, Arizona offered little that Jessie considered to be healthy for Hal. Perhaps she was also sentimental, having seen her family dwindle. Brother Clifford died in 1927, Albert died in 1928 from the same cancer that killed Hal's mother, and Oscar died of a cerebral hemorrhage in 1929.

Chase played some baseball in the San Joaquin Valley with Lindsay's team and the nearby Porterville team in the San Joaquin Valley League at the age of forty-five while he helped run the chicken ranch for his brother-in-law Frank Topham twelve miles northeast of Porterville.[2] Over the next few years, Chase would move between Lindsay and Oakland in California, Williams and Douglas in Arizona, and Reno in Nevada playing local baseball and scraping by on odd jobs that included prospecting in the Sierra Nevada Mountains. During the Depression, many had difficulty finding work. Chase admitted that during the decade of the 1930s, his excessive drinking threatened his health. It may not have been the cause of his troubles, but it certainly didn't help matters.

A similar fate befell former Santa Cruz superstar Mike Donlin, who like many former ballplayers tended to drink more than was healthful. After retiring from baseball after a tumultuous 12-year career where he achieved a career batting average of .333, Turkey Mike became an actor. He appeared in sixty-four movies; most parts were small. He was also frequently hired as a consultant on movies about baseball. He developed heart trouble in 1927 that required surgery, for which friends from the acting community paid. Six years later, at the age of 55, Turkey Mike Donlin died of a heart attack.

Conversely, in 1933 Harry Wolter was a picture of health. He continued to lead his Stanford Nine against the colleges of California. In 1927, he suggested the formation of a league called the Intercollegiate Baseball Association. In 1931, he led Stanford to its first title within the league with a record of 15-3. At the age of forty-nine, he still pitched batting practice and played in alumni games. He even starred in a game in February 1933 at his alma mater, where he led the Santa Clara alumni to a 22-16 victory over the regulars.[3] When he took Stanford to play USC during the regular season, legendary basketball and baseball coach Sam

Barry coached the Trojans. In February when Barry's baseball squad faced Stanford, the papers reported that the coach would shake up his lineup and send his flashy sophomore shortstop Rod Dedeaux[A] in to bat cleanup.

During this period, the lonely Chase looked to Baseball Commissioner Kenesaw Landis for some absolution for past indiscretions, even though Landis had never formally accused Chase or banned him from baseball. After spending his entire life in the game, Chase wanted to be a part of "the club." And as he considered his fate and reputation over a glass of prohibition alcohol, Chase summoned the courage or desperation to send a letter to Landis. He wanted to know where he stood with regard to Organized Baseball. He said he wanted to clear up misrepresentations connected with him. Landis diplomatically and even magnanimously replied, but baited Chase to provide additional facts surrounding the matters that had preceded Landis to office,

> As far as I know, you are in good standing with Organized Ball. You mention a certain mistake you have made. I should like to know more about this.[1]

Chase's lawyers advised that Chase not reply. If Chase had summoned lawyers regarding his letter, perhaps he had considered some legal action against baseball. Or perhaps the aging and prideful Chase, in an interview given toward the end of his life, simply mentioned he used "his lawyers" so that he would appear more distinguished. But there was nothing in Organized Baseball for Chase. Whether Landis or anyone formally charged Chase with wrongdoing, he had alienated himself from organizations. In time, the players within those organizations would change and the grudges would fade. Hal would also be welcomed back into the circles of California baseball. Through the years, owners, managers, and players alike struggled through the hurdles in life. And as time passed, fraternity won out over animosity. For as Fred Lange explained, after decades of playing baseball on the Coast, all that was left was an occasional old-timers game that afforded the players with a bit too much food, drink, and reminiscing that the wives threatened not to permit the husbands to attend anymore.

Neither the past nor baseball offered Hal Chase the source of income that all of America sought during Depression years. Even Doc Strub and the Seals continued to struggle financially through the early 1930s, requiring him to adapt. Two things would lift Strub out of his troubles – California's adoption of horse racing and the discovery of Joe DiMaggio.

Keeping creditors at bay and networking among the wealthy and influential of San Francisco, Strub kept abreast of current opportunities. The

---

[A] Rod Dedeaux coached the USC squad from 1942-1986 winning 11 College World Series titles, including five straight from 1970-1974, and 28 conference crowns.

Depression affected most businesses in America, including urban sports. Horse racing purses plummeted nationally by fifty percent. But in California, ironically the tax shortfalls created by the economic contraction forced politicians to think creatively about increasing revenues and consider adopting horse racing and pari-mutuel gambling. In 1933 the state voters passed a referendum to allow horse racing. The state would grant two licenses, one each for Northern and Southern California, which would essentially award a monopoly to two consortiums. Strub organized a large group from San Francisco, which included former Mission Reds owner Herbert Fleishhacker as well as wealthy magnates Folger and Sutro, to feverishly compete for one of the two licenses.

Ironies existed regarding Strub's pursuit of horse racing's gambling franchise. Technically, gambling on a sporting event such as horse racing differed little from gambling on baseball. Both involved wagering on athletic endeavors prone to corruption. That corruption in baseball was what Strub and others had worked hard to eradicate from the Pacific Coast League. One consequential difference between gambling in the two sports, however, was the illegality of baseball gambling. Even though the enforcement was lax, as an illegal activity, the illicit commerce fed organized crime, black markets, and non-taxable business. Venturing into horse racing didn't pose an ethical dilemma for Strub; rather, the proposition was purely business. He knew people loved to gamble on the outcome of sporting events. And he knew that owning the horse racing franchise would be profitable. He didn't so much oppose the idea of gambling; rather, he detested the unseemly influence gambling had on the game of baseball, the experience at the ballpark, and the integrity of the game. Because of his stellar reputation with the Seals during a period of pervasive gambling, Strub was uniquely qualified to oversee an operation that balanced the potentially derogatory elements of gambling with a decent and respectable experience for patrons. When compared with his competitors for the license, the State observed Strub as a superior candidate.

Another irony surrounding Strub's involvement in horse racing was that, as an owner of a baseball franchise within Organized Baseball, Strub was technically not allowed to participate. Yet, when he applied for special consideration from Baseball Commissioner Landis, the purportedly rigid administrator granted him special dispensation.

Strub was an insider, both in the social circles of California and in Organized Baseball. His franchise had provided the major leagues with great players for years, and his reputation earned him special consideration from baseball's highest official. And his record of finding stars reached new heights in 1933 when youngster Joe DiMaggio began poking around the ballpark to watch his brother Vincent play for the Seals.

Scout Spike Hennessey knew of the young Joe, having watched him play at the local San Francisco ball fields that the former Sacramento Gilt Edge first baseman frequented as the roving baseball instructor for the city's Park and

Recreation Department. Many conflicting stories existed about who and how Joe was discovered. Hennessey, who assisted over fifty players he called "his lambs" to the major leagues, including Hall of Famers Joe Cronin, Harry Heilmann, and Tony Lazzeri, told a story of DiMaggio watching a Seals game through a knot when Spike approached the 17-year old laying flat on his belly beyond the fence. Spike said he tapped Joe on the back and said, "You should never stay on the outside looking in unless it's jail." The two went to see "Uncle Charlie" Graham about getting a ticket.

Joe DiMaggio wanted badly to play for the Seals.

Joe later recounted in an interview late in life that one of the greatest thrills of his career was when he met Charlie Graham.

> ... the No. 1 thrill of those greenhorn days was neither the first nor the 61st game [referring to his hitting streak]. Maybe you've got to be a 17-year-old kid with baseball busting out of your boots to understand. But the heart-throb for me was that afternoon when I came out of a knot-hole to hear the owner of a professional club say, "Stick around, kid. Maybe you can practice with the team. [5]

The Seals signed the kid from 2047 Taylor Street near Fisherman's Wharf to a $225 per month contract.

Graham recollected, in his usual diplomatic manner, the young Joe, who often threw balls well over the head of the first baseman into the seats, "I'll say one thing about the kid. He's got a hell of an arm!"

Oscar Eckart of the Missions set a Coast League record in 1933 by hitting .417. But DiMaggio set a record of his own by hitting in 61 consecutive games.[6] The competitive youngster said he had never enjoyed baseball so much until he began looking forward to going to the ballpark for his daily hit.

The Coast League had produced its share of colorful characters over the years, including Ping Bodie, Hap Hogan, and Lefty Gomez who provided entertainment both on and off the field. Joe DiMaggio was different; he did all of his talking with his bat. In fact, he rarely spoke at all. A roommate lived with him for two weeks and said they never had a conversation. And when the Seals honored him for his hitting at an event, DiMaggio tersely delivered a speech he had practiced in front of the mirror for days. He stepped up to the microphone and said, "Thank You."[7]

According to his secretary, Doc Strub was similarly unsociable. But he was socially crafty. He networked incessantly among the wealthy Californians and put his contacts to use in seeking a grant from the State for a horse racing license. He battled many other influential figures, including parties from organized crime for the license. On August 8, he applied to the State Racing Commission for a permit to construct a plant on one of four sites, two located in San Francisco County and two in San Mateo County.[8]

Strub headed the St. Francis Jockey Club comprised of sixteen persons of high standing throughout the State on its board of directors and as many as another 150 significant contributors. He faced competition from the Oakland Jockey Club fronted by Gene Normile[A], Jack Dempsey's former business manager and a group called the San Mateo Jockey Club. In Southern California, various business front men including Al Uniack, Joseph Smoot, and Hal Roach developed plans. Roach, known for his successful "Our Gang" shows, originally planned to recruit two hundred investors who would put up $5,000 each for an honorary life membership in his Los Angeles Turf Club. Unable to line up the investors for various reasons, he persisted. Oakland, San Mateo, and Los Angeles Turf Club applications were denied. On October 14, 1933, the State granted Strub and the St. Francis Jockey Club a permit. The group began planning to spend $1,350,000 on a plant in Northern California.[9]

Opponents later claimed that the board showed favoritism in denying certain applications and favoring Strub's group. In March of 1934 in a 1,000-word letter, the board responded to an inquiry from the Governor stating that bookmaking and gambling interests attacked the board and questioned its impartiality. The report claimed that Strub represented the only applicants with finances and personnel who could be ready for operation no later than December 15, 1934. Strub represented the organizer who could deliver the state license – something nobody else could secure. And he didn't do it just once – he did it twice. The second time that he succeeded in obtaining a permit, he did so with a completely different group of investors; the influence that won Strub permits appeared to come from Strub and not necessarily those within his investor group.

Unforeseen complications at the Northern California site forced Strub and the St. Francis Jockey Club to pass on exercising the option granted in their license. Upon hearing the news, Hal Roach contacted Strub to discuss a partnership with the Los Angeles Turf Club. Strub turned his focus to Southern California.

Strub's personal finances were tenuous, and the organizer persevered with the diligence that demonstrated he understood his fragile financial predicament. But even though Strub's finances were in a precarious state, he always carried himself as if opulence was his birthright. When in Los Angeles to meet with Roach in January of 1934, Strub stopped to negotiate a contract with ballplayer Win Ballou, who Strub had offered $100 per month. When Ballou didn't sign, Strub visited his home in an effort to appeal to him in person, making the case that the team suffered financially due to the Depression. According to Ballou, Strub arrived at his home in an automobile "approximately as long as from home plate to first base, and a colored chauffeur hopped out and opened the door

---

[A] Normile would later operate horse racing in Tijuana at Agua Caliente where Southern California superstar horse Seabiscuit would race in 1938.

for the good doctor." Win said that Strub didn't appear to be suffering from the Depression, so he rebuffed the Doctor's offer.[10]

Strub had better success negotiating with the members of the Los Angeles Turf Club, which included investors from the North, and Southern Californians Hal Roach, local broker Leigh Battson, Nelson Howard, insurance broker Dwight Whiting, polo star Howland Paddock, Eric Halliburton, owner of Rosslyn Hotel Dwight Hart, Vice President of Southern Pacific Railroad Felix McGinnis, and Kenneth Kingsbury, President of Standard Oil. They agreed to make Strub the designated director-general of the club, as he maneuvered to secure its license.[11] Accounts have claimed that in the middle of the Depression, Strub went door-to-door seeking investment in the venture. In fact, no shares in the Los Angeles Turf club were sold to the public.[12]

Strub and his group did face competition in January. Fred Wilke, a local stockbroker, and Lou Smith, a horse racing promoter from the East prepared an application. And the State discussed granting two permits for Southern California.[13] But Strub presented a compelling, albeit self-serving argument that a single high-quality establishment served the State better because it would create stronger demand. As the State considered the applicants on January 9, Strub and the Los Angeles Turf Club were confident they would receive the license; they purchased 215 acres at the foot of the Sierra Madre Mountains on part of the Anita Baldwin estate from Ms. Baldwin for $236,500. The property was situated at the junction of Colorado Avenue and Huntington Drive just west of the site of the old Lucky Baldwin racetrack from twenty-five years before. The club planned to build one of the finest racing plants in the country. The city of Arcadia granted permission for construction to commence by February 15 to complete work by December 15. Strub planned to spend $800,000 in construction of the new facility that would incorporate revolutionary features including electronic timing and photo finishes. Strub insisted on "better than first class" and dedicated himself to providing an unparalleled experience.

The Los Angeles Turf Club received the sole license in Southern California. Strub signed an employment contract for five years as the executive manager of the club; he would receive 10% of net profits computed at the end of each fiscal year ending on March 31. With his payment computed in March, Strub decided to put one big egg in one big basket with a race held annually in February with stakes unmatched anywhere in the country, the Santa Anita Handicap, with a purse of $100,000. The race, and the first season of racing at Santa Anita, represented a make or break situation for Strub financially.

The Pacific Coast League continued to struggle. While the Seals situation was dire, Lew Moreing faced calamity in Sacramento. In February 1934, bankers holding the securities of the team gave Moreing one week to shore up finances before they took over the club. Moreing, in debt for $160,000, remained hopeful. The banks agreed to accept a loss of $35,000 if Moreing could raise

$125,000. A few weeks later, the banks took over the club in an effort to sell it. They agreed that if they received more than $160,000, they would give the difference to Moreing. However, Moreing lost the team. Within a year, he died, leaving his wife penniless.

Strub was not penniless, but he didn't receive a salary from the racetrack for all of his efforts during 1933 and 1934, as he meticulously supervised the development of the Santa Anita Racetrack. His compensation would be determined after March of the next year when the profitability of his efforts could be measured. That didn't stop Strub from continuing to think big, confident that Santa Anita would be a success. While still retaining ownership in the Seals, Strub resigned as President to focus his efforts in Los Angeles. He purchased a seven-story office building at the corner of Whittier Blvd. and Kern Avenue in the Belvedere Gardens district of East Los Angeles at a cost exceeding $100,000. The purchase demonstrated that in the midst of difficulty, Strub possessed an optimistic outlook, and he continued to invest in real estate. At the same time, an income tax lien was filed against Strub for years 1924, 1925, 1927, 1928, and 1929.

The Seals finished at the middle of the pack in 1934. Los Angeles won the title followed by the Hollywood Stars. Graham sold Augie Galan to Chicago and was expecting $100,000 for emerging superstar Joe DiMaggio. But Joe tore ligaments in his knee allegedly while stepping out of a car on the way to his sister's house for dinner. No team would touch him. Graham offered Chicago a no-risk tryout, but the Cubs passed. The Yankees offered $25,000. Disappointed, Graham accepted the New York offer, but negotiated for Joe to play for the Seals through the 1935 season. The move by Graham represented a boon for the organization. The Yankees agreed. Prior to 1935, attendance had dropped under 100,000, well below attendance levels that exceeded 500,000 in years prior to the Depression. In 1935, however, DiMaggio hit .398 with 154 RBI and 34 home runs earning MVP honors as he led the Seals to the league championship. DiMaggio's popularity bolstered the franchise and helped it weather economic hard times.

1935 marked a turning point for Strub in Southern California as well. Santa Anita opened for business on Christmas Day 1934. Thirty thousand crowded the racetrack's bleachers that holiday, including big stars of the era -- Clark Gable, Al Jolson and Will Rogers.[14] Writer Grantland Rice wrote, "The fans were packed in tighter than a tackle jammed against a guard." But the second day, the crowd dropped to 4,000. Doc's son Bob, who was sixteen on opening day, recalled, "My dad was concerned. It was a shaky feeling. He was not panicky, but he was deeply concerned."[15]

His friends considered Doc Strub a great poker player. He rarely revealed his hand to anyone. Certainly his son didn't realize the gravity of the situation at the time. Strub was broke.

On opening day the handle was under $100,000, leaving less than $5,000 net to keep the operation going. The next day was worse. On the third day there wasn't enough in the till to pay everyone, but Strub somehow borrowed it from a Los Angeles bookie.[16]

Strub called his publicist, Fred Purner, and demanded that he get some movie people out to the track quick or the track would close. Purner and Hal Roach brought out stars Lana Turner, Betty Grable, Charlie Chaplin, Mickey Rooney, Oliver Hardy, Jimmy Durante, Jackie Coogan, Pat O'Brien, Bing Crosby and many more who accepted invitations to have their pictures taken and featured in the local newspapers throughout Southern California.[17]

One paper later wrote that Doc Strub never allowed bankruptcy to stop him from making his next millions. Much of Strub's financial well being hinged upon the Santa Anita Handicap. He had yet to earn a penny from his efforts building the preeminent racetrack in the West. Los Angeles sportswriter Jim Murray would later contemplate how a $100,000 race would be received back in that Depression year.

Bread was a nickel, gas was nine cents-but nobody had the nickel or the nine cents. It was a daring, audacious purse for Dr. Charles Strub to post at Santa Anita. The bank he borrowed the money from sent its own armed guards. But he wanted instant credibility for his racing establishment and his daring had its desired effect: It lured the greatest horses in the country west.[18]

The big race drew a record 85,527 customers who wagered $12,611,400. The State of California received approximately $800,000 in taxes for just that one day. The track's first season was a success, a credit to the risky wager Strub and investors had made on the Santa Anita Handicap. At season's end, Strub was finally able to pay back creditors. And he became secure from the annuity offered by a successful horse racing franchise. In the coming years, investors in the track became accustomed to 25% to 30% returns per year. By 1947, the value of shares had escalated 1,300%.[19]

[1]   The Sporting News, September 18, 1941, Lester Grant (Oakland Post Enquirer)
[2]   The Sporting News, September 18, 1941, Lester Grant (Oakland Post Enquirer)
[3]   Bronco Old Grads' Nine Triumphant, Los Angeles Times, Feb 6, 1933, pg. 11
[4]   The Sporting News, September 18, 1941, Lester Grant (Oakland Post Enquirer)
[5]   Article "Day I'll Never Forget," Joe DiMaggio. Reprinted in Los Angeles Times, June 8, 1952; Jun 8, 1952; pg. K8
[6]   In 1941, DiMaggio would hit in 56 consecutive games, a record that has still not been broken.
[7]   Joe DiMaggio, David Jones, pg. 15
[8]   Seals' Prexy Planning on Race Track, Los Angeles Times, Aug 9, 1933, pg. A9
[9]   Commission Grants One Race Permit, Los Angeles Times, OCT 14, 1933, pg. 5
[10] Doc Strub Makes A Mistake, Los Angeles Times, Jan 25, 1934, pg. A9
[11] Racing Board Will Consider Permit Today, Gerald Pidge, Los Angeles Times, Jan 9, 1934, pg. A9
[12] Roach joined by Strub in Turf Venture, LA Times, 12/14/1933, pg. A9

[13] Southern California May Boast of Two Race Tracks, LA Times, Jan 8, 1934, pg. 11

[14] Mary Bender, Pasadena Star - News, Pasadena, Calif.: Dec 26, 2004.

[15] A Life at the Races Strub Helped Santa Anita Reach Prominence, but Now He Suffers From Lou Gehrig's Disease; BILL CHRISTINE, Los Angeles Times, Los Angeles, Calif.: Feb 4, 1993, pg. 1

[16] Art Rosenbaum, San Francisco Chronicle, San Francisco, Calif.: Mar 8, 1985, pg. 80

[17] Art Rosenbaum, San Francisco Chronicle, San Francisco, Calif.: Mar 8, 1985, pg. 80

[18] It's Like Sun Rising in the West: JIM MURRAY, Los Angeles Times, Los Angeles, Calif.: Jun 30, 1992, pg. 1

[19] City Games, The Evolution of American Urban Society and the Rise of Sports, Steven A. Riess, p. 188

Chapter 29

Promotion In the Golden Age of Sports

Perseverance and incessant promotion helped Doc Strub and Charlie Graham weather the difficulties of the Depression. Attention to detail and craftiness succeeded in filling the seats by delivering entertainment to the fan. And Graham soon learned that the "inside baseball" he had specialized in after the turn of the century wasn't what fans wanted to see. They wanted to see offense.

The Pacific Coast League had adopted a dead ball during 1934. Seeing the batting averages drop, "Uncle Charlie" petitioned the league to return to the lively ball used in prior years. The debate was not covert. Manufacturers, league administrators, and the media observed the discussions. The debate exemplified how baseball owners explicitly changed rules such as the strike zone, the height of the mound, and the qualities of a ball that impacted the results of the game over time.

Promotions also took the form of parades through the city streets, first pitches thrown and caught by celebrities and politicians, and Old-Timers games that showcased the tradition of the game in the respective towns. In San Francisco, local Ty Cobb frequently escorted his friend Charlie Graham, the chief of police, and the mayor in the parades that ushered in the new seasons. And the likes of Van Haltren, Fred Lange, and friends suited up each year into their eighties in front of fans who became increasingly more cognizant of current players such as Harry "Cookie" Lavagetto than the likes of Ernest "Kid" Mohler. The old-timers symbolized the tradition of great past West Coast baseball as coaches, scouts, managers, and umpires who trained and inspired future generations. For Graham, hosting the players created a special, traditional ambiance and ballpark experience for the fan. Particularly when a team adopted a new ballpark, the link to the past was critical for the franchise. And the exhibition games enabled Graham to pay tribute to his friends who had contributed significantly to the game.

Nostalgia and tradition appealed to the fans and helped create a brand for the teams and the league. To contribute to the branding effort, reporter and league statistician Leo Moriarty named an all-time Pacific Coast League All Star Team.

First All-Time Pacific Coast League All Star Team

Outfield	Arnold Statz / Paul Waner / Bob Meusel
Third Base	Willie Kamm
First Base	Hal Chase
Shortstop	Charley Hollocher / Kid Mohler
Catcher	Charlie Graham / Larry McLean
Pitchers	Doc Newton / Fay Thomas / Vean Gregg / Frank Shellenback
Manager	Hap Hogan
Umpire	George Hildebrand

After Lew Moreing's death in 1935, a young manager named Earl McNeely purchased the Sacramento PCL franchise. He partnered with St. Louis' General Manager Branch Rickey to make the team part of the Cardinals' minor league farm system. Bankers required only a small down payment to purchase the team; they agreed to future payments in the form of installments. McNeely, only thirty-five years old, became the youngest owner, manager, president, and player in the league.

At Stanford, Harry Wolter began his second decade as head coach of the baseball squad. He soon established himself as a leader both on the West and nationally in amateur baseball. Some called him the "patron saint of Coast Collegiate baseball." He became the western representative for the American Amateur Baseball Congress, which met in Chicago in July of 1935. In 1936, Wolter was selected as coach for the United States amateur national team that played exhibitions at the 1936 Olympic Games in Berlin.[A]

In Southern California, Doc Strub appealed to the State not to allow additional racing tracks near Los Angeles. He argued creatively and persuasively to maintain his profitable monopoly at Santa Anita. He stated that the State's revenues would ultimately suffer if the allure of racing became diluted by many, ordinary racing venues. He felt that by keeping purses higher in fewer races, the quality and appeal of the sport was better served. And most importantly, he felt that his prescribed formula would create more tax revenues for the State. He said that with two tracks, neither could afford to pay the large purses to attract the best and most famous horses from the East. The State had earned $1 million annually in taxes from Santa Anita. He pleaded, "Do you think that the public would like to see us cut our stake and have just ordinary racing?"

[A] Baseball did not become an official Olympic sport until 1984.

Indeed, Strub had created quality, high stakes racing in the West. The $100,000 Santa Anita Handicap was known affectionately as "The Hundred Grander." And in 1937, a special horse and its owners set its sights on a victory at the prestigious event. Seabiscuit had already run well in the East, at Bay Meadows in Northern California, and at warm-up races at Santa Anita. The horse, whose life-sized bronze statue would eventually grace the entrance of Santa Anita Racetrack for more than fifty years after the horse's retirement, lost by a nose to Rosemont in the 1937 Santa Anita Handicap. Following that race, however, Seabiscuit became a West Coast celebrity by winning eleven of fifteen races to become the leading money winner in the United States. Before television in the 1930's, the radio, newsreels, and newspapers not only delivered news of sporting events to the fan, but created heroes and icons. Like Babe Ruth, Lou Gehrig, and Joe DiMaggio, Seabiscuit became an icon. The same year, the great War Admiral captured the Triple Crown and was considered one of the greatest race horses of all time. The two horses would not meet in a race until 1938.

Sports promotion continued to reach new heights. Strub and Graham understood that as promoters, their responsibility was to deliver a quality show. They were leaders, and they understood that leadership, whether at Santa Anita Race Track or Seals Stadium, required an unwavering long-term commitment to service to the customer. From the time Charlie Graham was a young man, he organized and managed baseball teams. Early in his life, he chose the precarious career of baseball team ownership that offered few guarantees. In hindsight, even the wealthiest owners, including Hen Berry, Ed Maier, and Cal Ewing ultimately conceded to the next generation. And the enterprising, such as Harry Wolverton and Lew Moreing, lost fortunes during a few down years in spite of a string of successful campaigns. But Charlie Graham persisted for decades. A mathematician by education, Graham understood the calculus required for survival and success. He loved the game, felt that fans wanted to watch it, and dedicated himself to a product that the fans would embrace. A man of few words, Charlie Graham in 1937 made a statement that embodied the simplicity of his personal philosophy toward baseball promotion and ownership:

> *When the fans have money and you give them a show, baseball will never want for patronage. It is the greatest game of all and it will always be a national sport.*
>
> *I can remember in the days when they said the bicycle would ruin baseball. Then they said it was the automobile that was killing off the fans' interest. But baseball is having its greatest season this year since the depression. It's survived the bicycles and automobiles and I think the game is going to come back greater than ever in the next few years.*[1]

On September 13, Graham hosted another Old Timer's game at Seals Stadium. The vets played a three-inning game. The teams were named the Pioneers and the Haverlys. The Haverlys and Pioneers were two of San

Francisco's baseball teams in the late 1880s. Mike Finn, who had passed away in 1936, had managed the Pioneer team, which featured a player named Cooney, who may have been the same Cooney who "died at second" in the poem "Casey at the Bat." Hen Harris had managed the Haverlys, which won a string of titles fifty years before. Other teams in the league included the champion Stockton team and the Greenhood & Morans. The squad featured three participants at the game, including seventy-seven year old former manager Colonel Tom Robinson. Robinson managed the San Francisco team from 1886 to 1903 at which time he sold his interest to Cal Ewing when the Pacific Coast League formed. In his seventies, former G&M hurler George Van Haltren pitched the first inning and gave up just one single. He was joined by former teammate Fred Lange. Elmer Stricklett, Bill Lange, Kid Mohler, Cliff Blankenship, Tubby Spencer, Elmer Emerson, and Ben Henderson also played. Harry Hooper, not yet inducted into baseball's Hall of Fame, and Hal Chase appeared in front of the eight thousand fans that witnessed the Pioneers defeat the Haverlys 8 to 3.

The Hall of Fame had just formed in 1936 and inducted its first class that included Ty Cobb, Babe Ruth, Honus Wagner, Christy Mathewson, and Walter Johnson. Many of the old-timers at Seals Stadium in September of 1937 received votes the initial year. Ironically, future inductee Harry Hooper didn't receive any. Hal Chase received eleven votes, ahead of Frank Chance (5), John McGraw (4), and Connie Mack (1).[A] Bill Lange received six votes from the Hall of Fame's veteran's committee, the same as Charles Comiskey and former East Bay star Jerry Denny. George Van Haltren received one vote, as did one of Northern California's pioneer baseball players, Cal McVey.

In the second year of voting in 1937, Hal Chase received eighteen votes. Although still remembered, Chase lived in relative obscurity in Northern California. During the depression, Chase's sister Jessie Tophams and her husband Frank purchased a 900-acre ranch at 8th and G Streets in Willliams, California outside of Sacramento on which they grew rice, barley, walnuts, and livestock. Hal's father lived with them until his death from a cerebral hemorrhage in 1935 at the age of 88. Hal lived three years with his sister Jessie's daughter and husband in Alameda. When Hal's niece left her husband in 1936 to live with her parents in Williams, Chase moved into an apartment in Oakland. Chase worked for the WPA, the Works Progress Administration, part of Franklin Roosevelt's largest New Deal agency founded to create jobs after 1935. He handled assignments including plumber and carpenter's helper. He also received financial assistance from the State Relief Administration.[2]

Chase later admitted to considerable drinking during the 1930s. His drinking habits compounded the challenges everyone faced during the Depression.

[A] Every player who received as many votes as Hal Chase did in the initial voting eventually became a member of the Hall.

Times were difficult. Conditions in California, particularly in the farming regions of Central California where Chase's sister Jessie lived, were perhaps best described in the novel The Grapes of Wrath, penned by John Steinbeck while residing in the late 1930s in Hal Chase's home town of Los Gatos. Like the Okies who migrated to California during the Dust Bowl, Chase too lived a humble life. But he never lost his spirit in spite of obstacles. Charlie Graham recalled Chase coming to Seals Stadium and asking for a pass to a game. Graham was happy to give him one. Chase said, "I had a dime a little while ago. But I just spent it for a cigar." Graham remembered him puffing away and enjoying immensely the stogie for which he spent his last ten cents. "That was the way he was. Hard knocks didn't bother him, and maybe it was because he had so many of them he'd gotten use to them…. Trouble was his lot. But he never lost his smile."[3]

And Chase never lost interest in baseball. He kept up associations with baseball programs, including at the University of San Francisco coached by friend Bill Cunningham.[A] And wherever he lived, he attended and observed local youth games, probably still itching to put on a glove and take the field even though his body was worn beyond its fifty-five years of age. The years had purged him of his ability, but not his memories.

The memories of early Pacific Coast League ballplayers were kept alive in Southern California as well as in San Francisco. William Wrigley's Los Angeles Angels honored the late Hap Hogan on May 29, 1938 at Wrigley Field in Los Angeles. Wrigley and former nemesis Ed Maier buried the hatchet for the affair, as Maier took charge of the memorial more than twenty years after the popular Vernon Tigers' manager's death. Jim Jeffries and Barney Oldfield, two regulars along with Hap at Maier's parties at his ranch, assisted with the ceremonies. Included at the event were players Walter Carlisle, Roy Hitt, George Stovall, and Roy Brashear as well as long-time trainer Shine Scott. Scott had been with the Vernon team since it started in 1909.

Over eighty years of age, Scott still trained the Hollywood Stars. Hap Hogan had hired Shine many years before after seeing him playing piano in a dance hall. After Hogan's death, Shine remained with the team, even moving to San Francisco with the Mission Club in 1926.[B]

Hogan was remembered as the best bunter anyone ever saw. The Los Angeles Times reported that Hogan could "squeeze over runs and tell the pitcher

---

[A] Cunningham was born in San Francisco and played at St. Mary's from 1913 to 1917. He won two World Series titles with the New York Giants in 1921 and 1922 in a four-year major league career. He also coached in the majors.

[B] When the Hollywood Stars took over the Mission franchise in 1938, Shine returned to Los Angeles. In 1940, in failing health, Scott retired on a pension. Many players and officials worried how long he would last without being a part of the team. The first week of October, 1940, Shine Scott died of a heart attack.

338

he was going to do it." A few years later, Los Angeles Times columnist Dick Hyland named Hogan among the best "money players" in baseball history, along with Ty Cobb, Tris Speaker, and Frank "Home Run" Baker.

Just a week before Hogan was honored, a match race between the two greatest horses of the era, War Admiral and Santa Anita's most famous racer Seabiscuit, was postponed due to physical problems with the West Coast hopeful. A crowd of 40,000 was expected for the original race to be held on May 30 at Belmont Park. A subsequent showdown was scheduled for June in the $50,000 Massachusetts Handicap, but rain at Suffolk Downs made the track sloppy, and Seabiscuit withdrew. Fans became frustrated by the on again, off again dramatics that heightened the anticipation of an eventual meeting between the two great horses.

In August, rumors surfaced about War Admiral heading west to face Seabiscuit in a $100,000 stake race. At the same time, Seabiscuit raced head to head in a match race against Bing Crosby's horse Ligaroti at Del Mar. Seabiscuit won the race with a time that trainers felt exceeded the abilities of War Admiral. While a venue for a similar matchup between Seabiscuit and War Admiral was selected, newspapers contended that a match race could be fixed. At one time, gambling and impropriety in baseball attracted comparisons to horse racing. With discussion of jockeys being paid to throw a match race, horse racing began to resemble baseball.

> *All the hullabaloo following the Seabiscuit-Ligaroti duel at Del Mar probably helps explain why the War Admiral-'Biscuit match race never came off as scheduled. Match races may be wonderful things to settle arguments, but they certainly leave the gate wide open for scandal to come down under the wire first. Especially so would have been the Admiral-'Biscuit affair, in which millions of dollars would have been wagered all over the country.... Some of our nation's "outstanding" politicians have been guilty of crooked tactics, so it wouldn't be too much to expect a jockey to pick himself up a few thousand bucks by throwing a race and then retiring. After all, a jockey's life is a short if not a merry one, and he must gather the hay while he can keep his girlish figure. So why blame one if he double-crosses a few folks who might eventually double-cross him?.... But, to get back to match races, the racing boards all over the country would do well to ban them. Even those on which no public betting is allowed, as was the case at Del Mar. The racing game is on too shaky a foundation to invite trouble.[4]*

On September 14, the horses' two owners agreed to a race to be held the day after Halloween on November 1, 1938 at Pimlico. Each owner wrote a check for $25,000 that they agreed to forfeit as a token of good faith to the racetrack for hosting the event.^A Alfred Vanderbilt, the Vice President of the Maryland Jockey Club and director of the Pimlico track engineered the much sought after match up.[5] Sportswriters reported that the race was to take place at Santa Anita, but Sam Riddle, owner of War Admiral didn't want to go west for the race. The Los Angeles Times reported that from the excuses offered to Strub and the Santa Anita representatives, it appeared that Riddle "thought that western racing was a rodeo, or that Indians with tomahawks found their way into the races."[6] After the rowdy happenings at the racetrack between Seabiscuit and Ligaroti, Riddle was genuinely concerned that West Coast racing was too rough. In the Ligaroti race at Del Mar, the jockeys physically assaulted each other as they raced around the track. In spite of Strub's guarantees that rough riding would not be tolerated at Santa Anita, an eastern venue was chosen.

The Tuesday horse race was sandwiched by East Coast sporting events that received national attention as America sought distraction from the grim international news in Europe of Hitler's Germany invading Czechoslovakia. Still years away from entering into WWII, the U.S. military focused temporarily on the much anticipated football game between Army and Navy on Saturday. On Sunday the Washington Redskins battled the Brooklyn Dodgers on the gridiron, Henry Armstrong boxed Ceferino Garcia on Wednesday, and the next Saturday St. Mary's battled Fordham in football. Colorful radio broadcasters announced the events to fans across the country. The popular medium, however, experienced the most significant event in its history the day before the War Admiral vs. Seabiscuit affair.

On the eve of the race, Orson Welles broadcast a drama on CBS radio about Martians invading the East Coast. In a medium that in the past had clearly delineated between news and entertainment, "The War of the Worlds" became one of the first entertainment shows to become news. Countless citizens believed the mock report and momentarily feared the world's demise. The nation demonstrated a curious vulnerability to fiction that was delivered by a news source that had previously defined itself by credible, factual reporting. The next day's race was both cathartic and exhilarating for a nation in need of diversion.

Forty thousand fans packed the Pimlico Race Course 1 3/16 mile race. An additional forty million listeners tuned in for the radio broadcast. War Admiral was the heavy favorite at 1-4. The next day, sportswriter Grantland Rice described the victorious Seabiscuit,

> *A little horse with the heart of a lion and the flying feet of a gazelle yesterday proved his place as the gamest thoroughbred that ever raced over an American track... For almost a half mile they ran as one horse, painted against the green, red and orange foliage of a Maryland countryside. They were neck and neck -- head and head -- nose and*

---

^A When the previous race at Belmont was postponed, the track took a loss.

nose... I had seen him (Seabiscuit) before in two $100,000 races at Santa Anita, boxed out, knocked to his knees, taking the worst of all the racing luck -- almost everything except facing a firing squad or a machine-gun nest -- and yet, through all this barrage of trouble, Seabiscuit was always there, challenging at the wire. I saw him run the fastest half-mile ever run at Santa Anita last March, when he had to do it in his pursuit of Stagehand.

Seabiscuit left the Admiral so far behind that it wasn't even a contest down the stretch. War Admiral might just as well have been chasing a will o' the wisp in a midnight swamp. He might just as well have been a fat poodle chasing a meat wagon. He had been outrun and outgamed -- he had been run off the track by a battered 5-year-old who had more speed and heart.

America and California embraced the promotion of entertainment as it had done throughout its history. With each decade, the markets and the grandeur of the staging grew. And nobody was considered a better organizer of urban entertainment than Doctor Charles Strub. In 1939, San Francisco hosted a World's Fair on Treasure Island in the middle of the San Francisco Bay. Attendance was initially below expectations, so Strub was appointed Managing Director, a duty he performed unselfishly and without a salary as a gift to San Francisco, in an attempt to salvage the show. Perhaps Strub also offered his services to honor his mother, a native of San Francisco, who died a few months after the show concluded. Surely his mother was proud. His personality and dynamic plans were said to bring harmony to the staff. He organized a "Summer RE-opening" and followed the formula that had worked for him at Santa Anita; he booked big-name personalities from radio, screen, and entertainment worlds. Attendance surged and Strub was credited with the Fair's success.[7]

---

1 The Sports X-Ray, Bob Ray, Los Angeles Times, pg. A11
2 The Sporting News, September 18, 1941, Lester Grant (Oakland Post Enquirer)
3 San Francisco Examiner, May 21, 1947
4 The Sports X-Ray, LA Times, Bob Ray, Aug 18, 1938
5 Riddle Agrees to Match Race, LA Times, Oct 6, 1938, Pg. A14
6 Los Angeles Times, Oscar Otis, Oct 25, 1938 pg. A9
7 California-Magazine of the Pacific, Published by the California State Chamber of Commerce, 1455O

Chapter 30

The Greatest Defensive First Baseman in Baseball

In 1940, Hal Chase moved to Colusa, near his sister Jessie, to live with a friend George Messick who owned a local hardware store. By October, Chase entered the County Hospital to deal with the onset of Buri Buri brought on by a decade of drinking. He vowed sobriety on October 6, 1941 and remained so for the rest of his life.[1]

Hal then moved in with his sister and lived in a cabin behind the main house. He lived off Old Highway 99 between Theatre Drive and Crawford Road in Williams, near Colusa, northwest of Sacramento near the interstate 5 freeway heading north to Red Bluff. He took a job as a watchman in town.

Chase was still remembered. Whenever a first baseman came along who combined strong hitting with superior fielding ability, the newcomer drew comparisons to the greatest defensive first baseman yet to play the game. In October of 1941, it was the slick fielding San Francisco Seals first baseman Ferris Fain who drew comparisons to the skilled Chase. One reporter wrote of Chase,

> He'll be remembered for a few days and then forgotten, recalled only occasionally as some old-timer, fumbling for a comparison, will hail a phenomenally clever rookie as "the greatest first baseman since Hal Chase." [2]

Sportswriters would also refer to Chase when drawing attention to poor fielding first baggers. Since the end of the deadball era, power hitting replaced defense as a prerequisite for a first baseman. The defensive specialists of the dead ball era were long forgotten after strong hitting bruisers including Jimmie Foxx, Hank Greenberg, George Kelly, Johnny Mize, and Bill Terry took to the stage. Through decades of defensive dearth at first, writers referred to Chase as the ultimate.

1958

Musial was no Hal Chase around the bag.[3]

1967

... (Don) Clendenon, although not exactly a Hal Chase around the bag, batted .299 with 29 homers and 98 RBI last season.[4]

Legendary Los Angeles Times sportswriter Jim Murray referred to Chase for decades when seeking a metaphor for the gold standard in defensive first basemen. In 1984, Murray commented on how first base had tragically transformed over the years.

The most famous burlesque routine in baseball history, "Who's on first," is all right as far as it goes, except in terms of historical accuracy, perhaps it should be changed to "Who-Cares is on first."

First base is not a position, it's a retirement community. It's like a condo in Fort Myers, Fla. Instead of giving you a gold watch, they give you first base. It's a reward, not a challenge. It's like locking the family idiot off in an unused wing of the ancestral home and hiding the matches. Like sending the black sheep of the family off to India with a remittance. The baseball equivalent of the elephants' graveyard. When you can't play anything else, you play first base. It comes with a rocking chair....

When they get a guy who can hit but can't do anything else, they stick him on first. Some of the great lockwrists of the game – Dick Stuart, Zeke Bonura, even Babe Herman – played first, giving rise to the old Flatbush joke that the Dodgers had the only first sacker whose batting average was higher than his fielding average.

Murray harbored sentiment against hapless defensive first basemen for decades, and frequently alluded to the Chase as the emblem of grace at the corner more than sixty years after Chase had retired. Murray wrote,

1962

Baseball mitts today are a far hunk of leather from the palm-bruisers they wore in the old days. A trapper's mitt makes a Hal Chase out of a guy who can't see his shoelaces.[5]

1965

Whadda you mean calling that triple an error? I don't care if Dick Stuart DID drop-kick it into the stands. Hal Chase couldn't of handled that smash.[6]

1966

Look for a guy who looks like he's just finished two truckloads of fried chicken and is trying to decide where to go for lunch... (Boog Powell) may not be the niftiest first baseman – some say he plays the position more like Ilka than Hal Chase.[7]

1971

He (Wes Parker) was easily the most stylish first baseman the league has seen since Hal Chase.[8]

1981

Joe DiMaggio was the towering epitome of non-anxiety, not-to-worry baseball. No one played it with more grace and ease... Oldtimers say Hal Chase had this attribute...[9]

So what did Murray think about Chase? Murray wrote,

> *He had been a brash, impudent, cocky ball player who was completely aware of his own unparalleled skill. He was too aware of it. Chase could move faster and think faster than anyone else.*[10]

In 1941, the enigmatic Chase gave one of the most extensive interviews of his life to Oakland Post Enquirer reporter Lester Grant, who submitted three separate pieces to the Sporting News in September. At fifty-eight years of age, sober, and in failing health, Chase remained haunted by Organized Baseball, fearful of how it controlled his legacy. He tactfully and gracefully avoided directly criticizing the game, although contempt could be gleaned from his response. Chase felt that Organized Baseball lacked justice. But he was not interested in stirring up ill will. If he had not been a beaten man, defeated by Organized Baseball's assault and his own self-inflicted spiral, perhaps he could have stood up for players' rights. Alas, he was a broken man who had lost the will and ability to fight. He offered,

> *... baseball is even a better game now, a cleaner, healthier institution through and through. The days of wildcat ball and vicious exploitation of the player are gone forever. There may still be abuses. Club owners are still human and, being human, they'll wring the last dime of profit out of their talent. If they happen to ruin a kid's career doing it, their consciences won't trouble them too much. After all, they're business men. And there aren't many business men, in the strict sense of the term, who put human souls above pennies.*

In the past, the opposite of whatever Prince Hal said in public was closer to his genuine sentiment. He wanted to appear as a sage and diplomat, but he lacked the verbal acuity to hide his true feelings. In the quote above, his attitude toward baseball owners was conspicuously transparent. He meant,

> *Baseball has a history of viciously exploiting players. The condition may still exist. Club owners will wring the last dime of profit out of their talent. They have no consciences. As businessmen, they are heartless.*

During the interview, Chase obsequiously directed flattering comments toward Commissioner Landis. Still viewing Landis as the judge and jury for Organized Baseball, Chase demonstrated a desire to be accepted by the game by pandering to the baseball czar.

> *I wonder how many people realize just what Landis has done for baseball? Where would the game be today without him? His consistent championing of the underdog and his determination to see that justice prevails no matter what the cost has made him, in my opinion, the most valuable member of the whole baseball fraternity.*

Chase refered to a baseball fraternity as if he were an honorary member based on lifetime achievement rather than one who had been permanently subjugated to a status of "outsider." And perceiving himself as an esteemed member of the "club", Chase bestowed special recognition upon Landis in a manner akin to Judas complimenting Jesus for his contributions at the last supper.

Chase continued with his admiring monologue regarding Landis as the just protector of players' rights.

> ... *today the ball player has Judge Landis on his side and if I talked all day and all night about the value of having a Judge Landis on the scene, I don't think I could do justice to the subject. Landis is the champion of the ball player, the greatest single individual in the game today. He stands for justice for the worker, the player who gets out there and makes those base hits and catches those long flies and pitches those victories.*

Prince Hal, more the ambassador than the agitator as an aging man, shrewdly decided against contention toward Baseball and Landis, but to gain affection and favor by highlighting the Commissioner's merit as the "champion of the ballplayer." Once again, however, Chase likely meant the following:

> ... *Judge Landis represents the owners, and the players have nobody on their sides. Landis and the owners don't care about the players. Nobody stands for justice when it comes to the workers who play the game of Baseball.*

Perhaps unknowingly, Chase offered two stories during the interview depending on which side of his mouth one listened to. Some of the interview was cliché, including memories of players and plays that certainly interested the fan. He recalled his greatest thrills, one of which occurred during the 1905 season. Hal came to bat in the ninth inning with they tying run on third base. An excellent squeeze bunter, Chase attempted to bunt the runner home. But because fouling off a bunted ball with two strikes represented a third strike, Chase attempted to bunt by "half swinging" at the ball. He fouled off twelve straight pitches. On the thirteenth, he looped a ball into shallow left, and took second. He later scored the winning run.[11] Another great thrill was winning the batting title in 1916 by hitting .339 and beating out Rogers Hornsby and Honus Wagner for the honor.[12]

Other aspects of the interview revealed a remorseful and regretful man who had recognized his immaturity as a husband and ballplayer. Over a lifetime, the self-inflicted wounds caused by pride and indiscretion grew into dark shadows that consumed the Prince. He admitted that one of the biggest regrets of his life was not staying with his first wife Nellie Heffernan. Nellie remained close to the Chase family throughout their respective lives. As a fifty-eight year old man, Hal recognized he had lost the love of his life due to youthful impudence that led to their acrimonious divorce, which Hal allowed to turn into a soap opera played out publicly in the media.

He also took responsibility for his poor reputation in baseball.

> *You know, baseball was good to me, but I'm afraid I wasn't very good to*

baseball. Most of the grief I had during my career as a player was of my own making. At least, if it wasn't of my own making, I could have prevented it, had I acted more wisely.[13]

Writers have referred to the quote above as Hal Chase's admission of guilt. However, once again Hal speaks out of both sides of his mouth. He said the grief he caused was of his own making, and then said perhaps he didn't directly cause it. Then he said that he could have prevented the grief. The grief he referred to in the quote was the fix of the 1919 Worlds Series, which he admitted to knowing about. Showing contrition, he stated that he could have acted more wisely by notifying league officials regarding the fix.

During thousands of sleepless nights since 1920, Chase had tossed and turned, rehearsing and preparing for the opportunity to address his critics during an interview such as the one offered by Lester Grant. Considering the conditions in baseball in 1919, however, Chase's response regarding reporting the World Series fix didn't hold water. Not for a moment should anyone believe that Chase or almost any other player would have reported a gambling scandal. Gambling had been prevalent throughout the game for decades. Players frequently heard about and knew about fixes, but most didn't ever notify league officials. Even in the interview, Chase stated that he wasn't one to turn in fellow players. Referring to the opportunity to notify the President of the National League, John Heydler, about what he knew, Chase disingenuously said he "pulled a terrible boner" by not saying anything. Being more truthful, he went on to say what nearly every ballplayer would say,

... I have never had any use for a stool pigeon or a squealer.[14]

During the interview, Chase chose the tack of gaining favor by admitting to human frailty and showing remorse rather than by painting himself as a victim. He did not deny betting on games, which he indicated was a common custom when he played. He didn't attempt to appear righteous. And how could he? If the incident with Spider Baum was true, then Chase had become so caught up with gamblers by 1920 that he betrayed "home" – he betrayed his friends in California and the Pacific Coast League. Much like an addict, Chase likely rationalized his actions because the PCL was part of Organized Baseball that opposed him. The perceived lack of justice in the game perhaps justified in Chase's mind unethical behavior on his part. Regardless, while not proven in court, the Spider Baum incident likely occurred as Baum explained, which demonstrated that Chase took an active role in cavorting with elements that cast doubt on his reputation. And by doing so, Prince Hal had cut himself off from the home that had provided support throughout his career. Hal was not a victim. He took action that brought harm to himself, in his first marriage, interactions with gamblers, and other aspects of his life.

Chase attempted to convey in his interview emotion more than fact. To his adversaries, he was willing to raise a white flag and show remorse. If he had caused grief, he was willing to convey penitence and regret. Reading between the lines of the interview, one can hear Chase's message:

> *I was right. Those owners were bastards. Things haven't changed. But I am fifty-eight years old, sick, and not looking for a fight. If I caused anyone or any institution harm, which I am not sure that I did, I am truly sorry.*

Chase gave a different kind of interview about the same time to a youngster in Colusa named David Smith. Smith recalled a tearful Chase tell his parents that he was innocent in the Black Sox incident.

> *He denied vehemently that he had anything to do with the Black Sox. He had tears in his eyes when he said it.*[15]

The young Smith remembered Chase affectionately for his goodness. He recounted how Hal handed him a first baseman's glove as a gift.[16] It was not the first time that Hal had handed a young ballplayer a first baseman's glove as a gift, no matter how down on his luck Chase had been at the time. For many, Hal Chase defined first base as a player. And through his life he handed out the gloves to inspire children to love playing first base as much as he had. And it didn't matter whether they played first base, or even if the glove fit them. When Chase handed Smith the glove, the youngster told Hal that he wasn't left handed. Chase told him to learn because all of the best players are left-handed.

[1]   The Sporting News, September 18, 1941, Lester Grant (Oakland Post Enquirer)

[2]   The Tragic Figure of Hal Chase, Arthur Daley, New York Times, May 20, 1947, pg. 31

[3]   Frank Finch, Here's the Pitch, Los Angeles Times, Dec 6, 1958, pg. A2

[4] $2 Million Price Put on Halo Infield, John Hall, LA Times, Apr 2, 1967

[5]   The Glass Menagerie, Jim Murray, LA Times, Feb 14, 1962, pg. B1

[6]   All Hail the Heel, Los Angeles Times, May 16, 1965, pg. B1

[7]   All Together Now, Let's hear it for Hero Boog!, Jim Murray, Los Angeles Times, Oct 11, 1966, p. B1

[8]   Stylish Miscast, Jim Murray, Los Angeles Times, Mar 28, 1971, pg. B1

[9]   He Could Play in Top Hat and Tails, Jim Murray, Los Angeles Times, Mar 22, 1981, pg. D1

[10] The Tragic Figure of Hal Chase, Arthur Daley, new York Times, pg. 31

[11] The Sporting News, September 18, 1941, Lester Grant (Oakland Post Enquirer)

[12] The Sporting News, September 18, 1941, Lester Grant (Oakland Post Enquirer)

[13] The Sporting News, September 25, 1941, Lester Grant (Oakland Post Enquirer)

[14] The Sporting News, September 18, 1941, Lester Grant (Oakland Post Enquirer)

[15] The Black Prince of Baseball: Hal Chase and the Mythology of the Game, Don Dewey and Nick Acocella, pg. 409

[16] The Black Prince of Baseball: Hal Chase and the Mythology of the Game, Don Dewey and Nick Acocella, pg. 409

Chapter 31

Legacies Are For The Living

When Chase gave his interview to Lester Grant in 1941, World War II raged in Europe, but Franklin Roosevelt and the United States remained uncommitted. Nonetheless, the nation, particularly those on the Coasts, feared an attack. Frankly, the U.S. military was ill prepared if an attack were to occur. Entering the War would require immediate and massive expansion of the armed forces. Charlie Graham readied his team in the event wartime would once again claim the many young ballplayers from the Coast, as it had done during WWI. Throughout the 1941 season, Graham required that his San Francisco Seals team march every day in practice to prepare for war.

In 1941, ambient light from the cities wasn't as significant as it would later become, but citizens and city officials were notified to dim lights during the night to diminish as targets the metropolises along the Coast, particularly San Francisco, for Japanese submarines and ships. All Pacific Coast League stadiums, including Seals Stadium, which possessed the most powerful lighting system in the West, were told to dim the lights at night and to play only day games.

On December 7, 1941, "a date which will live in infamy," the Japanese attacked Pearl Harbor. Immediately, Roosevelt reported that U.S. ships were being torpedoed between San Francisco and Hawaii, confirming suspicion of a threat close to the mainland. On January 14, Commissioner Landis wrote to President Roosevelt to inquire whether continuing to play baseball during wartime was appropriate. The next day, Roosevelt replied that, for the sake of the national spirit, the season should be played. The major leagues and the Pacific Coast League continued to offer their much-desired entertainment to America, demonstrating the importance of sport to the citizens of the country.

In Los Angeles, Doc Strub had little choice than to provide Santa Anita Racetrack as a temporary Japanese Interment Camp after the outbreak of war. The Japanese, eventually sent to permanent internment camps throughout the West, were gathered in the interim in regional "Civilian Assembly Centers," mostly fairgrounds and racetracks. Many who arrived at Santa Anita in April came from San Francisco, and were eventually relocated to Manzanar, once it was built, in the hot and dry Owens River Valley approximately two hours to the Northeast of Santa Anita.

In July of 1942, the fifty-six year old Hal Chase suffered a heart attack in Oakland. He was reported in critical condition at Highland Hospital, but was conscious and coherent. Chase survived the attack, but it highlighted his frail condition and deteriorating health.

In 1943, Charlie Graham irked the other Pacific Coast League owners by announcing that he didn't expect to play this season as they had the previous year because of the War. Not only would the season be a financial burden, the players had a duty to serve. Twenty San Francisco Seals players reported for service in March of 1943. Many major leaguers also reported after the 1942 season, including Joe DiMaggio, Ted Williams, and Bob Feller. Both Graham and the owners were correct; the season began in spite of the drain of talent to the War, but was cut to one hundred fifty-five games rather than the normal schedule of more than two hundred.

On December 13, 1943, the former owner of the Vernon Tigers and the Maier Brewing Company, Eddie Maier, died. The sixty-one year old expired fighting a fire at a beach cottage in Malibu at 18724 Old Malibu Road. The long-time owner, who inherited the baseball team after graduating from college following the death of his older brother, brought a youthful exuberance unchecked by financial constraints to the Tigers, Los Angeles baseball, and the Pacific Coast League. Each year he had hosted Shriners, Elks, and his many friends to large banquets at his 10,000-acre ranch. In the years preceding the sale of the ranch in 1934, more than 5,000 guests were served the traditional western barbecue and treated to boxing bouts and the landing of the Volunteer, Goodyear Rubber Company's dirigible. In 1932, in the midst of the Depression and prohibition, Maier Brewery went bankrupt (he later re-acquired the brewery). Tragedy struck in 1933 when Maier's wife, Kathleen, died of injuries in an auto accident. In 1934, Maier sold Maier Ranch to Dr. W.R. Livingstone of Oxnard.[A]

The newspaper reported that Maier was intimate over the years with celebrities, including Jim Jeffries, Jack Dempsey, William Essick, Frank Chance, Hal Chase, and the late Hap Hogan, who were considered at one time "the elite of the sporting world here." He was known as a charitable man, as evidenced by his banquets for the citizens of Los Angeles, a label to which he replied, "They need it and I've got it. Maybe someday I'll need a hand."

In 1944, Doc Strub no longer needed a hand, but he didn't want to be too charitable with the California State Board of Equalization. The Board filed a tax lien on him and his wife Vera for past due taxes from 1934 and 1935. In the fledgling years of Santa Anita, Strub would have lacked the ability to pay back taxes. But Strub was now in a financial position to pay the debt in the event his defense was overruled. Strub argued that although he received compensation in 1935 from the new Santa Anita Racetrack after a successful first season and Santa Anita Handicap, much of the compensation was accrued from work performed in 1934, a period of time for which he received no compensation while he obtained licenses, built the racetrack, and opened for business in December. Strub

---

[A] In 1947, the property was purchased to become what is now the American Jewish University Brandeis-Bardin Campus.

attempted to allocate some of the income received in 1935 to 1934. The bonus Strub received in 1935, representing his ten percent cut of the profits from the first season from the Los Angeles Turf Club, was $99,320. Strub felt that only 1/3 of that belonged as 1935 income, and that 2/3 should be considered 1934 income, particularly since he entered into employment with the Turf Club with a five-year contract commencing on February 28, 1934. Strub's argument was credible, but most accountants would advise, as did the tax commissioner, that Strub owed back taxes. His rebuttal was overruled.

In 1945, Jackie Robinson signed a contract with the Brooklyn Dodgers and was assigned to the minor leagues. Strangely, although the War drained talent from the major and minor leagues, Organized Baseball had yet to allow African Americans to play. That same year, Strub and Graham considered selling a portion of the San Francisco Seals to Paul Fagan, who would eventually purchase the team outright. But during the War, the franchise was appraised at just $225,000. In an effort to bolster the franchise, which had not won a championship since 1935, Graham established a working relationship with the New York Giants. His first deal was an option granted to the Giants for outfielder Neill Sheridan in return for $50,000 worth of talent.[1] Graham felt that with the alliance, he could better compete with the Los Angeles Angels club that had been bolstered by its relationship with the Chicago Cubs, a relationship established years prior by former owner Frank Chance. Instead of selling the club, Graham and Strub sold Fagan a partial ownership share in 1946 and remained as owners.

In February of 1947, the New York Turf Writers' Association voted Doc Strub as the man who had done the most for racing. A month later, Hal Chase suffered a stroke. He was in a coma for three days, but recovered.

That same month, the USC Trojan's baseball coach, Sam Barry, traveled to the East for personal reasons during the baseball season. On March 24, he had his assistant Rod Dedeaux, who later became one of the greatest collegiate baseball coaches, serve temporarily as head coach in a series against Harry Wolter's Stanford Indians.

About three weeks later, ill and in bed at the Colusa County Hospital, Hal Chase listened on the radio to the announcement that at Ebbets Field on April 15, Jackie Robinson became the first African American player to play in the major leagues. A week later, Hal gave his final interview to J.W. Sehorn, who published the report in the Sporting News. At the interview, Chase's sister, Jessie, who had lovingly cared for favorite brother Hal throughout his ill health in recent years, proudly showed off scrapbooks containing clippings she had kept of her brother since he played with the Angels in 1904. She was indignant of the press coverage since Chase retired. She said,

> ...everything derogatory said about him for 28 years adds up to one thing - make Chase the goat.

Hal no longer had anything to prove. He would never know a life without his ass hanging out of a backless dressing gown in a county hospital. Regarding betting on games, Chase said,

> *I could have made a million dollars out of baseball on bets and gambling. I used to bet on games. My limit was $100 per game and I never bet against my own team... Like others, I had to have a bet on the side and we used to bet with the other team and with gamblers who sat in the boxes. It was easy to make a bet.*[2]

By this point in his life, Chase was smart enough to understand and summarize his legacy. Sure, he wanted acceptance and recognition. Sure, he wanted vindication. And if he weren't called the greatest, perhaps he would be known as "damned good." But he knew the reality. As the scapegoat, he would not likely ever be recognized for being a player who made great plays. The following expressed not so much how Chase viewed himself, but how he knew that others would view him.

> *I know I was a wiseguy, a know-it-all, I guess ... I lived to make great plays. What did I gain? Nothing. ... You note that I am not in the Hall of Fame. Some of the old-timers said I was one of the greatest fielding first basemen of all time. When I die movie magnates will make no picture like Pride of the Yankees, which honored that great player Lou Gehrig. I guess that's the answer, isn't it? Gehrig had a good name; one of the best a man could have. I am an outcast, and I haven't a good name. I'm the loser, just like all gamblers are.*

One of the most competitive men in the deadball era had no more fight in him. The bravado that at one time fueled him to challenge Comiskey and the reserve clause was gone. Now penniless, powerless, and dying, he conceded defeat. Maybe in a healthier body, he would not have uttered that his admirably outspoken and justified oppositions to Organized Baseball were the acts of a "wise guy." But Hal was not a rebel by choice; he gained his resolve by resisting the unnatural, such as when Organized Baseball told him where or when he could play ball. He didn't value being a "wise guy." He didn't prefer the moniker as part of his epitaph. Like most others, Chase would rather have been part of the status quo and have been loved. He would have wanted an endless number of leagues and owners vying for his services without constraints until he could no longer play. But that wasn't how things were. Chase wore out his welcome in the very small world of Organized Baseball until he had no other options. Yes, Organized Baseball won. So perhaps Chase was a "wise guy" thinking that he could burn bridges in an oligopoly and not suffer the consequences. In the end, he did suffer. And that is what Chase likely came to grips with – how the perception of him being a "wise guy" would endure - as he saw nothing on the horizon to the contrary.

And as a defeated man, the shadow of his years gambling seemed to consume him, like the many regrets facing a dying man before his final confession. He admitted that his gambling was insignificant. But as a defeated man, he could only consider how, if he had not been a gambler, he would perhaps have been remembered differently.

On May 18, 1947, Hal Chase died at the age of sixty-four. His funeral was held in San Jose. His pallbearers were University of San Francisco coach and former New York Giant Bill Cunningham, Santa Clara ballplayers Thomas Feeney and Chauncey Tramutolo,[A] William Benson, and lifelong friends George Poultney and Frank Farry. His son, Hal Jr. and his first wife Nellie attended. Also in attendance were Casey Stengel and Lefty O'Doul. Joe DiMaggio and Ty Cobb wrote letters of condolence to Hal's sister Jessie.[3] He was buried at Oak Hill Cemetery in San Jose.[B]

---

[1] Sportraits, Al Wolf, Los Angeles Times, Jan 25, 1945, pg. A9
[2] The Sporting News, J.W. Sehorn, April 23, 1947
[3] The Black Prince of Baseball, Don Dewey and Nick Acocella, pg. 414.

[A] Feeney played with Chase. Tramutolo played 1911-1912 (perhaps other years).

[B] As much as Chase's illness appeared to be brought on by years of drinking that resulted in his sister Jessie having to care for him, the cruel irony was that Jessie died less than a year later from the same hereditary illness that afflicted her brother.

Chapter 32

A Half Century of Service to California Baseball

In 1948, Charlie Graham continued as President of the San Francisco Seals, a post he filled for over a quarter century. Many Seals' fans knew him from his photo, which appeared in every program sold at Seals Stadium, showing the smiling, grey-haired, and bespectacled "Uncle Charlie" in a business suit beside long-time manager Lefty O'Doul, who appeared in his uniform.[A]

Graham always recognized the need to surround himself with individuals who complemented his skills. He continued that practice with O'Doul. Like Hap Hogan from years before, Lefty O'Doul was a bon vivant around town. His abilities as a baseball ambassador transcended San Francisco, the Pacific Coast League, and the North American continent. In the 1930s, O'Doul had taken interest in promoting baseball in Japan. He led teams of Americans to the island country prior to the Second World War that both instructed and inspired a generation of baseball players. Baseball in Japan had been banned during the War, and in 1948, the nation was in ruins. But soon thereafter, local teams once again began to form. And in 1951, O'Doul resumed trips to the country, taking former Seals stars including Con Dempsey, Dino Restelli, and Joe and Dominic DiMaggio.[1] Through O'Doul's efforts, and the efforts of the former Seals ballplayers, a common bond was established between the two former enemies. General Douglas MacArthur called the visit by the players "the greatest piece of diplomacy ever."[2] While O'Doul has yet to be voted into the Baseball Hall of Fame in the United States in spite of possessing the fourth highest career batting average in the history of the game, he did become the first American inducted into the Japanese Baseball Hall of Fame.

In the late 1940s, the Seals continued to develop talent for the major leagues, and Charlie Graham, a longtime President of the National Association of Professional Players, had influence on a national level regarding the issue of the draft, an issue that he had battled as a minor league owner for forty years. In January of 1948, Graham approached Happy Chandler, who had replaced Landis as Baseball Commissioner following Landis' death in 1944, about altering the current rules. Graham and Chandler were similar in many ways. Chandler was a former Governor and Senator from Kentucky who was selected by Franklin

---

[A] Lefty O'Doul managed the Seals from 1935 through 1951. He won five league championships over those seventeen years. He owned the bar and restaurant called Lefty O'Doul's on Geary Street, around the corner from the St. Francis Hotel on Union Square, which is still in operation. Hanging on the walls of the restaurant is a pictorial museum of ballplayers, many of whom are mentioned within this book.

Roosevelt during wartime to preside over Organized Baseball. Like Graham, Chandler had zero tolerance for aberrant behavior. Just as Graham had neither tolerated gambling in the Pacific Coast League nor the alleged indiscretions of the otherwise successful manager Nick Williams, Chandler also exemplified a dedication to an ideal of purity in Baseball. In 1947, for example, Chandler had suspended the popular Leo Durocher for the entire baseball season because of "conduct detrimental to baseball."[3] On the issue of the draft, Graham appealed to Chandler to:

> 1) Exempt players from selection until they had been in the game for six years (instead of the current four years), and
> 2) Arbitrate the draft price rather than set it at a flat $10,000.[A]

The same day that Graham made his appeal to the Baseball Commissioner, the Pacific Coast League announced that the league's Most Valuable Player Award would in perpetuity be named the Charles Graham Cup in honor of the seventy-year old Seals' President.

On August 27, 1948, Graham suddenly became critically ill from what was believed to be food poisoning. He was rushed to the hospital. The next day, pneumonia developed and Graham was placed in an oxygen tent. Dr. Anthony Diepenbrock, the physician, said that Graham was "very gravely ill." "Uncle Charlie" Graham passed away the next day.

Among the mourners was Stanford baseball coach Harry Wolter. A short train ride south on the Southern Pacific on the Stanford Campus, Coach Harry Wolter prepared for his final season. Wolter would retire after the 1949 season because Stanford imposed a mandatory retirement age of sixty-five for its faculty. And while Wolter could still pitch batting practice and hit as well as some of his pupils, the University made no exceptions for the many academicians who were still vital in their respective fields.

Wolter's team would not earn a berth in the College World Series that year.[B] But the coach could take pride that he was responsible for the championship's formation in 1947; he was instrumental in persuading the NCAA to set up the national playoff. And he could take pride that he and his cronies, now gone or aged, had contributed to the unparalleled development of the sport in California and the West.

The University of California won the first championship in 1947. USC won in 1948.[C] Cal won again in 1957, as did USC in 1958. And after being

---

[A] When the draft was implemented in 1904, the owners argued over the flat $750 price.

[B] Stanford would not play in the World Series until 1953.

[C] Yale was defeated in both '47 and '48. In '47, Cal's superstar Jackie Jensen led the Bears to victory. The captain of the Yale team for both World Series games was first runner-up in 1960, USC won the championship behind coach Rod Dedeaux in '61, '63, '66, '68, '70-'74, and '78. Santa Clara was runner up in 1962. Cal State Fullerton won in '79, '84, '95, '04 and was runner up in '92. Stanford won in '87, '88 and was runner up in '00 and '01. Pepperdine was champion in '92. And Fresno State was champion in '08. In sixty-two years, California schools were champions or co-champions twenty-seven times (44%). Including Arizona schools, the percentage was 69%.

When Wolter retired, the University honored him with a varsity/alumni baseball game followed by a barbecue in April. In the game, the still-fit Wolter pitched. He had served as head coach for twenty-seven consecutive years.[A] He had won a league championship in 1925 behind the heroics of Ernie Nevers. He also developed future major leaguers Bobby Brown and Lloyd Merriman. And in 1927, he persuaded West Coast schools to form the Intercollegiate Baseball Association. He and Stanford won that league's crown in 1931 with a 15-3 record.

The month of his retirement, Wolter received a letter from former Santa Clara classmate Raul de la Guardia, who hailed from Panama. In the letter, Mr. de la Guardia remembered the days at Santa Clara when he had watched Wolter play as a young man. De la Guardia wondered whether Wolter remembered him. And whether he did or not, the letter was considered important to Harry. Wolter submitted the letter to the University Archives. He also submitted a collection, the source of which is unknown, of photographs of ballplayers from the College dating back to the 1860s. The letter from de la Guardia reveals the reminiscent older man, a young boy still contained within, remembering fondly the wonderful memories of days past.

Dear Friend;

Perhaps you do not remember me. I am one of the four De la Guardia Brothers that attended Santa Clara College from 1901 to 1905 as day boarders. My other brothers graduated from Commercial Department y 1904 and 1 finished in 1905. At that time Rev. Father Kenna was President and later succeeded by Rev. Father Norton. Other teachers were Father Riordan, Cavennaugh, Hays, MacCarthy, Raggio and many others. 1 was 19 years old and hailed from Panama.

As 1 was very fond of picture taking 1 bought myself a big Camera 7x10 and became almost the official photographer of the college. 1 took all the

---

baseman George H. W. Bush. George Bush and Hal Chase shared the rare distinction of being first baseman that threw with their left hand but batted right-handed.

[A] The Stanford basketball coach, Everett Dean, who coached players including All-American catcher Jack Shepard and who continued to gradually develop a tradition of baseball at the University after 1949, succeeded Harry Wolter as baseball coach. Dean had won three Big 10 championships in basketball as a coach at Indiana University.

pictures of the Varsity Teams and all the pictures concerning Montgomery's airplane the Santa Clara 1 and 11. In fact Mr. Montgomery died owing me 24.00 for pictures[A] furnished him for publicity and propaganda.

Among the other pictures 1 still have in my scrap book several taken of your now prominent figure. Reading over our newspaper the Panama American 1 came across and with pleasure read a news from Santa Clara mentioning you as the veteran coach of from Stanford and nevertheless an alumnus from Santa Clara.

1 could not help buy rejoicing whenever 1 hear from Santa Clara College, now University. My son and nephews attended and graduated from Santa Clara University. 1 am now old with gray hair but 1 cheer up when 1 talk about Santa Clara. 1 am sending you clippings from my scrap book as 1 am sure you likewise will be happy to remind old days.

Your friend,

Raul de la Guardia '05[4]

In 1970, Harry Wolter died of cancer in Palo Alto four days short of his 86th birthday.

- - - - - - - - - - - - - - -

Dr. Charles "Doc" Strub's persistence to create a quality experience for the fan at the Santa Anita racetrack paid dividends to him throughout his life. He lived in a mansion with his wife Vera and their family overlooking "the Arroyo," within walking distance of the Rose Bowl and downtown Pasadena. He frequented the inner circle of the social elite in Los Angeles and its entertainment industry. Nicholas Schenk, head of MGM and uncle of CBS President William Paley, played poker with Strub and claimed "Doc" was one of the three best in the country – besides himself and Irving Berlin.

Strub became involved in countless philanthropic activities, often focused on the tradition of developing Los Angeles into a city possessing the cultural accoutrements of the greatest cities of the world. To that end, he worked with CBS on a beachfront amusement park. He was also named Director of the Los Angeles Metropolitan Opera.

In 1950, Strub sold his one-third interest in the San Francisco Seals to Paul Fagan. The remaining one-third remained in the family of Charles Graham.[B]

[A] Montgomery, the airplane pioneer, died tragically in a plane crash.

[B] Graham had three surviving children, sons Charles J. Graham and Reverened Robert A. Graham, and daughter Mary Claire Smith.

Strub continued to live the life that others dreamed about. He had taken risks, worked hard, and reaped the rewards sown from the seeds of his labor. He had experienced highs and lows, but persisted throughout as the consummate "host" for the citizens of the West – at Seals Stadium, Santa Anita Racetrack, San Francisco's World's Fair, and the many social events he celebrated. And much like the jockey who mounted his horse one day after the other - giving blood, sweat, and tears - holding nothing back from any race, Strub was satisfied with his accomplishments, having given his all. In an interview in 1958, he had little more to say than, "It's been fun."[5]

In the interview, perhaps Strub had uttered his epitaph. For two weeks later, on March 28, 1958, Charles Strub died of a stroke at seventy-three years of age.

One might see irony in the life of Charles Strub, when compared with his one-time teammate Hal Chase. Strub made a career in baseball even though he wasn't good enough to earn a living as a player. Association with gambling disgraced Chase; yet Doc Strub amassed a fortune from sports gambling. Organized Baseball ostracized Chase because of his association with gambling; Strub received special dispensation from Commissioner Landis to participate in both horse racing and baseball. And one might say that Chase created his own bad luck due to his associations with organized crime and illegal gamblers. But one will never know to the extent that Strub, who in 1934 in the middle of the Great Depression needed a loan from a "bookie" to keep operating Santa Anita, associated with organized criminals.[A]

Strub did not necessarily have involvement with crime mobs; the evidence indicates otherwise. But perhaps if any records did exist, they were destroyed when Strub's office at Santa Anita caught fire six months after his death.

After Doctor Strub's death, his wife Vera Wood Strub continued a lifelong commitment to philanthropy, which included active involvement with Santa Clara University. Serving on the Board of Regents, she influenced the school to become coeducational in 1961. In 1963, Mrs. Strub was honored with the dedication of a women's dormitory in her name. On November 15, Strub Hall became one of four halls that comprised the University's first dormitory for women. It became part of the larger Charles H. Graham Residence Center for Women, named in honor of the former owner of the San Francisco Seals and her husband's partner.[B]

[A] Organized crime at racetracks was the norm rather than the exception. Mobster Meyer Lansky, for example, listed on his tax returns that he earned a living gambling legally at Santa Anita.

[B] The other halls are Campisi, Sanfillipo, and Swig.

By 1963, three generations of Graham had attended Santa Clara University. Over a period of a half-century, Charlie Graham had been a student, teacher, baseball coach, and trustee at the school.

Ironically, when Strub Hall and the Graham Residence Center were dedicated, a fellow member on the Board of Regents was San Francisco Giants owner Horace Stoneham,[A] who had moved his team in 1958 from New York. Perhaps the irony doesn't reside in the fact that Strub, Graham, and Stoneham represented the center of baseball in San Francisco for fifty years, but that by moving to San Francisco, the Giants supplanted the Seals in San Francisco. In 1910, California Angels owner Hen Berry had wanted to be the first to bring major league baseball to California. Two decades later, John McGraw told Graham that he would soon have a major league franchise in San Francisco. But nearly three more decades passed before a major league team arrived in the Bay Area - the team would be "McGraw's Giants."[6]

- - - - - - - - - - - - - - -

In July of 1951, Ty Cobb testified in front of the House of Representatives regarding monopoly power in baseball and it's violation of federal anti-trust laws. He was asked if the reserve clause violated the players' rights to bargain freely. Cobb said, "Hell, yes!"[7] Cobb's suggestion that players remain reserved for a period of only five years was not taken seriously at the time. But nearly a quarter of a century later, his suggestion was implemented when free agency took hold.

In 1952, the decision passed down by Oliver Wendell Holmes and the Supreme Court favoring the reserve clause was reaffirmed in the case of Toolson v. New York Yankees. When Curt Flood, in the case of Flood v. Kuhn, once again challenged it in 1972, the courts again supported the original ruling.

On December 23, 1975, Judge Seitz finally ruled in favor of players Andy Messersmith and Dave McNally, ending the grip of the reserve clause on baseball players, and ushering in an era of free agency. The ruling came sixty years after Hal Chase challenged and defeated Charles Comiskey in a similar seminal suit.

- - - - - - - - - - - - - - -

The pioneers of California Baseball, including Donlin, Chance, Graham, Wolter, Stricklett, Arellanes, Hogan, Shafer, Johnson, Van Haltren, Lange, Denny, and Fogarty who played on skinned diamonds in places like San Pablo, Alameda, Stockton, and Olinda back in the 19th century, inspired brilliance in the game that has endured and grown for more than a century. Their impact and

---

[A] Horace Stoneham was the son of Charles Stoneham, previous owner of the New York Giants.

example mount with time, although their names are often forgotten. The weather has had much to do with the culture of elite baseball in California. But weather alone could not provide what only leadership and service could build. The game needed Harry Wolter to coach twenty-seven years at Stanford, forming the most elite collegiate league in the country and starting the national playoff system. It required Cy Moreing to be a rogue outlaw owner in Stockton, churning out one championship team after another solely motivated to create a winner for his hometown. It needed Hen Berry to love baseball so much that he would save the Los Angeles Angels after the 1906 earthquake, handing out tickets to people on the street and abandoning concern for profit. It required Walter Johnson to grow like a weed and become a legend that decades of fathers and sons would recall with awe. It needed Spike Hennessey to patrol the parks and recreation centers in San Francisco finding players such as the DiMaggio brothers. It depended upon Charlie Graham to choose a precarious career as baseball manager and owner in Sacramento and San Francisco. The game of baseball in California needed its pioneers to teach and inspire generations to pursue greatness, thus creating a legacy that will outlast the memories of their names.

Similarly, the memory of Hal Chase fades with time even as current players enjoy increasingly more lucrative contracts because individuals such as Chase, Nap Lajoie, and Curt Flood germinated the prospects for free agency long before its adoption. But Chase didn't just fight so that players could make large contracts. Granted, he would not have turned one down. But more important to Hal Chase, he fought to have a choice about where and when he could play. Because Hal Chase just wanted to play ball. And nobody could tell Prince Hal he couldn't play. Nobody.

---

[1] Through A Diamond: 100 Years of Japanese American Baseball, Kerry Yo Nakagawa, 2001
[2] O'Doul Created Baseball Bridges, Oakland Tribune, January 29, 2009
[3] Dodgers Handled Unrest to Start '47, The Washington Times, Dick Heller, April 10, 2006.
[4] Santa Clara University Archives, Letter to Harry Wolter from Raul de la Guardia, pp-small alpha box 18 f. Harry M. Wolter - biographical material.
[5] Family Closeup, Los Angeles Times, March 16, 1958, pg. D1
[6] "McGraw's Giants" in the figurative sense. John McGraw passed away in 1934.
[7] Cobb, A Biography, Al Stump

Appendix A

The Case for Chase in Baseball's Shrine

Chase had been one of the best players. Perhaps he was the best defensive first baseman to play the game. Babe Ruth said about Chase:

> *... [he] wasn't just the best defensive first baseman, but the smartest ballplayer he ever saw. His only flaw was that he was so quick he often was way ahead of his other teammates. He played before the ball was juiced up. Gehrig had more power and could run. But Prince was also a very fine hitter. He couldn't run; he could fly. Aside from Ty Cobb, he was the greatest base runner that ever played. He was worth the price of admission just to watch him toe-dance around first base and pick those wild throws out of the dirt.*

Some argue that Ruth gushed about Chase to demonstrate his knowledge of "old school" baseball as he stumped for a manager's role at the end of his career. Or perhaps the young Ruth was impressionable and star-struck as an upcoming pitcher for Boston in 1916 when he witnessed the older, slick-fielding Prince Hal win the batting title. But Ruth was not alone touting Hal Chase as one of baseball's greatest former players.

Chase was named on the rosters of the game's all-time best by and impressive group of writers, umpires, and baseball men including Miller Huggins (1929), Hugh Fullerton (1935), Ed Barrow (1935), Jack Kofoed (1938), Bill Dinneen (1938), Bill Klem (1939), E.A. Batchelor (1939), Zack Wheat (1941), Bill Coughlin (1941), Nick Altrock (1942), Cy Young (1943), Tris Speaker (1944), Frank Graham (1947), Art Shires (1947), Clark Griffith (1952), Tom Connolly (1953), Bobby Wallace (1954), Nap Lajoie (1956), Casey Stengel (1959), Fred Clarke (1961), Sam Crawford (1961), George McBride (1964), Davey Jones (1964), and Jimmie Austin (1964).

They would recount feats that included Chase crossing all the way over to the third base line to gather up a bunt and throw the runner out at first. Or he would cut in front of the pitcher to field a bunt along the third base line and force the runner out at third. Or he would charge a bunt, grab it barehanded, tag the runner on the way to first base, and then throw to second or third to complete a double play. Or he would charge squeeze plays, challenging himself to catch the bunt before it hit the ground and use his momentum to tag the runner at home plate.

The former President of the Bay Area's Mission League, Jim Nealon, who banned Chase from his league, knew well Prince's skill after playing against him for years.

Chase not only was the greatest first baseman I ever saw, but he was also the greatest RIGHT FIELDER. Many's the time Chase played short right field, trapped perfectly legitimate base hits and, with the pitcher covering the bag, threw the runner out at first base.[1]

A young batboy for the Oakland Oaks in 1935, now in his eighties, remembered asking Oaks manager Oscar Vitt about Prince Hal.

My interest in Hal Chase was started by my father and uncle who used to see him play in old San Pablo Park in the East Bay and would relate how fast he was... In 1935 I was a batboy for the Oakland Oaks and Oscar Vitt was manager. Oscar had just finished reaming someone out, as was his habit, and I asked him about Hal, who by this time was long gone from the major leagues. His expression changed, mellowed and asked, "Who told you to ask me about him?" I said my Dad had seen him play. He said my Dad was lucky cause we wouldn't see anyone who could play like that again. I was only thirteen when I talked to Oscar but in the middle fifties I got to ask both Ty Cobb and Swede Risberg about him and the reactions were the same; no one was even close in their book.[2]

Ty Cobb took pride in telling a story about how he once fooled "the greatest defensive first baseman the game has ever known."

Cobb was known to go from first to third on infield bunts. He did that 19 of 21 attempts one season. So Chase told his third baseman that if Cobb was on first, hang close to the bag and he would nail him and not pay attention to the hitter at first. So the next game, with Cobb on first, Crawford bunted to Chase. Chase fielded the ball and threw to third, but Cobb was standing on second. He had overheard the two New York players scheming the day before as he was getting a drink of water. So he double-crossed Chase...[3]

If Hal Chase had been such a great player, shouldn't he then be voted into the Hall of Fame? First, did Hal's exploits between the lines earn him the distinction as one of the game's greatest? And second, was he guilty of actions that deserved exclusion from baseball's shrine?

In terms of ability, the case for Hal Chase clearly hinges on his defensive prowess at first base. Most consider Chase the best, or one of the best, to ever play the position. Others receiving recognition include Gil Hodges and Keith Hernandez, two first sackers who haven't entered the Hall of Fame. Defensive first basemen haven't received the recognition that fielders at other positions have. Six ballplayers from other positions have entered the Hall of Fame largely due to their defensive prowess. They include Brooks Robinson at third base, Ozzie Smith and Rabbit Maranville at shortstop, Bill Mazeroski at second base, Ray Schalk at catcher, Harry Hooper in left field.

Defensive Specialists in Hall of Fame (with exception of Chase)

NAME	YRS	AB	AVG HITS PER 500 AB	AVG RUNS PER 500 AB	AVG RBI PER 500 AB	SB PER 500 AB	LIFE AVG	LIFE OB %	LIFE SLUG %
Hal Chase	15	7,417	145	66	63	25	0.291	0.319	0.391
Harry Hooper	17	8,785	140	81	46	21	0.281	0.368	0.387
Brooks Robinson	23	10,654	134	58	64	1	0.267	0.322	0.401
Ozzie Smith	19	9,396	131	67	42	31	0.262	0.337	0.328
Bill Mazeroski	17	7,755	130	50	55	2	0.260	0.299	0.367
Rabbit Maranville	23	10,078	129	62	44	14	0.258	0.318	0.340
Ray Schalk	18	5,306	127	55	56	17	0.253	0.340	0.316

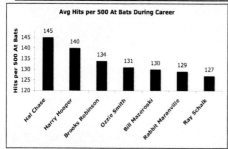

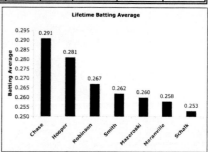

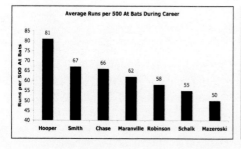

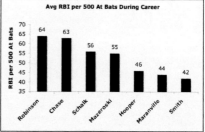

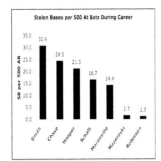
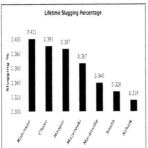
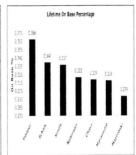

Hal Chase compares favorably as a hitter to other defensive specialists already in the Hall of Fame. Few can argue that the others are undeserving. Gold Glove Awards or All Star teams didn't exist back in the deadball era. But more recently Brooks Robinson and Ozzie Smith were selected to fifteen All Star teams and won sixteen and thirteen Gold Glove Awards, respectively. Robinson also won the league MVP distinction in 1964 hitting .317 and leading the league in RBI with 118. Mazeroski won eight Gold Gloves, earned seven All Star team nods, and was the 1960 Major League Player of the Year. Some on the list not only won championships, but earned distinction for their play in the post-season.

But Chase not only compares well against this elite group of athletes offensively, he stands head and shoulders above them. His lifetime batting average is considerably higher than all of the defensive specialists, which demonstrates that Chase was not merely a "no hit, good glove" type of player. He even won a batting title beating out Honus Wagner and Rogers Hornsby. He ranked fourth or higher in the league in hits four different seasons. He was in the top eight in RBI seven seasons; in the top three from 1915 to 1917. His 363 stolen bases ranks third all-time among first basemen; the other two, Frank Chance and George Sisler, are in the Hall of Fame. Critics point out that Chase had a poor on-base percentage and was simply a singles hitter. Indeed, his on-base percentage was low, but it was not significantly dissimilar from the others in the group. And the slugging percentage that ranks second in the group only to the powerful Brooks Robinson, even though Chase played in the deadball era, highlights that Prince Hal had a knack for extra base hits.

An aspect of Chase's ability offensively that set him apart was the mastery of the hit and run play. Many players attested that Hal Chase was the greatest hit and run batter in the history of the game. And in the deadball era of "small ball", the hit and run was arguably akin to a home run in today's game.

In terms of fielding, few can argue that Hal Chase could be the greatest defensive first baseman of all time. Many baseball historians name Chase as the first baseman on their all-time defensive roster. The precedent has been set, with the inclusion of the likes of Bill Mazeroski and Ozzie Smith, that the best defensive players at their respective positions should be recognized in the Hall of

Fame. But more important, Chase not only was one of the great defenders, he redefined how the game was played at first base. He ushered in a new era that has been emulated for nearly a century by defense-minded first sackers.

In 1952, baseball fan John Herbold from Hollywood stated his case in a letter to the editor soon after former San Francisco minor league greats Paul Waner and Harry Heilmann were elected to Cooperstown.

Baseball fans throughout the country were greatly pleased to see those two fine outfielders, Harry Heilmann and Paul Waner, selected for Baseball's Hall of Fame at Cooperstown, N.Y.

But why the delay in naming that great Calfornia boy Hal Chase for the honor? Is it because most of those making selections never saw this player perform? Or is it on account of some prejudice against Chase? In the long history of baseball the National and American Leagues have had a long list of fine first basemen – Beckley, Hoblitzel, Bransfield, Kenetchy, Gehrig, Foxx, Chance, Bottomley, McIness, et all – but Hal Chase made plays in and around first base that others never attempted.

Years ago, Fred Tenney came out of Brown University to join the New York Giants and initiated a new technique of playing first base, which was improved on and perfected by Hal Chase of the New York Highlanders ...

So the next time selections are being made for the Hall of Fame, let's hope that Hal Chase, the king of first basemen, is chosen.

John O. Herbold, Hollywood.[4]

To understand the greatness of Hal Chase, one must ask those old enough to have heard from their fathers, and father's fathers, such as Mr. Koch who is approaching ninety years of age.

Hal has been dead for just a little over sixty years and I find it a little disgusting having people younger than sixty trying to tell us what kind of a man he was... Then we have the other experts saying he couldn't have been that great a first baseman because of his batting average; what the hell does batting average have to do with what Ruth, Cobb, Walter Johnson and others were talking about [that Chase was the greatest]. It was the way he played first base defensively... [from comments from statistical analysts] you'd think Earl Sheely was the greatest of first baseman because he hit over ,300 every year although he never ventured more than 42" from the sack in any direction and had to hit the ball on the fence to get a base hit because he was so slow... my father and uncle who used to see him play in old San Pablo Park in the East Bay would relate how fast he [Chase] was.[5]

Aside from any ethical objection due to actions taken by Chase off the field, it is difficult to fathom that Chase, the man widely regarded the greatest first baseman ever, the man who changed forever the way first basemen play the game, the man many thought to be the most talented, intelligent and graceful man in the game, would not have been otherwise voted into the Hall of Fame. He played enough seasons, had enough talent, and had enough recognition. His batting really was not so very awful that it would exclude him from the Hall. In the field, he had titanic skills; he was considered better than many greats including Chance, Anson, Sisler, and Gehrig. And during an era when defensive ability was considerably more important than it is today, Chase's contributions to the game are all the more considerable. And on the basepaths, another important facet of "inside baseball," Chase was also superlative. Clearly he would be in the Hall if not for exclusion caused by alleged gambling.

Yet all gambling claims, in terms of him throwing games, still remain allegations. No evidence has been presented. Organized Baseball, in fact, took all measures not to provide proof in court. It acted as its own judge and jury, not needing proof to determine guilt. Thus, there is nothing other than conjecture to condemn Hal Chase in the hearts and minds of future generations.

Certainly in the period before 1920, before Organized Baseball made Chase into a symbol of corruption, his contemporaries understood the prevalence of gambling in the sport. Chase was not the exception. In any wrongdoing, the existence of wrongdoing by others does not excuse one's actions. But wrongdoing by Chase was never proven.

Discrediting Chase as a ballplayer because of involvment with gambling is akin to discounting the contributions of Thomas Jefferson because he owned slaves when slavery was legal. It wasn't right, it may diminish from the perception of his good character, and it may have been antithetical to the ideals that he espoused. But his ownership of slaves was indicative of the prevailing conditions of those times. He was not the exception, and many consider his contributions in spite of his personal practices.

One might also argue that Chase earned consideration because of his courage challenging the reserve clause during a period when players were shackled by its clutches.

Perhaps after a century, one can understand that, although flawed like the game he played, Chase was good. And from among the tens of millions of young boys who laced up cleats for over one hundred and fifty years, Hal Chase was perhaps the greatest first baseman. And for that, he should be in the Hall of Fame.

What do we know, and what is conjecture?

WHAT WE KNOW	ALTERNATIVE VIEW	CONJECTURE
Chase admitted to gambling on baseball games when it was legal to do so, and claimed to never have bet very much.	His ex-wife, not altogether a reliable source after going through a divorce, claimed that Chase gambled considerably and squandered his money.	Like many players, Chase gambled. Perhaps he gambled quite a bit at some point in his career.
Many individuals named Chase as being involved with game fixes that didn't involve throwing games.	All involvement is alleged, and unlike many other ballplayers who could have been implicated, the instances with Chase were blown out of proportion and memorialized by those in Baseball who targeted Chase as the scapegoat in the gambling scandals of the era.	Chase probably created some of his bad luck by associations with gambling concerns. For many years, gambling on games and arranging fixes to assist one's own team was commonplace.
Chase has been identified as a cause of the gambling problems in Baseball	The gambling issue in baseball precedes Chase by decades; there is nothing other than circumstantial evidence regarding Chase's negative influence on the game.	Chase played for Devery and Farrell, two unsavory Tammany Hall characters, for years. Prior to that, baseball and gambling had been inextricable for decades. Chase was drafted into a shady environment; he didn't create it. But he likely was involved in gambling, perhaps more than he later claimed.
Many other ballplayers and baseball personnel, including many stars, were involved in fixing games.	As with Chase, there is no proof.	Gambling and game fixing was prevalent throughout the era and involved many baseball personnel.
Ballplayers fixed and threw games on a regular basis, particularly at the end of each season to help a team win a pennant, secure Worlds Series pay for finishing toward top of the league, or for other reasons.	The money given to other teams at the end of the season was in appreciation for good play against opponents during the season.	It takes two to tango. If a game was fixed, it required a perpetrator to throw the game on behalf of the gambling interest. Fixes were prevalent, and they required many ballplayers to participate, including by throwing games.

WHAT WE KNOW	ALTERNATIVE VIEW	CONJECTURE
There is perception that Chase distinguished himself as particularly unsavory because he threw games throughout his career.	There is no proof that Chase ever threw a game.	Game fixes were prevalent during Chase's career. Under those conditions, any play made by any player could raise suspicion of a fix. Sportswriters speculated about many players and plays. For years, they suspected Chase at times. But there is not only no proof, but little evidence that Chase threw games prior to 1917. After that time, he came under more scrutiny, particularly from Christy Mathewson. But nothing was proven and Chase and Mathewson reconciled.
There is perception that Chase arranged fix of 1919 and made $40,000	Chase had minimal involvement other than being at the bar when the plans were discussed.	Chase likely knew gamblers and individuals, such as Arnold Rothstein, and probably acted as a go-between when players looking for financial backing. Chase likely didn't organize anything. He likely just made introductions as a facilitator.
Chase did gamble on the 1919 because he knew of the fix	He admitted to gambling a small amount on the World Series after learning that a fix was likely	Chase did bet on the World Series, as did many others such as John McGraw, which heightened suspicions of a fix.
Chase knew of the 1919 fix and didn't report it to League Officials	Chase admitted to knowing about the fix in 1919 and of betting on it.	Chase admitted to knowing about the fix in 1919 and of betting on it.
Chase was a persona non grata in the American League after jumping to the Federal League after telling Ban Johnson and Charles Comiskey that he would not. They also resented him challenging and defeating Comiskey in court after he jumped.	Chase created his own bad luck by cavorting with gamblers and lacking respect for the institution of Organized Baseball that was the source of his livelihood.	Johnson and Comiskey admittedly never forgave Chase for jumping to the Federal League, and became resolute to make him pay, particularly when he became involved in the fix of the Chisox in 1919. They smeared Chase in the media and influenced all of Organized Baseball, including the Pacific Coast League, to banish Chase.

WHAT WE KNOW	ALTERNATIVE VIEW	CONJECTURE
Chase was banned by the Pacific Coast League	After the meeting between Chase and Spider Baum in the midst of a war on gambling in the PCL, Baum misinterpreted Chase's comments. Chase was looking for a tip from Baum on how to bet and make some money on PCL games.	Baum seems credible, and while he may have taken Chase's comments out of context, in this case Chase did create his own bad luck. Nonetheless, after hearing the report from Baum and after being considerably influenced by a smear campaign of Chase coming out Ban Johnson's office, the PCL chose to ban Chase. It could have been a case of "better safe than sorry." And indeed Chase was involved in gambling, which was what the PCL was trying to eradicate from the league. But if Chase actually attempted to fix a game, we will never know because he was never given the opportunity to defend himself.
Chase was banned by the Mission League	Chase did nothing wrong.	Mission League followed the Pacific Coast League and didn't have any additional claims against Chase. And arguably, the PCL was influenced by the smear campaign of Ban Johnson.
Ban Johnson and major league baseball felt that Chase fixed games, threw games, and fixed the 1919 World Series.	There was no proof of any of those claims.	Ban Johnson kept a file on many occurrences in baseball for years. Nobody knows for sure what he knew and what evidence he had. It appears, however, that all the activity known to Johnson didn't serve to promote the games' brand, which was his main priority. So if there was evidence, it was never fully vetted by any parties that didn't have a vested interest in the outcome; i.e., there was no justice.

1 The Sporting News, September 18, 1941
2 Baseball Fever Blog, R. Koch, Jan 17, 2009
3 The Sport's Parade, Braven Dyer, LA Times, Feb 22, 1943, Pg. I3
4 Why Not chase, The Sports Fan Speaks, Los Angeles Times, February 17, 1952, Pg. B11
5 Baseball Fever Blog, Entry by sports fan R. Koch

Index